Entrepreneur.
MAGAZINE'S

ULTIMATE

GUIDE TO

PROJECT

MANAGEMENT

for Small Business

Get It Done Right!

SID KEMP

EP Entrepreneur. Press

Editorial Director: Jere Calmes
Cover Design: Beth Hansen-Winter
Composition: CWL Publishing Enterprises, Inc., Madison, Wisconsin, www.cwlpub.com

This publication is designed to provide accurate and authoritative information in regard to the subject matter covered. It is sold with the understanding that the publisher is not engaged in rendering legal, accounting, or other professional services. If legal advice or other expert assistance is required, the services of a competent professional person should be sought.

–From a Declaration of Principles jointly adopted by a
Committee of the American Bar Association and
a Committee of Publishers and Associations

ISBN 1-932531-72-6

Library of Congress Cataloging-in-Publication Data

Kemp, Sid.
   Ultimate guide to project management for small business / by Sid Kemp.
      p. cm.
   Accompanying CD-ROM provides worksheets, graphs, and forms.
   ISBN 1-932531-72-6 (alk. paper)
   1. Project management. 2. Small business--Management. I. Title: Ultimate Guide to project
   management for small business. II. Title: Project management for small business. III. Title.
HD69.P75K4554 2005
658.4'04–dc22

                                                                    2005011212

Printed in Canada
10 09 08 07 06 05   10 9 8 7 6 5 4 3 2 1

Contents

Preface

I F YOU'RE IN CHARGE OF A BUSINESS— whether a small company, an independent franchise, or an office or division of a medium-sized company— then this book is for you. Why? Because businesses depend on projects. Project management is the art of making change work, and small businesses are swimming—or sinking—in a sea of change. In a small business, we can't afford to make many mistakes—we have to get it right the first time.

A project is "a problem scheduled for solution," according to the management pioneer Joseph M. Juran (*Juran's Quality Control Handbook*, 4th edition, with Frank M. Gryna). Or, it may be "an opportunity scheduled for realization." Any one-time job we do that we've never done before is a project. Selling the same item off the shelf over and over isn't a project. Balancing your checkbook isn't a project. But launching a new product line or taking care of a sudden inventory shortfall are projects—as is planning next year's success for your business or department.

There is an art—and a science—to getting things done right. This book distills and scales down the best practices of the *Fortune* 500 and the major consultants to make them work for you—whether you are alone or you manage a team of five, 15, or 50.

Entrepreneur Magazine's Ultimate Guide to Project Management for Small Business is for you whether you are in a for-profit business, a not-for-profit business, government, or education. Any organization has goals and wants to meet those goals without wasting time and money. This book will help you do that. The most important question is: What is *your* bottom line? It may not be money, even if you are in a regular, for-profit company, partnership, small business, or one-person shop. My goal is to offer my customers the keys to success. What's yours?

Why Learn Project Management?

Why do small and medium-sized businesses need project management? Because, all around us, things are changing. And that leaves us only three options:

- Bury our heads in the sand and hope the change goes away before we go out of business.
- Launch a project the wrong way, waste time, lose money, and go out of business.
- Get it right the first time with best practices from *Entrepreneur Magazine's Ultimate Guide to Project Management for Small Business.*

If you want to succeed, learn from the best so you can do your best.

What Is a Successful Project?

A successful project solves the problem, cashes in on the opportunity, and improves the business. Have you ever heard the saying, "The operation was a success, but the patient died"? Well, thanks, but no thanks. My appendix may be out, but if I'm not around to enjoy the experience, what's the point? It's the same way with a project. For a project to be good for our business, it has to do the following:

- Define and solve the right problem.
- Add value—be worth more than it costs.
- Be good for us, our customers, and our vendors.
- Leave behind a solution that makes our business better off.

Good project management helps every part of our business. Whether you manufacture or buy from suppliers, a good project will get you better products faster. Whether you sell products or services, a good project will improve them and reduce the cost of providing them. A project will help you grow your business—and will help you shrink it to survive, if you have to. Whether you're planning and running a whole marketing campaign or you're designing a single ad, it's a project.

How Do You Make a Project Work?

Project managers go through a series of steps to make a project work. The big challenge is that a project is like an airplane. Every part has to work or the whole thing goes boom! And you don't want to be up in the air when you learn the landing gear won't work. In this book, you'll learn how to manage a project from start to finish.

- Define the real problem.
- Design the right solution.
- Choose among alternate solutions.
- Figure out how much the project will cost.
- Figure out how long the project will take.
- Pull together the right team—your own employees, consultants, or whoever is best.
- Plan for quality—make it good.
- Plan for risk—make sure it's going to get done.
- Launch the project.
- Keep it on schedule and on budget.
- Handle the bumps in the road with risk and change management.
- Communicate effectively so the project succeeds while your business keeps rolling along.
- Deliver success with solid, measurable results that make for happy customers and a better bottom line.

Project Management for You

So, if you want to fix your business problems and make things work—in production, marketing, sales, finance, or customer service, for a store, a school, a service firm, a manufacturing company, or a wholesaler—*Entrepreneur Magazine's Ultimate Guide to Project Management for Small Business* is for you. We'll get you jump-started in plain English. And if you're planning a big, complicated, risky project, we'll give you all the techniques that matter. Even more, we'll provide you with real-world examples of success to emulate—and disasters to avoid. At the end of the project you'll be able to say, "Mission accomplished! Bottom line improved! Customer delighted!"

Again, and again, and again, as life keeps changing.

HOW TO USE THIS BOOK

I hope that, by the time you finish this book, you will be a better problem solver, a better leader, and a better project manager. I'm an author, but I'm also a trainer and coach. I know that—unfortunately—most people don't use books as well as they might. I've done all I can to give you what you need, but it is up to you to *use* this book, and not just read it.

If you want to be entertained and informed by stories of success and failure, just start reading. If you want to get a good idea of what project management (PM) is all about and how it might help you, then read carefully.

But I hope you want more than that. I hope you want to change the way that you work. If you want things to get better, you have to change what you do. In fact, one definition of insanity is to keep doing the same thing and expect differ-

ent results. If you're ready to get out of the endless loops we all fall into—paying for useless solutions, starting projects that never finish, complaining but never changing—then get everything you can out of this book.

This book has visual aids, questionnaires, forms, sidebars, and a CD-ROM full of tools and templates. When you see a visual aid, a table or figure, slow down and make sure you get the idea. Then go back to the explanation in the text. The questionnaires are included to help you know where you are and plan which way to go next. Fill them out, read the key, and follow the advice to stay on course. When you see a form, think how you would use it in your business or on your project. Then go to the CD and copy the editable version of the form to your computer and start using it. You can also explore the many other tools, templates, and links to resources on the CD.

There are several types of sidebars. Here's what they're called and how to use them:

- *In This Chapter.* Review this to make sure the chapter makes sense to you. Use it later to find stuff you need.
- *Focus!* These ideas will help you target your learning on what is most important.
- *Key Terms.* Some key terms are precise definitions of everyday words like *task*, *product*, or *service*. Others are the jargon of project management—what I like to call *fancy words*. These give you definitions you can use to talk with experts, understand project management gurus, and entertain people at parties. The fancy words don't matter much; it's the *ideas* that make all the difference.
- *Smart Thinking!* These are examples of the best way to succeed. Use them in your business.

- *Bottom-Line Basics.* Always remember these things. Forgetting these points when you are on a project is like forgetting gravity when you are climbing a mountain. Remember them—or you'll be headed down fast!
- *Be an Expert!* These are high-end extras. Skip them if you are in project management boot camp. But use them when you're ready.
- *Something Slipped!* These are examples of mistakes to avoid.
- *Think for Yourself!* This is where the work starts. Don't skip these. Stop, read, think, and write down your answers. This is a chance to start changing the way you work.
- *Boost Your Business!* These make the book work *for you.* Answer the questions. Think about your own business and the projects it needs. Make a plan—and *get it done right!*

It's all here and now it's up to you. This book is like a toolkit: it works only if you use it. I have a toolkit in my garage and I also had a screen door that was broken until last week, when I got out the toolkit and used some tools to fix the door. My toolkit was good—in theory. But I had to put the tools into practice.

There are problems all around us waiting to be fixed and there are profits all around us waiting to be made. So turn the page and get right to work!

RESOURCES FOR LEARNING

The field of project management is always growing. Your needs are changing, too. To help with that, we've included a CD in the back of this book and—even more important—set up a web site where you can go for the latest tips, tools, templates, and other resources about project management. My company, Quality Technology & Instruction, maintains the web site at www.qualitytechnology.com/doneright.

When you open the CD, you can look at the file DoneRight.htm or the document DoneRight.doc. Either one will show you how to use the files on the CD and how to get to my web site to get the newest versions.

I keep learning, too. And I learn most from my readers like you. I'd love to hear your stories of success and your challenges or answer any questions. Maybe you can even send me a case study of how you took an opportunity and got what you wanted or solved a problem, planning and doing what you needed to do to *get it done right!* E-mail me at sid@qualitytechnology.com.

The Basics of
Project Management

Are you ready to *get it done right?* In Part I, we'll show you how. We dive right in with Chapter 1, Get It Done Right! where we walk through planning, doing, and delivering a small project from beginning to end. Then, in Chapter 2, we step back and look at the big picture of *why businesses need successful projects*. In Chapter 3, you will learn to solve the right problem, because one of the most common mistakes in business is to throw a lot of time and money away solving the wrong problem. We tie all that together in Chapter 4, Your Business and Your Projects.

So, sharpen your pencil, put on your thinking cap, and get ready to master the art of getting things done.

CHAPTER 1

Get It Done Right!
Solving Problems and Realizing Opportunities

IN THIS CHAPTER

- *Start where you are,* including a questionnaire that will guide you in learning project management.
- *Get it done right!* Word by word. What does it mean to get it done right?
- *Pick a project.* How to decide what to do first.
- *Define the problem.*
- *Define a good solution.*

- *Make a plan.*
- *Do and check.* Are we doing what we planned and heading for success?
- *Deliver the results.* The right way to finish a project.
- *Evaluate the project.* There's always more to learn.

THE GOAL OF PROJECT MANAGEMENT (PM) can be summed up in just four words: *get it done right!* This chapter will show you how to do that. The rest of this book will explode outward from there, showing you why project management matters for your business, what you have to do to get it done right, and how to avoid all the ways project work can go wrong. When you're done reading, learning, and using this book, you will be able to solve problems and grow your business with confidence.

START WHERE YOU ARE

One time, as I finished teaching a two-day project management class, a student came up to me and said, "Sid, everything in this course was great! But there's more here to learn than I can learn in six months. Where do I start?"

The answer is: Start where you are. How could you start anywhere else? Any good plan starts where we are and takes us where we want to go.

So, where are you in relation to this book? Answer the questions below below to see.

▼ Focus!
Problems and Opportunities

A problem is something that gets in our way. We want to remove the roadblock and keep going. We want to solve the problem once and for all; we don't want it to get in the way again. An opportunity is a chance to do something new, to grow our business, to serve more, and, yes, to make more money. We want to seize opportunities and make the most of them.

Often, our customers' problems are our opportunities. Solving our customers' problems is a great way to grow a business.

GET IT DONE RIGHT!–WORD BY WORD

So, let's learn how to get it done right. We'll start by taking a close look at what we mean by "get it done right!"

- "It" is a problem to be solved or an opportunity to be realized. Defining the problem or opportunity is our first step. Solving the wrong problem would be one of the biggest mistakes we could make.
- "Get done" means deliver. We're going to deliver a solution to the problem or a new product or service that takes advantage of the opportunity. Getting things done is about change, about improvement.

▼ QUESTIONNAIRE
Are You Ready to Learn PM?

Instructions: Write down your answers to the questions. Then go to the survey key (page 6) to interpret your answers and plan how you can best use this chapter.

1. Why did you pick up this book?
2. What are the biggest problems and challenges you face in your business or department? (List one to three.)

   -
   -
   -

3. What are the biggest opportunities for you, your department, or your business right now? (List one to three.)

   -
   -
   -

4. How much do you know about project management? (Pick one.)
   - ❏ Zip. I don't even know what a project is.
   - ❏ I know what a project is, but nothing about how to manage one.
   - ❏ I've got the basics down: goals, time, cost, planning–but I really don't know how to get a project done on time.
   - ❏ I can do a project myself, but I don't know how to lead a team.
   - ❏ I'm pretty good, but I want to be able to get projects done on time and within budget more often.
   - ❏ I'm a good–or great–project manager, and I'm looking to grow.

5. How important is learning to get jobs done on time to you and your business?
   - ❏ Crucial. Without it, I'm likely to lose my business or my job.
   - ❏ Very important. I'm sure that this is where my company or department is stuck.
   - ❏ It matters a lot. The improvements would be a big help.
   - ❏ It can help. It's one of the things that we need.
   - ❏ Right now, there are other priorities, but I want to get a handle on this.

❏ I'm not sure.

❏ Actually, now that I think about it, I'll give the book to someone who needs it more than I do.

6. How much time do you have to read and *use* this book?

❏ Two or more hours per day: I'll make the time—I'm desperate.

❏ A few hours a week.

❏ I'll kind of read it around the corners, as I get time.

❏ I have to get some other things done first, and then I can put in some good time. But I'd like to get a handle on it now.

❏ Help! I'm so buried in work that I don't have time to learn how to do a better job!

7. What do you hope to learn from reading and using this book?

8. What do you hope to do differently after reading this book?

9. What projects would you like to get done soonest?

■ "Right!" means lots of things. Things go right when:

– *We solve the right problem* and take care of it so it doesn't come back again. That's being *effective.*

– *We plan the job well.* That includes planning what the project will give the business—the *solution*—and what it will take from the business—the *resources.*

– *We deliver on time and within budget.* That's being *efficient.*

– *We think ahead and handle change well.* That's managing project *risk* and *change.*

– *We have the right people doing the right job.* We use people with the right talents and give them the right training, skills, authority, and resources to do the job well. That's *leadership* and *empowerment.*

– *We make things better.* That's adding *value.* We do that by planning, managing, and delivering *quality.* We can also see that as being *effective.*

KEY TERMS

Project Joseph M. Juran, the Total Quality Management (TQM) guru, gives us the simplest definition of a project: "a problem scheduled for solution." We can add, "an opportunity scheduled for realization." We'll look at fancier definitions later on.

Manage When we manage, we define the job, plan the work to be done, and control the work according to plan. A project manager takes responsibility for planning and managing to deliver success on a project.

Subproject Sometimes, a project is too big and it gets messy. To prevent that, we break it up into smaller projects. Each smaller project gets part of the job done; we

call these small projects *subprojects* of the big project.

Problem Something that gets in the way of good work and success. Problems have *symptoms, consequences,* and *causes.*

Symptom A sign of a problem, a result. Taking care of a symptom isn't enough; we want to solve the problem.

Consequence The end result of an action. All actions have consequences. A problem left unsolved usually has the consequence of leaving us in a worse situation—or out of business altogether.

Cause The reason for something. When we solve a problem fully, we eliminate the cause of the problem.

Opportunity A chance to do something new, to make things better, to serve more, or to make more money.

Effective Producing a desired result.

Planning Thinking through—and writing down—what we're going to do.

Efficient Obtaining maximum results with minimum resources. We can measure efficiency against time—if it's done quickly, it's efficient—and against cost—if it doesn't cost much, it's efficient—and in relation to other resources.

Risk In general, the possibility of unexpected events. In project management, any event or situation that could prevent us from finishing the project, reduce the value of what we deliver, or force us to alter our plan, schedule,

or budget is a project risk.

Leadership Setting direction for a group of people.

Empowerment Giving people what they need to get the job done, including tools, skills, information, authority, and resources, and letting them do it themselves.

Value A better result or situation. For a customer, value is what he or she will pay money for. (A customer buys when he or she thinks, "This is of value to me, this is worth the price.") For an organization or business, we increase value by accomplishing our mission, serving our customers, making more money, spending less money, and improving our ability to continue operations and grow.

Quality That which adds value.

You learn from this book by doing. Right now, you're going to pick a project and get it done before you finish the chapter!

If these situations sound like your company, don't feel bad. This country has an epidemic of bad project management; maybe you've caught the

▼ QUESTIONNAIRE

Key: Are You Ready to Learn PM?

Check your answers against the following comments.

#1. *Always keep the answer to #1 in mind.* Stay connected with your reason for reading this book and applying what you learn from it. Read it aloud to yourself every time you open this book.

#2 and #3. *These lists of most important problems and opportunities form the list of projects you will do.* Solve big problems and help your business grow.

#4. *Plan your learning.* If you checked box 1 or 2, then read Part 1 to learn the big picture. If you checked box 3 or 4, then skim Chapters 1-4—and stop if you see something you need to learn or use. Then go on from Chapter 5 to the end of the book. If you checked one of the last two boxes, then skim Part 1 and turn to the part of the

book that will give you what you need.

#5 and #6. *Make sure that the amount of time you're willing to invest matches your need.* If getting things done—or getting things done right—is your challenge, then the answer is here. But if you're overwhelmed, then you'll have to organize a bit and maybe set some other things aside to really use this book. But it will pay off. You'll complete a project in Chapter 1. After that, every page will offer quick little tools that will save you time.

#7, #8, and #9. *This is your list of goals.* Think of it as your finish line in a race. Keep your eye on the prize and check your progress. Whenever you finish reading a chapter, assess your progress against your answers to #7, #8, and #9 and set your direction toward your goals.

▼ **QUESTIONNAIRE**

Conclusion: Use Your Answers Well

Now, plan how to read, learn, and apply this practical guide to solving problems and seizing opportunities. Review the table of contents and plan your reading schedule. Write it on your calendar. I'll tell you why. If you need this book, one of three things is going to happen.

- You'll put time in your calendar, read it, and change the way you work. After that, you'll be solving problems and seizing opportunities—and you'll get better and better at it for the rest of your life.
- You won't set aside the time or you won't read it. Then you'll take a course or call me for coaching. It will cost you more, but it will work. Instead, save time and money by doing it yourself. One of the best tips I ever learned was to set time aside for myself in my calendar.
- You'll let this drop and miss an opportunity. You'll keep doing the same thing and hoping for a different result.

Most of us do that. Most of us don't get much of what we want. *If you want to succeed, dare to be different.* What most people do defines mediocrity. Do you want to be mediocre? Or, think of it this way: if everyone got things done right already, the world would be a much better place and none of us would need this book. But we do need it. And now is your chance to use it.

Don't read another word. I mean it. Don't read another word until you've made this book your own by starting to use it.

Now, for the really good news. Learning project management is a project. If you've done the survey, reviewed the table of contents, and set some goals and a schedule, then you've just planned your first project. How are you doing so far?

bug. Feel good—the medicine is in your hands.

PICK A PROJECT

With so many ways to get it done wrong (see sidebar, So Many Ways... to Get It Wrong), we can see why PM is complicated. As I said before, a project is like an airplane flight—one little thing goes wrong and—Boom! we miss our goal. In the rest of this chapter, you'll get your first taste of everything it takes to get it right.

How do you pick a project? Go back to your survey and look at the list of problems (question 2) and the list of opportunities (question 3). Look at each one and answer these questions.

- Do I understand this problem or opportunity?
- Do I think it is solvable? That is, do I have enough people who are smart enough to do the job?

▼ **BOTTOM-LINE BASICS**

Experience and Expertise

When we've done something, we have experience. When we think about what we've done and we can explain it—to ourselves and to someone else—we have expertise. If you try something the first time and get it right, that's called beginner's luck—and we don't want to rely on luck. So, we learn by doing—getting experience—and then thinking about what we've learned—turning experience into expertise.

Expertise is more than knowledge. Knowledge is great—in school. Knowledge lets us answer questions and explain things. Expertise goes beyond knowledge—we can answer, we can explain, but we can also do and deliver—and lead a team that does and delivers what the company needs.

▼ SOMETHING SLIPPED!

So Many Ways … to Get It Wrong

I'm going to take the list of how to do a project right—and flip it on its head. This is the way most companies—perhaps 80 or 90 percent of them—generally do business. To me, sometimes it's amazing that they stay in business. So, take a look at your company. Are any of these the way you do things now?

- *Never pick a project.* Just run around, putting out one fire after another.

- *Just get it done, OK!?* Has anyone ever yelled that at you when you wanted to make a plan? Planning can be a quarter or even half of a successful project. Jumping in and doing leaves important people and essential thinking out of the process.

- *Declare a project without seeing if it's the one that really matters.* Announce an initiative that's going to make everything better—only it has nothing to do with your company's real problems.

- *Tell everyone the project is really important—and then, next week, tell them to do something else.* Many organizations start with enthusiasm, but don't back the project and the team all the way through. Instead, they pull people off the project they said was important to go run around putting out other fires.

- *Solve the wrong problem.* This is a big one. Would you go to the doctor and get a prescription without a diagnosis? That's what most companies do when it comes to projects. We pick solutions without really finding out what is wrong and just waste lots of time and money.

- *Use the solution of the day.* Instead of finding the best solution to our problem at our company, we grab a solution from the latest guru, consultant, or fad in a one-size-fits-all mentality. And just like after Christmas, we end up returning our gift to the store because we can't use it.

- *Whatever you do, don't talk with … the customer, the IT group, a project management expert.* The department goes ahead without getting good technical advice. The technical group builds a solution without asking the customer what he or she needs. Everyone jumps in without asking for directions. Or, we have meetings, but they aren't run well and we never get on the same page. Sound familiar?

- *Just turn it on and hope it works. It's "user-friendly." We don't need training; it has an "intuitive interface." It's their job to learn how to do it.* If those statements are familiar, then checking, testing, and training aren't happening—and there isn't a lot of success going around, either.

- *What! Didn't you know we finished the project? We've got a solution. It's around here somewhere.* How many solutions have you bought and then left sitting on the shelf?

- *I think everyone liked it. Well, at least there aren't any complaints.* Maybe people aren't complaining to you because they gave up on you the last time!

- Is this project reasonably small? Pick something that can be done in a few days or weeks with one, two, or three people.
- Can I picture the solution?
- Can I see that having the solution will be good for my business?

If you can answer "yes" to all of these questions, you've got a good first project.

If nothing from your list works, then you might have been thinking big when you made your list. Can you think smaller? Look at the problems and opportunities again and ask, "Is there one small part

▼ **SMART THINKING!**
Start Small

Remember: you're just starting to learn project management. Start with small, short projects. You can tackle larger projects when you have more experience.

If you're just learning to drive, you're better off in a go-cart than in a race car. There's less chance of an accident and less damage if you run off the road. And what you learn on the go-cart track will give you the basics; it will make you ready to race.

Or, think about throwing a party. If you try to cook five or six new dishes, you're likely to run into trouble. With that much going on, something won't work. But if you make one nice, new fancy dish and serve it along with the usual things you cook (or pick up at the store), then your party will be a success and you'll survive the preparation and be there to enjoy it.

Likewise, it's better to keep regular, production work running and do one small project at a time than to do a lot of projects and get overwhelmed.

▼ **SOMETHING SLIPPED!**
Right Program, Wrong Language

I met a computer programmer who saw his company had a problem. They needed to do some fancy financial calculations and they didn't have a program that would do that. So he wrote the program. Unfortunately, when he started writing the program, he wrote it for computers with the UNIX® operating system, because that's what his company had. He didn't ask around and find out that the company was planning to replace UNIX with the Windows® operating system. By the time he finished writing the program, everyone had Windows, no one had UNIX, and no one could use the program.

deeper. You can also describe the environment, the situation around the problem. This is especially important if outside experts—people not in your company or not in the department with the problem—are going to help out.

DEFINE A GOOD SOLUTION

When you've defined the problem or opportunity, you know your starting point. Now, describe where you want to end up. What does the solution look like? How will it work? What will people be doing differently when the solution is in place? What will the benefits be? Or, what will the new opportunity—product sales, new contracts, new services—look like? Be as specific as you can. You should describe it so well that somebody else could do it.

It's kind of odd. When we go to a restaurant and order dinner for $20, we take the time to say exactly what we want. We name the dish, we choose the side dishes, and we give special directions on the preparation—low salt, please, or no oil. But when we are spending $2,000 or $20 million, we just say, "Fix the problem." We don't take the time to spec-

of this I can do now?" Check that smaller problem or opportunity against the questions and see if you get all yeses.

Now, if you've picked your project, give it a name. That will help you keep track of it.

DEFINE THE PROBLEM

In plain English, to define the problem, we ask some simple questions. What's wrong? What is happening now that shouldn't happen? Or what isn't getting done that needs to get done? What does the mess look like?

Or, if it's an opportunity, what is it? What would you sell or deliver? Who would buy it? How much would they pay? How much would you make?

Those are the basic questions, but you can dig

ify what we want. And it's no surprise when what we get isn't what we really wanted.

Time and again, on thousands of projects, I've seen that a clear definition of our goal is the first step toward success. And—you guessed it—a vague definition is the first step toward failure. A clear goal lets people come together and work together. It also keeps others from interfering and changing the goal to get what *they* want, instead of what *we* want. Project managers call a clearly written description of the goal a *requirements specification*.

MAKE A PLAN

If you want to get something done, make a plan—a written plan. In our daily lives, we can plan to do something with family and friends without writing it down, but that's not a good idea at work. At work, there are too many interruptions and distractions. Also, people don't know each other that well. If my wife says she wants to go out to dinner, I can prob-

ably guess which restaurant she wants. But our employees can't guess exactly what we want to do. We have to tell them. If I say, "Don't spend too much money," one employee will be scared to spend $20, while another will think she can spend up to $100. So, in planning, we need to write things down—and write them down clearly. In this section, we'll learn what a plan is and then we'll learn how to plan projects from three angles: the business side, the technical side, and the project plan.

You can use the templates on the CD to create project plans that lay out your problem, your goal, and your path to success.

What Is a Plan?

Once we know where we are and where we're going, the most important part of planning is the steps that get us from here to there. What do I mean by a *step*? A step, also called an *action* or a *task*, is a piece of work to be done. When that work is finished, there will be something to show for it. The finished

---

▼ SMART THINKING!

Cutting to the Root

Henry David Thoreau wrote, "There are a thousand hacking at the branches of evil to one who is striking at the root." This is as true of waste, delays, and poor quality as it is of evil. When we see a problem, we should ask, "Why did this happen?" Instead of just cleaning up the mess, we should make sure that the mess won't happen again.

For example, suppose the purpose of your project is to fix a broken printer. If you fix it, it might break again. If you ask, "Why did it break?" you might find that you bought a cheap brand to save money—and that sure didn't work. So, then you decide to buy a reliable printer to replace the cheap one. Or maybe you consider leasing or getting a service agreement.

But let's go one step further. Do you want to re-eval-

uate your policy for purchasing equipment? Could you prevent this problem throughout your entire company, instead of with just this one machine? That thinking is the basis of continuous improvement, which the Japanese call *kaizen*. We make everything better every day as we learn from each problem.

Then our project might be to create an office policy for buying services and equipment. The policy might say, "Figure out what we need. Figure out if we can get it as a service, so we're not relying on equipment that might break. If we can't, then we buy equipment that is reliable. And, if we use it all the time, we might just buy two."

So the real project wasn't to fix the printer. It was to fix the way we run our company.

---

result of a step of work is called a *deliverable*.

When we work as a team, each thing we complete, each deliverable, goes on to the next person. My deliverable, or *output*, becomes your *input*.

Say we're preparing a dinner for friends. You'll do the cooking and I'll do the shopping. The food I bring home is the ingredients for the dish you are going to cook. If I bring home the wrong ingredients or the wrong quantities or if I forget something, you won't be able to cook the great dinner we planned.

So who should make the shopping list? Not me, the person who is going to the store, but you, the person who will be using the ingredients. You should make the shopping list and I should make sure I understand exactly what you want. If my outputs are your inputs, you are my customer (within the team) and I should give you want you need to do your job well.

We waste a lot of time and make a lot of mistakes because we don't define our inputs and outputs clearly. We give people what we think they want, instead of communicating effectively and giving people what they really want and need. That goes both for our customers and for the people we work with—our customers on the team. If I could pick one thing to teach my entire team, it would be this: Define your deliverables clearly and ask the next person on the team, "What do you need to do a good job?" Then, deliver it, doing good customer service within the team—and with the customer.

As we define each step of work and each deliverable, we are building the steps of our project plan. The project plan steps are the core of our plan. But, just as a tree has to have more than a trunk, a plan has to have more than a list of steps. Now, let's look at how to build a complete plan: one that works for the business, succeeds technically, and works as a project.

KEY TERMS

Step, task, or action The smallest part of the work on a project. One job, done by one person or a small team, with a clearly defined deliverable.

Deliverable An end result to a step of work. It must be clearly defined and someone else must be able to use it without calling on the person who made it.

Requirements specification A detailed statement of the exact results we or the customer want to get from a project.

Process A defined series of steps that gets us from where we are to where we want to be.

Project plan A document that includes our starting point, our goal, the process that will get us to where we want to go, and anything else that will help us make the project work.

Planning for the Business

A project is good only if it is good for our business. Here are the basic questions we must answer in our project plan to make sure that the project is good for the business and fits in well with our other work:

- *What's the value?* When this project is done, how will the company be better off than if we didn't do the project?
- *Is it worth it?* Is the value greater than the cost?
- *Is this the best project to do?* Or is there a better use of our time and money?
- *Can we do this project?* Do we have what it takes?
  - Do we have the expertise inside the company?
  - If not, can we hire it from outside?

- Do we have the time to do this, given everything else we are doing?
- Do we have enough money to do this? If we don't, can we borrow it?

■ *Is this the right time?* Does this project fit in with our work schedule and our other projects?

If we can answer "yes" to all these questions, then the project is a go—we should do it. If not, then the project will run into trouble. And the main goal of business planning for a project is to prevent trouble, to avoid starting something we can't finish.

So, if it's a go, we need to declare it so. We need to create a *project charter,* which is an official statement from the company saying, "We are doing this project. It is important. We will make sure we give it all the money, people, time, and other resources it needs." And we should also name a project manager. The project manager is the person who has the responsibility to make sure the project gets done. And the project manager can do only that if he or she is given authority and resources to match the responsibility. The project charter does just that.

The other important person on a project at the beginning is the project sponsor. The *project sponsor* is an executive who makes sure the company stays committed to the project, makes sure the money is there, and resolves conflicts between the project and other work if something is getting in the way. The sponsor doesn't run the project day to day; he or she is the person we go to when a problem is too big for us, as project managers, to handle.

We'll talk more about all of this in Chapter 4, Your Business and Your Projects. For now, just know that the project manager, who runs the project day to day, needs the authority and resources to get the job done.

Technical Planning

Every project has a technical side. Sometimes, this is obvious. If we're remodeling a building, then the technical side is construction. If we're getting new computers, the technical side is information technology. But I would argue that there is always a technical side. If a marketing department is planning a new ad campaign, then the technical side is knowing good ways of writing copy and designing ads. Whatever kind of work we are doing, we are better off working smart—using the best expertise in our company or the best expertise our company can find.

> ▼ **BOTTOM-LINE BASICS**
> **Even a One-Person Project Is Still a Project**
> On a small project, you may be the sponsor, the manager, and half the team—or even the whole team. We can plan, do, and complete small projects by ourselves, but a project, no matter how small, is still a project. It still is a good idea to have a written plan, a stated goal, a start date, and an end date. That keeps us from wasting time.

Every industry and profession has its own technical skills and standards. When we use those skills and follow those standards, we are planning the technical side of the work. And the better we plan, the better our results will be. A good technical solution gives us what we want, is of high quality, comes at a reasonable cost, and can be delivered on time.

At the beginning of a project, once we've defined the problem, we should figure out what technical skills are needed. Then we get the right people doing the right job—and that's the mix for project success.

Project Planning

Let's go back to our dinner party. We have a basic plan—a number of guests, a menu, and a date set for the party. That's the business side of planning. We've got good cooks, they've selected the best recipes, and they have all their kitchen tools. That's the technical side of planning. Now, there's one more type of plan we need—the project plan. The project plan will take care of nine things:

- *Scope.* Exactly what are we making?
- *Time.* When do we start? When do we end? Who comes at what times? Which job is done each day or each hour?
- *Cost.* How much will it cost?
- *Quality.* How do we make it good? How do we prevent mistakes?
- *Human Resources.* How do we get the right people? How do we keep them and help them improve?
- *Communications.* What information do we need from each person? What do we need to tell each person? How will we keep track of all that information and get the word out?

That may sound simple, but a project manager can easily spend 90 percent of his or her time communicating, making sure people are on the same page and making sure people have the information they need to do their jobs.

- *Risk.* Once we've planned for what we want to do, then we plan for the unexpected. What if it's an outdoor dinner party and it rains? What if one of the cooks gets sick and can't cook? What if the store doesn't have the right ingredients? Expecting the unexpected and figuring out how to succeed anyway is the focus of project risk management.
- *Procurement.* What do we need to buy? How will we get it? If we're hiring services, what expertise do we need and how do we get it? How do we handle invoices and legal contracts and all that stuff?
- *Integration.* Sometimes, a change in one place causes a change in another. Suppose, for example, we have a procurement problem: there's no hamburger meat for the picnic. So, we upgrade to steak. But that costs a lot. So we buy some steak and some chicken. Now, we

▼ **BOTTOM-LINE BASICS**
Plan as Much as You Need to, and No More

All of these areas of planning are important—except when they're not. If I'm doing a small project, such as writing a new ad to put on my web site, I don't need to buy anything. I don't need a contract. If this is something that is part of my regular workday, I don't need to do any special cost management or procurement management for this project. Risk management is minimal. It's all pretty simple. We don't want to overburden ourselves with planning. The most important thing is to make a choice. If money is important, do cost management. If the project isn't routine, put extra time on risk management. If it has to be just right, focus on quality. We don't always need to do all nine areas. We need to think about each of the nine areas and do the ones that matter.

When we make intelligent choices about planning, we save time and money, things go right, time is not wasted, and the job is done well. But we should always do some planning. When I do a two-hour project, I spend half an hour planning. I find that I get a two-hour project done in two hours that way. If I don't plan, I usually end up with a five-hour mess instead.

need a recipe for steak. And steak takes longer to cook, but there's no time spent making hamburger patties. The adults are happier, but the kids are less happy. Just one change in procurement created a change in cost, time, scope, and quality. Integration management is how we keep track of all the ways a change to one part of the plan changes other parts of the plan.

Putting the Plan Together

We've talked about the three parts of the plan: business, technical, and project. Although we talked about them one at a time, they actually all have to be done at once. Why? Because a change in one creates a change in the others. A good project consists of a clear business problem or opportunity, a good technical solution, and the project plan to make it work. We develop all of them together and they all work together.

How much of a project should be spent in planning? Would you believe that it could be more than half of our time! Honest.

Here's an example. Way back in the 1970s, it was found that the cheapest way to run a project for writing a computer program was to spend 60 per-

cent of the time planning, only 10 percent of the time writing the program, and the remaining 30 percent testing and fixing it.

Suppose you decide to buy a new car. You spend a lot of time thinking about what kind of car you want and what you want to do with it (especially if you've got a family and everybody has to plan together and agree). Then you spend time talking with friends about kinds of cars and learning who the best dealer is and looking at cars you might buy. All that time is planning; buying the car—doing the work of the project—takes just a few hours. But aren't you glad you did all that planning and got the car you wanted?

▼ **BOOST YOUR BUSINESS!**
Plan Your First Project

Right now, before you turn the page, plan your first project. A few pages ago, you chose a small project. Now, stop reading and start planning!

Write up a three-part plan—business, technical, and project—for your project. Your plan might be three paragraphs, three pages, or 30 pages—whatever is right for the job. Make that plan right now! For guidance, see the templates in Chapters 3 and 4, the examples in Part III, and the tools on the CD that accompanies this book.

DO AND CHECK

After planning comes doing. The project team gets to work: building, making, writing—whatever the work is. And we check our work as we do it. We need to check the work on three levels—that's right, you guessed it—technical, project, and business.

- *Technical—Does it work?* We test parts, then put the parts together. We test components, then put the components together. We test

---

▼ **THINK FOR YOURSELF!**
Does Planning Matter?

Remember a time when something didn't work. Pick something small—a meeting that didn't go well or a shopping trip where you forgot something or didn't get what you wanted. Now, ask yourself, if you were doing it again right now, how would you make sure it goes right this time? Would a little more planning help?

Let your own experience tell you how much planning you need. It might be more than you would think.

> ### ▼ SMART THINKING!
> #### The Cost of Connecting
>
> One time, a client asked my company to build a computer network link between two of its Arizona offices, one in Phoenix and the other in Tucson, that they needed to run their trucking company. Everyone else told them that a solution would cost at least $10,000. That was four times more than they could afford. I looked at what the business really needed and I found a technical solution that cost $2,500, including equipment and labor. So, good technical planning changed the business decision from "No, we can't do this" to "Yes, we can." Careful project management got the job done on time and within budget.
>
> A good solution brings together smart thinking from the business, the technical people, and the project manager.

the whole thing. If it doesn't work when we test it, we find out what's wrong and fix it right away. This is called PDCA—plan, do, check, act.

- *Project—Are we following the plan?* We track each deliverable and make sure it is done. Then we ask questions. Is it done on time, within budget, and with quality? Have any unexpected events (risks) changed our plan? Are we taking care of teamwork, communications, and procurement in a good way? We track the project in all nine areas that we planned and we take care of problems as soon as they pop up.
- *Business—Is the project still good for the company?* Most of the time, on a small project, the business side doesn't present too many problems. But we need to keep an eye on two things. First, if the business needs change before the project is done, we might need to change the project or cancel it altogether. Second, if the business is thrown off schedule or is short of money, it may be hard to get the people, time, and money we planned for. If we can't get what we need to make the project work, we have to find a way to adjust the plan or we have to fight for what we need to make it work.

Week by week, we track progress on the project, find and resolve technical and business problems, and work until we've completed the plan—we've made what we set out to make. But we're not quite done.

DELIVER THE RESULTS

When the product is ready, we have to deliver it. Delivery can include installation, final testing by the customer, or training. It *must* include whatever it takes to put a smile on the customer's face. When the customer is happy and knows he or she has what he or she wanted from the project, then the product is delivered and the project is over.

At that point, there is some cleanup work to do. If there were contracts, we pay them off and sign off that work is done. We gather our paperwork and make a file that others can look at later. At last, our project is done.

EVALUATE THE PROJECT

Even though the project is done, we and our company might get a little more out of it. Remember that a project is unique work—it's something new. And whenever we do something new, we have a chance to learn something. What did we learn? And what did we get out of the project? We can find out by doing a *post-project review.* A post-project review has two parts:

- *Lessons learned from the project.* Here, we look at what worked and what didn't work. And we decide how to do even better on our next project.

- *Proof of the business case.* When we planned the project, we said it would be good for the business. It would launch a new product line, make money, save money, or something like that. Well, is that happening? Are people using the new product or service? Are they working in new ways? If not, why not? What can we do to make it work? If they are using the product or service, is the company benefiting in the way we said it would—more sales, more income, lower cost, or whatever other changes we expected? And what is the next step?

DO YOUR FIRST PROJECT!

Now it's time to put down this book. You should even take off your thinking cap! Now is the time for action—for doing.

Go ahead and do your first project. This first chapter has provided enough guidance for you to complete a small project that would take two to four hours or a larger one if you have done projects before. Plan, then do the work and keep track of it, then follow through and deliver. If you want some extra help, look at the templates in Chapters 3 and 4 and on the CD.

CONCLUSION: WE CAN GET IT DONE RIGHT

We really can get it done right! Step by step, you can learn how to make a project work. When you put it all together, you'll be solving problems and growing your business like nobody's business—but yours.

What Can PM Do for Me?

Now that you have a sense of what project management can do, it's time to ask, "What can PM do for me?" Think of some things you have tried to do or someone in your company tried to do that didn't work out as expected. Maybe you came up with a plan to save money, but never implemented it. Maybe you bought a new printer, but never installed it. Maybe someone started something and then left the company. It happens all the time. Lots of projects fail.

Keep that in mind as you look at Chapter 2, Why Businesses Need Successful Projects.

Why Businesses Need Successful Projects

IN THIS CHAPTER

- *What is a project?* Projects are about unique work and changing your business.
- *Projects change your business.* You see your business as a system and you manage change.
- *Life cycles.* Our products, our business, and our projects are born, grow up, change, and come to an end just the way people, plants, and animals do. Looking at business and projects in terms of life cycles helps us succeed.
- *It's bad out there.* Many projects fail. Do yours? We can do better.

DO YOU WANT TO:

- Take advantage of opportunities?
- Define and solve problems?

If so, then project management (PM) is for you!

Business is all about problems and opportunities. In business, we want to seize each opportunity—offer a new product while it's hot, solve our customers' problems right away—so we can grow the business and make money. To do that, we have to get the roadblocks out of the way: we have to identify and solve problems. Success in business equals seizing opportunities and solving problems. PM keeps us successful at getting things done, seizing opportunities, and solving problems.

As mentioned in Chapter 1, Joseph M. Juran, one of the founders of the Total Quality Management (TQM) movement, defined a project as "a problem scheduled for solution." To that definition we added, "an opportunity scheduled for realization." If you want to get the most out of your opportunities and solve your problems in the best way, then PM is the way to do it.

Unfortunately, we can't hire a project management company the same way we can hire a CPA firm or an attorney. If we need our taxes done, we can shove all of our financial records into a couple of shoeboxes and let the CPA do his or her magic. A lawyer can represent us and create contracts for us—spend hours of his or her time and hundreds of our dollars—with little direction from us. But our problems are inside our business and we can solve them only by doing good work inside the business. So, if we run a small business or a department in a medium-sized business, we have to learn PM ourselves or hire managers who know PM to make it work inside the company. It's even better if everyone on our team knows what project management is and how to work together to solve problems and get good work done.

WHAT'S A PROJECT?

Any time we solve a problem, we complete a project. Anytime we realize an opportunity, we com-

plete a project. And any time we make a change to how our business works, we complete a project.

Projects are any work activities that are not routine. Table 2-1 shows some examples of projects and some examples of routine work.

Most of what is taught in business school is about the routine work of production management or maintenance and operations. But the more unique work we are doing, the more we need project management methods. Sometimes, we can say clearly, "This is a project" or "This is routine work." But a lot of what we do falls into a gray area in the middle. For those items, we can use some routine management skills and some project management skills.

Here are some tips for when project management helps:

- *If you're starting something new, make it a project.* For example, if you're launching a newsletter or magazine, treat the first four issues as a project. Once you've got it going well, then you can make it routine, write up instructions, and delegate it to someone who can do it regularly, all the time, as production work.

- *If the field is changing, use more project management.* Plumbing is a pretty routine business and fixing a leaky faucet is routine work. A plumber might take one look and say, "It needs a new washer," and probably be right. But fixing a broken computer may not be routine. Because computers are constantly changing, it may be more difficult to know what is wrong. Faucets have been leaking for decades, but just 30 years ago computer viruses didn't even exist. If we need to diagnose what is wrong with a computer before we fix it, more project management thinking is needed.

- *If you need to bring experts together, make it a project.* For an accountant, handling a finan-

Area of Business	Project	Routine Work
Executive	▪ Annual strategic planning meeting leading to new strategic plan ▪ Creation of a new division or special team	▪ Reviewing business status and keeping things running ▪ Routine hiring and professional development
Financial	▪ Installing a new financial system ▪ Annual closing of books, annual taxes, inventories, and audits	▪ Bookkeeping, accounts receivable, accounts payable ▪ Routine tax payments
Product/Service Development	▪ Developing new products or services	▪ Maintaining efficient product manufacturing and delivery
Marketing	▪ Creating a new ad campaign	▪ Running an ad campaign
Sales	▪ Preparing a proposal for a unique product or service for a major customer	▪ Selling many of the same small items to many customers (sales clerk in a store or low-end telemarketing)
Customer Service	▪ Expanding a help desk to handle a new product or service ▪ Announcing and managing a recall	▪ Handling routine questions on a help line or web site ▪ Handling routine customer returns
Research and Analysis	▪ Analysis of the marketability of a new product	▪ Regular, scheduled customer surveys
Infrastructure	▪ Major renovation or construction of a new building ▪ Planning and purchasing a new computer system to run your business	▪ Keeping a building clean and safe ▪ Keeping the computers running

TABLE 2-1. Projects vs. routine work

cial problem is routine. For a computer expert, installing a new computer program is routine. But, if you need to bring an accountant and a computer expert together to install and configure a special computer program to handle a particular financial problem, that's a project. Building a team and coordinating a special effort that isn't part of people's regular work calls for good project management.

- *If you're changing the way you work, make it a project.* Project management can help you plan and deliver changes to your business and make sure that the end result is better—not worse—than before.

- *If you're trying to get jobs done on time and on budget, use project management tools.* Many businesses need to control costs or keep on a tight time schedule—from a plumber doing an emergency repair with only one trip to the hardware store to a team producing a weekly TV show. These are routine jobs, but project management tools help control those budgets and meet those deadlines.

In short, the more unique the work, the better off we are considering it as a project and using project management tools.

BE AN EXPERT!
The Eggheads of Project Management

The Project Management Institute (PMI) defines a project as "a temporary endeavor undertaken to create a unique product, service, or result." The PMI, a global professional association with over 150,000 members in 150 countries, is the world's foremost advocate for the project management profession. To put it another way, the PMI does for project management what the American Bar Association does for lawyers.

Though I call us PMI members "eggheads," I mean that with affection and admiration. Eggheads are people who care about sound theory. The PMI consists of theoreticians and also good-hearted, hardheaded business managers. In this book we'll turn sound theory into good work and business success.

When the PMI calls a project a "temporary endeavor" it simply means that projects have due dates and deadlines. Every project delivers something and there's a time when it's got to be there. Basically, we're going to decide what we want, plan for it, put in money, smarts, and effort, and deliver it on the due date or by the deadline.

The resources we put into a project can be measured in dollars. We will buy materials and equipment, we will pay our staff while they do project work, and we may pay experts or consultants, as well. So projects have a budget.

But it isn't good enough to spend money within our budget and deliver something on time. That *something* has to work: it has to solve the problem or give us what we need to realize the opportunity. And it has to improve the bottom line.

So, projects aren't just about delivering on time and on budget. They are about delivering *value* on time and on budget. In Chapter 3, Solving the Right Problem, we'll take a long hard look at delivering value. For now, think of value as the benefit we gain from:

- Defining a problem, coming up with the best solution we can find, and delivering that solution
- Making something in our business work better
- Delivering a new or improved product or service
- Taking advantage of a unique opportunity

PROJECTS CHANGE YOUR BUSINESS

Projects have a delivery date, but they don't just go away after that. They leave something behind. Usually, they leave behind a new way of working. If

BOTTOM-LINE BASICS
The Wrong Change Makes Things Worse

Suppose that you told me that you wanted a trailer on your car and I went out and bought a trailer, found your car parked in your driveway, and hooked up the trailer. When you saw it, you'd probably be upset. Why?

- I haven't taught you how to drive with a trailer. Now, you can't even back out of your driveway until you find me.
- You discover you need new shock absorbers to haul the trailer, so you have to unhook the trailer and take the car to the shop before you can use the trailer.
- Your gas mileage is going to go down and you haven't budgeted for that.

The lesson: A project is likely to make things worse unless it includes good communication, training for people to adjust to the change, and planning to make sure everything works when the project is done.

that new way of working is better, then you get more done, make more money, and realize more value. If that new way is worse—as it is all too often—then the job gets harder and we end up worse off.

Sometimes, one little change is simple and doesn't cause any trouble at all. Another time, a small change can make a huge difference. When one light bulb on a Christmas tree goes out, it doesn't matter much. But when the string on a bead necklace breaks, the beads roll all over the floor and the necklace is gone. One dent in the body of a car doesn't keep the car from running. But one small problem with the engine, transmission, drive train, axles, or wheels and the car can't go anywhere.

To understand this difference, we need to understand what a system is. And if we want to understand why project management is so important, we need to understand how one change to a system can fix or improve—or break—the whole system. And this matters because—you guessed it—your business is a system.

A *system* is a bunch of parts that work together to perform a specific function inside an organism or an organization. Those parts can be procedures, components, or smaller systems. When one system is inside another, we call it a *subsystem*.

▼ KEY TERMS

System A set of components (bunch of parts) that work together to perform a specific function inside an organism, organization, or larger system.

Component or **part** One element in a system. This could be a process (such as a set of instructions), a physical object or tool (such as a computer or car), a person or team, or a subsystem.

Subsystem A system that is part of a larger system.

▼ FOCUS!
Systems and Subsystems: Your Body and Your Business

Your body is a system made up of subsystems. For example, you have a circulatory *system* that moves oxygen and nutrients to all your cells and takes away carbon dioxide and waste products. You have a respiratory *system* to receive oxygen and release carbon dioxide. These systems and others together form your body. And your body is part of you. And you are part of society, which is part of the human race, which is part of our lovely planet Earth, which is part of the solar *system*....

Similarly, your business has subsystems. Even if you are a one-person shop, you do different work that has different functions. For a list of the functional systems within a business, turn back a few pages to Table 2-1 and look at the left column. Areas like sales, marketing, executive, and financial are all parts—subsystems—of any working business. And your business is part of an industry, which is part of the economy, which is part of society.

The lesson: If you start to see your business as a system, it is easier to define and solve problems.

So, a business is a system made up of subsystems. So what? Well, there are some fundamental rules about systems that make all the difference.

- If we change one part of a system, we change the way the whole system works.
- When the parts of a system don't communicate or don't work together well, the system fails.
- When a system has problems, the symptoms are in one place, but the source of the problem is likely to be somewhere else.
- When things around a system change, the

system has to change to adapt and keep working.

Since projects change the system of our business, we'd better make sure the whole system works better after the change. When we think in terms of systems, we can solve the right problem, instead of just running in and tinkering and hoping things get better. And we can work to make sure that the solution doesn't create more problems than it solves.

Many projects fail because the people involved don't consider the consequences of the fundamental rules of systems. Here are some examples of what can go wrong.

- A small company lands a huge new contract. The company grows quickly to serve the big client. But management can't find good people quickly enough. Old customers, used to prompt service, are upset at the new delays. The new contract falters. The company had a great opportunity, but as a system it wasn't able to change to take advantage of the opportunity and ended up worse off.
- Can you remember a meeting or event for which the schedule or location changed at the last minute and not everyone got the news? Some people didn't make it or were very late. Without good communication, the team as a system can't get the job done.
- Suppose sales of your product are falling. Are salespeople doing a worse job? Is your new ad campaign getting a bad reception? Or was a batch of product bad and word has gotten around that what you sell is no good? Before rushing ahead to solve the problem, find the real source and solve the right problem.
- Until yesterday, you ran the only coffee bar in town. Starbucks moves in down the block. Now what? You'll have to change your business to stay in the game.

There are so many ways to handle change badly. You need to learn how to manage change in a way that works.

EVERYONE NEEDS A LIFE CYCLE

Everything has a beginning, a middle, and an end. Living things must grow, mature and serve a purpose, and then pass away. Birds must grow inside eggs before they can survive out in the world. After they hatch, chicks depend on their parents. Then they learn to fly from their parents. At last, they go off on their own as adults. The same is true for products, companies, and projects.

- A product must be developed inside the company before it is released (hatched). Then it must grow in the market, perhaps losing money when sales are low and sales costs are high, until it breaks free and, as a mature product, flies into the market and makes money for the company.
- Many companies now start up in business incubators funded by local governments, which helps reduce start-up costs. When the business grows, it can fly on its own.
- A project begins when we give birth to a new idea or a new way to solve a problem. Our planning stage is the crucial, early stage equivalent to the time in the egg. When we finish planning and start work, we are making something new and the product, service, or system is real, but still under development, still growing. We help it grow and we test it. When it passes all the tests, it is ready to fly to the customer and it doesn't need us, the project team (its parents), any more. It moves into a productive (adult) life and we move on to bring up new projects.

Thinking in terms of life cycles helps us plan product marketing and plan business growth. These plans include problems and opportunities, so they lead to the definition of new projects that will help our business. When we are working on just one project, we can think about the life cycle of the project as well. That helps ensure project success.

Product Life Cycles

Marketing, as a field of study, offers a standard model for the life cycle of a product or service, shown in Figure 2-1. In the first phase, the product is under development and there are no sales. In the introduction phase, sales may grow slowly and then climb rapidly in the growth phase. Sales are stable during maturity and then go down as the product enters the decline phase.

This diagram can describe a single product from a single company (say, the Dodge Neon) or a class of products from many companies (say, four-door cars). It applies to services in the same way. In fact, for our purposes, everything we say applies to products, services, and solutions—to anything we sell to our customers. In general, whenever you see the word *product* in this book, you can replace it with *service* or *solution*—whatever your company offers. And what we say here applies to not-for-profit organizations, government agencies, and any other organizations that provide products, services, or solutions. For example, a university provides educational services and the U.S. Postal Service provides mail and package delivery services.

When we plan to produce and market a product, we should be aware of two things:

- *Where is our product in its own life cycle?* Is it still under development? Have we introduced it? Are sales growing or are they leveling off into maturity or heading into decline?
- *What is the stage of the life cycle of this type of product in the market?* Are we the first to introduce this product? Is the market growing? Are we competing in a mature market? Are we trying to stay in business with a product in decline?

Our project plans for producing and selling our

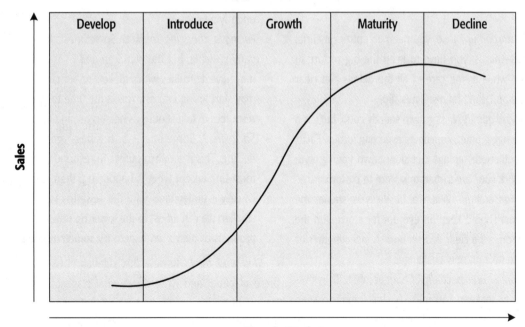

FIGURE 2-1. The product life cycle

▼ KEY TERMS

Customer A company or a person who pays for a product, service, or solution. Individual customers are often called *consumers*. *Business customers* may use what we sell or, if *resellers*, sell it to their customers.

Product A physical thing that a company sells.

Service An activity that a company sells.

Solution A combination of products and services that solves a problem for a customer. Some businesses see themselves as *solution providers* for their customers, rather than simply as providers of products or services.

Industry All of the related companies that produce, sell, or service a related set of products or services.

product will be based on the answers to these questions. For example, if our goal is to be first to market and competitors are developing similar products, then delivering quickly makes time a priority on our project. If we are making changes to our marketing strategy because product sales are in decline, then we may have more time, but we will have less money to work with, so we will want to keep project costs tightly under control.

Of course, in the real world, the situation is often more complex. We may face a declining market in North America and then discover that we can introduce our product to Eastern Europe or South America, where it's the hot item with rapid growth. We may think the market is declining, but actually sales are in a slump due to the season or to a need to revamp our marketing campaigns. Most of the time, if we understand the product life cycle

▼ BOOST YOUR BUSINESS!

Where Is Your Business?

Is your business …

- *Just starting up?* If so, you need an entrepreneurial focus—that is, you have to keep the big picture in mind while taking care of all the details. Set clear goals and don't let deadlines slip.

- *Growing quickly?* Fast growth sounds good, but it is a challenging time, sometimes even dangerous. Focus on bottlenecks—things that slow down your growth or block your production or service to customers.

- *Holding steady?* When a business is stable, the owners should keep an eye out for storms on the horizon, set a clear course, and choose whether or not to take on new challenges.

- *Changing unexpectedly?* Changes of staff, ownership, or location can make it challenging to keep the business going—and growing—steadily. Identify these changes, face them head on, and look for

underlying causes.

- *Facing a changing market?* Sometimes, the company is stable, but the world around us is not. We may have difficulties with suppliers or our customers may start losing interest. This is the time to use our resources to adjust our business to outside changes.

- *Shrinking?* Sometimes, a business goes into decline. This is a difficult time. To respond well, we must first accept what is happening, then study it. Once we understand why the business is getting smaller, we can adjust to the lower demand for our products or plan a strategy to try something new.

Stop and think! Review this sidebar now. Grab a piece of paper and write down what stage of the life cycle your business is in. Then ask, "If that's the situation my business is in, what's the biggest problem I can solve to make my business work better?"

and apply it with a bit of common sense, using our own experience, we'll make the right choice about what to do.

Business Life Cycles

Companies and organizations also have life cycles. They are, of course, a good deal more complicated than product life cycles. If we understand where our company is in its life cycle, we can plan better projects to solve the company's problems and to seize the opportunities in a changing market. To see where your company is in the business life cycle, use the sidebar, Where Is Your Business?

Project Life Cycles

Projects have life cycles, too. As project managers, we define and control each project from beginning to end. This allows us to define our project life cycle. The most basic reason for defining a life cycle is that a project is simply too big to think about all at once. It is much easier to plan and deliver a project if we do it in stages.

To make the stages clear, we end each one with a clear set of deliverables. We then review all of these deliverables and make sure that we've done a good job in that stage. The review time is called a *gate*. If the deliverables are all in good shape and the company still needs the project, then we approve the completion of the stage we just finished and we approve the start of the next stage.

The simplest life cycle (Figure 2-2) has three stages: plan, do, and deliver. Keep the life cycle that simple unless you have a good reason to make it

---

▼ SMART THINKING!

One Solution After Another

A friend of mine has been running a stock photography business, selling pictures to advertisers and textbook publishers, for over 30 years. The last seven years have been one challenge after another. First, he had to get a new computer system before the year 2000, when the old one would stop working. Then he went through a major ownership struggle. Then the whole industry moved to the Internet and he had to move too or lose the business. At the same time, the bigger companies were buying the smaller ones left and right. His customers went through a big downturn in late 2001 (after September 11). Then, due to changes in technology, his whole industry moved into a declining phase.

In the middle of all of this, he had to keep his business running from day to day and to keep producing books, brochures, and catalogs as marketing tools. And, like any other business owner, he faced the routine problems of computer system failures and staff changes.

He's still in business. How did he do it? I see him do four things:

- He always thinks and decides what the biggest problem is.
- He's pulled all the members of his team together; they've all become a great bunch of problem solvers.
- He keeps an eye on his industry and the economy by reading and by going to general trade shows, so that he knows where his business and the industry are going.
- He confers with experts to think through problems and relies on experts to get technical jobs done.

The lesson: My friend thinks through problems and defines projects. He succeeds by realizing opportunities. He is a businesses owner who uses project management to move through challenges and succeed. You can do it too.

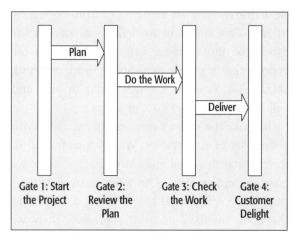

FIGURE 2-2. Simplest project life cycle

more complicated. For tips on choosing the best life cycle, see the sidebar, What Makes a Good Project Life Cycle?

In Table 2-2, we make the life cycle real. Here, we apply the simplest life cycle to three types of projects: solving a problem, realizing a new opportunity (such as increasing sales through a trade show or marketing campaign), and developing a new product or service.

▼ BOTTOM-LINE BASICS
What Good Is a Project Life Cycle?

Defining a life cycle for each project does a lot of good things. With our project broken up into stages, we can:

- *Save money* by planning early, reducing costly mistakes.
- *Reduce risk* by setting up gates between the stages, where we make sure the project is on track.
- *Grow the team,* using fewer people early on and then bringing more people on board as we finish planning and begin the work. If our team is rightsized all the way through the project, we'll save money.

▼ KEY TERMS

Stage (or phase) A large, defined piece of a project that ends with a clearly defined set of deliverables.

Milestone A defined set of deliverables due at the end of a phase or stage. The term comes from the markers along roads that tell us how far we've come—and how far we still have to go. The PMI has a similar definition of a milestone: a significant point or event in a project, usually completion of a major deliverable. I'm looking at milestones in terms of our work process; the PMI is looking at milestones in terms of reporting project status.

Gate A review process at the end of a phase where we make sure the deliverables are all in good shape and we decide whether or not to continue the project. We can also put a gate at the beginning of the first phase to make sure everything is lined up and our project is ready to go.

Planning is our chance to make our mistakes on paper, instead of in the middle of our work. It is easier to change a blueprint than to change a building under construction. And the same rule applies to computer software, ads in a marketing campaign, and everything else we do.

▼ BOOST YOUR BUSINESS!
Apply a Life Cycle to Your Project

Pick one problem, opportunity, or new product or service that you're working on right now. Think about your work plan. Have you defined your stages and gates—checkpoints where you make sure everything is going right? If not, would the project run better and would you be more confident of success if you added some stages and gates?

Project 1: Solving a Problem						
Gate 1: Start	**Stage 1: Plan**	**Gate 2: Review the Plan**	**Stage 2: Do the Work**	**Gate 3: Check the Work**	**Stage 3: Deliver**	**Gate 4: Customer Delight**
Work to be done						
Name the problem. Launch the project.	Describe the problem. Define the solution.	Ensure the plan is complete and the project is worth doing.	Do the work to create the solution and test it.	Make sure the solution is good.	Deliver the solution. Train people as needed.	
Deliverables						
Project charter	Project plan	Approved plan, schedule, and funds	Workable solution past initial tests	Solution ready to put into place	Solution in place, people working in a new way	Problem solved!
Project 2: Realizing an Opportunity						
Work to be done						
Name the opportunity. Launch the project.	Describe the opportunity. Define the work to be done.	Make sure the plan is doable and the project is profitable.	Prepare for the event. Work on the campaign.	Final check before the event or launch.	Launch the campaign or run the event.	
Deliverables						
Project charter	Goal statement and work plan	Work plan approved and team launched	Ready for opportunity (event, campaign)	Everything ready to go	Customer contact	Customer delight, company profit
Project 2: Developing a New Product or Service						
Work to be done						
Create a short description of the product. Launch the project.	Describe the product, its purpose, and its market. Plan how to develop, test, and produce the product.	Ensure development plan is complete and workable. Ensure product is good for company.	Develop and test the product. Develop and test the marketing plan.	Complete all product tests. Ensure the product is ready for market. Improve and approve the marketing plan.	Produce the product for sale. Perform marketing before launch date.	Introduce the product to market.
Deliverables						
Project charter	Product description, product development plan	Approval and funds to launch product development	Product ready for production, marketing plan ready for launch	Product enters production, marketing begins	Product launch and beginning of sales	Customers delighted with the product

TABLE 2-2. Apply a simple life cycle to your project

▼ Focus!

Planning Saves Money—and Saves Your Project

Study after study shows that the more we plan well early, the less the whole project costs. With good planning, it costs much less to deliver the same thing!

How much less? Would you believe ten times less? That's right: study after study, in all kinds of industries, shows that fixing an error during planning costs one tenth of what it would cost to fix the same error during the project. And that's true for constructing buildings,

making cars, or writing computer programs. Planning always pays off.

In fact, poor planning often leaves the project so badly off that it fails altogether. So, to save money, deliver sooner, reduce the chances of failure, and allow your team to focus on making it good (instead of just making it through), here's what you have to do: plan, plan, plan.

IT'S BAD OUT THERE—PROJECTS ARE FAILING ALL THE TIME

"Aw, come on," you say, "it can't be that bad." But it is: projects get into trouble and get their businesses into trouble all the time.

There are many definitions of project *success* and project *failure*. For example, is it a failure if the project is late and over budget, but still delivers the product? Or is it a failure only if nothing gets delivered at all? If a project is canceled for a good reason, is that a failure? Different studies use different definitions, but overall, we find that 50 percent to 75 percent of all projects fail. I could cite statistics from one state's information technology projects that would show that $100 million more was spent in one year than was budgeted. The cost overruns on some military projects, such as the missile defense shield, are staggering. Maybe government and big

▼ Be an Expert!

What Makes a Good Project Life Cycle?

Larger companies and government agencies put a lot of time, energy, and brainpower into creating life cycles. At small and medium-sized businesses, we can keep it simple, but still learn from the best.

- *No more than six stages.* Harold Kerzner, author of *Advanced Project Management: Best Practices on Implementation,* recommends that we keep the life cycle simple—six stages or fewer. I've seen life cycles with ten or 12 stages, but if there are too many stages it tends to create delays as we try to get each stage approved by everyone.
- *Remember: "life" is the key word.* A good life cycle is modeled on the success of the biological life cycle.

- *At one company, every project uses the same life cycle.* Remember how, as kids, we would get together to play a game and then argue about the rules. The same thing will happen if different projects and different project managers use different life cycles. We should train the whole company to use the same life cycle so that, as people move from one project to another, the rules stay the same.
- *Use the best life cycle in the industry.* In each industry, there are project life cycles that work well for the type of work being done. If you really want to get ahead, learn what life cycles are used in your industry and pick the one that works for your company.

▼ SMART THINKING!

Storyboards Make It Better

Before the filming of the three movies in *The Lord of the Rings,* every single shot was planned in a drawing called a *storyboard.* That is, the script was turned into a visual layout–one camera shot after another–showing all of the action and special effects. All that careful planning paid off. The movies were delivered on time and on budget and won multiple Academy Awards.

Was there a connection? You bet. The storyboards:

■ Allowed directors and actors to block (plan) each scene, saving time on the filming.

■ Allowed stunt crews to plan stunts safely.

■ Gave special effects people advance time to figure out the least expensive way to produce great effects.

■ Guided the post-production crew in putting the whole film together to create great movies.

■ Let the whole team work together, contributing creative gifts to the final product.

The lesson: Good plans keep everyone on the same page, letting everyone focus on quality, reducing time and cost while improving the result.

▼ THINK FOR YOURSELF!

Project Success at Your Business

What's happening at your business? Are projects being defined? If so, are they delivering on time and within budget and giving good results?

Make a list of projects that have been completed or are ongoing. What can you say about your company's success rate?

If you haven't defined projects, how has that worked for you? Do problems get solved? Do they come back again? Can you realize new opportunities and grow your business?

---

business can afford to throw money away like that. But small and medium-sized business can't.

And that is what this book is about. We need to solve problems without wasting time and money. Let me say that clearly, in full: we need to seize opportunities and define and solve the real problems of our businesses, getting the job done right the first time, almost every time. Otherwise, our business falters.

So, the bad news is that lots of projects fail and lots of money gets wasted.

The good news is that you can do it differently—and the answer is in your hands. A few companies (I would estimate maybe one in ten or one in 20) do good project management. Project after project, these companies solve the right problem. In these companies, problems get solved and things move ahead. When an opportunity comes, they see it, take advantage of it, and grow. These companies adjust to changing market conditions, they improve products or services, and they solve their own problems and their customers' problems. If you want to run your organization like that, then this is the right book for you. Because we're going to learn from the best and make it work for you. In business, when you've solved all your problems, what's left is success!

Well, what's left is success until the next day, when more problems turn up. But that's OK. We learn to walk by falling down and getting up. We grow our business by winning some, losing some, and staying in the game.

Now, you know why you need project management. Read on! In Chapter 3, you'll learn how to apply project management to solve the right problem.

▼ BE AN EXPERT!

Three Good Reasons to Cancel a Project

Very often, we get locked into the idea that we have to complete a project. But there are times when it's better to quit. The fact that we've already spent money on the project is not always a good reason to continue; it doesn't make sense to throw away good money after bad—after money that's already gone. Sure, it's embarrassing to cancel a project. But isn't embarrassment better than losing your shirt?

So, at every gate, we should ask, "Is there a good reason to cancel the project?" Here are some good reasons to consider:

- *It's going to cost too much.* If the project cost exceeds any amount of benefit we can expect from completing the project, it's time to stop.
- *Better never than late.* Usually, we say, "Better late than never." And usually, that's true. But for some projects, it's better to call it quits instead of delivering late. For example, the owners of a chain of supermarkets realized that they could not get all of their computers up to date before the year 2000. Instead of trying, they quit. That's right—they sold the whole supermarket chain to a larger company

that already had a computer project that was going to make it on time. And, instead of spending lots of money and then going out of business, they made money on the sale of the business.

- *We don't need it any more.* Sometimes, the company's needs change before a project is done. If the new product or new way of working isn't going to help the company, then stop the project before you spend too much money. For example, over ten years ago, IBM was planning to acquire some software companies and develop a word processing program to compete with Microsoft Word. The day before they bought a certain company, the guys upstairs at IBM changed their mind and closed down the whole division. They realized that competing with Microsoft Word wasn't the direction they wanted to go in, so they canceled the project and freed up the money for something else.

The lesson: It's never easy to cancel a project, but sometimes, it's the best thing to do. And when a project should be canceled, it is better to cancel it sooner than to let it keep running until it runs into the ground.

Solving the Right Problem

IN THIS CHAPTER

Chapter 3, Solving the Right Problem, is organized around two basic ideas. The first idea is the four questions we need to answer to define a project:

- *What* is the problem or opportunity?
- *Why* should we solve this problem or seize this opportunity? What makes it worth doing?
- *How* should we solve this problem?
- *Whether* we should do this project. Is it worth doing? Is it the best use of our team's time and our money?

The other key idea in this chapter is *gap analysis,* the idea that we can define any problem, opportunity, or project as a gap between *where we are now* and *where we want to be.* You'll learn to use these ideas as we go through the four sections of this chapter:

- *Which problem do I tackle first?* Sometimes, we're so overwhelmed it's hard to know where to start.
- *Defining the problem or opportunity.* You'll learn how to cut a problem down to size. Then we'll

look at diagnostic tools for moving from symptoms to the source of a problem and marketing tools for defining your customers' problems. Our customers' problems are our opportunities.

- *Picking a solution.* Sometimes, there are multiple ways to solve a problem: some slower, some faster; some cheaper, some more expensive; some basic, some offering extra advantages. The best solution is the one that fits your business needs.
- *Will this really work?* Before we start the project, we'd better be sure it's going to work. There are three questions. Technically, can we make this solution happen? As a project, is it well planned and supported? And, for the business, is it a good fit?
- *Is it really worth doing?* Before you buy stocks or bonds, you evaluate what you're getting for your investment. A project is no different. We'll look at how to calculate return on investment (ROI) for a project.

I N MANY COMPANIES, RUNNING AROUND PUTTING out fires has become a way of life. That's good—if you're a firefighter. But fires are bad for most of us—at home or at work. If we want our business to do good work and make good money, letting fires happen is a big problem. Most of our resources—and often, all of our profit—go into putting out the fires and cleaning up the mess. If we learn to prevent fires, then we focus on serving our customers and seizing opportunities for growth.

So where do we start? As always, we start where we are:

- *If you have lots of fires to put out,* start by putting out the most important ones before your company is toast. See each fire—each crisis—as a problem to be solved. This chapter will show you how to knock out those problems one after the other, so you have some space to take control of your business.
- *If things are going well and you have time to choose what to do next,* then this chapter will teach you how to prioritize your problems and opportunities. Then you'll know which project will give you the biggest bang for the buck.

Solving the right problem means knowing what all the problems are, figuring out which ones are most important, and then looking at each problem or opportunity so that we can decide what to do. This is illustrated in the project funnel (Figure 3-1).

We start by brainstorming, talking to people, and doing research to find as many problems and opportunities as we can. We cast our net wide—the more problems, the better. Why? Because if we don't find the right problem, the most important thing to be doing, then we can't fix it. After brainstorming to get lots of ideas, we prioritize them. This begins the winnowing process, the process of separating good ideas from bad ones, important

▼Focus!

Fix the Problems That Matter

Too often, we spend our time running around putting out fires. We need to get on top of our problems and see what really matters to our business. When we do this, we catch problems before the crisis. Let's do fire prevention, instead of firefighting. Fire prevention costs less and does less damage than letting fires burn, then putting them out, and then cleaning up the mess afterwards. If we can get one step ahead of our problems, we can focus on making our business grow, instead of running ourselves ragged as we jump from one crisis to the next, trying to keep things going.

problems and opportunities from ones that won't really make a difference to our business. As we do this work, we move down the funnel until we have some project plans.

Then we look at each plan and ask, "Can we do it? Is it feasible, workable now? Or is it too expensive, or too risky, or just plain too much hassle?" That takes us further down the funnel, to a short list of projects that we can do. Then we sort them out, asking which projects are worth doing right now.

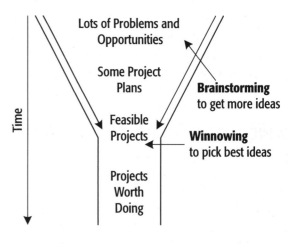

FIGURE 3-1. Project funnel

The small business project planning process (Figure 3-2) shows the work of this chapter as a flow chart instead of a funnel. Here, you see the processes you will learn in this chapter. If you're not familiar with flow charts, just follow these guidelines as you read Figure 3-2:

- *Arrows are the work flow.* Start at the top and work your way down.
- *Rectangles are processes,* where you do work and create output. Since these are planning processes, your outputs will be documents.
- *Boxes with wavy lines at the bottom are documents.* In this case, each document shows the number of the table in this chapter that is the template you will use to create documents with descriptions of problems, opportunities, and projects.
- *Diamonds are decisions.* When we get to a diamond, we evaluate a document, answering the question in the diamond. If our answer is "no," we follow the "no" arrow. If our answer is "yes," we follow the "yes" arrow.

If you compare the flowchart in Figure 3-2 with the list of topics in this chapter, you'll see how the flowchart is a road map of what you're about to learn. This chapter will give you all the processes and tools you need to be able to do all the tasks, create all the documents, and make all the decisions in the small business planning process. When you get to the end, you'll really know how to make project management work for your company. So, let's start at the top and follow the flow together.

WHICH PROBLEM DO I TACKLE FIRST?

Sometimes, we have just one big project or one big problem. If you book half your sales for the year at the annual exposition for your industry and it's coming up, then making sure that your presentation at the expo works is number one. If you have

a department of five positions with three vacancies, then hiring is your highest priority. But don't be fooled. Sometimes, the urgent thing that we're working on is not all that important.

In fact, *urgent* and *important* are two completely separate ideas.

> ▼ **KEY TERMS**
>
> **Urgent** means that a thing must be done by a certain time or it has no value. For example, if you are delivering a proposal to a customer and the customer doesn't accept late bids, then it is urgent to finish the proposal and deliver it on time.
>
> **Important** means that a thing matters, that it makes a difference. If we can measure the value in dollars, then the bigger the difference to the bottom line, the more important. Things we can't measure exactly, like customer goodwill and employee retention, can also be very important.

So, let's say that you've cleared your desk and you have a little room for planning what to do next. Here's how to decide which project matters most:

1. Make a list of problems and opportunities. (You can review your questionnaire results from Chapter 1 and you can also use the sidebar, Five Ways to Make a List of Problems and Opportunities.)
2. For each thing on your list, decide how important it is.
3. For each thing on your list, decide how urgent it is.
4. Organize the list using Table 3-1. (Instructions for using this tool are at the bottom of the table.)
5. Delegate anything you can to someone else.
6. Come up with a plan to take care of small things.

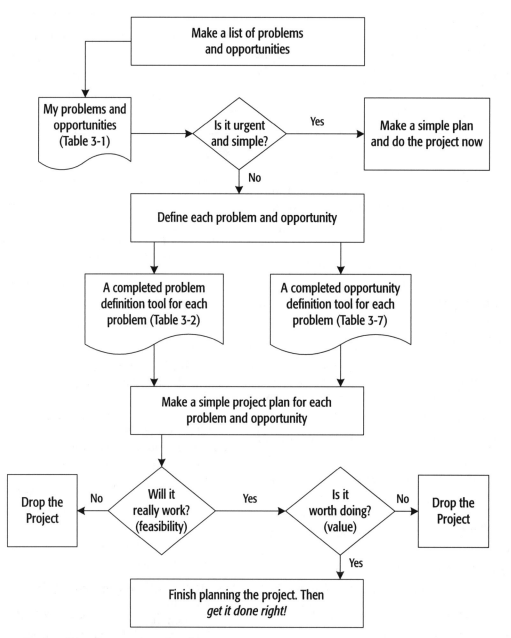

FIGURE 3-2. The small business project planning process

7. Pick one big thing that is important—and maybe urgent—and make that your next project.

8. Go through the planning steps in this chapter. If that project turns out to be too difficult to do now, go back to your list and pick a different problem or opportunity.

Company name:		
My name:		
Date:		
Urgent		**Important (but not due soon)**
Item	*Due date*	*Item*

Instructions:
1. Write each important item on a separate 3-by-5 card or sticky note.
2. Pick a date and put all items due before that date in one stack, called Urgent Items.
3. Organize the Urgent Items stack in order of due dates, with the item due first at the top.
4. Put all the other cards or notes in a separate stack, called Important Items.
5. Organize the Important Items stack in order of importance, with the most important item at the top.
6. List the urgent items in the left column of this table, from most to least, with the due date next to each item.
7. List the important items in the right column, from most to least.

Now, you're ready to turn each item—each problem or opportunity—into a project.

TABLE 3-1. Problems and opportunities

▼ BOOST YOUR BUSINESS!
Five Ways to Make a List of Problems and Opportunities

There are many ways to make a list of problems and opportunities. Here are some of my favorites.

- Write down your worries. Then organize them into a bulleted list.
- Write down the things you'd like to do. Then organize them into a bulleted list.
- Bring your team together for a brainstorming session. Keep it practical. Sometimes, it's good to keep it specific, too. You can bring up a question such as "How can we sell more of Widget model 102?" or a more general question, such as "How can we improve the sales department?" The more experience your team has working together, the more general the question can be. (See Chapter 11, Focus on Success, for how to run a brainstorming session.) (continued on next page)

- Listen to your customers. See the sample project, a customer survey, in Chapter 10, Delivering Customer Delight.
- Look at results. You can look at sales results, productivity reports, employee retention rates, or measures of productive work hours. Compare present results with past results. Are you where you want to be? If not, plan to get there. That's a project.

So, if you've followed the steps above, then you have goal—a problem you want to solve or an opportunity you want to seize. If not, go back and do one of them now! Why wait?

DEFINING THE PROBLEM OR OPPORTUNITY

In this section, you will learn how to think about and understand problems and opportunities. We'll include tools for defining a problem, describing an opportunity, and understanding the root cause of a problem.

Defining a Problem

How do we understand a problem? A problem has some or all of these five parts: a crisis, a symptom, a consequence, a cause, and a root cause.

If there is a crisis, we take care of that first. Then we look at the symptom. We separate the symptom from the consequences of the problem and we evaluate the consequences. If the consequences are costly enough, then we decide the problem is worth fixing. (Otherwise, we choose the least expensive solution—live with it!) If we decide to fix the problem, we look at the cause and the root cause. Understanding those will help us develop the best solution.

Let's take a closer look at each of these ideas:

- *What makes a problem a problem?* A situation is a problem only if it gets in the way of doing what we want to do. Some people can make big problems out of situations of no real consequence, making a mountain out of a molehill. Business problems basically come in two forms: barriers to ongoing business and barriers to realizing new opportunities.
- *A crisis requires urgent attention.* Sometimes,

▼ KEY TERMS

Problem A situation that, if not resolved, will create results we do not want or prevent us from doing what we do want.

Crisis A situation that must be not handled immediately or things will get much worse. All crises are problems, but not all problems include a crisis.

Symptom A sign of a condition. In this case, a sign or indication of a problem.

Consequence The result of an action or an event, whether negative or positive.

Cause A reason that something else happens. A cause leads to a consequence. Be aware that most problems have more than one cause.

Root cause A deep underlying cause, a cause of other causes.

Permanent preventative solution A change in the way we work that eliminates a root cause, so that the problem and similar problems cannot happen again in our company or our department.

part of a problem requires immediate action: if we don't do something, things will get worse. We may not be able to solve the problem. We take care of a crisis so we can buy time to fix the problem.

- *The symptom tells us about the problem.* The symptom is something we can see or smell or measure that tells us that there is a problem. Where there's smoke, there's fire. The smoke is the symptom and the fire is the cause. Doing something about the smoke does nothing at all. We have to look deeper than the symptom to find the cause. Then we can make a real difference.

- *The consequence of a problem is the unwanted results if we do nothing.* When we describe a problem, the consequence is the possible future of the problem. If we solve the problem, we won't have that unwanted consequence.

- *The cause is the center of the problem.* The most basic project is to define the cause of a problem and change that cause so that the problem stops happening. Sometimes there's more than one cause that we may have to fix.

- *The root cause is the cause of the cause.* Sometimes, we solve one problem after another, yet the problems keep coming back. It's just like pulling up dandelions: if we don't get out the whole root, dandelions will keep coming up. If we can find and dig out the root cause, then the problem will never happen again.

- *A permanent preventative solution puts an end to a root cause.* If we remove all the dandelion roots from our garden, then the dandelions never grow back. If we remove all the root causes of our problems from the way we work, then our problems don't come back any more.

When we encounter a problem, our first question should be "Is there a crisis?" If so, then take care of the crisis. If not, then relax and look at the problem before you try to solve it. If there's no cri-

---

▼ THINK FOR YOURSELF!

A Sticky Situation

Sometimes, we can learn an idea from a silly example. Let's try that now. Suppose you've gone for a long walk on a hot day. As you're walking, you notice something sticky on the back of your leg. You take a look: it's lemonade. You remember that you brought a bottle of it to drink if you got thirsty. The bottle must be leaking.

Now, here's the exercise. Take a piece of paper and do the following:

1. Write down as many bad ways to solve this problem as you can.
2. For this problem, write down:
   a. The symptom

   b. The problem
   c. The cause (or one possible cause)
   d. The likely consequence if you do nothing
   e. The worst possible consequence of doing nothing
   f. A possible crisis that could be part of this problem
   g. A good solution to the problem
   h. A possible root cause of the problem
   i. A good permanent preventative solution, assuming that your answer to *h* was the root cause
3. After you've written your answers, look at my answers (on next page).

Sid's Answers to a Sticky Situation

Don't read my answers until you've written your own!

For #1: five bad ways to solve the problem.

- Lick the juice off my leg. That's taking care of the symptom without addressing the problem.

- Just not worry about it until things get really sticky. That's ignoring the problem.

- Pull the bottle quickly out of my backpack, not noticing it's upside down, so that all the lemonade spills out all over my backpack. That's a solution without planning that makes things worse.

- Throw away the bottle of lemonade. That's a wasteful solution.

- Decide never again to take lemonade or water on my walks. That's giving up what we want, not solving the problem.

For #2:

a. The sticky juice I feel running down my leg is the symptom. It tells me about the problem.

b. The problem is that my lemonade is leaking from its bottle.

c. The cause could be that the lid of the bottle is loose or the bottle could be leaking.

d. The likely consequence: my leg and my backpack will get stickier and I'll lose my lemonade.

e. The worst-case scenario: I'll stop when I'm too tired to walk. Then, fire ants will come to get the sweet lemonade and I'll get bitten all over my leg. Then I'll try to walk home, but, without my lemonade, I'll die of heat exhaustion. (I naturally think like this. That's probably why I've become an expert in planning.)

f. A possible crisis: I'll get very hot and thirsty and have nothing to drink, leading to heat exhaustion.

g. A good solution: Drink the lemonade now, and wipe off my leg.

h. A possible root cause: I used a bottle with a lid that doesn't lock down.

i. A permanent preventative solution: Get a good bottle that is leak-proof and has a locking lid and always use it when I go for walks. Even better, get more than one so that I always have a clean one available.

The lesson: Learn to break a problem down into symptom, crisis, consequence, and cause. Then you will be able to solve the right problem in the best way. If you're already good at this, teach your team to do it, too!

---

sis, we've got some time to understand the problem and come up with a really good solution. When we can describe a problem's symptoms, consequences, and causes, we can say that we understand the problem. For practice, see the sidebar, A Sticky Situation. For a tool that will help you describe a problem, see Table 3-2.

Sometimes, when we've defined the problem, there is one clear, obvious, easy solution. In that case, we should just do it. All too often, though, the situation isn't that clear. If a problem has multiple causes, we might need to fix one of the causes, some of the causes, or all of them. If a problem is really expensive to fix, then we might be better off living with the problem and managing it rather than solving it. For example, if we have dandelions in our garden, it might be easier, cheaper, and healthier to weed the garden once a week than to dig up all the dandelion roots or use weed killer. So, instead of solving a problem, we can *bring it under management.*

Finding Multiple Causes—the Ishikawa Diagram

Sometimes, one problem has many causes. Let's say, for example, that you find that you are staying

Name of the problem:
My name:
Date:
Company name:
Problem Description
Is there a crisis? Yes ____   No ____ (If yes, take immediate action, then come back to complete this form.)
What are the *symptom(s)*? (What tells me there is a problem? What do these symptoms tell me about the problem?)
What are the *causes* of the problem? (List one or more causes.)
What are the *consequences* of this problem? (What will happen if you do nothing? List one or more consequences.)

TABLE 3-2. Problem-definition tool

▼ **BOOST YOUR BUSINESS!**

What Problems Are You Living With?

Take a look at your company or your office. Talk to the people on your team. Ask yourself and them, "What problems are we living with? What things do we have to take care of or fix or adjust over and over?" Write down a list of problems that you are living with, titled *Problems Under Management.* Next to each problem, write down the name of the person who knows the problem best. (That's usually the person who has to fix it all the time.)

For each problem under management, give a copy of the problem definition tool (Table 3-2) to the person who knows the problem best. Have him or her describe the problem. Then you and your team are ready for the next step, picking a good solution.

late at work more often than you like. Something that used to be normal is becoming a problem. You decide that, from now on, you'll always leave work at 6:00 p.m. So, you want to find out *all the reasons* why you work after 6 p.m. and then change all of those causes so you can go home earlier.

If you came to me and asked for some guidance on this problem, I'd introduce you to the *Ishikawa diagram*, also called a *cause-and-effect diagram* because it shows many causes for a single effect. So, let's make an Ishikawa diagram together.

The first thing I would have you do is gather some data. Until now, you've had no reason to ask, "Why do I stay at work after 6 p.m.?" Now, you want to know. That requires some simple research. I'd ask you to set a timer or alarm clock at work to ring at 5:30. When it rings, you stop whatever you are doing and fill out the answers the questions in Table 3-3.

When we have ten or 20 or more sheets on which you've recorded why you stayed until 5:30 or would need to stay past 6:00, we analyze them. Our first step is to combine similar instances and do a tally, counting the times that each reason was a cause. We can show the tally in a table (Table 3-4).

With this data in hand, I ask you to enhance it by using your memory of your experience. Can you say more about any of these instances? Are there any other reasons you can remember from the last year or two? When we talk about it, you realize that work often piles up while you are at the Wednesday afternoon staff meeting. You also remember that, before you began keeping track,

you were working late quite a bit during your company's busy season, from October through Christmas. Then you create an updated version of the table, based on those changes (Table 3-5).

Sometimes, it is easier to see things in a picture, instead of a table. The Ishikawa diagram in Figure 3-3 lays out the information from Table 3-5.

As the diagram shows, most of the causes are related to fulfilling client requests. That's no surprise, as making the customer happy is your job. But what do we do about it?

Once we see all the causes of a problem, we can decide what steps to take to solve the problem. But do we need to address every cause or just some of them? That depends on two things:

- *How much improvement is enough?* If our goal is to make the situation better, but it's not cost-effective to eliminate the problem, then we need to remove only enough of the causes to obtain the desired result—doing more would be extra work with no real benefit. On the other hand, if we want to completely fix the problem so it doesn't happen again, we may have to address every cause. In our example of leaving work earlier, if our goal is to leave later than 6:00 no more than twice a month, then we may not need to address every cause. But if our goal is to leave at 6:00 every night, then we need to address every cause.

- *What happens to the system when we make a change?* In Chapter 2, we introduced the idea of a system, where causes and effects interact

Sample Cause-and-Effect Data-Gathering Tool: Why I work after 6 p.m.
Date:
Why am I still at work at 5:30?
Will I need to stay past 6:00?
Why will I need to stay past 6:00?

TABLE 3-3. Sample cause-and-effect data-gathering tool

Sample Cause-and-Effect Data-Gathering Tool: Initial data for staying late at work	
Reason for staying late at work	*Number of times it happened*
Too much work piled up	13
Got a client phone call late in the day	7
Filling rush request for client	5
Arrived late and had to make up time	3

TABLE 3-4. A sample cause-and-effect data-analysis tool

Sample Cause-and-Effect Data-Analysis Tool: Revised data for staying late at work	
Reason for staying late at work	*Number of times it happened*
Stayed late during busy season	20
Too much work piled up	8
Got a client phone call late in the day	7
Too much work piled up after weekly staff meeting	5
Filling rush request for client	5
Arrived late and had to make up time	3

TABLE 3-5. Revised data for staying late at work

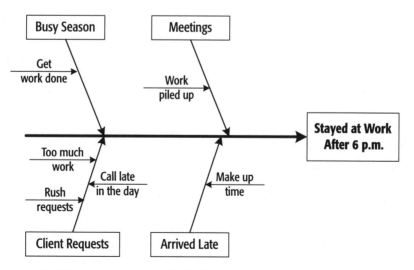

FIGURE 3-3. Sample Ishikawa (cause-and-effect) diagram

in a complicated way. In a system, multiple causes may be required for a single instance. For example, a part will fail only if three different things go wrong at the same time. Perhaps my car fails to start only if the temperature is below 40 degrees, it rained during the night, and I haven't driven the car in 24 hours. In that case, even though there are three causes, I can simply start the car twice a day and be sure it will always start. I've addressed only one of three causes, but I've solved every instance of the problem. On the other hand, we find some problems, such as leaving work after 6 p.m., where any one of several causes can create the problem. In a case like that, to eliminate the problem we have to deal with every cause.

In our example, let's say that it is essential to always leave by 6 p.m. and also essential to complete all rush requests from clients. And, as much as possible, we want to keep the backlog small at work. Given those goals, we need to address every cause. Table 3-6 shows how we might do that. Note that for some of the causes there is more than one solution. For each cause, we put the best solution first; if we can't make that one happen, we have other things to try.

Sometimes, our problems seem overwhelming. It would be easy to imagine someone saying, "How am I ever going to leave work every day at 6:00? I stay late half the time and I don't even know why!" If we take the time to break down the problem and find all of the causes, though, good answers often just pop right up.

Of course, this kind of analysis requires an understanding of the issues involved. If we're trying to

Leaving by 6 p.m.	
Causes (reasons for staying late at work)	**Solutions (ways to be sure to leave by 6 p.m.)**
Stayed late during busy season	▪ Arrange to have an evening assistant during busy season. ▪ Come early most mornings during busy season.
Too much work piled up	▪ Leave at 6 p.m., but come in early the next day.
Got a client phone call late in the day	▪ Don't take phone calls after 5 p.m. Let clients know this, then check messages when I get home.
Too much work piled up after weekly staff meeting	▪ Ask the boss to move the meeting to the morning. ▪ Come in early on Wednesdays and get all work cleared before staff meeting.
Arrived late and had to make up time	▪ Work up list of problems and solutions so I don't arrive late. ▪ Arrange with boss so that, if I arrive late, I can make up time by coming in early the next morning, instead of staying late.

TABLE 3-6. Leaving by 6 p.m., causes and solutions

solve a technical problem, we need the right expertise. I can usually figure out why my computer breaks down, because I spent 15 years as an IT technician. But when my car breaks down, I call my brother: he's the auto mechanic in the family. At the same time, the right technical expertise isn't enough. Technical experts need to be given tools like the ones you've seen in this section—including the Ishikawa (cause-effect) diagram—so that we have a structured process of defining our problems. So, practice these tools and give them to your team and you'll all be tackling problems before they tackle you!

To summarize what we're learning about problems and solutions: these are the keys to success in defining multiple causes, performing root cause analysis, and implementing permanent preventative solutions:

- Don't let yourself be overwhelmed by the size or difficulty of the problem.
- Use the right experts, people who know the environment and work processes well.
- Take time to really look at the situation and gather data.
- Think of the situation as a system of multiple causes creating multiple effects.
- Define clear, workable goals.
- Define your solution—how you will reach those goals.
- Do it—*get it done right!*

▼ BE AN EXPERT!

What Problems Can't Be Solved?

Many problems that look impossible can be solved, once we define them clearly and get the right expertise. But some can't—at least not within our organization or not within the time and money available. In fact, when a problem can't be solved, it's almost always for one of these three reasons:

- *There really is no answer—yet.* Science and engineering have not yet solved some problems. The good news is that, for most of us in small and medium-sized businesses, we rarely run into such problems. In business, it pays to solve problems, and someone, somewhere, probably already has a solution. If we can't fix it ourselves, we can probably get the help we need.
- *We don't have the time, people, and money.* Sometimes, we can't fix a problem in time to meet a particular goal. Maybe the government is requiring us to report certain employee information, but we just can't afford the computer software upgrade that will get the job done in time. So, we may face

paying a fine and then fixing the problem when we can afford to fix it.

- *The corporate culture won't allow a solution.* Unfortunately, our own corporate culture is all too often the barrier to good solutions. Consider our example of wanting to always leave work by 6 p.m. In some companies—often called family-friendly—this would be easy. At these companies, everyone respects our home life and the organization makes allowances for balanced lives. However, at some other companies, the culture may simply say, "If you don't work late, you're not right for us, you're not showing the dedication to the job that you should." That may not be true at all—maybe you can get more work done in eight hours than most other people can in 12—but the culture sets the rules and those rules are hard to challenge and change. So, sometimes, the organization and the people are unwilling to accept a good, easy, cost-effective solution to the problem.

Finding the Root Cause

Once we've defined a problem, we can ask whether we want to solve just this one problem or go after a bunch of similar problems all at once. To go after many problems at once, we will need to do more work. We'll need to understand the root cause of the problem and design a permanent preventative solution.

What is a root cause? As we've seen, problems have many causes. If we go one step further, each cause has a cause—something that made that happen. And, of course, those causes have causes as well. We can always go back and find an earlier cause. Doing that is the first step in a root cause analysis.

Our second step is to look at the causes we've found. We try to find one cause that is a cause of many causes of many problems.

Suppose we find water damage in our warehouse. That's the symptom. We look around and find water damage in many places. At each location, we trace the cause. When we do, we find that the roof above the leak either is patched or has an opening for a vent, door, or chimney. Around all of these openings, the roof is leaking. So, we talk with a roofing expert. He tells us that old roofs, before they wear out totally, become difficult to patch. Our roof has gotten old and it will continue to leak at seams and patches.

In this case, each wet spot in our warehouse is a symptom. Each situation where water is leaking in is a problem. Each leak is a cause. But the one root cause is that we have an old roof.

At this point, we have two choices. If we just want to solve each problem, we can patch the leaks. That would solve the problems and not cost too much. But we could be pretty sure that those patches, and all the other seams, would break open again. Our other choice is to tackle the root cause: our roof is old and can't be patched well. So, our solution is to get a new roof. We call the solution to the root cause of a problem a *permanent preventative solution,* because, if it works, we will have no more leaks.

In some cases, it is obvious that we need to solve the root cause. In other cases, we may find that we have a choice—to solve the problem and live with similar problems for now or to go after the root cause. Near the end of this chapter, we'll ask the question, "Is it better to just fix the problem or to go for a permanent solution?"

When we have a technical problem with a car or a leaky roof, finding the root cause is fairly simple, because the problem is physical. An expert could hear the story about the car and say, "There's your problem!" A roofer takes one look at your old, worn, patched roof and says, "There's your problem!" Unfortunately, when we're looking for a problem inside a business, we can't see a physical source of the problem. When we look for the root cause, we're not looking for a hole in the roof; we're looking for a hole in our system, a process that doesn't work right.

One key to finding the root cause is to realize that it might be in one of three places. The root cause might be:

- *Inside our own business.* This is good. If the root cause is inside our business, then we have control of the process that isn't working—fixing the problem is up to us.

- *Inside a vendor or customer.* This is not quite so good, but it's not all bad. We don't have control to make the change happen, but we have influence. If we can convince the vendor or customer to make the change, then we can solve the problem permanently. Or, alternatively, we may find that we're better off getting a new vendor or even firing the customer.

- *Out in the world at large.* Sometimes, we've done all we can inside the company and with those whom we can influence (our area of concern). At that point, the causes are a part of the larger business world or society. We want to make changes, but we cannot. We have to live with the problem.

We may find multiple causes or even multiple root causes. If we do, we are always better off working first in our own business—our area of control—then in our area of concern, and last accepting the world at large and working with the problem as best we can. There is a very simple way to do this. When we identify a root cause, we ask, "What can I do about this?" When we figure out what we can do, then we take control of the problem and work toward a solution.

For example, let's say that we're tracing all the reasons for defective products going to our customers. At first, we identify the mistakes we're making inside our own company. We might find root causes like poor inspection, poor training of new workers, and pressure to deliver defective items to meet production quotas. Maybe it takes us three years to straighten out all those problems. Then we start all over again: we do an analysis of why customers receive defective products. This time, we find that our vendors are supplying us with parts that aren't good enough; that's the source of most of the bad products. It would be easy to say, "There's nothing we can do about that." But it wouldn't be true. After all, these vendors are our suppliers, so we are their customer. We can evaluate how we choose our vendors and we can share with them our methods of eliminating defects.

Japanese car companies began doing that back in the 1970s and American car companies followed suit in the 1980s and 1990s. Product quality improved a great deal during those years; profits improved as well. The process was called Total Quality Management. Even though most U.S. companies dropped it because they thought it was a passing fad, the companies all around the world that kept doing it are getting better and better every year. And you can do it to.

▼ BOTTOM-LINE BASICS

Here and Now

The causes that matter are the ones that are happening right here, right now. Psychologists look for causes that happened years ago, in our childhoods, but what can we do about those? For a business—and for us as individuals—the causes that matter are the things we can change. They are the choices we make and the ways we do things that just don't work for us. When we aren't getting the results we want, it's best to ask, "What can I do differently that will get me what I want?"

▼ SMART THINKING!

The Only Problem Left Is the Time Zones

Dr. Harold Kerzner, a recognized world expert in project management, asked his best clients what problems they were having managing their projects. These are companies that have been improving their project management skills continuously for 30 years. In the past, they reported problems such as adjusting to different cultures around the world and bringing vendors on board with their projects. However, recently, the best companies are saying that their biggest problem is time zones. When a project spans the U.S., Europe, and Asia, someone is going to have to wake up very early in the morning to make the weekly project status meeting. As long as the world keeps turning, that's a problem we'll just have to live with.

The lesson: If we keep improving, over time, we can solve *almost* all of our problems.

Defining an Opportunity

An opportunity is a chance to make things better. In business, that's usually, but not always, a chance to make more money. To make more money or get more customers or grow the business or whatever, we need to change what we are doing. Our actions cause our results. Only if we change what we're doing can we seize the opportunity and get the better results.

Defining an opportunity means defining the new results and defining the new ways we are going to work to get them. This is all part of planning. After we define the opportunity and plan how to get there, we may decide that it isn't worth it. So we'll define the opportunity, plan how to get there, and then evaluate it to see if it's worth doing.

So, the key to defining an opportunity is to ask, "What will be different?" Specifically:

- *The results.* How will your business results be different once you've realized the opportunity? Will you make more money, gain new customers, have customers buying over the Internet instead of by phone?
- *The process.* For each person, describe the

▼ SOMETHING SLIPPED!

Bigger Isn't Always Better

A friend of mine told me this story. He knows someone who owns a landscaping business. The man enjoys the work and does an excellent job. He had lots of happy customers—so many that he realized he could grow his business. He thought he could make a lot more money if he hired other people to do the landscaping while he got new customers and managed the work.

He grew the business and it was successful. He had many more customers and many people working for him and a lot more money coming through the business. And he spent the time managing the customers and the schedule and keeping everyone happy.

But there were two problems. First, although a lot more money was coming through the business, he wasn't bringing home more money at the end of the month. His income was higher, but with paying workers, his expenses were higher, too. In the end, his profits were no higher than before. The second problem was worse: he didn't like being a manager. He enjoyed working outdoors and running equipment, like backhoes and mowers and tractors. He didn't like spending all day indoors at a desk on the phone getting other people to get their backhoes where they were supposed to be. It was as if he had quit a job he loved to take a job he couldn't stand—for the same pay.

Many business owners find the same thing—that growing the business means doing less of what they love and that it usually isn't worth it. This story, though, ends well. The landscaper saw that what he was doing didn't work for him. So, he shrunk his business back to what he wanted it to be: himself, one assistant, and a backhoe keeping a few customers happy.

The lessons:

- *Bigger isn't always better.* More money coming in (gross revenue) does not mean more money you get to keep (profit or net revenue).
- *When our businesses change, we have to change what we do.* So, let's make sure we're going to like our new jobs before we make the change.

Defining and planning opportunities gives us the chance to see these changes *before* we make them, so that we only make changes that really leave us better off.

---

difference in *how* he or she will work. Maybe you'll spend more time selling to customers while others work more in other areas. Or, maybe you'll do work more in other areas while others spend time doing sales. Maybe you'll all do the same jobs, but on laptops and with cell phones, working from home and on the road, instead of coming into the office.

You can use Table 3-7 to describe and define an opportunity.

The best way to describe a new opportunity combines creativity with good analysis. To ensure creativity, write down your idea in one or two paragraphs before you use Table 3-7. Write it so that anyone in your company could understand it. Don't write more than a sentence about *why* you want to do it; that will come later. Then add good analysis to your creativity by filling out a copy of Table 3-7. You can get an editable copy of the tool from the CD that came with this book.

Show what you've written to everyone whose job will change with the new opportunity. Get their ideas and make it even better. In fact, make it as good as you can. Come up with a realistic, solid plan that makes your business better.

How much time should you spend defining an opportunity? That depends on several factors:

- *How big is the expected change in results?* The bigger the chance for growth, the more time it's worth exploring the idea.
- *How big is the change in the way you work?* Note that this can be different for different players. For example, in the sidebar, Bigger Isn't Always Better, the change for the company was small. But the owner's whole job changed—and in a way he didn't like.
- *How big is the risk?* If this opportunity is a real challenge, if it relies on things outside your control or if it may just be too big or too

difficult, then plan it and evaluate it closely before you go ahead.
- *How much will it cost?* Time and money spent on planning should be proportional to the investment.

Put lots of planning, thinking, and research into a new opportunity—look before you leap. Why? Because every opportunity you invest in cuts off other opportunities. Moving your business into the future is like climbing a huge tree with many branches. Every time you step out on one branch, you leave all the other branches behind. You move ahead, but you limit your choices to the branches of this branch. It is very costly to go back to another branch and very risky to leap from one branch to another. So, before we set a new direction, we should be sure that that branch will take us where we want to go.

When you've described and defined your opportunity well, you are ready to prepare an initial project plan for realizing the opportunity. When you have the opportunity defined and the plan sketched out, you can make a final evaluation of the opportunity and the plan before you go ahead. The most important tool in evaluating an opportunity is *return on investment* (ROI), which we will learn later in this chapter, in the section where we ask, "Is it really worth doing?"

KEY QUESTIONS IN DEFINING A PROBLEM

So far in this chapter, we've defined problems with their symptoms, consequences, causes and root causes. And we've defined opportunities with their changes in results and changes in the way we work. In doing this, we've defined *what* the problem or opportunity is. To fully understand a problem and whether or not we should make a project to fix it, that is one of four questions we should answer.

Let's take a closer look at the four key questions in defining a project and deciding whether to do it:

The Question	How It Is Now (before they change)	How It Will Be After the Opportunity Is Realized
The Results of the Opportunity This section describes business results before and after the change.		
Money		
Gross revenue		
Net revenue		
Customers		
Number of customers		
Type of customers		
Staff		
New staff		
People in different jobs		
Jobs that will be lost		
Products and Services		
New products or services		
Products or services that will be eliminated		
Changes or upgrades to products or services		
Tools and Equipment		
New tools and equipment		
Tools and equipment that will go away		
Tools and equipment that will be replaced or upgraded		
The New Way of Working This section describes our work process—how we do our work before and after the change.		
Executive Leadership Functions		
How will owners', executives', and senior managers' jobs change?		
Product and Service Development		
What will change in the ways we create our products and deliver our services?		

TABLE 3-7. Opportunity-definition tool (continued on next page)

The New Way of Working

This section describes our work process—how we do our work before and after the change.

The Question	How It Is Now (before they change)	How It Will Be After the Opportunity Is Realized
Marketing		
What will change in the ways we market?		
Sales		
What will change in the ways we sell?		
Client Services and Customer Support		
What will change in the ways we serve clients and respond to customer support requests?		
Financial Operations		
What will change in the ways we do accounting and financial work?		
Research and Analysis		
What will change in the ways we do research and analysis?		

TABLE 3-7. Opportunity-definition tool (continued)

▼ SOMETHING SLIPPED!

It's the Starter—Not!

On the radio show *Car Talk,* a woman told a story of how her car wouldn't start and it made a peculiar grinding noise whenever she turned the key. Every local mechanic—and a few local know-it-alls—said, "It's the starter." Well, she had the starter replaced three times—which cost a bundle—before she called the show to find out what the problem *really* was. Following the advice from Click and Clack, the show's hosts, she went on to replace the gear that was broken—and was breaking one starter after another.

The lessons:

- Fixing the wrong problem is expensive and useless. I'm sure you've had experiences like that. Can you think of one that is happening in your business right now? Would it be worth the time to stop and figure out what the real problem is before trying another quick fix?

- If we don't fix the root cause, then the problem keeps coming back. In this case, the gear that was stripped was destroying starters, one after the other as she replaced them.

- *What* is the problem or opportunity? In project management language, we are defining the *scope* of the project.
- *Why* should we solve this problem or seize this opportunity? Here, we are talking about value, benefit over cost, and return on investment.
- *How* should we solve this problem? For now, we'll be answering this question at a very high level. We'll be sketching out the basic ideas of the project plan, but we won't spend the time to create a full plan until we decide to do the project.
- *Whether* we should do this project. Is it worth doing? And, of all the things we might do, is this project the most important and the most valuable?

By the end of this chapter, we will have answered all of these questions. We'll have created a list of possible projects and then chosen which one to do first. And, for that project, we'll have a very good understanding of what it is we're doing and the beginning of an understanding of how we're going to do it.

We can round off the topic by introducing an approach called *gap analysis*. After that, we will look at some templates that I call *problem-definition tools*. As you'll see, a lot of project planning involves writing down ideas and asking questions to expand and clarify those ideas. Templates are a great way to do this: they tell us which questions to ask.

After that, we'll work to make a clear picture of our project—our problem and its solution—by looking at how to evaluate market opportunities; how to bring the customer, business, and technical team together with good *architecture*; and how to define the *driver* of a project and project *constraints*. When we've done all this, the project is well enough defined so that we can move on to the last section of this chapter, where we look at the project and ask, "Is this really worth doing?"

▼ BOTTOM-LINE BASICS

The Three Things You Need to Know to Get Anywhere

If you want to get anywhere, you need to know three things:

- *Where you are.* If you want to reach my house and you call for directions, I'll ask where you are. If you're lost, we'll have to figure out where you are before we can get you going in the right direction.
- *Where you want to go.* If you ask for directions as you leave my house, I'll ask where you want to go. If you haven't decided where you want to go, you can't get there.
- *The territory.* If you don't know your way around town, you're going to need to get a map.

This is just as true of a project as it is of a road trip. We plan a project by knowing where we are, knowing where we want to go, and knowing the territory. If we don't know, we learn and decide. Then we plan how to get there—and go!

Gap Analysis

From the beginning of this book, we've been doing gap analysis. Now it is time to understand the general idea. Any problem or opportunity can be defined as a gap. A gap is a space between two places. In gap analysis, the two places are *where we are now* and *where we want to be*.

When Evel Knievel decided to do a motorcycle jump across the Grand Canyon, he had a project. The start of the project—the first side of the gap—was him and his bike on one side of a very big gap—the Grand Canyon. The end of the project—the other side of the gap—was him (still alive) and his bike on the other side. Early on, he decided that that gap was too big, so he redefined the project to a smaller gap—the Snake River Canyon, which is narrower.

No bike in existence could make that jump, so now he had a problem on his project. And we could see that as another gap. He had to close that gap by creating a better bike, one that might make the jump. He got that far and he tried the jump. The bike didn't make it. However, with the help of a parachute (a good contingency plan!), he survived and got some pretty good press in the process.

This example makes four points:

- Every opportunity in our business can be seen as a gap between where we are and where we want to be. A project will close that gap.
- Every problem in our business can be seen as a gap between where we are and where we want to be. A project will close that gap.
- Every problem we encounter within a project can be seen as a gap, also. The small problems—not having the right tool or the right person for a job—are gaps that we can fix with a little planning and a little work to keep the project rolling along.
- We can keep going with gap analysis, defining and closing smaller and smaller gaps. Suppose the project is a road trip and the gap is from here to our destination. The first problem is that the car isn't working. The gap for that problem is from car not working to car ready for the trip. Then we have a second problem: we can't get the part to fix it. The gap for that problem is between no part and part. Breaking things down into finer and finer steps like this is called *progressive elaboration*.

Using gap analysis—thinking about where we are and where we want to be—has important advantages:

- *It keeps us focused here and now, on the present and the future.* It keeps us away from the blaming questions like "Whose fault was it?"

> ## ▼ KEY TERMS
>
> **Gap analysis** The approach of seeing any problem or opportunity as a gap—a space to be crossed between where we are now and where we want to be.
>
> **Progressive elaboration** Defining something very broadly at first and then in more and more detail as we go along. Progressive elaboration allows us to rightsize our problem solving.

Blame only wastes time we could be using to make things better.

- *It keeps things simple.* We can always picture where we are, where we want to be, and the path to our goal. This makes it easy to plan, to lay out our project the way we would plan a road trip.
- *It brings the team together.* If I disagree with someone, I can apply gap analysis. The gap isn't between the other person and me. It's a gap for both of us, between where we are—not agreeing—and where we want to be—in agreement or respecting our differences and working together.

Making a habit of gap analysis is a good idea. Then the team can always work together to solve problems and no problem is too big to solve. If we add progressive elaboration, the small problems won't trip us up along the way, either.

PICKING A GOOD SOLUTION

In this section, we'll put together everything we've learned so far. We'll put it together into templates—blank forms you can use to define problems and projects. As you use the templates, whenever you see "Where am I now?" and "Where do I want to be?" think *gap analysis*. Also notice that each template usually asks the basic questions about a project: what, why, how, and whether.

▼ KEY TERMS

Template A form with spaces for you to write in, where you spell out key ideas clearly.

Checklist A form with checkboxes that helps you make sure you don't miss any steps.

Templates and checklists are the easiest way to learn new and better ways of working. If you've used them in your office, you probably already know that. If not, see the sidebar, Templates Make Your Life Easier, for tips on how to get started.

Using Table 3-8, the template for the simplest project plan, we can put together all the good planning we've done so far this chapter. I suggest you fill out one copy of Table 3-8 for *each* of the problems and opportunities you listed at the beginning of this chapter. When you're done, you'll have a clear understanding of each project and they will all be defined in the same way. That will make it easy to evaluate each project and to compare one project against another so you can decide which one to do first.

Table 3-8 can also be used for a quick project you're going to do right now. You can write it up and then follow the steps, checking off each step when you finish it. If the project is going to take

▼ BOTTOM-LINE BASICS

Templates Make Your Life Easier

I use templates all the time, in more ways than you can imagine. I probably go a bit too far when I have my shopping list on the fridge with separate boxes, one for each store, and a master list of things to check if I have before I go to the store. But, in business, I don't think we can go to extremes with templates. Here are some ways I use them:

- To define projects
- To give out work assignments
- To think through problems clearly
- To teach my staff how to do their jobs
- To help my staff learn how to think clearly
- To put an idea in front of everyone, so that we're all on the same page (literally), with the same understanding of the problem, project, or issue
- To make a good comparison between or among projects by describing each project in the same way, filling out a template for each project

If we use templates well, they help us work smarter and faster. For some people, templates are quick, easy, and obvious. But others have attitude problems with them. Here are a few problems and suggestions for getting beyond those attitudes.

- *The problem:* Templates make me nervous. They're intimidating. They feel feel like an exam: I have to fill in every box and get every answer right the first time. *The solution:*
  - Templates just show you a good way of thinking. Think of a template as a PM coach, guiding you in thinking through your problems.
  - Each box is a question to help me with my thinking.
  - I don't have to answer all the questions at once.
  - If I'm not sure, I can write down an answer, then put "??" next to it, to remind me to check on it later.
- *The problem:* Templates are just paperwork for someone else. In a bureaucratic environment, templates are going to seem like a waste of time. *The solution:* Templates are for me, to help me think more clearly.

- *The problem:* These templates aren't my own. I don't feel like some of the words are appropriate. There are some boxes that I don't need. I need other boxes. *The solution:* Make the templates your own. Rewrite the templates, revise them, change them any way you want. Make them work for you.

Even if you don't feel resistance to using templates, they may still not feel familiar to you. So, here are some practical tips for working with templates.

- *If you can, use a computer.* Word-processing programs like Microsoft® Word are great, because we can fill in each space on a template with as much writing as we want and, even better, we can move our ideas around easily, with cut and paste instead of scratch out and rewrite. Spreadsheet programs like Microsoft® Excel take a little practice, but they are very good for sorting lists or doing calculations.

- *If you can't use a computer, keep copies of the templates around.* You can photocopy the templates from the book and keep a stack available for use.

- *Make sure you understand the templates.* The best way to understand a template is to read the book so you understand each idea through explanations and examples and then use it a few times. The CD that comes with this book includes detailed explanations and examples for each template.

- *Use the templates as a team.* Templates are a great way to get team members to all think in the same way and work together easily. They eliminate a lot of misunderstanding. Once team members understand a problem the same way, a good solution is close at hand.

less than four hours, this project plan is probably the only one you're going to need.

For larger projects, we start with this plan. Then, we take each project through the two questions at the end of this chapter: *Will this really work?* and *Is it really worth doing?* At that point, we can sort our simple project plans into three groups:

- *Toss it into the trash.* This is the group of projects that are not worth doing and will never be worth doing.

- *Wait until later.* In this pile, we have the projects that are either not important or too big or challenging to take on right now. For example, if you're in the middle of a busy sales season and you get a good idea for a new product to develop, you can set the project aside until the summer lull, when you'll have time to work on it. We can make a note on each project plan saying when might be a good time to do it—either a date, like "next summer," or a situation, such as "after we hire a new marketing manager and he or she builds the department"—and file it for later.

- *Consider doing now.* These are the projects we might just start today. This stack is the input for the next chapter, Your Business and Your Projects. There, we'll look at how you can set up your business to keep running and make projects succeed at the same time. We'll then take this stack of simple project plans and turn them into full-blown projects in Chapter 5 and carry them through to success in Chapters 6 and 7.

Are you ready for the next step? We're going to look at two key ideas. The first is *architecture,* a poorly understood idea that can make the difference between an easy, low-cost success and an expensive disaster. The second idea is *constraints and drivers,* which are important to understand so that you don't end up with confused project team members pulling against one another in different directions. Then we'll tie this section together by

▼ BOOST YOUR BUSINESS!

Train Your Team with Templates

I hired a college student as an administrative assistant. I offered him the templates I used, but I didn't insist. However, I required that he write down all his work so that we wouldn't lose track of what he had done and what he still had to do. At first, he didn't want to use templates or use the computer; he kept a large pad with notes and numbered items and a lot of scratching out and rewriting. Occasionally, he lost track of things. We discussed this and he saw the value of putting an organized list on the computer. I showed him how templates like the ones in this book made it very easy to keep track of multiple jobs and projects all at once. He used the templates and read books about the ideas behind them for a couple of months.

When he started, the assistant was bright, but he couldn't always think his way through a problem clearly. As he practiced with the templates, he was more and more able to complete project plans by himself.

After that, I encouraged him to write a job description for the new job he wanted at my company, director of marketing, and also job descriptions for other market-ing positions we will need to fill as we grow. He did an excellent job. He designed a whole department and showed sharp, clear thinking in the process. He showed he was ready to seize an opportunity that will give him a career and help my business grow. As a result, he earned a promotion from administrative assistant to director of marketing in eight months.

I asked him how he had learned so much in just a couple of months. He said that by doing three things—working with the templates, studying the ideas, and using a computer to keep things organized—he had learned how to think about and organize all of his work.

The lesson: People who want to grow, learn, and solve problems can really get ahead by working with templates. Why? Because templates condense a lot of useful knowledge into practical tools that let us work smart, quickly, and easily. If you and your team make practical use of templates, you can go from overloaded and struggling to effective, efficient, and growing in just a few months.

building an example of a project that gives us some new ideas about how to sell things to our customers.

Architecture—Bringing Together Customer, Business, and Technical Views

As we said in Chapter 2, a project is a system: if one part of it doesn't work, the whole thing can fall apart. Given that each project always has three aspects—business, project, and technical—there is a big risk that something will go wrong. Very few people can keep all three aspects of a project in mind at one time. That talent is called *architecture*—and it is worth learning to do it well.

If you and your family have bought a piece of land and are hiring an architect to design your dream home, she will look at the building from three perspectives:

- *A home for you—her customers.* This is the business perspective for the architect, whose job is to understand your family, your activities, and your needs and to create a picture and a plan of the home that will make you most happy.
- *As a project to be completed on time and within budget.* You, as the customer, will tell the architect how much you want to spend and when you want to move in. She will have

Project name:
Company name:
Date:
Your name:
Why am I doing this project?
Where am I starting?
What is my goal?
Do I know my way around? (For the next three boxes, enter any questions you need to research or expertise you need to get.)
Business issues:
Project management issues:
Technical issues:
How will I do it? (Enter the major steps below.)
Instructions: Use this template for a quick, simple project that you can do alone or hand to someone who can do it in a few hours or a couple of days. Use one of the more complicated templates if you need to set deadlines, track cost, or assemble a team to do the work. If you like, you can start with this form and then shift to one of the bigger forms later. 1. Fill in the first four lines. 2. Answer *Why am I doing this project?* with business benefits and value, not technical features. 3. Answer *Where am I starting?* in terms of both the business situation and the technical situation. 4. Answer *What is my goal?* in terms of the business results, the new way of working, and the new technical solution. 5. Answer *Do I know my way around?* by considering whether you need some information (a map) or expert assistance (a guide) in relation to the business issues, the technical issues, or planning and managing the project. 6. After you do any research or get any expert assistance you need, write up the steps that take you from where you are now to your goal. 7. Review the whole project plan. Is everything in it clear? If someone else is going to work with you or do this work for you, is it clear to both of you? Could you put this in a drawer, take it out a week from now, and know exactly what to do? If not, revise it until it is completely clear. 8. Review the plan again. Is it complete? Does it solve every part of the problem? Does it cover every major step from the starting point to the goal? If not, add whatever is needed. 9. If you've reached this step, then your project is ready for evaluation so that you can decide whether or not this project will work and whether you want to do the project or not. This project is ready for the final two sections of this chapter, Will This Really Work? and Is It Really Worth Doing? 10. If you decide to do the project, follow the plan. If it is a simple, small project, you've done all the planning you need. If it is large or complicated, then you can build a more detailed project plan using Chapter 5.

TABLE 3-8. Simplest project plan: template

▼ **KEY TERMS**

Architecture The ability to design something while seeing it several ways at once—and to explain it to others who can see it only one way. Architecture particularly includes the ability to work within constraints of different types.

Constraint A limit on how the project can be done. A constraint can be created by the business, from the project management perspective, or as a result of a technical requirement or limitation.

Driver A direction for a project, such as soonest delivery, lowest cost, or highest quality.

to design the house within those constraints and come up with the beginning of a project plan, including a list of materials, so the project can deliver the house on time and at the right price.

■ *As a technical design called a blueprint.* The architect will produce blueprints—technical diagrams of the house—that you won't understand at all. But an engineer and a builder will understand them and those blueprints will allow them to design and build the foundation, walls, floors, ceilings, heating and air conditioning, plumbing, electricity, and other things that are part of the technical side of building a home.

As you can see, a building architect can put together three perspectives on a building. You will see your dream home in a model, a drawing, or a computer rendering. The construction manager will see it as a list of supplies to order and steps of work to do on time. The engineers and builders will see it as technical plans to complete and to use as a guide as they build your home.

Just as there are architects for buildings, there are also architects for computers, called computer system architects, and architects for businesses. In fact, it pays to become a good architect for your own business, as you can see in the sidebar, Your Business: An Architectural Perspective.

Architecture gets really interesting when there are constraints, limitations on what can be done. If

an architect didn't have to worry about a budget or a schedule or the demands of climate and geography (such as snowstorms and earthquakes), it wouldn't be a very interesting job. Constraints are challenges; creating a solution that works within all the constraints is the key to good architecture. Constraints come up in each of the three areas and, because the project is a system, constraints in one area create problems in another area.

A good architect can come up with affordable solutions that will work for the long haul—and warn you about bad solutions as well. For example, I own a house that was built on a gentle slope in the 1940s. Now, water is draining under the house. If we don't do something, that will ruin the foundation in a few years. Architects have told me about two solutions. The less expensive one is a French drain. Installing a French drain means putting a gravel bed with a drainpipe around the house. The more expensive one is a concrete patio that slopes away from the house. At first, the French drain sounded like the better solution. But an excellent home renovation expert pointed out that, while it would save money now, in the long run, pipes clog and break and French drains are very expensive to repair. He was able to see the long-term effect of each way of solving the problem and help me choose the best solution. How was he able to do this? He understood the technical issues of French drains, the project issue of cost compar-

▼ **BOOST YOUR BUSINESS!**
Your Business: An Architectural Perspective

We can look at your business during a project the same way we look at a building being renovated. Table 3-9 shows the similarities.

A Building	A Business
People have to keep using and living in a building during renovation, so you can't turn off the plumbing for long to replace the pipes.	People have to keep working during a project, so you can't turn off the phone system for long while you're upgrading the telephone switch.
The longer and bigger the renovation, the more chance that it will interrupt people's lives.	The longer and bigger the project, the more chance that it will interrupt people's work.
If the renovation involves core infrastructure (plumbing, foundation, roof) or many rooms, it will interrupt the lives of more people.	If the project affects business infrastructure (building, computer systems) or many departments, it will interrupt the work of more people.
When the renovation is done, people will use the building in a different way and, we hope, will be better off.	When the project is done, people will work in a different way and, we hope, be more productive.
If the renovation runs over budget, the owners have to pay for it.	If the project runs over budget, the business owners have to pay for it.
To succeed, a renovation must achieve all the owners' goals and resolve the project problems and the technical problems.	To succeed, a project must work for the business, meet its goals, and resolve project problems and technical problems.
Coming up with the right solution early through good architecture makes the renovation less expensive and more effective.	Coming up with the right solution early through good architecture makes the project less expensive and more effective.

TABLE 3-9. Building and business architecture

The lesson: The success of your projects depends on your ability to think like an architect—to see business, project, and technical sides of the problem and possible solutions all at once. Practice this as you plan your projects. For big, complicated, risky projects that are crucial to your business, get the architectural and project management expertise that you need by using consultants.

ison of solutions, and the business issue of the total cost of installing *and maintaining* a solution.

Constraints and Drivers

Above, we defined a *constraint* as a limitation imposed on the project. There can be business, technical, or project constraints.

When President John F. Kennedy said, "This nation should commit itself to achieving the goal, before this decade is out, of landing a man on the moon and returning him safely to the earth," he defined the mission of the National Aeronautics and Space Administration (NASA) and imposed a time constraint—the end of the 1960s—on what became the Apollo projects.

From a project management perspective, these kinds of constraints are common. As you'll see, constraints can be categorized according to the knowledge areas defined by the Project Management Institute in the *Project Management Body of Knowledge:**

- *Time constraints.* The project must be completed by a certain date.
- *Cost constraint.* The project must be finished for a certain amount of money.
- *Scope constraint.* Certain work must be completed or specific functionality must be delivered.
- *Quality constraint.* Project results must meet certain quality requirements.
- *Risk constraint.* There is a limit on the risk of project failure acceptable to the customer.
- *Human resource constraint.* Certain people must (or must not) be on the project team.
- *Procurement constraint.* Certain procurement guidelines, such as bidding rules on contracts, must be followed.

In addition to project constraints, there are business and technical constraints. An example of a business constraint would be that the project not interfere with ongoing, regular operations. Technical constraints are defined by the situation and the type of work being done. For example, a construction site—its size, shape, and type of soil—set constraints for a construction project.

*Copyright and all rights reserved. All material from this publication in this chapter has been reproduced with the permission of PMI.

Defining all of the constraints for a project in writing keeps everyone on the same page. It helps ensure that everyone understands the project and that, as the project goes forward and new people join the team, everyone understands the rules of the game and how the work will be done.

A constraint is a limitation on the project. The opposite of a constraint is a *driver*. A driver is a force that pushes the project in some way, a priority that determines what the project team should try to do most. Typically, a project will have one of four drivers:

- *Time.* If a project is driven by time, then it should be done as soon as possible, even if that means using all money available and including only the minimum required scope, with no extras. Time is often a driver when a company wants to launch a new product and be "first to market," ahead of the competition.
- *Cost.* If the project driver is cost, then total cost should be kept as low as possible, even if that means that the project takes more time or includes only the minimum required scope, with no extras. We should use cost as a driver when money is tight and either we have to borrow money or the money would be very valuable for other things.
- *Scope.* When scope is a driver, then we deliver as much as we can, including extra features, within the available time and budget.
- *Quality.* Quality is a driver when we want to make the best possible product, given scope, time, and cost.

If you are doing a project for a customer, it is very important to understand what is driving the customer, that is, what the customer thinks the driver should be on the project. Otherwise, even though we start on the same page, we end up going in the wrong direction.

For example, I do a lot of projects for state government agencies and state universities. For most of them, cost is the driver: they want me to get the job done as inexpensively as possible. One time, though, I was planning a project for a medical school at a state university. At the beginning, I tried to keep costs down because I figured that was what they wanted. When I sat down to meet with them, I asked, and the department director made it very clear that he was willing to spend as much money as it took to get a good solution to his problem. Then I realized, "This may be a state school, but it's a *medical school* too—and medical schools have lots of money." I shifted my focus from cost to quality. Or, to put it in technical language, instead of running the project with a driver to keep costs to a minimum, I chose the project driver to be delivering the highest possible quality solution.

Generally speaking, it doesn't work to have two drivers on one project. If part of the team is trying to include as many features as possible and part of the team is trying to get the work done as fast as possible, the result is going to be confusion, wasted time, and wasted money.

An Example: Evaluating Market Opportunities

So far, we've focused mostly on projects inside our business. Now, it's time to turn our attention to the customer.

There are several kinds of projects that involve our customers. Some companies do custom projects for customers as a service—a catering business would be an example. We also focus on our customers when we are defining a new product or service. If we figure out what the customers will want and how much they will pay for it, we can decide what to make. Or, if we design or invent something, we can use a project to test-market our idea and find out who would want to buy it. That kind of project can do more than define what we

> ### ▼ BE AN EXPERT!
> #### Changing Drivers in Midstream
> Although, as a general rule, there is only one driver on a project, I've found an exception to this that works very well. I often begin a project with a focus on quality—on making the product and the project plan as good as possible. Then, during the work phase, once I see that the results are indeed going to be very good, I shift to put the focus on time, working to complete the project as soon as possible. Often, this gives the highest quality along with the earliest delivery.
>
> Why does this work? Because we can save a lot of money by focusing on high-quality planning. As we will discuss in Chapters 5 and 6, an early focus on quality prevents a lot of problems and saves a lot of money and time.
>
> *The lesson:* Focusing first on increasing quality and then on saving time or money can give you the best of both worlds.

will sell; we can also use it to define *how* we will sell—what our marketing, our advertising campaign, and our sales program will look like.

Let's take a look at a simple example of market research. Let's say we own a restaurant. We have two good managers who've been with us for a number of years and we realize that we can grow to open a second location. In this case, we already know the name of the restaurant, the menu, and the décor and style. Our only concern is location: where should we put the second restaurant?

We look around town and we find two vacant restaurants. Both are the right size and about the same price. How do we decide which location is better for our restaurant? Since opening a restaurant is a new opportunity, we start with the opportunity-definition tool. Table 3-10 shows the definition of the new opportunity of opening a second restaurant.

The Results of the Opportunity
This section describes business results before and after the change

The Question	How It Is Now (before any change)	How It Will Be After the Opportunity Is Realized
Money		
Gross revenue/month	$45,000	$90,000
Net revenue/month	$10,000	$20,000
Customers		
Number of customers/night	90	180
Type of customers		No change.
Staff		
New staff	Total 10	Total 20. Hire one new manager for each restaurant
People in different jobs		No change, except one manager moves to new location
Jobs that will be lost		None.
Products and Services		
New products or services		No change.
Products or services that will be eliminated		No change.
Changes or upgrades to products or services		Full menu now served at two locations, instead of one.
Tools and Equipment		
New tools and equipment		Fully stocked second restaurant.
Tools and equipment that will go away		None.
Tools and equipment that will be replaced or upgraded		None.
The New Way of Working This section describes our work process—how we do our work before and after the change.		
Executive Leadership Functions		
How will owners', executives', and senior managers' jobs change?	Owner always at one restaurant. Managers usually supervised by owner.	Owner splits time between two restaurants. Manager will need to be able to run restaurant 3 nights/week.

TABLE 3-10. Opportunity definition: opening a second restaurant (continued on next page)

The New Way of Working This section describes our work process—how we do our work before and after the change.		
The Question	**How It Is Now (before they change)**	**How It Will Be After the Opportunity Is Realized**
Product and Service Development		
What will change in the ways we create our products and deliver our services?	Cooking at one restaurant.	Cooking at two restaurants.
Marketing		
What will change in the ways we market?	Advertise one location.	Advertise both locations. If one location is full, recommend people go to the other.
Sales		
What will change in the ways we sell?		Add sales effort to new neighborhood.
Client Services and Customer Support		
What will change in the ways we serve clients and respond to customer support requests?		No change.
Financial Operations		
What will change in the ways we do accounting and financial work?		Bookkeeper will split time between two locations.
Research and Analysis		
What will change in the ways we do research and analysis?		No change.

TABLE 3-10. Opportunity definition: opening a second restaurant (continued)

Laying out the opportunity on this template gives everyone a very clear idea of what we are doing. Of course, the whole project of opening a new restaurant is huge—it involves construction, hiring, and a major advertising campaign. So, for our example, we will focus on just one small subproject: choosing the location.

We can now rephrase what we said above, in the first paragraph, as a set of business constraints on the project:

- We will open only one new location.

- To save money and time, we will open only in a building that has already been a restaurant and is the right size.

Our first paragraph also shows that we've done some legwork—perhaps with the help of a real estate agent—and we've discovered a technical constraint. There are only two possible locations available at this time. Let's go one step further and say that we've arranged for a 60-day option on each property. So, we have 60 days to make up our minds and choose one of the two locations. This gives us a project—a time-limited, unique problem to solve. Which is the better location? Table 3-11 shows a project plan for answering that question.

This is a good start on the project plan. It would make sense to do two other things right upfront. One is to think about drivers and constraints. The best driver for this project is quality: we want to make the best decision we can by our deadline, July

15. We only have one shot—and a wrong choice could mean a failed restaurant and less income every year for years to come. This is one decision we want to get right. It wouldn't make sense to rush the decision or refuse to pay a reasonable consulting fee, given that the right decision could be worth $240,000 in net revenue per year, every year.

The second thing we might do is design some

Project name: Choosing a restaurant location
Company name: Sid's Mountain Pizza
Date: June 2005
Your name: Sid Kemp
Why am I doing this project? I want to choose the best location for my second restaurant. I want the location that will be more likely to succeed or, if both would succeed, be more likely to have more customers and make more money.
Where am I starting? I've already found two locations that would work.
What is my goal? A decision by July 25: which restaurant should I lease?
Do I know my way around? (For the next three boxes, enter any questions you need to research or expertise you need to get.)
Business issues: Somewhat. I know the restaurant business. But I inherited this location and it has always worked, so I don't have a lot of expertise in the exact issue: evaluating the location of the restaurant.
Project management issues: I need to plan this around my regular work schedule and around other planning related to opening the new restaurant. However, I don't think it will take a lot of time, and it is important.
Technical issues: I need to learn more. What makes a location good for a restaurant? Why did the previous restaurants at these locations close?
How will I do it? (Enter the major steps below.) 　1. Do some reading in industry journals about restaurant locations. 　2. Find experts to talk with–someone in the restaurant industry and a business real estate expert. 　3. Walk around the neighborhoods at different times of day and night. Find out what happened to the previous restaurants at each location. 　4. Talk with my current customers–see what they think. 　5. Perhaps do some kind of survey or focus group. 　6. Get ideas from my employees. 　7. Write down and organize my thoughts. 　8. List key determining factors. 　9. Rate the two locations. 　10. Make a decision and then arrange for the lease.

TABLE 3-11. Simplest project plan: choosing a restaurant location

data tables. Maybe we could make a table that shows the number of customers and total revenue per night, each night of the week, at our current restaurant, with spaces for estimating the numbers for each of the two possible new locations.

This will be an interesting project. Some restaurant owners, people who have scouted locations and who know the neighborhoods, would find it fairly easy. Others, who've always worked at one location, might find it very difficult. There might be something that would make one site obviously better, such as a movie theater located in the same mall as one of the potential locations. Or there might be a reason that would rule out one location, such as a history of six restaurant bankruptcies at one location. Or we might end up with a really difficult choice.

One thing that makes this a very good plan is its honesty. The restaurant owner states very clearly what he doesn't know and what kind of help he's going to need to get. Many people have a hard time doing that. But, as Clint Eastwood said in *Dirty Harry*, "A man's got to know his limitations."

Here's the most important point of this example. With a bit of thinking and a bit of writing, we're ready to do our best. Now that we've taken a thorough look at defining problems, opportunities, and projects, let's turn to evaluating them by asking if our project plan will really work.

WILL THIS REALLY WORK?

Now that we have a simple project plan, it's time to evaluate it. Some good ideas just won't work and other ideas won't work for our business, or within the time and money we have available, or within technical constraints.

Business Evaluation

First, we have to evaluate whether this project works with our business. Do we have the time and the team to take on this project right now? Or are there too many other urgent priorities? Do we have enough staff? If the project requires our own personal attention or the attention of a specific expert, do we or that person have the time to work on it? To put it simply, we should avoid doing too many things at once and we should avoid biting off more than we can chew.

Each year, I write an annual plan. I usually end up doing about half of it. Some years, I simply plan to do more than one person could do. But I'm learning. Each year, I make a smaller plan and get more of it done. Recently, when I don't finish part of my plan, it's usually because a better opportunity came along.

In this first, short evaluation, we are only asking if we can do this project and keep the business running. We'll have more to say about the business evaluation of a project below in the next section (Is It Really Worth Doing?) and in Chapter 4, Your Business and Your Projects, where we look at how to choose some projects over others and how to organize all the projects that we're going to do over time.

Project Management Evaluation

When we evaluate a project from a project management perspective, there are three key questions:

- *Is the plan clear?* Vague or ambiguous plans are likely to fail. Different people will think we're doing different things and everything will fall apart. So, review the plan for clarity and, if others are involved, make sure that they understand it as well as you do. Revise the plan until everyone understands it. Get expert help if you need it. If you can't make the plan clear—either because people can't agree or because you lack enough technical or business knowledge—then cancel the project. For the project to work, the plan must be clear on all three levels—as a plan for the business, as a project plan of steps laid out in time, and as a technical plan that experts or engineers can evaluate and approve.

- *Do we have enough of the right resources for the work?* Here, we need to do two gap analyses. The first is about expertise. Do we have people who can do this job and do it well? If not, how will we close the gap between the skills that the project needs and the skills that we have? Will we get some training for our team? Will we hire an expert? Once we've closed the expertise gap, we have to look for a time gap. Does the project team have enough time available to do the project and get all the work done on schedule? If not, can we get extra people, move the deadline, or delay some other work so that we have enough of the right people with enough time to do the work?
- *What could go wrong?* The third evaluation from a project management perspective is about risk—about events that could make the

project fail. We cover risk management next.

Starting Project Risk Management: Making Sure We Can Succeed

Recently a project manager and I met to develop a plan for a big event. I said, "Send me the plan and I'll lead a team to make the risk plan." He replied, "There is no plan without a risk plan." Really, we were both right. I was thinking of the work plan, the set of steps we would do to get the job done. And the work plan is a very good place to start when risk planning—it's the key input to the process of risk planning. He was also right: no plan is complete until we add a risk plan, until we ask, "What could go wrong?"

So, when we have our simple project plan, and we know it is clear and that it makes sense to everyone, that the business can do it, and that we have enough of the right people, that is a great time to begin project risk management. We begin by asking, "What could go wrong?"

▼ SOMETHING SLIPPED!

Oops! Wrong Genius

I know of a start-up company that failed. The team was two MBAs and a scientist who had a new way of treating wastewater. In his small, experimental model, the wastewater treatment method was effective and was less expensive than any other method on the market.

Their business plan was simple. A wastewater processing facility gave them some space to build a full-scale model. The inventor would build it and install it and make it work. With a working full-scale model, the company could get venture capital to manufacture the system and sell it. It would sell easily because it cost less to run than anything else on the market.

They made one mistake in their plan. They figured that the scientist who invented the device was the best

person to build the full-scale version and make it work. That turned out to be a bad idea. Inventing new things is the expertise of scientists. Making something work at a new size is the realm of a very specialized engineering discipline called *scaling*. So, they used the wrong genius. They had a scientist when they needed an engineer who was an expert in scaling a device up to a larger size.

The scientist built the full-sized test system and it did not work. He didn't know what to do about that and, before they could find the right expert, they ran out of time and money.

The lesson: Don't assume that you know everything. Instead, find out who knows what you need to know. Get the right expert.

Risk management is about planning for events that might happen, planning for uncertainty. It is a simple fact of life that we don't know what might happen.

Project risk management is about planning for uncertain future events that could change the delivery of the project. We're looking for things that could delay the project, make it cost more, or cause it to fail altogether. Those are called *negative risks.* We're also looking for things that could make the project easier, reduce its cost, or enable us to finish sooner. Those are called *positive risks.*

If we don't do risk planning, unexpected events will change our plan, mostly putting up obstacles on our path to project success. The only reason most of those events are unexpected is that people don't take the time to ask, "What might happen?" In risk planning, we're thinking ahead, learning to expect—and plan for—the unexpected.

We'll cover risk management in depth in Chapter 7, Ensuring Success by Completing the Plan. At this point, all we need is a list of risks and a sense of how much risk is a factor on the project.

This early in the project, it is probably enough just to do good risk identification and a little risk assessment. Remember: we haven't even decided yet if we're going to do the project. So, our goal is not a full-blown risk plan; it's a good sense of what the risks will be and how risky the project is overall, that is, how likely it is that unexpected events will create problems for the project.

Risk Assessment. Risk assessment begins very simply with *risk identification,* that is, with making a list of risks. We want to move from a statement of uncertainty, "something could go wrong," to a clear, written list: "Here's most of what could go wrong."

I like to think of risk assessment as "proactive worry." We're asking what could go wrong, but it's not a doom-and-gloom session. Instead, the best perspective is "We want this project to succeed. To make sure it does, we're going to plan for what could get in the way." Risk assessment is best done as a team brainstorming session. Here are some questions you can bring to the team:

- *What has gone wrong in the past* on similar projects or on any projects at this company or with this team?
- *In the plan, where are we relying on people outside the team?* Any time we rely on anyone outside the team—a vendor or even the customer—to tell us something or deliver something to us, there's a chance that they won't get to it, that they will delay the project, or that they will give us something that doesn't work.
- *In the plan, what are we not expert at?* Any step we might not know how to do is a risk. And we're expert only if we've done it before—several times. If someone says, "Oh, I've done that," ask, "How many times have you done it?" If the answer is less than three, it's a risk. If the process is open heart surgery, it's still a risk even if the person has done it a hundred times.

▼ KEY TERMS

Uncertainty The fact of life that we don't know what will happen. It is the starting point for risk management.

Risk management The attempt to bring uncertainty under our control.

Project risk management The work of planning for, monitoring, and controlling unexpected events that might have an impact on project outcomes.

Risk planning Creating a list of risks, describing each risk, and planning a response to each risk.

Risk identification Creating a list of risks and naming each risk.

- *What outside events could interfere with the project?* Rain is a risk for a picnic. A sudden rush of business can be a risk for a project. Or a sudden drop in business, so there isn't enough money to finish the project. An executive who changes his or her mind too often is a source of risk, as well.

- *What could happen that would make the project easier than we expect?* Here, we're looking for positive risks. Suppose our project includes some renovation on our building and we've heard that it is very hard to get building permits in our town. But, when the time comes, city hall has gotten its act together and it takes just an hour, instead of two weeks. As a result, we can start construction sooner and finish the project sooner.

A successful risk brainstorming session involves reading the project plan and any other project documents as a team and asking all these questions about each point of the plan. The result is a written risk list. You'll find templates for project risk management in Chapter 7.

Once we have our list of risks, we need to step back and ask, "Overall, how risky is this project?" Here are some things to consider.

- *How big is this project relative to the company or department?* Any project that takes up a lot of time and resources is high risk, because other events in our business may pull us away from the project.

- *How stable is the business?* If the business is going through change or is subject to challenges outside its control, it will make it hard to finish the project.

- *How expert are we at what we're doing?* It is a lot less risky for a company that already publishes three magazines to launch a fourth than for a company to launch its first magazine.

- *How expert are we at the details of what we are doing?* Often, it seems that we have the expertise, but then we realize that we don't. As we saw in the example earlier in this chapter, just because I know how to run a restaurant doesn't mean I know how to choose a good location for a restaurant.

- *How much are we relying on unknown outside help or expertise?* If we need a particular product, service, or consultant, then that item might not work or that person might not be able to show up or might not work well with us. Relying on people or things from the outside is a big risk.

- *How much leeway do we have, in time or money?* If a delay or a need for more funds would kill the project, then it is high risk. If we could put the project on hold and come back to it or add a bit more money to get help and make it work, that lowers the overall risk of project failure.

When you are done, prepare a short summary—one or two paragraphs—describing whether the project is likely to succeed (low risk), moderately risky, or very challenging (high risk), and why. Attach your initial risk list. These two items—the executive risk summary and the initial risk list—are inputs to the executive decision about whether or not to launch the project.

Technical Evaluation

Our final evaluation is technical. This requires technical expertise and it will be different for projects in each application area, each field of business. This is where the architect says, "This building will stand up," the marketing director says, "This is a great ad campaign," or the computer expert says, "This new computer network will meet your business needs for the next three years."

There are three keys to a successful technical evaluation:

- *Use the right expert.* You need to be sure that the expert knows what's needed for the project. That's true whether you hire an outside expert, use someone in your company, or rely on your own expertise. See if the expert can make a clear, convincing case to you and others and can demonstrate examples of both success and failure, showing why your plan is like past successes and different from past failures.
- *Avoid bias.* We all want to think things will work out. And, if we're going to be paid to work on the project, so much the more so. That is, we're biased toward thinking that our ideas are good and that our plans will work. Be very clear that, when we're deciding whether or not to launch the project, we want the truth. If there are risks, we want to know about them. If we're courting disaster, we want to hear it. If necessary, we should get outside experts to give us unbiased opinions of our project concept and plan.
- *For big projects, test the waters.* For a small project, it is enough to think, write, plan, and decide. But, for big projects, we may want to test the waters, to try out our idea in a small way, before we dive in and commit to a large project, a whole new product line, new division, or new way of running our business. That is the subject of the next section.

Ways of Testing the Waters

In this section, we'll look at specific ways of deciding if our project plan is good and at some techniques that big companies use to try out ideas before committing a lot of time and money.

Creative Solutions—Better or Worse? As we look at the solution to our problem, we should ask, "How creative is this solution? Have we found a solution that is routine at other companies: everyone's

doing it and we just haven't done it yet? Or are we going off into the wild world of woolly ideas and untried experiments?" Creative ideas are great—when they work. But, by definition, the more creative an idea, the more innovative, the less it has been done before. And the less it has been done before, the higher the risk that it just won't work.

There is a certain type of narrow, focused creativity that is very good for a small business. If we know two things that work and we're the first company to put them together, that can be very good. If we take a solution from a similar industry, but we're the first to do it in our industry, that can be very good. In general, small companies succeed with innovation by finding one creative idea and making it work well.

On the other hand, it just doesn't make sense to do everything in a new, creative way. Why write a custom software program to run your business when there is an off-the-shelf application that is good enough for the job? Why build a better mousetrap when you can get a good mousetrap at Home Depot really cheap?

I recommend choosing creative solutions when:

- We can focus the creativity, doing just one innovative thing per project.
- We don't just reinvent the wheel for no reason or to make it just a little rounder.
- The innovation is part of our core business.
- The creativity and risk are a good fit for the way we do business.

Just Fix the Problem or Go for a Permanent Solution? When we discussed root causes, we said that first we find the causes of the problem and then we find the causes of the causes, the root cause. That gives us a question: Is it worth going after the root cause or should we just fix the one problem we have today?

In the case of the leaky warehouse roof, it clearly costs more to replace the whole roof than to patch

▼ **THINK FOR YOURSELF!**

Would Creativity Be Good for Your Company?

Some companies—Sharper Image, Boeing, and 3M come to mind—thrive on innovation and creativity. Others, like Radio Shack and Baskin-Robbins, do well by delivering the same thing year after year. What works for you and your company? Here are some questions that may help you decide if a little innovation will boost your bottom line. Pull out a piece of paper, write down your answers, and decide if your company is ready for a creative leap.

- *Do you like new ways of doing things?* Or do you prefer to keep a routine?

- *Do you like solving problems?* Or do you want someone to hand you a solution?

- *Do your team members like solving problems?* Or do they just want to come to work, do their jobs, and go home?

- *Is being first at something new, being different, important to you and your team?* If not, what is most important?

- *Is your company strong enough to invest in risky ideas and projects?* If you're struggling to make payroll or dealing with constant changes from outside, a creative leap is must riskier. Take that chance only if you have to. Otherwise, focus on solving your problems in a simple, practical way and building a robust business that's ready for a jump into the unknown.

Here's another way to ask this question. If you went for a day of sailing, which would you prefer—a steady wind and calm water or a bit of chop on the sea, a shifting wind, and a challenging day at the helm?

---

a few leaks. What makes it worth getting a whole new roof? The cost of all the damage caused by all the leaks we'll have until we go out and get a new roof later. If the costs of that damage—including damage to goods in the warehouse, the cost of patching the roof, and work time lost to interruptions—are greater than the cost of getting a new roof now instead of later, then it's better to put the permanent preventative solution in place now: get a new roof over our heads before we get wet again!

Companies that get into the habit of thinking in terms of root causes and permanent preventative solutions are starting on the path of continuous improvement. *Continuous improvement* is an approach to business where we seek to work smarter every day. We don't like *same old, same old*. We always try to do everything the best way we know to do it. Once a whole team gets into that habit, it is easier and less costly and a lot less hassle to grow and change than to live with problems that we already understand and could leave behind.

A Little Research Can Go a Long Way. Now, we'll take a look at ways of doing research and running small tests to see if a big project is a good idea. Any research or analysis we do to find out if a project will work can be called a *feasibility study*. Here are several types of feasibility studies:

- *Learning the territory.* In this case, we talk with experts, read, and study. We get to know our way around. The results may not be specific, but they help us with our thinking, planning, and decision-making. One result may be a decision that we don't know enough, that we're going to need expert help on the project.

- *Gathering data.* As we've seen in some examples, it can be good to get good data, well-organized numbers that really show what is going on. For example, if we know at what

▼ SMART THINKING!

Wait for a Hailstorm—or Not?

I own a house with an old roof like the one described in the text: it is likely to keep springing leaks. I thought it would be a good idea to get it replaced sooner rather than later. But someone pointed out to me that an old roof like this would get punched full of holes in a hailstorm. And, if that happened, my insurance company would pay for a whole new roof and I wouldn't have to pay anything.

It's an interesting idea: wait for a disaster to happen and then let an insurance company foot the bill. I'm not sure it's a bad idea. But I generally prefer taking good care of the things I own—my homes and my business. I'd rather not live through the mess of flood and fixing. So, I think I'll call my roofer sooner rather than later.

The lesson: When choosing a solution, be sure to ask five questions:

- *How much will it cost to fix the problem now?*
- *How much will the hassle cost?* One hassle is the problems that continue until you solve them later. The other is trying to work during the project. Especially for a small company, reducing hassle can be more important than reducing cost.
- *What is the best time for permanent preventative solutions?* Some companies are very seasonal. If you sell Christmas decorations, make it through the season by fixing problems; then, start putting your permanent preventative solutions in place in January.
- *How much will it cost to fix the problem later—* including taking care of any additional problems before we put our permanent preventative solution into place?
- *Who will pay?* We can sometimes get insurers to pay for work or share costs with customers or vendors.

times movies start and stop at the theater, we can decide when to put extra waiters on at our restaurant we're going to open up next door.

- *Market research.* Beyond just gathering data, we can do organized surveys and studies of our customers and potential customers. Market research is a whole field of expertise on its own. Creating good surveys and analyzing the results is a challenging specialty. Sometimes, though, it is worth getting the expertise and doing an entire market research project.
- *Gathering opinions.* This is a less formal, less expensive version of market research. Here, we get information from some group—experts, customers, or potential customers—using a structured interview or using a *focus group.* A *focus group* is an organized group of people who represent potential customers. We can introduce them to a new product—usually with a prototype, as you'll see in the next section—and get their reactions. Gathering opinions informally is quicker and easier than careful market research. If our idea is not too innovative, it might be enough. We gather opinions when a formal study is too expensive and we're willing to take the risks that our research may give us somewhat biased information.

- *Prototypes, proof-of-concept systems,* and *pilot projects* are more advanced techniques described below.

A *prototype* is an early model of something. There are two types of prototypes and several ways

> ▼ **KEY TERMS**
>
> **Prototype** An early model of something we plan to make.
>
> **Mock-up** A prototype that is not fully functional.
>
> **Working model** A fully functional prototype.
>
> **Proof-of-concept system** A working model of an idea or concept that shows it can be done, but doesn't show that the idea is worth developing.
>
> **Pilot project** A small project that tests the waters for a larger project that we might do later.

of using them in evaluating a project that will make a finished version of the product or service. The two types of prototypes are *mock-ups* and *working prototypes:*

- A *mock-up* is a partial example of a product or service, where everything isn't fully working. Examples:
  - A body of an aircraft with no jet engine or controls that can be tested in a wind tunnel
  - Several recipes of similarly flavored pretzels, ready for taste tests
  - A set of computer screens that show what a new program will look like, but don't actually work or hold data yet
- A *working prototype* is one-off complete, functioning model of something we hope to mass-produce later. Examples:
  - Car companies will build one fully functioning sample of a new model to show at car shows and test drive. It is very expensive to make just one car. But showing and testing the prototype lets the companies make changes to solve problems that show up in the tests and changes that will make customers like the final product more.
  - Seymour Cray, the inventor of the supercomputer, spent $20 million building the first prototype supercomputer. He sold it to the U.S. Navy for $20 million, recovering all of his development costs in one sale. He then went into business producing and selling more supercomputers just like the prototype.

Here are ways of using prototypes to improve our final product and add information to our decision about whether it is worth going ahead with the project.

- *We can show working prototypes of new products to customers.* We can display them, run focus groups, or loan them out for a trial run.
- *We can run a prototype of a new service for one customer,* offering it even at a loss or offering a money-back guarantee, and then use the results of this as a case study. If the customer is happy, the case study is used for marketing. If the customer is not happy, it is used to redesign the service before we try again.
- *We can show mock-ups of new products or services to customers or potential customers* and we can get their opinions.
- *We can build and test mock-ups of new systems inside our company.* This is very useful in designing new software. We can test a prototype and then programmers can add functionality. We can review it again and they can improve it. In software development, we might see prototypes several times on the way to a final product.
- *We can create a prototype of a web site or advertising campaign* and then show it to some experts or customers before finishing the site or campaign and going live with the general public.

Although prototypes were first developed for very large, expensive projects such as new cars, computers, and jet aircraft, we can use them in small businesses as well. We might be able to build a prototype in just a few days and show it to our customers at a trade show or in a display at our store. Showing a prototype and gathering opinions gives us a surprising amount of information. People have very different perspectives and very different reactions to new ideas. Even without a formal study, we'll get a better idea of what people like if we let them try it out.

A *proof-of-concept system* is even more basic than a prototype. A concept is an idea—in this case, a new innovative idea, one that most people would scoff at, saying, "That will never work" or "No one would buy something like that." Inventors make one example that proves the concept. It doesn't prove that the concept is worth doing. A prototype can be used to say, "This is worth doing," but a proof-of-concept system just says, "It can be done."

We could say that the Wright Brothers' first airplane was a proof-of-concept system. For centuries, people hoped that we could fly in heavier-than-air craft. The Wright Brothers' plane proved it was possible. At that point, it wasn't worth anything. The first plane couldn't carry passengers or cargo and it would crash in a high wind. It took a few more years to show that, not only could airplanes fly, but also that it was a good business proposition to use them for war, for commerce, and for entertainment.

Today, we are at a similar stage with commercial space flight. In October 2004, the Mojave Aerospace Team won the X Prize by being the first private company to launch a spacecraft carrying a person to the edge of space (100 kilometers up, about 62 miles) and back, proving the concept that a private company can build spacecraft and fly them safely. Now, that concept is proven. But is it worth doing, if there is no big prize at the end? Is it commercially viable? We don't know. And that's the difference between a proof-of-concept and a prototype.

The third advanced technique for proving something new is the *pilot project*. This is any project that is a small test run of an idea before the idea goes into full production.

We can see pilot projects all the time at fast-food chains and on the candy bar shelves at grocery stores. In the early 1960s, McDonald's tried

---

▼ SMART THINKING!
Project Management—When They Try It, They Like It!

As I started writing this book, I wondered if it would work to create seminars on project management for small business. I had a friend who runs a small business discussion group in rural Texas, up in the Hill Country. When we floated the idea to the group, several of them said, "No one in this town would pay that much money for a seminar."

So, we took a different approach. I offered a short version of the seminar for free. It gave me a chance to try out my new ideas and to get their reactions.

I got a total turnaround. By the end of the two-hour lunch meeting, they were total project management fans. They thought I could offer seminars and people would pay. One of them asked me to design a course for his business incubation program. Others offered to send people or to help promote the class.

The lesson: People will often say "no" to a new idea, then love it when they see it. As a result, we get more information from letting people play with a prototype than from just presenting an idea and asking what they think.

out the Hulaburger—a slice of grilled pineapple in a toasted bun, covered with melted American cheese, mustard, ketchup, and a pickle—and it was a big flop. (Everyone said, "I see the hula, but where's the burger?") More recently, fast food restaurants are testing low-carb menu items and Tex-Mex salsas. The Hershey Company pilot-tested white chocolate candy bars in 2002 and 2003 and made Reese's® white chocolate peanut butter cups and KitKat® white chocolate wafer bars permanent items in 2004.

Maybe your business could do the same. Is there some new product or service you think would sell? Could you make a little of it at a reasonable price and see if it sells? You might lose money on the first batch, but you'll gain a lot of information. Sometimes, we only have three choices with a new idea: run a pilot project, drop it without trying anything, or jump into a big, expensive project that, if it fails, will be a big loss for the company. In those situations, a pilot project makes a lot of sense.

A pilot project is more than a prototype. Usually, we don't sell prototypes; we just show them around. A pilot project is a full-blown test of a new product or service. If the results of the project are positive, we'll be out there selling the product or service. And we'll be learning if the product or service is worth keeping. If it is, we can make more of it—usually at lower cost—and sell it to more customers in larger markets.

A medium-sized company can also try a pilot project for changes to internal operations. For example, let's say your company has a dozen stores. You're considering a new computerized cash register system to automate inventory and ordering. You could try it at two of the stores. If it works, if it's easy to use and saves enough time and money, you can put it in at the other ten stores. In this situation, a pilot project is a lot better than installing the program in all 12 stores at once for two reasons. First, you get to try it out before committing

to the expense. Second, you will learn some things about setting up and using the system before you interfere with work at the other ten stores. In a case like this, you should find enthusiastic people ready to try the innovation when you choose the location for your pilot project.

IS IT REALLY WORTH DOING?

If our project has made it this far, we have a basic plan clearly defined and we know it will work—for our business, as a project, and technically. But not everything that will work is worth doing. In this section, we do a business evaluation of the project. Here are the tools we will use:

- *Return on investment (ROI) analysis.* ROI was first developed for financial investments, to answer questions like "Am I better off investing in the stock market, mutual funds, or government bonds?" Now, we can apply the ROI method to projects, asking, "Am I better off doing a big project (project A), two small projects (projects B and C), or no projects at all?" An older, simpler version of ROI is called *cost-benefit analysis.* A warning—ROI is probably the most challenging idea in this book. Reading the next few pages may feel like wading through molasses, but it will be worth it. ROI may be challenging, but it is one of the best new tools for business planning.

- *Evaluation of fit.* Some products, services, and ways of working are right—but not right for us. We need to evaluate the project results to see if they really work for us and for our company.

- *Alignment with values.* Every company has values—and some business owners know what those values are. If a new product, service, or way of working is in alignment with our values, it is likely to be good for our company. Otherwise, it won't be and it's likely to confuse our customers about who we are or even damage our reputation.

- *Gut instinct.* Anyone in a small business knows that our feelings can guide us to success. So, how do we combine our feeling of what is right with all of our ideas and plans?

Return on Investment (ROI) Evaluation: Will the Project Make More Than It Costs?

ROI models and methods can be very complicated—too complicated for a small business, if you ask me. However, we can keep the idea simple. There are just a few important things to remember:

- *Keep a level playing field.* Whatever method you use to define value and calculate ROI, be sure to use the same method for every project. That way, comparing one project against another—which we cover in Chapter 4—will be fair and accurate.
- *Make all estimates realistic.* Don't inflate estimates of potential profit or estimate costs low to make a project look better. We want a good picture of the future, not a sales hype for the project.
- *Define hard-dollar value and soft-dollar value.* This early in the project plan, we can't be sure exactly how much money we will make. Some estimates will be pretty accurate; we call those *hard-dollar values. Soft-dollar values* include estimates that we can't nail down and benefits that can never be measured exactly, such as increased goodwill or wider name recognition.
- *Be realistic and specific about what is good for the company.* In evaluating a project, we have to move beyond generalities like "more efficient" or "a better way to do things." We need to compare the new product, service, or way of working and then *define* what makes it

better and *measure* how much better it will be.

- *Take into account the time cost of money.* On a project, we spend money now, but we don't start making (or saving) money until the project is over. If I have $1,000 right now, I can put it in the bank at five percent interest and have $1,050 next year. On the other hand, if I get $1,000 next year, I'll have ... $1,000. A dollar next year is worth less than a dollar now. This is the *time cost* (or *time value*) of money.
- *Remember that ROI doesn't include risk.* Our ROI calculation assumes that the project will work, will be on time, and will cost as much as we expect. The risk of delays, excess cost, and project failure has to be considered separately, after we calculate and evaluate ROI.

With these ideas in mind, we can build a process for calculating ROI:

- Determine the value of the project, assuming it succeeds.

▼ KEY TERMS

Return on investment (ROI) A method that creates a number we can assign to a project that shows the ratio between the benefits and the costs of the project or how soon we will get our money back.

Hard-dollar value Value we can measure and put a number on.

Soft-dollar value Value that we can't measure exactly, either because it is too early in our project to estimate accurately or because it is a type of value that we can recognize but cannot measure.

Time value/cost of money The idea that, due to interest rates, a given amount of money in the future is worth less than the same amount of money now.

▼ **KEY TERMS**

Life cycle cost The total cost of a product, service, or system, including development, maintenance during its productive years, and, if appropriate, decommissioning costs.

Present value The value of money we expect in the future, adjusted for time, so we can compare all money at different times as if it were money today.

- Calculate the life cycle cost of the project, plus maintenance of the product or service.
- Adjust for the time value of money, using *present value.*
- Perform the ROI calculation, which will tell you the date by which the project will pay for itself.
- In presenting ROI, also present the issue of project risk.

Determining Project Value. A project is worth doing only if it adds value to our company. We need to be able to define and measure that value. There are three basic ways to increase value:

- *Increase revenue.* The equivalent for a not-for-profit organization or government agency is to *increase ability to perform our mission.*
- *Decrease cost.*
- *Reduce fiduciary and liability risk exposure.* If we can reduce our risk of getting sued, by improving security on employee and customer data, for example, that's good for the company. The benefit may show up in reduced insurance costs, in lower legal expenses in the event of a problem, or in being able to sleep better at night.

The starting point for estimating project value is Table 3-7, the opportunity-definition tool. Whatever our project, we have to turn each differ-

ence in our before and after columns into a hard-dollar change in net revenue or a soft-dollar statement of some value or benefit to the company.

Calculating Life Cycle Cost. We introduced life cycles in Chapter 2. Now we'll expand that idea into calculating the total life cycle cost. There are three basic elements to the cost of the life cycle of any product, service, or process that we create by doing a project:

- *Development cost.* This is the cost of the project.
- *Maintenance cost.* This is the cost during the production years: the cost of producing the product, providing the service, or maintaining the equipment or system we've put into place.
- *Decommissioning cost.* This is the cost of shutting things down when the product, service, or system is no longer of any value. Companies often ignore this cost, figuring it is too far in the future to worry about and too hard to estimate. Often, that is true. But, in some cases, decommissioning cost should be considered from the very beginning. For example, if you are setting up a manufactur-

▼ **SOMETHING SLIPPED!**

Nuclear Power Didn't Pay

The idea of life cycle costing made the news about 20 years ago when someone did a study of U.S. nuclear power plants. They measured energy, rather than dollars. They calculated the total energy it took to build the plant, to run the plant every year for 30 years, and then to decommission the plant. It turns out that a nuclear power plant used more energy than it generated in its whole life!

So, we didn't know it until it was too late, but nuclear power never paid off.

▼ BOTTOM-LINE BASICS
Net Revenue Is What Matters

Net revenue is total (or gross) revenue—all the money coming in—minus total expenses—all the money that goes out. Ultimately, what is good for the business is an increase in net revenue. This is important to remember in three ways.

- *Increased revenue is worthless if it costs too much.* More money coming in doesn't necessarily mean more profit. We must increase revenue more than we increase expenses.

- *Cost cutting works only if it doesn't cut our revenue.* If we can cut costs while delivering the same product or service, with the same quality, in the same quantity, that's good. But if cutting costs means reducing quality and losing customers or not having enough product available and losing sales, then we lose revenue while reducing expenses and net revenue doesn't go up.

- *Sooner or later, vague ideas have to become hard dollars.* We must understand how and when good ideas will pay off. Here are some examples.

  - *Increased goodwill.* You might hear that, as a small business, if you help out with a volunteer or social benefit project in your town, people will appreciate you. That goodwill is very important. But goodwill becomes dollars only if it keeps or attracts customers. For example, you might donate to a local charity and issue a press release about the donation, so that customers link your charity with your business.

  - *Reduced cycle time.* The time it takes to bring a product to market, to close a sale, or to complete any other business activity is the *cycle time* of that process. In general, reduced cycle time is a good thing. It makes a company more flexible: if there's a change, it can respond faster. For example, if we automate our inventory and cash register system, we shorten cycle time on price changes. This allows us to adjust for inventory overstocks, competitors' price cuts, and changes in customer preferences and then lower prices for a sale more quickly. But, before installing the new system, we'll need to estimate exactly how this faster cycle time will increase net revenue. If we can estimate the change in dollars, that's a hard-dollar value. If we can only describe and estimate the benefit, that's soft-dollar value.

---

ing plant that will create toxic waste, then you should consider final cleanup costs before you start the project.

Adjusting for the Time Value of Money. Now, we've calculated the value (gross revenue) of the project over its useful life and we've calculated the cost over three periods: development (before its useful life), production (the useful life), and decommissioning (after its useful life). We can think of this as the projected income and expense of each year of the product, service, or system we are putting into place. Income minus expenses is net revenue. The first three lines of Table 3-12, product life cycle net value, adjusted for time, show these numbers for a simplified project. A minus sign in net revenue indicates a loss for the year.

We're developing a product for sale and its product life cycle looks like this:

- The beginning of year 1 is when the project starts. Product development (the project) will take one year, during which time we will make no money and we will spend the total project cost. So year 1 shows a loss equal to the project cost.

	Year 1	Year 2	Year 3	Year 4	Year 5	Year 6
1. Gross Revenue	$0	$60,000	$100,000	$100,000	$40,000	$0
2. Expense	$50,000	$60,000	$60,000	$60,000	$10,000	$10,000
3. Net Revenue	–$50,000	$0	$40,000	$40,000	$30,000	–$10,000
4. Adjustment for Time Value	97.0%	94.1%	91.3%	88.5%	85.9%	83.3%
5. Net Present Value of Revenue	–$48,500	$0	$36,507	$35,412	$25,762	–$8,330
6. Cumulative Net Present Value	–$48,500	–$48,500	–$11,993	$23,419	$49,181	$40,851

TABLE 3-12. Project life cycle net value, adjusted for time

- At the beginning of year 2, we will introduce the product and start selling it. Initial sales will be light, but will grow rapidly, supported by our marketing effort. Expenses include the costs of production and initial marketing.
- Years 3 and 4 are the mature phase of this product's life cycle. Sales and gross revenue are high and steady. Expenses include the costs of production and our ongoing marketing program.
- In year 5, we expect a rapid decline in revenue and expenses, as this product is replaced by a newer model. We will stop selling the product at the end of the year.
- In year 6, we will decommission the plant that produces the product; we expect no revenue and we include costs for decommissioning the production plant.

If we simply add up Table 3-12, line 3 (net revenue) for all six years, we find that, with losses the first and last year, breaking even in year 2, and making money in years 3, 4, and 5, we come out ahead $50,000. When we don't consider the time cost of money, we are using an older method called *cost-benefit analysis*. Our benefits over cost (net revenue) equal $50,000. That seems like a pretty good deal.

But, as we mentioned above, future money is worth less than present money, because we could earn interest on present money if we kept it in the bank, instead of spending it on our project. Line 4 introduces that adjustment. Each year, the money is worth less and less. But how much less? Most companies use the current prime rate (an interest rate set by the U.S. Federal Reserve Bank) as the measure for ROI. As I'm writing this book, the prime rate just hit three percent. So, we'll adjust the time value of money to decline at three percent per year. After 1 year, the value will be 97 percent of the value in 2005. (A dollar at the end of 2006 is worth the same to me as 97 cents is at the end of 2005.) Each year, the amount declines by another three percent. That creates the percentages in Table 3-12, line 4. At a decline of three percent per year, a dollar six years from now is only worth 83 cents today. (Looking at it the other way around, if I put 83 cents in the bank today and earn at the prime rate, I'll have a dollar in six years.)

Line 5 for each year is calculated as line 3 (net revenue) times line 4 (factor for adjusting the value). It shows us the value of net revenue in present-day dollars, also called the *net present value*.

Line 6 shows us how the expenses and then the revenue accumulated over the years. At first, we pay money out. In year 2, there is no change, because net revenue is $0 for the year. In year 3, we start to earn back the cost of the project. Early in year 4, we break even on the cost of the project and start to make money. We keep making money until the end of year 5 and then lose a little during decommissioning in year 6. Overall, we end up $40,851 ahead over the whole life cycle of the product.

We can do the same calculation for any product, service, or new system. We're simply finding out the value of the project results compared with the project cost.

Calculating ROI. Table 3-12, above, shows all the numbers we need to calculate return on investment. We can then express the return on investment in a number of ways:

- *As the final number, revenue over expenses, adjusted for time.* This is the last figure, in year 6 of row 6, cumulative net present value: $40,851. This is, simply, how much money we will make, after expenses, in present-day dollars, over the whole life of the product. It is the simplest expression of ROI.
- *As the date we have finished paying for the project.* In this example, we can say, "We will have paid for our project early in year 4, and everything after that will be our profit, until we have to pay for decommissioning." In general, the sooner we reach the payoff date, the better. Note that this measure does not take into account decommissioning costs. If we are comparing projects and some have much higher decommissioning costs than others, we should not use this method.
- *As a ratio of net revenue to project cost (including decommissioning).* Here, we consider the ratio of the net value of the years that we made

money against the net loss of the years we lost money. Years 3, 4, and 5 have net revenue of $36,507, $35,412, and $25,762, totaling $97,681. Years 1 and 6 have losses of $48,500 and $8,330, totaling $56,830. The ratio of $97,681 to $56,830 is an ROI value of 1.72.

- *As a ratio of gross revenue to total life cycle cost.* We can also separate out revenue and costs year by year and then adjust for net present value. The yearly numbers we need for this calculation are shown in rows 5 and 6 of Table 3-13, ROI ratio by gross revenue and expense. Note that we've added a column on the right to show totals. To calculate the ROI ratio, we divide the total net value of gross revenue by the total net value of gross expense. $270,600 divided by $229,749 is an ROI ratio of 1.2.

ROI calculations are complex. In fact, this is probably the most complex thinking in all of this book. The advantage of ROI—the ability to make apples-to-apples comparison of the value of projects of different types, sizes, and length—makes it worth the effort. You may want to review the section with someone familiar with financial management and choose which method of ROI calculation you want to use.

Considering ROI Plus Risk. The ROI value is just one number that describes our project. It can't be the only thing we consider when choosing which project to do. For example, ROI assumes that the project will succeed as planned, right on schedule and within budget. To put it another way, ROI doesn't consider risk: the ROI value of a project doesn't say anything about how risky it is.

Certainly, in choosing among projects, we should look at both ROI and the executive risk summary and initial list of risks we prepared earlier in this chapter. In addition, we can think about the relationship between ROI and risk.

	Year 1	Year 2	Year 3	Year 4	Year 5	Year 6	Total
1. Gross Revenue	$0	$60,000	$100,000	$100,000	$40,000	$0	$300,000
2. Expense	$50,000	$60,000	$60,000	$60,000	$10,000	$10,000	$250,000
4. Adjustment for Time Value	97.0%	94.1%	91.3%	88.5%	85.9%	83.3%	
5. Net Present Value of Revenue	$0	$56,454	$91,267	$88,529	$34,349	$0	$270,600
6. Cumulative Net Present Value	$48,500	$56,454	$54,760	$53,118	$8,587	$8,330	$229,749

TABLE 3-13. ROI ratio by gross revenue and expense

For example, we could ask, "What if the project comes in 50 percent over budget? How would that change the ROI?" Using the last ROI formula, we change the project cost from $48,500 to $72,750, add up the rows, and calculate an adjusted ratio of 1.1 instead of 1.2.

Adjusting for a project coming in late is more complicated, because we have to adjust every year, as our product launch will happen later.

Of course, we can also ask about the results of positive risks on the project and on our projected product income. What if we finish the project three months early, for only $40,000, and sales are 20 percent higher for the life of the project? If we want to, we can create two ROI values. One would plan for the project with the lowest likely cost and the highest likely revenue, giving us our best likely ROI ratio. The other would consider the most expensive, longest project that would succeed, with the lowest net revenue for the product. That would give us our worst likely ROI ratio. We could then present a range, saying, for example, that ROI will be between 1.1 and 1.3. If every project is presented with such a range, executives will have a very good comparison tool for choosing which projects are the best ones for the company.

Congratulations! You've survived learning about ROI. Now we can go back to some easier

SMART THINKING!

Watch Your ROI–You Might Be Held Accountable!

Any ROI calculation is a projection–a statement of what we think will happen in the future. Some project managers and consultants take advantage of that, claiming very high ROI figures to convince companies to sign onto a project. Remember, though, that a few months or a year after the project is over, anyone can calculate the *real* ROI from your project. If it comes in a lot lower than what you said, then you may have to explain. So, don't tinker with the numbers to make them look better. Give the most honest figures possible. Then, when the time comes, you're likely to be right. Or, if something goes wrong, you'll be able to give an honest explanation of the difference between your estimates and the results.

The lesson: Businesses need people who will make realistic, fair, unbiased assessments of the benefits, costs, and risks of doing projects. If you play with numbers to get what you want, your company will end up worse off–and so will you.

ideas—fitness for your company and alignment with your company's values.

A Good Fit for the Company

Money isn't all that matters. Every company has a personality—a sense of purpose and style. This is especially true of small and medium-sized businesses. In the U.S., big companies often try to make money by mergers. Sometimes, they buy up other companies just because they are profitable. It works for a while, but it usually falls apart sooner or later, simply because nobody—executives, stockholders, customers—can say what the company is doing any more.

In considering any change, we should ask if it is a good fit for ourselves personally, for the company's way of doing business, and for the image our customers have of who we are. When we go to an Italian restaurant, we expect Italian desserts. Chocolate mousse may be all the rage and every restaurant in town may have it, but it may still not be a good choice for your Italian bistro.

Here's another example. You sell accessories for luxury cars. A vendor who installs and stocks soda machines explains how much money you can make by having sodas available for your customers. The money is good, but you decide against it, because a soda machine would make your store look cheap. On the other hand, you consider installing a high-end cappuccino bar and serving Italian sodas—a good match for the Lamborghinis, Fiats, and Alfa Romeos that you customize.

To understand what is a good fit for your company, you have to think about what defines your company. A particular product or service? A particular location? High quality? Low price? Convenient hours and service? Once you have a sense of who you are, it will be easier to see which project is right for you.

Alignment with Values

In addition to fitting with the image of our company, we want to make sure a project is in alignment with our values. Some values, such as honesty and integrity, should be universal. Others are different in different industries, cultures, and locations—and *vive la différence!* For example, some industries—project management is one—have very strict rules about what counts as a conflict of interest. Other businesses allow multiple relationships between companies without it being a big issue. Remember that a project will change the way that you work. You want to make sure that you will feel good about the new way of working when the project is over.

When thinking about values, we should also consider what we value—what matters to us. I like to see people succeed in business. From time to time, I've thought of products or training classes for people in their personal lives, rather than at work. But I've always decided to cancel the project. I really want to work with people in business. Similarly, I've done some work with *Fortune* 500 companies and with big government agencies. I can learn a lot on those jobs. But what I really like doing is what I'm doing right now—sharing the best ideas I can find with owners and managers in small and medium-sized businesses. It's what I value, and every project I take on—every product and service I develop—is going to make my business more of what I want it to be.

Trust Your Gut

You've probably guessed by now that I do a lot of planning and thinking. But that isn't right for everybody. Some folks run their business on gut instinct. And that is a good way to go. We know our businesses and we have good instincts about them. Sometimes, we can't say why a particular idea is good or bad, but we just know it feels right. And we should always take that feeling into account.

I think we can learn to combine careful planning and realistic evaluation with gut instinct and intuition. When we bring them together, they may line up: the plan looks good on paper and the idea feels good, too. Or the reverse: the plan looks problematic and the project doesn't feel right either. In those cases, our choice is easy.

But what do you do when a project looks fair and feels foul or it feels foul and looks fair? I suggest you take some time, think about it, sleep on it, and feel your way through the problem. After a day or two or maybe even a week, come back and reread the plan. More often than not, you will see what is bothering you—why a good plan isn't right for your company or why a plan that looks way too risky on paper is totally the right thing to do.

This may surprise you, but I change plans and follow my intuition all the time. Each year, I have a plan of how to grow my business *if nothing better comes along*. And, several times a year, something better does come along. It may be a new customer or a new potential employee. I'm free to seize the opportunity, because I know what I was going to do if the new possibility hadn't turned up. I know the ROI of what I'm giving up or setting aside. And if the ROI and risk look better on the new opportunity, I'm ready to jump for it. I don't have to follow my plans if something better comes along: planning doesn't get in the way of whims, gut feelings, or instinct. Planning and instinct combine to help me know what is best for my company.

▼ SMART THINKING!

Good Idea ... or Bad Feeling?

I heard this idea from a project manager whose friend owned a cookie company. The cookie company's specialty was that every order—and almost all the business was mail order—was custom. People could pick as many cookies of each flavor as they wanted—a dozen chocolate chips or five chocolate chips, four hazelnuts, and three peanut-butter raisin cookies—and a delightful gift box would be on its way.

That signature customization drove the bakers crazy. They never knew how many of which type of cookie to bake. And it led to a lot of waste—a lot of cookies left unsold by the end of the day.

The project manager had a practical solution. He asked his friend, "What if you offer a standard assortment? People can still pick their own if they want to. But some people—maybe half—will just go with the standard assortment. The bakers can plan on that and waste a lot fewer cookies."

The idea felt all wrong to the owner. She was very attached to the idea of selling only custom cookie assortments. Eventually, though, she saw she had to try something or go out of business. So she set it up, just to try it out. In project management language, she did a pilot project.

It worked! Over 90 percent of callers chose the standard assortment. They were actually happier, not having to make up their minds among so many delicious choices. Orders could be filled a lot faster, the bakers knew what to make, there was a lot less wastage at the end of each day, and the company became profitable again.

The lessons:
- Learn to tell the difference between good intuition and attachment to ideas that don't work.
- Be willing to test with a pilot project.
- Face your problems before it is too late.
- When you have a problem, be open to other people's ideas and suggestions.
- Give your customers choices and see what works.

CONCLUSION

If you've taken the time to work your way through this chapter, you've learned a lot—not just about project management, but also about your business and its needs. You have a prioritized list of problems and opportunities for your business.

If you've just read through, you might go back now and make that list and then practice making a few simple project plans. The sooner you plant your crop, the sooner you reap the harvest. And the sooner you plan your projects, the sooner you finish them and watch your problems go away and your profits head upwards.

In Chapter 4, we'll take the next step in putting together your business and your projects. If you've got several good projects but not the time to do them all, you'll learn more about how to pick just one project. If you're planning to do several projects at once, you'll learn how to keep your business running while fixing all those problems. And you'll learn how to share project management with your team, so everyone in your company can run a project.

CHAPTER 4

Your Business and Your Projects

IN THIS CHAPTER

Once you start to think about projects, you start to see problems and opportunities everywhere. It's like the old saying, "When you have a hammer, everything looks like a nail." To a project manager, everything looks like a project. So which nail do we hit first? Which project should be at the top of our list to schedule for a solution? We'll answer that question in the first section, Choosing Which Projects to Do. You'll learn several techniques, including work flow analysis, strategic planning, program management, portfolio management, and matrix management.

In section two, we turn to keeping track of all your projects. You'll learn the art of managing multiple projects, how to delegate tasks and projects, and how to train your whole team to get it done right.

I HOPE THIS CHAPTER WILL BE AS MUCH FUN— and as useful—for you as it is for my clients and me. I've taken the best leadership and strategic ideas on how to run a business from the *Fortune* 500 gurus and think tanks and scaled them for our small and medium-sized businesses. It gives me a lot of confidence to know that the tool I'm using to solve a problem on a $10,000 project has been used to solve a $10-million problem.

All too often, small businesses face big problems. A big company can add a product, lose a few million bucks, and then try again. For a small company, each product, each hiring decision, each new location, or each new product can be a make-or-break decision for the whole company. In this chapter, we'll use the best methods from the big companies to tackle problems like these:

- Should I focus on my core business or should I launch a new product?
- Reading Chapter 3, I made a huge list of problems. Now, I don't know where to start.
- We just moved to a new office. Every time I turn around, things just aren't

▼ Focus!

Organizing the Projects at Your Business

As you bring project management into your company, division, or department, you'll face questions like these:

- Which project should I do first?
- How many projects can I run at once without running into trouble?
- If I let a team member run a project, how do I know if it's going well or if the project got stuck?

You can face these issues and plan ahead to get the biggest bang for your buck as you invest in learning project management. In Chapter 4, Your Business and Your Projects, you'll plan how to make your business better and how to move to success, project after project.

working. How do I figure out what's wrong?

- To launch this product, I need to develop it and plan marketing and advertising at the same time. I also need to hire some new staff. How do I coordinate all of that at once?
- I just got big contract offers from two clients.

I can't do both. How do I choose which one is the best opportunity?

- When I try to assign projects to my team, they tell me that they're too busy—all their time is filled up with their regular work. How can I get them working on production and projects at the same time?
- I've got so many different things going on, I don't know which end is up!
- At my company, everyone has a different way of doing things. We each do good work, but we can't work together, because we don't understand one another. How can we get on the same page and become a real team?
- My team tells me I don't let them manage their own work. I think they make a mess every time I let them do it their way. How can I give work to my team and have them do it right?

If any of these problems sounds familiar, the answer is in your hands. Read on!

CHOOSING WHICH PROJECTS TO DO

In Chapter 3, we poured a whole bunch of problems and opportunities into a funnel and, by

▼ Bottom-Line Basics

With the Right Tool, the Job Is Easy

I've learned something from trying to scrub out burned pots and install washing machines. If the job is hard, I'm probably using the wrong tool. I've scrubbed a pot until I was blue in the face and the result was a dirty pot and some pretty good muscle building. Then I changed cleansers and, one good wipe later, the job was done. Or, if you ever try attaching a washing machine hose without using a pipe wrench—watch out! Your clothes won't get very clean, but you'll get soaked head to toe. On the other hand, one quick twist with a pipe wrench

and the job is done right.

The lessons:

- If a job is too hard, get a better tool.
- It's worth learning the tools that are right for each job.

As you read Chapter 4, Your Business and Your Projects, take the time to learn each tool well— and then apply it right to the problems and opportunities at your company.

> ### ▼Focus!
> #### Get The Work Flowing
>
> We often talk about work flow, but we don't stop to picture what it means. Work flow planning uses methods first designed for chemical factories that made sure that their pipes were the right size and turned on at the right time, so that chemicals would mix together correctly and produce the right products on time. We've adapted that idea so that we can move anything—products, services, paperwork, signatures and approvals, even information and ideas—through our companies.
>
> *The lesson:* If you learn to picture your company as a system with information and other things flowing through it, you'll be able to keep it all flowing. When the whole system works, work flows out and money flows in. When one part jams up, the work—and the money—stop flowing.

defining and evaluating those projects, we came up with a list of projects that were worth doing. That list of projects is the input for Chapter 4.

If you just read Chapter 3 and didn't make the list of projects, you might want to go back and do that now. Using the techniques for defining problems and opportunities in Chapter 3, list your problems and opportunities and put them into a copy of Table 3-1, problems and opportunities.

That list, plus the problem definitions, descriptions of opportunities, and simple project plans from Chapter 3, are all inputs into the work we are about to do. If you have them ready, then you can do more than just read and learn—you can organize all the projects in your company or department.

Work Flow at Your Company

As we said in Chapter 2, a business is a system and, following the fundamental rules of systems, a symptom in one place may be a sign of a problem somewhere else. For example, if sales have dropped, that doesn't mean that your sales team is doing a bad job. Maybe they are. But maybe the problem is with your advertising campaign, or the design of your web site, or the fact that people don't like your product. To fix the right problem at a company, we have to view the company as a system and then be able to trace symptoms back to their causes.

Unfortunately, many companies can't do this. Large companies get blocked by a stovepipe mentality: each division puts up high walls and doesn't want to hear about how other divisions do their work. Sales managers think, "We know the product is crappy, but we have to sell it anyway." Production teams think, "We've got a great product, but the salespeople just don't know how to sell." No one talks to anyone else and the problem doesn't get solved.

The same thing can happen in a small company, but for a different reason. Many problems in a small company come up because we don't like to admit that we don't know something. Very few people are good at every part of running a company. But we small business owners all too often like to think that, just because we're in charge, we have to look like we know what we're doing. We don't want to admit that we're good at selling but bad at hiring people or good at developing new products but bad at bookkeeping. As a result, we develop blind spots. Those blind spots lead to problems and—by the fundamental rule of systems—those problems could show up anywhere in the company.

Work flow analysis is a powerful tool that is not a part of the traditional MBA program. One reason that we get so much benefit from work flow analysis is that gives us a clear, coherent picture of our business. The knowledge from the traditional MBA program doesn't do that. The traditional

---

▼ SMART THINKING!

Rewriting All the Rules at Once

Back in 1994, Gordon Bethune took over as CEO of Continental Airlines. He had a big job in front of him, as the company was nose-diving into its third bankruptcy and was, by every official measure, the worst airline in America. He did a lot of things to turn the company around and succeeded in under two years.

One thing he did, we can learn from. He literally burned the old Continental company rulebook. Then he said to his employees, 'You know how to run an airline. Work smart. Write your own rules. Just one thing–anyone who has to work with your new rules, make sure you talk to them.'

Route planners talked with the customers–travel agents–and came up with new proposed flight destina-tions. They asked schedulers to make the new flights work. Schedulers talked with maintenance people first, to find out how much time planes needed between flights, and then put together workable schedules. Every part of the airline reorganized and all the parts worked together and made the whole company work. Within two years, Continental was the best airline, according to all official ratings, and was profitable again.

The lesson: If we see our business as a system, we can fix each part so that it works right–and all the parts work well together. Then our company's departments mesh like the gears in a finely tuned watch and, running smoothly, we run straight to success.

MBA program was assembled from a bunch of separate experts working in separate areas—finance, operations, marketing, and so forth. There's a lot of useful stuff in an MBA program, but it leaves blind spots. Work flow analysis can get us past the blind spots.

A few years ago, I hired a young man with an MBA but not a lot of work experience. As many other entrepreneurs have discovered, I saw that what people learn when they get an MBA is very different from what we learn by running our own businesses. It's not better or worse—just different. My assistant told me that one of his professors warned him that business school gave students some pieces of the jigsaw puzzle, but never put them together or told the students what pieces were missing. So, just using an MBA education and trying to run a business is like trying to finish a jigsaw puzzle with a bunch of missing pieces and no picture of what the puzzle should look like.

Work flow analysis will show you what pieces of the jigsaw puzzle are missing. A work flow diagram shows you how information, products, and money flow through your company to the customer. First, we create two maps: one of how our business is flowing—or stuck—and the other of how our business *should* flow. Then we compare the two. The comparison shows us what's stuck—where the bottlenecks are. And those bottlenecks are usually the areas that MBAs don't learn about in school or part of our business that maybe we didn't think were important, or we didn't think anybody could do well, or we thought someone else was taking care of.

Note that a work flow diagram is not just a different way of drawing an organizational chart. Organizational charts show hierarchy of authority—who reports to whom. Work flow diagrams show the flows of information, products, and money. Businesses succeed or falter on the steadiness of that flow. Seeing and then freeing up the bottlenecks improves the bottom line.

As you can see, Figure 4-1 is not your typical picture of a business. The circles describe functional activities—work, jobs to be done. The arrows show the movement of information, products, and money. The boxes show storage areas for ideas, products, and money. (A storage area could be a computer data file, a database, a warehouse, or a bank account.) The functional areas—circles—on this diagram first appeared in Chapter 2 as the functional parts of a business. Now, we're seeing how the parts fit together.

Let's start at the left side of the figure and work our way around counterclockwise. In any company, someone develops products and services for the customer. In a retail business, it would be the buyer. In a manufacturing business, it would be the assembly line at the plant. In a service company, it would be the people—consultants or construction workers—who can describe what they do and how much it will cost. That group—product and service development—defines a set of products and services the company can give to the customer. Marketing takes that information, develops marketing materials, designs a marketing campaign, and develops sales support materials. Marketing gets the word out to the customer. Sales responds to customer requests and closes deals—arranging contracts and closing purchases. Customer service provides service in a service business or product support for companies that sell products. Finance takes in the money. The executive function keeps everybody working together and heading in the same direction. (That's called leadership.)

That's the core of our business. But it is smart to know what our customers think about our products, to learn about other potential customers, and to make good use of that information. That brings in research, which goes out and gets information, and analysis, which studies the information and comes up with good ideas and support for executive and other decisions.

There is one functional area that doesn't appear on the page—infrastructure. Infrastructure includes human resources, computer systems, and building facilities. It's not on the diagram because these areas support every part of the company, so adding it would just put too many arrows on the page.

This is how I think about a business. It works really well for me and for my consulting clients who come to me with problems that they can't figure out. However, most people look at this diagram and their eyes glaze over. Maybe that's why business schools have never tried to come up with a picture that includes all the pieces of the business puzzle! I suggest you read the last seven paragraphs two or three times, trace out the diagram, and ask yourself, "Does this make sense to me? Is this how my company works?"

So, this picture of business functions and flows is impressive, but is it useful? You bet! When we have a good picture of how our business works, we can do some troubleshooting.

For example, we can trace out the problem I raised at the beginning of this section: sales are low—we're not closing contracts. The source of the problem could be in the sales department. But maybe the salespeople aren't getting the marketing materials they need. Or maybe marketing is trying to sell products and services that aren't very good. Or maybe research and analysis didn't do a good job, so our information about our target market and acceptable pricing is off. Any of the circles that feed information to the sales area could be the source of the problem.

Let's take another example. Suppose that customers are complaining about our services, saying that they don't like what they got. Where's the problem? Well, it could be in product and service development; maybe we've got a bad batch of products. But it could be in marketing or sales; maybe we promised or promoted something the

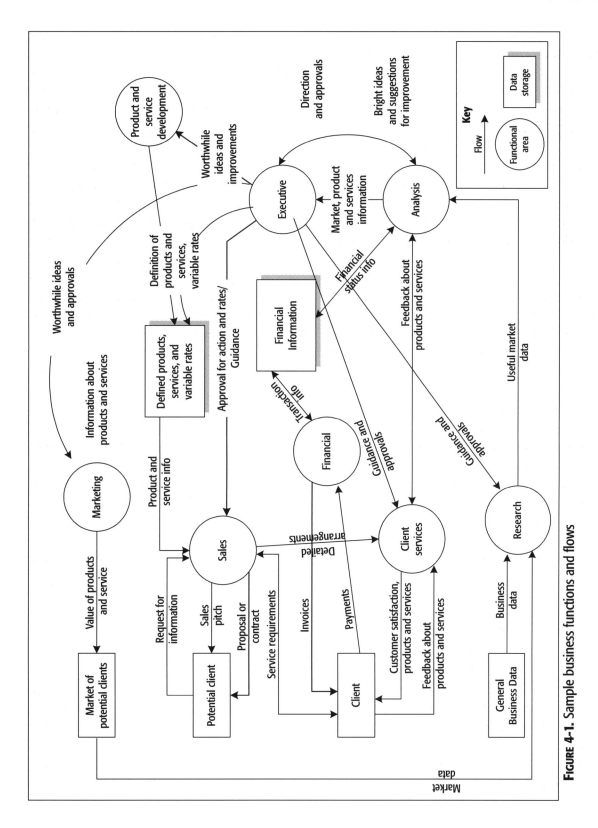

FIGURE 4-1. Sample business functions and flows

▼ **SMART THINKING!**

I Can Sell, I Just Didn't Market

A few years ago, I made a big change in my company. For the first seven years, I worked with a marketing company that promoted my training services. Then, five years ago, we went our separate ways. I was going to have to do my own marketing and sell my services. I wondered if I was any good at sales. It seemed like I wasn't—I was having trouble getting enough work.

I have two friends who are excellent sales managers and sales coaches. I called them up and had them grill me. They agreed that I was a great salesperson. So, that wasn't the problem.

That's when I first drew the diagram you see as Figure 4-1. And I saw my problem.

My problem was that I knew what I was selling. Since I did all the work myself, I had no trouble describing it, so I'd never bothered to write it down.

My customers were impressed, but I didn't leave anything behind and they didn't know what to do next. What was missing wasn't sales; it was marketing. So I beefed up my marketing. I created a new web site and wrote proposals and a brochure. Sure enough, once people could read about what I can do for them, business picked up and I never looked back.

The lesson: Find the function that isn't functioning and fix it, and the problem goes away.

---

product couldn't deliver. Or maybe our product—if it's perishable—spent too much time in the warehouse and went bad. If you trace the circles, lines, and boxes on this page, you'll find all the possible sources of your problem. A diagram like this one is an excellent help when you apply the multiple-cause analysis and root-cause analysis methods you learned in Chapter 3.

In the next section, we'll work together so that you can make a picture of how work flows at your company. Then you'll learn how to find clogged pipes and create a project to fix them.

Making a Picture of Your Company. Every company works a bit differently. Figure 4-1 may describe your company very well. Or, maybe all your product sales are directly from your web site, so sales is really part of marketing. Perhaps one of the functions—such as finances (bookkeeping and accounting)—is outsourced, the responsibility of another company. Pick up a blank piece of paper and a pencil with a good eraser and let's try to figure out how your

company works. Here are some tips:

- *Don't think about who does what job or how big a department is.* The diagram for my company doesn't change whether I'm working alone or I have a team of five—and it wouldn't change if I grew to have 250 people.
- *Find the inputs and outputs.* When people do a job, where do they get what they need to do it? If they get it from inside the company, you've found two circles and an arrow from one to the other. If they get what they need from outside the company, then you've found a circle that has an arrow coming in from outside—probably from a customer or a vendor.
- *Ask what people give to other people.* Who gives information or products to customers? Who gives information, money, or products to other people in the company?
- *Separate out the infrastructure.* Leave out groups like human resources and computer

support that help everyone. They are important, but it's just not easy to fit them on the page.

- *Trace your diagram.* Can you follow information and work from one circle to the next? Does it make sense?
- *Define your storage areas.* Where is information kept?
- *Explain your diagram to someone else.* When you can explain it to someone else, then you're ready to use it yourself.

Now, compare your diagram with my Figure 4-1. What are the differences? Why are they there? Try to understand the unique, special aspects of how your business works. Sometimes, the difference is just a name. I know one company that calls its product development group Ingestion. (That's better than *indigestion*, I guess.) Seeing how your company is different from my standard diagram will help you define the most important areas to think about and plan for.

Next, ask, "Is there a better way to do this?" Are there unnecessary steps in your flow? Are there things going back and forth between two people in different departments, when it would be easier if they worked together in the same department? Do you have any pieces that are missing altogether, as I did when I parted ways with my marketing company? To put it another way, "What isn't flowing?"

Finding the Bottlenecks. The tool we just used is called *data flow diagramming,* a child of a tool called *flow diagramming,* which was first developed for chemical processing plants. If you want to make a complicated chemical—such as glue or plastic or artificial flavor—you need to mix chemicals in the right time and right amounts. You do this with processing vats (the circles) connected by pipes (the arrows). The pipes let the right things flow in at the right time and the vats mix the chemicals, cook them, or cool them off.

If everything flows in at the right time and mixes right, you get a good batch of plastic or glue or artificial flavor. If a pipeline runs too slow or too fast, you get a bad batch. If something sits too long without mixing, you get a bad batch, too.

Information, products, services, and money work just the same way inside our company. If products and services don't reach our customers, we don't make money. If bad information goes to a department director or executive, he or she makes a bad decision and things start to go wrong. If money doesn't flow to where it is needed, problems don't get fixed and supplies don't get bought.

So, the key to finding the problems in your company is to find the flow that isn't flowing. Either work is being done badly, resulting in poor products or bad information, or work isn't happening fast enough and we have a bottleneck—a narrow point in a flow, a point where things are moving too slowly.

The challenge is that the bottleneck may be in one place and the symptom may be in another. But as soon as we find the bottleneck and fix it, the whole company runs better. Fixing an information bottleneck is like opening a clogged gas line in a car: fix it and, as soon as the gas reaches the engine, you're off and running.

In addition to fixing your business, you can use your business functions and flows diagram to make your business grow. I've found that we can do that in five steps:

1. Make sure each area is running well. Clean up any backlogs and fix any small problems.
2. Find the area that is weakest and work on that one. Define a project that will fix the problem. Does that function need to deliver better results? If so, focus on quality. Does it need to deliver faster or at lower cost? Then focus on efficiency and reducing cycle time.
3. Find the next bottleneck and fix that.

4. When everything is running smoothly, look for an opportunity to grow. It might be taking on a big client (more customer service) or growing the marketing function. Or, if demand is already exceeding supply, you might increase your ability to produce prod-

BE AN EXPERT!
Technology Changes, but Businesses Keep Flowing

People say that changes in technology make us change the way we work. In obvious ways, that's true. But it is also very important to see the ways in which businesses do not change, no matter what technological change happens. In almost all cases, changes to technology will not change the flow diagram of your business. The question will be "How does my *same* business flow through the new technology?" If we look at the familiar history of the video rental business, we'll see this.

New technology can give birth to an entire industry. For example, when the VCR tape was invented, movies could fit inside a plastic box the size of a book. That meant that people could rent movies to watch at home the same way we can borrow books from a library. The video rental business was born: a small company started renting 50 movies. Video Station was first, but Blockbuster and other companies soon jumped into the game.

That was a big change. For the first time, we could watch movies we wanted to see when we wanted to see them, instead of going to the theater or waiting for the movie to be on TV and rearranging our schedule to match the times that the theater or TV station set.

After the VCR tape, DVDs didn't seem like such a big innovation. But DVDs, along with the rise of the internet, gave birth to a whole new way of delivering movies that is putting an end to the era of video rental stores. DVDs survive in the mail and weigh less than an ounce. You can order over the internet and get them by mail. Hello, Netflix! Now, instead of choosing from a few thousand titles at my local store, I can browse over 20,000 titles

and have the ones I want in two days. Pretty cool!

Of course, the change in technology didn't mean a change of which company is the leader in a business. Netflix beat out Blockbuster because Netflix saw the opportunity and jumped first. But it doesn't always go that way. Sometimes, the old company makes the new technology work first. For example, Netscape saw the power of the internet before Microsoft did, but Microsoft still beat Netscape to the punch with its Internet Explorer.

And now the movie delivery industry is changing again. Soon, high-speed internet and servers with huge libraries of movies will enable us to download movies on demand. What company will win out: Netflix, Blockbuster, or someone else?

So, everything seems to change when technology changes. But does it really? If you draw four pictures—one of an old movie theater, one of Blockbuster, one of Netflix, and one of the new movies-on-demand service—each as a set of business functions and flows of information, money, and products, you'll find that all of these businesses are just the same. The technology has changed, but the basic process of providing services, marketing, selling, and delivering to customers hasn't changed at all.

The lesson: At the core, business doesn't change. Business delivers products and services to customers. We just change the way we do business, keeping up with new technology, but not racing ahead too fast. And if we don't change the way we do business at the right pace, someone else will and take our place.

ucts. If you're in a fast-changing market, you may need to produce new products and services. Whichever of these you choose, you're seizing an opportunity—and that means that a well-defined project will get you where you want to go. Remember, though, that when you enlarge one area, you'll have to adjust all the other areas to handle the demand. For example, if you run a new advertising campaign, will you be able to provide service for all the new customers?

5. Keep an eye out for changes in technology in your industry. Are there better ways of taking orders, tracking information, or even delivering products to your customers? These days, smart uses of technology—especially the internet—can save a business from disaster and give it a chance to grow. A business—like a person or an animal—can adapt to a changing world to live and grow.

Now, we'll look at a more traditional way of understanding our business and leading it to success: strategic planning.

Strategic Planning

In the good old days, we didn't need strategic planning. Great-grandpa was a blacksmith, grandpa was a blacksmith, and dad was a blacksmith. Guess what I'll grow up to be—a blacksmith. But things have been changing faster and faster. A century ago, running a business was like walking down a road: our way was laid out in front of us. Now, running a business is like driving a fast car. If we don't watch the road, we won't notice a turn and we'll crash. And every fork in the road is a choice that might help the business grow or might bring it down. So strategic planning and leadership—looking ahead and setting direction—are crucial parts of running a business in the 21st century.

Strategic planning usually starts at the top. Unfortunately, it often ends there as well. A strate-

> ### ▼ KEY TERMS
>
> **Strategy** Setting goals, based on *why*, on reasons for doing things.
>
> **Strategic planning** Taking time aside from work to look at the big picture, to define why, and set long-term goals.
>
> **Tactics** Deciding which tools and methods we will use to reach our goals.
>
> **Implementation** Deciding how we will use the tools to reach those goals.
>
> **Execution** Actually doing the job.

gic plan is no good if a few people at the top write it on a retreat and then it goes into a drawer and nothing is done. Successful strategic planning starts at the top and then works its way down. It

> ### ▼ BOTTOM-LINE BASICS
> #### It's Not All About Money
>
> A few years back, a professional association of young millionaires—people under 35 years old who owned businesses worth more than a million dollars a year—met and discussed why they were in business. Not one of them was mostly in it for the money. Instead, they loved what they did and the money was secondary. How did they know that? Obviously, some of the businesses were bigger or more profitable than others. But not one person would trade his or her business for someone else's, even if it was making more money.
>
> *The lesson:* If things other than money drive us or bring us satisfaction, it's a good idea to know what those things are. Otherwise, we may make a business decision or let an opportunity slip by and end up going in the wrong direction, being much less satisfied than we are now.

goes from vision and values to mission and goals. Then we move into tactics and implementation to plan how to meet those goals.

We can also get to strategy from the bottom up. We take our list of problems and opportunities and decide that solving those problems and realizing our opportunities defines our goals. From those goals, we grow our vision and values.

If we want to build a strong company, it is good to involve everyone in this process, planning from top down, and then from bottom up. Like a spider building a web, we weave threads of our plan down and up, pulling together a flow of communication that makes the team flexible and strong. Let's do this together now.

Top-Down Planning. The highest level of our business plan is expressed in vision, mission, and value. In *Built to Last: Successful Habits of Visionary Companies,* James Collins and Jerry Porras demonstrate that companies seen as truly visionary over a long time—companies like Boeing and Hewlett-Packard—consistently live by an unchanging core vision, mission, and values. Many of these companies write up their mission and publicize it; some do not. I think writing it down and looking at it is a good idea, even for a small company. If we have a reason for doing what we're doing, it's good to be able to say what it is. Here are ways I use my company's vision, mission, and values statement.

- I read it regularly. That helps me stay focused and motivated.
- I share it with potential new employees and collaborators. If they understand my vision and share my values, it increases the chances we will work well together.
- Whenever I have a big decision to make, I decide based on what is in alignment with my vision, mission, and values.

Having a written statement of vision, mission, and values gives a company focus the same way as

KEY TERMS

Vision A picture of where we want to go.

Mission A statement of who we are and how we serve.

Values Key principles we live by and key terms that define what matters to us.

having a project plan keeps a team focused on a project.

The vision, mission, and values statements are the pinnacle of a company's planning. Our first step down brings us to our current mission and our strategic goals.

If the owners of a company ask me to help them with annual strategic planning and they already have a mission, a vision, and values, I would propose this agenda.

- Review the vision, mission, and values to see if any changes are necessary and make sure we all understand them the same way. This review also introduces these documents to new team members.
- Ask how that mission interacts with the current business environment—customer needs, changes in technology, and competitor activity—to create specific current missions and define goals. From that, we draft a current mission statement with long-term goals.
- Ask what major problems are getting in the way of our ability to do our mission and then set goals, scheduling those problems for solution.

The process can be quite linear or we can get creative and explore new ideas in many ways. When we're done, we have a strategic plan that can define which projects the company needs to do to achieve its mission, realize opportunities in the marketplace, and resolve problems.

Once we have a strategic plan—typically looking ahead one to five years—we work our way down from strategy to tactics.

Seeing problems and opportunities as projects is a tactic, so we'll focus our discussion of tactics in terms of project management. Using project management as a tactic means:

- Defining the process that takes us from where we are now to a date in the future where we say "mission accomplished" as a project or program. (We'll talk more about programs later in this chapter.)

- Defining projects to achieve objectives.
- Defining projects to resolve problems and clear away barriers.

After tactics, the next step of making our business plan is implementation. OK, so we're going to use project management. How will we use it? The answer to that is our implementation plan. Here are some examples of implementation decisions:

- We'll teach every manager and team leader how to manage projects the same way.
- In a medium-sized company, we might implement a project management office, a group that sets project management standards.
- We'll choose one PM method for the company. For example, we might agree that the company uses *Entrepreneur Magazine's Ultimate Guide to Project Management for Small Business: Get It Done Right!* (Sorry, I couldn't resist the plug.)
- We decide we will assign a project manager for each project and make sure he or she is responsible for getting the job done and also has everything needed to do the job.
- We make those assignments, naming a project manager for each project.

When we've finished with implementation, we're done with planning. Now, we have these plans:

- A statement of unchanging vision, mission, and values
- Our current strategic plan: a statement of our current mission and objectives, looking one to five years ahead, including objectives that further our mission (opportunities to realize) and objectives that remove roadblocks (problems scheduled for solution)
- Our tactical plan, naming the tools that will help us reach those objectives
- Our implementation plan, saying how we will acquire, learn, and apply those tools and assigning people to lead projects to meet the

---

▼ SMART THINKING!
Good Planning Saves Time and Money

I realize that the amount of planning I just recommended is a lot more than most companies want to do. My experience, though, is that this is the right amount of planning—the most efficient amount. If we plan less than this, then we end up moving into execution—doing projects—and then running into big delays in the middle of the projects. We get stuck and have to ask, "How are we going to do this?" (an implementation question) or "What are we doing?" (a tactical question) or "Why are we doing this?" (a strategic question).

Each time we have to answer one of those questions during a project, it will take ten times longer to answer it than it would have if we had answered the question before starting. Also, in companies with more than 20 people, if we are asking these questions in the middle of projects, then we are asking them over and over again. Someone else has probably already answered the question, but the answer got lost in the shuffle. Without knowing it, we're wasting time reinventing the wheel.

The lesson: Projects go straight from starting point to goal fastest and at lowest cost when we already know why we are doing them (strategy), what we are doing (tactics), and how we're going to do it (implementation).

---

objectives by realizing the opportunities and solving the problems

That's enough planning! The next step is execution, which means no more planning. Now, we do it and *get it done right!*

Maybe top-down planning isn't your style. Maybe you're a hands-on person who likes to work in the trenches. In that case, we have a different approach—bottom-up planning.

Bottom-Up Planning. Sometimes, we start with our problems. You know how that is. You show up for work and, as soon as you walk in the door, there's a problem—or three, or five, or ten problems—waiting for you.

Even when things are like that, there are ways to work with implementation planning and tactical and strategic thinking. Note that I put the terms in reverse order. Because that's how we're going to do it this time around, in this section. We're going to take a problem and plan it from the bottom up.

Let's walk through an example of bottom-up planning. Here's the situation. Two sales reps are

▼ FOCUS!
Fast Planning Is a Lot Better Than No Planning

Bottom-up planning gives us the advantages of good planning right in the middle of a problem or crisis. When we do that planning, we make our project ten times more efficient—reducing cost and delivering a solution a lot sooner.

---

arguing and the sales manager comes over to find out what the problem is. It turns out that a new potential client had talked to both of them. The client called this morning and said, "If you get me a contract by noon and deliver the first products by 6 p.m., you've got me as a client. Otherwise, you're out." Each rep wants the customer and is accusing the other of trying to steal him.

Here's how a savvy sales manager would use bottom-up planning to solve the problem.

- He starts by listening. and understanding. He makes sure he understands each person's problem. Then he says, "OK, each of you have a problem: you think the other is stealing your client. We'll have to take care of that. But first, the company has a problem. What's the company's problem? A client wants a contract and some products, but my salespeople are standing around arguing!" He gets them to agree to solve the company's problem first and then resolve their own problems.

- He focuses on implementation. "OK, the two of you will split the commission on today's order, but one of you is going to get the contract and deliver the goods. I'll decide based on what's best for the company." He asks what each of them would do if the order hadn't come in. Whoever is doing the more urgent or more valuable work doesn't get the new client. That is, the sales manager makes an implementation decision (who will do the work) based on opportunity cost—what other work won't get done if one or the other takes on this job. (I'm assuming each sales rep would be equally good at fulfilling the new order. Otherwise, the one more likely to succeed would get the job.)
- The sales manager moves up to tactics. He makes sure the assigned rep understands what he or she has to do to make the client happy.
- Everyone agrees on *why* they're handling the situation this way (strategy). The company is better off if salespeople are serving clients than if they're arguing with each other and losing clients.
- Now, we're at the top of the pyramid: we've moved up from implementation planning through tactical thinking and strategic thinking. But there's another issue—an issue of values. The issue is fairness. What is the fair solution? Which rep should get the client

from now on? The sales manager defines the issue and makes these decisions:

- The company has a system that should prevent this problem: salespeople have territories. The system didn't work. The sales manager will find out why. He will do a root-cause analysis and, if the problem is likely to repeat, he'll introduce a permanent preventative solution that will ensure fairness without conflict in the future.
- The sales manager will review the history of client contact. If one salesperson did a lot more work to land the client than the other, then he or she will get this client. If the work was about equal, then he'll work out a fair solution with both reps. Maybe one will get the client, but the other will share the commission on him or her for a period of time. Maybe the senior salesperson will get the client, but then she will help the junior salesperson close contracts with three more clients where he's having some trouble. That would be a win all the way around.

Does all that thinking and planning seem like a lot of work? It is. But take a moment and consider the alternative. Here are some typical shortcuts the sales manager might have taken and the problems that would have resulted:

- The sales manager says, "You two work it out." They don't and the customer doesn't sign the contract.
- The sales manager picks one person and gives him or her the client, based on his feelings or a seniority rule, but ends there. There is no acknowledgment that what happened was unfair or he acknowledges it but does nothing about it. The other salesperson feels the manager is unfair and lives with resentment or quits. Either way, the company loses sales and is worse off.

Yes, good thinking is hard work. But it is good thinking that solves problems, creates workable plans, and, most importantly, creates a fair, healthy work environment where good work gets done and people stay with the company a long time.

Our example with the sales manager shows how we can solve a problem by turning it into a project and planning it from bottom up, asking how (implementation), what (tactics), and why (strategy).

As a team, we can do the same with all of our problems at once. A bottom-up team strategy session works like this:

- Before the meeting, have every member prepare a list of problems he or she is working on and another list of problems he or she knows about, but is not working on. You can help them do this by working with them using the problem-definition tools in Chapter 3.

- At the meeting, have each person describe the problems on his or her lists and put all of the problems into one list on a white board, on giant sticky notes, or on a computer display.

- Group the problems into related areas.

- For each set of problems, ask the implementation questions: *Who* will take responsibility for solving this problem? *How* will we solve it? Write down the answers to these questions.

- For each set of problems, ask the tactical questions: *What* is the goal? *When* do we plan to reach that goal? Write down the answers to these questions. That's how you define your projects.

▼ THINK FOR YOURSELF!
Growth Isn't Always a Good Idea

American society seems to always think bigger is better. So, when we talk about opportunities, we usually think of growing the business, getting new clients, or making more money.

But maybe that simply isn't what we want to do. Here are some examples of opportunities that aren't about growth:

- *Leading a balanced life.* If my business has just been through a difficult time, I might have been working 65 hours a week. Maybe I need a vacation and time with my family. Maybe the whole team needs a break. Those are opportunities to realize.

- *Working smarter.* Becoming more effective and efficient means making more money in less time. Maybe we can develop *passive income* product sales that come in over the internet without any effort on our part, which some people call *making money in your sleep.*

- *An exit strategy.* Do you plan to keep running this business for the rest of your life? If not, design an exit strategy. How will you leave your business with the reputation, the money, and the situation you want so that you can do whatever you want to do next? Some entrepreneurs want to start a new business every few years. Others want to stay with the business until they retire. Some people want to close their business when they retire, others want to pass it on in the family, and others want to sell it. What are you planning to do next? Is your business oriented toward your reaching that goal on schedule? That's your exit strategy.

The lesson: For the greatest satisfaction, find the opportunity that means the most to you.

■ For each set of problems, ask the strategic questions: *Why* are we doing this? Is it really worth doing? What's the benefit to the company? Be sure to ask *whether* this is the direction you want to go and whether the problem is worth solving. Write down the answers to these questions as the "why" or "purpose" section of your project plan. Knowing the purpose will keep people focused on getting the project done.

A bottom-up strategy session to define and organize all of our problems into projects is a very good start. If—like most businesses—you're very busy and have a lot of problems to solve—go for it. Organize your problems and take care of them.

There is another step after fixing our problems. We shouldn't forget about opportunities. I've seen this happen. Companies walk through their idea of vision, mission, and values, but something is missing. The strategic plan looks good at first, but, when I look at it closely, all they've really done is listed all of their problems.

We can do better than that. We can focus on opportunity.

Once we've cleared the problems out of the way, it's time to focus on our purpose, new goals, and the opportunities to fulfill our mission in a larger way. We can do a bottom-up opportunity session the same way we did a bottom-up problem-solving session. Have each person bring two lists, one of opportunities he or she is working on and the other of opportunities he or she has thought about, but isn't working on yet. Then work through the same steps as we did for problems, in the bulleted list just above, focusing on the opportunities as you earlier focused on the problems.

Weaving Top to Bottom. Now, we've learned two methods of planning—from the top down and from the bottom up. Either one works, so go with how you usually think. If you're a hands-on, just-get-it-done person, don't try to change that; plan from the bottom up. If you're a visionary person with lots of ideas, go top-down.

A team works really well if it can do both top-down and bottom-up planning. In the middle of things, we ask, "What's the problem?" Then we make sure we know *who* will fix the problem, *how* they will do it, *what* the goal is, and *why* it is worth doing. When we have more time, we step back and say, "OK, let's reread our mission statement and reconnect with our purpose." Starting with *why* we do things, we decide *what* we will do and then ask *who* and *how*. In both cases, be sure to ask *whether* this is worth doing, so that you do not fall into simply assuming that the problem is worth fixing or that the opportunity is the right one for the company.

Working top down or bottom up, we cover all the bases, answering all the questions that let us define a problem and develop a solution or identify an opportunity and find a way to make it real.

▼ **Focus!**

Use Program Management to Organize Your Big Goals

Program management was first developed for the government, military contractors, and big business. Its value for small and medium-sized businesses is that we can take a little time to think like the big organizations and organize our company and our team to succeed with our biggest goals. In addition—especially for medium-sized businesses—we can pull the team together and make sure that we aren't starting up projects that conflict with one another. For example, we probably don't want one project taking us into a new market and another one making a new product for the old market.

Program Management

Now, we're going to look at three planning methods that the Project Management Institute (PMI) says define the context for project management. That is, these three topics—*program management*, *portfolio management*, and *matrix management*—define how projects will be organized inside our company.

A *program* is bunch of projects and possibly some production work that all fit together. There are two types of programs, as illustrated in Figure 4-2.:

- *A group of related projects, each of which accomplishes part of our mission.* The classic example here is the Apollo Program at NASA, which was a series of projects that got men to the moon and engaged in exploration and research on the moon. The whole pro-

gram was a series of projects. Each Apollo rocket launch, with a Saturn V rocket sending a three-man capsule into space, was one project. Early projects tested the system by orbiting the Earth and then going to the moon and back without landing. In June 1969, the 11th Apollo mission put men on the moon. After that, additional missions (projects) landed at different locations and performed different activities, included driving around in the Lunar Rover and performing different experiments. All program objectives were met by doing a series of projects. But there was also a support group—people managing the finances, negotiating contracts, and maintaining Cape Canaveral,

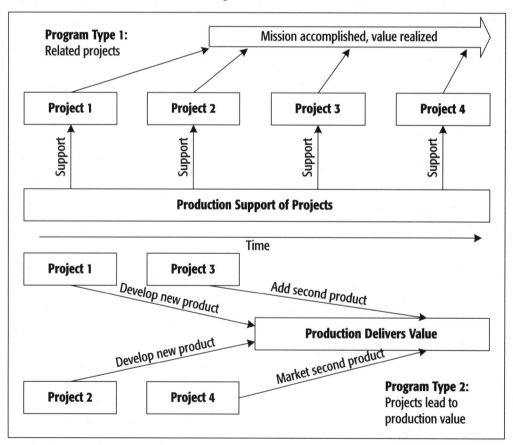

FIGURE 4-2. The two types of programs

the Johnson Space Center in Houston, and other locations. These people were not assigned to projects; they were doing routine work that supported the projects.

- *Several related projects that create ongoing production work.* Here, the classic example is the development and marketing of a new line of products. Computer printers are a good example. A company like HP or Epson will have several similar printers. Maybe all of them are color ink jets that scan, fax, and print. Developing the first one was a big R&D project. Naming the line and deciding what would make each printer unique was a big marketing project. Developing each additional model—an inexpensive one for the low-end market, one optimized for speed and simple office graphics, and a model that prints photographs well—is a smaller project. Developing a marketing campaign for each printer is another small project. As soon as one model is in production and being marketed, then the product life cycle—production work—begins. In this kind of program, the value is realized through the production work, not through projects. After all the projects end, the production work goes on through the product life cycle, generating revenue for the company.

Most programs fit into one of these two types, though some things are called programs that are really, in PMI's terminology, just very large projects. That's particularly common in the U.S. military and with military contractors. What makes a program different from a project is that for a project the schedule is very tight. A one-day delay on one task might mean that the whole project runs a day late and the customer gets delivery a day late. On a program, related work is tied together, but it's not all kept on a tight schedule. For example, if an Apollo rocket wasn't ready for launch due to one technical problem, the launch had to be delayed. But when Apollo 13 ran into problems and didn't make a moon landing, its payload and experiments could be moved onto the next projects within the program by adjusting the payload schedules of Apollo 14, 15, and 16.

When we look at large companies that run projects of the second type, several related projects that create ongoing production work, we may find that the person who runs the program is called a product manager, rather than a program manager. Or, some companies organize their programs by customer and the program manager might be called a customer relations manager. For example, a large computer consulting firm like EDP or Computer Associates might run a program that manages every contract it has with a big client like General Motors.

Why Think About Programs? How is our company better off if we use program management? There are several benefits:

- *We don't get our fingers into too many pies.* A small or medium-sized company can't grow in all directions at once. By organizing our strategy and projects into programs, we can make sure that we keep things running and make one or maybe two big improvements at a time. Otherwise, we may start several things and then not be able to finish them all. For example, we might choose between opening a new store and developing a new product line, instead of doing both at once.
- *We increase efficiency by coordinating projects.* If we have several related projects, we can hire someone with the right skills to work on all of them or we can give several people training and then realize the benefit of that training across all the projects. Also, if we create really good project and technical plans for the first project, we can reuse parts of those plans for other projects throughout the rest of the program.

- *Product development and marketing programs give our customers a clear sense of who we are.* When we define a line of products or services, we can give it a name and we can use that branding or trademark in all of our advertising and promotions. We become known for what we do for our customers. That leads to success.

Obviously, when an agency like NASA or a company like Hewlett Packard designs a program, it is setting up plans that run for years or even decades. Program management was designed for the big organizations. In *Project Management for Small Business,* we are looking at much smaller programs. In the next section, we'll see how to scale program management down to size.

Planning and Running Programs for Small Businesses.
In my own business and with my consulting clients, I've found several good ways to use program management ideas on a small scale.

- *In top-down strategic planning, I will usually focus each year by creating a program to improve one functional area of the company that year.* For example, if my customers want me to head in a new direction, if my industry is changing, or if my own interests are changing, I'll focus on product and service development. If I'm working too many hours for too little money, I'll develop a marketing program that will sell more products and fewer services. With product sales over the internet—passive income—I make money while I sleep. So, if I haven't been getting enough sleep lately, it's the perfect solution.
- *A program can cut across functional areas to help us align our company with our customers and increase revenue.* Customer needs define the direction for our success and our business should follow. If a new product or service is selling well, we may need to rearrange a

lot of things to improve our profit margin. The sales team should focus on the new market. Marketing should expand its ad campaign. Product and service development should develop new products or services in the new area. To do all this, we may have to decide to let go of some of the things we've been doing. Grocery stores need to get rid of the Halloween candy to make room for Christmas decorations. In the same way, we may need to change what we make room for in our store or our business to meet customer demand. I call this *aligning the company to the customer,* and it works well as a program. In the program, I create one or two projects in each functional area and then coordinate them.

- *Entrepreneurial ventures do well as programs.* As I've mentioned earlier, I've seen start-up businesses with good business plans fail because, although they planned well for the investors, they didn't do good project management inside the company. They set deadlines, but didn't do enough work to figure out how to meet those deadlines. When we're starting a new company or division, we would do very well to see it as a program, set up the resources, and fund and schedule a series of related projects to pull it all together and get everything done on time.

When we do program management in a small business, what do we actually do? It's different for each of the two types of programs.

If we are creating the kind of program where the projects deliver the value—like NASA's Apollo Program—then we set up an inexpensive infrastructure that supports the projects. Companies that do consulting or custom work for clients benefit from this approach. Each client job—a custom home renovation, a business web site, or whatever service we provide—is one project. And we set up a client manager, a way of scheduling the work so all the jobs get done, and whatever infrastructure, such as equipment and training, the workers will need. We schedule and manage each project for maximum net revenue. Then we use program management techniques to fill in the gaps between or among projects or provide extra support when we have too much work.

For this kind of program, the most important thing is to manage the work flow. We need to know which customers can accept a delay and which ones require delivery on schedule. We need to let some jobs at the office pile up and then make sure we do them when work is slow. The program manager can make it easier to balance the workload by arranging discounts for clients who book in advance or who accept a flexible schedule. He or she also keeps track of all project work and assigns people as they move from one job to the next.

For the other kind of program, where we are setting up a new product line or making other major changes to our production work, our first focus should be on ensuring that the new product or work process is really better than the old one. For that, we start with the opportunity-definition tool in Table 3-7 of Chapter 3. We then research the opportunity and calculate the ROI, ensuring that the change in the way we work is worth the cost and risk of the projects required to make the change.

If we decide to go ahead, we define the work as a program. There are several important things we can do in program management for launching a new product line or changing our ways of working. The most important ones are listed first.

- *Make sure that we're ready and we're not tackling too many things at one time.* The biggest cause of program failure for a small business is those daily problems—the fires we have to put out—that put our projects way behind schedule.
- *Make sure we have the right expertise.* If no

SOMETHING SLIPPED!

A Day Late and It's All Gone

In my collection of examples of programs gone wrong, I have a lovely invitation to an opening of a new art gallery. Clearly, someone put a lot of effort into creating many pieces of fine art over several years, finding a location, opening a gallery, planning the opening, getting together a mailing list, and sending lovely invitations clearly designed by an artist, with my name and address in a lovely script font.

I think it was the script font that tripped them up.

The invitation—promising delicious hors d'oeuvres and fine art—arrived two days after the event. Either their mailing simply ran late or the organizers did not take into account the extra time the post office needs to read fine script fonts. Either way, months of preparation and a lot of money went out the window because of just one tiny error in their advertising campaign.

The lesson: Good program management supports each project and also keeps an eye on every project, to make sure that one small mistake doesn't ruin months of work.

one in the company knows how to do the work well, then hire an expert or pay to get some training. If this opportunity is worth doing, it's worth doing right.
- *Make sure we have enough money to finish the job.*
- *Schedule the work so that it can get done without interfering with routine business operations.*
- *Plan the program schedule to deliver results a few weeks or months before we need them.* If we want to be ready for the Christmas sales season, aim to finish all projects by early

---

August. That will give you some leeway if things fall behind.

- *Plan every project and keep an eye on every job.* It is very easy to let one project slip. But success depends on each one getting done right, so that the new system will work all together.

Portfolio Management

In portfolio management, we look at the content of a program—all the projects, production work, and resources in the program—but from a different perspective. Program management focuses on unifying the program, pulling together the resources to make sure that all the projects work and that they meet the goals effectively and efficiently. That is, program management focuses on realizing and increasing value.

Portfolio management focuses on managing resources and reducing risk. Portfolio management was first developed in the financial industry, as a technique for making the most money from financial investments. That was called maximizing return: portfolio managers would look at your money and figure out what selection of stocks, mutual fund, real estate, bonds, and other investments would give you the amount of money you wanted when you wanted it at an acceptable level of risk.

We learned the most important tools of portfolio management in Chapter 3—return on investment (ROI) and comparative risk analysis. Both of these tools were first developed to look at financial investments. Now, they have been adapted to help us look at a company's investment of resources—of time and people—into programs and projects.

Portfolio management of programs and projects is a good deal more complicated than portfolio management of a financial portfolio, for several reasons:

- *Future return is harder to estimate.* In financial management, we are looking at probable return from stocks, bonds, and mutual funds, which have a historical rate of return over many years. In project management, we are looking at the value of something we've never done before and we have less historical information on which we can make our judgment of how much money we will make in the future.
- *Value is harder to define.* At the end of our financial investments, we get money. At the end of a project or program, we may get many types of value. Money is certainly one. Reputation, goodwill, an excellent working team, expertise, and market leadership are others. It is hard to compare the soft-dollar value of one project or program with another.
- *Managing many resources and people is harder than managing just money.* In financial management, we are moving money around. Our

basic question is "Do we put more here and less there?" If we want to change our mind, we can usually sell one investment and buy another. If not, we can borrow against one to buy another. In portfolio management of programs and projects, our resource management is more complicated. We are limited in two ways:

- *We can't stop a project in the middle.* We can buy and sell a mutual fund at any time and we earn as much money as the time allows. But if we invest in a project or a product development program and stop partway through, we may not get anything at all.
- *We have to make sure we have enough of every type of resource, especially people with expertise.* Sometimes, a program seems just fine, but if we look at the plan and particularly the specific knowledge and expertise needed to do each project, we find that every project is relying on the expertise of just one person, who cannot do all five projects at once. We've found a

bottleneck. If we hadn't done portfolio planning, that bottleneck would have slowed everything down—or brought it to a grinding halt.

Using Portfolio Management in a Small Business. There are three ways we can apply portfolio management methods when planning programs and projects in a small business:

- *Apply ROI evaluation to our strategic planning choices.* If we're setting direction for the company, we should take the time to calculate the ROI of each idea for new products, services, major client relationships, and initiatives. For example, we might have a chance to accept a client contract that brings in lots of money, but the expenses would cause the net revenue from the contract to be low. Worse, the contract will use up so many of our service people that we'll have to stop doing smaller, more profitable jobs and we'll be putting all of our eggs in one basket. Is the contract still worth doing?

▼ SOMETHING SLIPPED!

Hot Java

Java is a computer programming language introduced in 1995. Java programming was a big part of the internet boom a few years ago. I know two entrepreneurial ventures—two small companies with a lot of money invested in them—that failed because they couldn't get a good Java programmer when they needed one.

Java was very hot: everyone needed Java programmers and Java was so new that there weren't a lot of people who could program in Java well. Each of these companies needed a real expert, not just someone who had been trained in school, and they couldn't find the right person *at any price.*

In both cases, the companies could have succeeded with better planning. If they'd looked ahead and seen that Java programmers would be hard to find, they could have started with a larger team of less experienced programmers. The teams would have learned as they worked and been expert in the kind of programming necessary to get the job done.

The lesson: It pays to examine our resource needs at the beginning of a program or project, find potential bottlenecks, and prevent the bottlenecks before it is too late.

- *Know the cost of resources and plan to have all we need from the beginning of the project.* If you hire flexible people who are dedicated to the job and want to learn, then they will become experts on the projects—learning the right skills for your company—from the beginning of the first project. This increases the chances that you'll have the expert people you need for the whole program.
- *Know our resources and evaluate programs to make sure we have enough of what we need.* In particular:
  - *Use knowledge transfer.* If only one person knows how part of the company works, our company is at risk. Any growth or change in that area relies on that person: that's a potential bottleneck. Worse, if that person leaves, the company has to relearn what he or she knew. The solution to this is *knowledge transfer.* Have people document how their jobs are done and cross-train one another. The team transfers into the company the knowledge of how the members do their jobs, so that anyone can take a vacation or leave of absence and others can keep the company running. If you do that, you'll also have extra resources for projects in critical areas.
  - *Get detailed about expertise.* Knowing a job in general often isn't enough to be able to do good work on a project. Create an environment where people want to be honest about what they can and can't do and support them in learning new things. Then explore the exact type of knowledge, ability, experience, and expertise needed for each project.

Portfolio management doesn't end with planning. It continues with tracking and control. So, track and control your resource needs as the project moves ahead. *Keep an eye out for resource bottlenecks or limitations on expertise all the way through the project.* If a project is running behind and someone says, "I didn't get the work done," ask, "Why?" Normally, we don't do that. We say, "OK, but get up to speed." Instead, we should identify the cause of the problem. If we don't take care of the cause, the problem may happen again and the project may go out of control.

Here are two examples of reasons people don't get work done in a small business. I'm sure they'll be familiar, because they are very common. But maybe you've never looked at them as portfolio management issues:

- Perhaps the person was pulled away to deal with some other problem or an increase in regular work. That's a resource bottleneck and it's likely to repeat if you don't address it. Consider assigning someone else to help with either the routine work or the project.
- Perhaps the person didn't want to focus on the project because he or she didn't feel able to do it. That's a missing resource, expertise, and the resource won't become available until you get it. Have the person get some training or bring in some help.

For the tracking and control side of portfolio management, we can focus on helping our team identify problems and come up with permanent solutions before the problems repeat, creating longer delays. If a cause is unresolved and problems start repeating within a project, the project usually spirals out of control and fails.

Matrix Management

There is one more way of looking at management issues that is helpful on our projects—*matrix management.* It's how we ensure that projects get done when they cross lines of responsibility on our organizational chart.

▼ FOCUS!

Get Production and Projects Done

Matrix management is all about solving one very simple problem: both production work and projects need people. How do we assign work and make sure that the production work and the projects both get done on time?

Many of the ideas in matrix management—such as organizational charts—may not seem too important for a small business. But after I present the ideas, I'll show you how they apply to your company, no matter how small and no matter what you do.

▼ KEY TERMS

Matrix management The art of balancing the needs of functional managers and project managers.

Functional manager The ordinary manager of a department, responsible for production work.

Project manager The manager assigned to run a project and make sure it gets done.

If all the work of a project is within one department, matrix management may not be a big issue. The department head just has to make sure that production work and project work both get done. Matrix management becomes an issue when we have multiple departments working together on a project.

The problem is when a person is assigned to a project and now has two jobs and two bosses. For his or her regular work, the person reports up the usual chain. For the project work, he or she reports to a project manager in another department. What happens when both people ask for 100 percent of the person's time?

▼ SOMETHING SLIPPED!

I Work Only 300 Percent of the Time

One time, I was teaching project management to several hundred IT managers in a *Fortune* 500 company. They told me that their company used matrix management and that they were assigned to multiple projects. I asked how many of them had how much of their time assigned. Almost all of them were booked 200 percent to 300 percent of their time. That's not matrix management; that's chaos.

The lesson: If we don't plan and supervise production and project work with matrix management, we won't get our projects done.

If the functional manager—the person's regular boss—and the project manager don't come to an agreement, that puts the worker in an impossible situation. The two sidebars, I Work Only 300

▼ SOMETHING SLIPPED!

He Was Working Half Time For Full-Time Pay—and No One Knew

A small department—17 people doing 40 audits per year—assigned workers to multiple audit projects. One worker was assigned to two audits. At the end of the week, his time report showed that he'd spent ten hours on the first audit and ten hours on the second audit. Both project managers were happy with his work and each assumed that the auditor had worked 30 hours on his other project. In fact, he'd only done 20 hours worth of work that week. No one knew what he did with the other 20 hours or even that he hadn't been working.

The lesson: If we don't plan and supervise staff time with matrix management, we don't know what our employees are doing—or not doing.

Percent of the Time and He Was Working Half Time for Full-Time Pay—and No One Knew, illustrate problems that happen if we don't pay attention to matrix management.

Matrix Management Concepts. From the project management perspective, this is the key issue in matrix management: the reporting structure of an organization determines how much authority the project manager has over the project and the people on his or her team. Table 4-1 shows the five types of organizations and the strength of authority of the project manager.

Matrix Management for Small Businesses. There are several ways to use matrix management in small and medium-sized businesses. First, decide which type of organization you have. Most small businesses fit into one of three types:

- *Traditional.* If you have a few workers or managers, each with a job title, and each does his or her work, you probably have a traditional organization. For example, I worked for a magazine that was almost all managers—an editorial manager, an art manager, a subscription manager, a sales manager, an advertising manager, and a book sales manager. The art manager and editorial manager each had an assistant. We each did our job, the publisher kept everything running, and the magazine came out every month. We rarely had to work with each other; instead, we each worked out problems with the help of the publisher.
- *Projectized.* If each job for each customer is a project—such as in a home remodeling firm, a consulting agency, or a doctor's office—you have a projectized work environment. The organization focuses on getting each job done and making each customer happy.
- *Not organized at all.* If you run a one-person company or have a small team where every-

one does what needs to be done, then you don't have any particular organization.

Once you've figured out what kind of structure (matrix) your organization has, you'll want to ask, "What kind of organization *should* my business have?" The best way to use program management and matrix management for your business depends on whether your organization makes money from projects or makes money from production work. Look at the two types of programs presented earlier in this chapter and decide. If your company makes money from production work, use the sidebar, Manage Production, Manage Change. If your company makes money from projects, use the sidebar, Projects to Success!

KEEPING TRACK OF IT ALL

Even though the terms "program management" and "portfolio management" contain the word "management," they focus mostly on planning. But having a good plan isn't enough. We also have to *execute* that plan, that is, do the work. And we have to monitor the work as we're doing it by tracking its status and then control it—change direction as needed to stay on course.

Here are the skills that will enable you to keep track of all your projects:

- *Self-management.* All of us can improve at keeping track of our work, preventing poor quality, and making good use of our time so that we get it done right one job after another.
- *Multiple-project management.* For one person, this is the art of doing many things at once. For the owner of a company or head of a department, it means helping each employee stay on track with his or her projects.
- *Assigning work.* We need to be able to assign work to others with confidence that they will get it done right. On a larger scale, this means assigning projects to project managers. On a

	Description	PM Authority	Advantages	Disadvantages
Functional	Traditional, hierarchical org chart by department.	None or very low	Each functional area gets its jobs done.	Change through projects and interdepartmental communications are very difficult.
Weak Matrix	Traditional org chart, with some allowance for projects.	Low: PM has to request resources, decision is up to FM.	Good for a stable company with occasional needs for projects.	Hard for PM to get resources and hard to be sure of keeping them until the project is done.
Matrix	Equal balance between FM and PM.	Moderate	Allows PMs and FMs to meet on equal footing. Good for projects.	Who decides when FMs and PMs disagree?
Strong Matrix	PM has more authority than FM.	Strong	Easy to do projects, even cross-functional projects.	Production work may not get the resources it needs.
Projectized	Traditional divisions don't exist; everything is done by project.	PM is the only person in charge.	Organization is totally geared toward project success.	When projects end, there is no work and layoffs may be necessary.

TABLE 4-1. Matrix management: the five types of organizations (FM = Functional Manager, PM = Project Manager)

small scale, it means delegating individual tasks within a project and getting the results we need to keep the project moving.

- *Running a program full of projects.* Here, we'll look at the key skills needed to move a program to completion.

KEY TERMS

Functional organization An organization with a traditional hierarchical structure of departments and no provision for cross-departmental project management.

Weak matrix organization An organization where functional managers have more power and authority than project managers, who can ask for people to be assigned to a project.

Matrix organization An organization where functional managers and project managers have equal authority in assigning people to routine work or projects.

Strong matrix organization An organization where functional managers have less authority than project managers: project managers get first pick in assigning people to projects and functional managers have to negotiate for people's time with project managers.

Projectized organization An organization where everything or almost everything is run as programs and projects by program and project managers.

▼ **BOOST YOUR BUSINESS!**

Manage Production, Manage Change

If your company makes money through ongoing operations—for example, a store or a manufacturing plant—follow these steps to take advantage of the basic ideas of program management and matrix management. You'll be able to streamline your company and improve the bottom line.

1. Build or clarify your organizational chart and make sure that the data flow and work flow are managed well and running well.

2. Ask yourself, "How often do we need to run projects to set up new product or service lines, upgrade our products, or change the way we work?"

3. If you do projects very rarely because your industry is stable (you've been selling widgets since your grandfather started the business), then keep a functional organization. Then, when a project comes around, run it yourself as owner of the company. If your company is a bit bigger, assign a project manager for the daily work; let everyone know you've given him or her full authority and then be very involved and available.

4. If you do projects more often, create a matrix organization with responsibility balanced between stable production work and changes introduced by projects. Make every manager responsible both for continuing production work and for ensuring improvements through projects.

▼ **BOOST YOUR BUSINESS!**

Projects to Success!

If your company gets value by completing projects for customers, follow these steps to take advantage of the basic ideas of program management and matrix management. You'll be able to streamline your company and improve the bottom line.

1. Organize your company by programs or projects. The people who control resources—whether you call them client managers, customer managers, program managers, or project managers—are responsible for defining what the customer wants and completing a project to ensure customer satisfaction.

2. Ask the question, "How can we build an infrastructure—production support—that will get us clients and supply the company with the ongoing work we want?"

3. Build that organization. It may include salespeople or a marketing team.

4. Make sure that there is good communication between the salespeople and the project managers, so that salespeople don't commit the company to impossible or unprofitable projects.

5. Define an organization that provides support and resources—people and equipment—so that projects can be done. Make sure that organization gives project managers what they need to get projects done right.

6. Plan whether and how you want the organization to grow. Chart a strategy that manages demand, by booking contracts of the right type far enough in advance, and resources, by ensuring that the project managers have what they need.

7. As owner or chief executive, make sure the programs and projects get what they need from the marketing and sales group and from the infrastructure support group and that work and information flow smoothly through the organization.

■ *Team training in project management.* Projects work best if we know how to work well together.

Self-Management: The Art of Getting It Done Right

Some psychologists and HR consultants will tell you that people are either well organized and task-oriented or not and that we can't change that. They'll say that the key is to hire good workers.

I won't disagree with the second part of that—hiring good workers is essential. In fact, the more customer service or unique project work we do, the more important it is that our team be made up of capable, flexible people.

However, I have found that a good manager can

▼ **FOCUS!**

Keeping Track of All Your Projects

In this second part of Chapter 4, we're going to focus on keeping track of all the projects that we're doing. You'll learn some simple, practical tools and ideas for tracking your projects. The sooner you know something is wrong, the sooner you can start fixing it. Early fixes are less expensive and more likely to work. It's just like driving a car: the sooner you notice that you are drifting, the sooner you can correct and the less likely you'll you go too far off course.

The lesson: Learn these tools and keep on top of your projects with your team. Then you'll have success after success, instead of crash after crash.

▼ **SMART THINKING!**

Make Money from Production and Projects

Most small businesses that make money from production work have very high overhead. Most of the money that comes in goes out in expenses. They can't raise prices much, because what one company can produce other companies can produce: that drives the prices down.

Most small businesses that make money from projects have low overhead and make more money per job. But the money isn't steady. It's hard to do the jobs we have and also market ourselves to get the next contract, so every busy time is followed by a lull when work is hard to get.

There are two solutions to this problem. One—the one we discuss in most of this book—is to solve our problems and remove bottlenecks. For production-focused companies, that reduces costs. For project-focused companies, that smoothes out the work flow. But there is another solution you might try.

If you're very well organized, you can do a mix of production work and project work. That gives you the best of both worlds. You make some steady money from production work—selling products or doing routine work—and you make good money from doing projects. The times of low revenue are less frightening when you know that production work will pay the bills.

Take my company, for example. I make some money selling books. Writing a book is a project; after it's finished, the sales bring in revenue with no work at all from my company. Then I earn money as a project management trainer and consultant. Some of the training is routine, long-term contracts and some of the training and all of the consulting is short-term, highly paid work. The result of this mix of products and services is a steady income and a shot at a high net income.

The lesson: Once you get organized and take care of your problems, you can design a mix of products and services or of production work and projects that provides a steady income and high net revenue.

▼ **Focus!**

What if Everyone Did a Good Job?

How well would our companies run if everyone did a good job, delivering what was needed when it was needed? What would it be like if every job were clearly described and every worker knew how to do that job?

It would be great. We would save huge amounts of time and money and our profits would shoot up.

It also is impossible—it is a goal that we can work toward, but never attain. My experience tells me that it's worth reaching for that goal. As we get better and better, there are fewer mistakes, cost goes down, and customer satisfaction goes up. It is easier to keep customers, to stay in business, to adjust to change, and to grow.

There are two basic challenges:

- *Everything is changing so fast that we have to constantly learn new things.* It's hard to do things well the first time. But projects are unique work. It's an exciting challenge to do something we've never done before—and do it well.

- *We have to change childhood habits.* By the time we reached school age, most of us had set reactions to jobs—ways of doing chores or ways of avoiding them. Working effectively means revising these habits—becoming better listeners, learning to be focused on work and committed to excellence without excessive self-criticism, learning to enjoy a job and feel good about delivering the results. For some of us, this can mean changing habits we didn't even know we had.

The lesson: The things in this section are simple, but are sometimes hard. When we become good at this stuff, we master jobs we never thought we could do and we grow together with our businesses.

---

help people become more organized and more capable of getting the job done right. There are two key points: defining the job clearly and providing training with time for learning.

Defining the Job Clearly. Figure 4-3 illustrates what we need to define to make sure a person has everything needed to do a job. (The Key Terms sidebar defines each of the words in the diagram.)

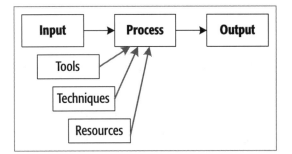

FIGURE 4-3. The parts of a job

The easiest way to understand this picture of a job is to think of something familiar, such as baking a cake.

- *The inputs* are the ingredients: flour, milk, sugar, and so forth.
- *The process* is cooking—mixing the ingredients and baking the mixture.
- *The outputs* are the cake and a cleaned-up kitchen.
- *The tools* are the mixing bowl, the mixer, the spatula, the cake pan, and the oven.
- *The resources* are the electricity for the mixer, the gas or electricity to heat the oven, the cook's time, and the time in which the kitchen is used for the cake project.
- *The technique* is the recipe.
- *The work environment* is the kitchen.

So far, the input-process-output idea is pretty

> ## ▼ BOTTOM-LINE BASICS
>
> ### Is It Done?
>
> Project management is about getting things done. In Chapter 1, I introduced the ideas of a task and a deliverable. I said that if you are doing one step and I'm doing the next step, then your output, your deliverable, is my input. If you don't do your job right, I can't start my job on time.
>
> Now, I'm going to rant about this for just a minute. Why? Because I want to save you a lot of time and frustration.
>
> Here's my rant: *project management won't work unless every team member understands tasks and deliverables.* You could spend thousands of dollars on project management training and get everyone professionally certified, but if these really simple basics aren't a habit for everyone, then you're all spinning your wheels, wasting money and time, and getting nowhere. Here are the things everyone needs to understand:
>
> - *Either it's done or it's not.* There is no such thing as "nearly done." That means nothing; it's like being "a little bit pregnant." If you're done, you have nothing
>
> else to do. You could put your deliverable on a shelf for six months and then a total stranger could pick it up and use it with no problems. When your task is done, you've delivered: you are not needed any more for that task; others can do it without you. If there is one tiny loose end, it isn't done and you say, "No, it's not done."
>
> - *All deliverables should be written down clearly, so that everyone understands them.* In a small business, there is no room for "Oh, just one more thing" or "I thought that was what you wanted."
>
> - *Plan your time, do what you say you're going to do, and get it done on time.* It takes a lot of practice to get good at this, but it pays off in credibility, respect, and the bottom line. In fact, it's worth working on every day, for the rest of our lives.
>
> Consider writing a credo like this one and making sure everyone understands it. Help all members of your team see their strengths, weaknesses, and next steps of growth in these basic skills.

simple; I think anyone can understand it easily. The next three ideas are crucial, but most people don't understand them or maybe they don't see how important they are:

- When we can fully describe each of the seven parts of a job, we have fully described the job.

> ## ▼ KEY TERMS
>
> **Input** Something that goes into a process and ends up as part of the product.
>
> **Process** Work that changes inputs into outputs.
>
> **Output** Something that is an end result or deliverable of a process.
>
> **Tools** Things that are used in a process, but not used up, so they can be reused.
>
> **Technique** A method or an instruction, a way of doing a process.
>
> **Resource** A thing that is used up in a process, but does not become part of the output.
>
> **Work environment** The surrounding situation in which a process is accomplished.

- If any one of the descriptions of any of the seven parts of a job is vague, unclear, or assumed, the job is not described well and we're likely to run into trouble.
- If each part of a job is described well, we can perform a gap analysis to see if a particular person can do a particular job. If we find a gap, we can work with the person to figure out how to close the gap.

Let's look closely at each of these three issues.

A Full Description of a Task. Table 4-2 is a template you can use to describe a task or even a small project. It is organized to make it easy to assign the job. Each of the seven parts of the job has a place— or more than one place—on the form. The questions on the form will help you and your team define the job well. You know that the person is ready to do the work when he or she says clearly that he or she understands the written answer to each question on the form.

Describing Each Job Clearly. There are three things we can do to make sure each job description is clear.

- *Write it down.* Use the template and write down a description of the job. The person assigning the job can do it, he or she can have the worker write it up and check it with him or her, or they can work on it together.
- *Make sure it is clear to the worker.* The worker should read the task description and make sure it is all clear. It helps if the worker pictures doing the work and asks, "Do I know how to do this?" and "Do I have everything I need?"
- *Organize all your work this way.* For a project, these descriptions are the small steps, or tasks, that make up project plan. For routine production work, each repeated task can be written up and called a *standard operating procedure* (SOP).

Gap Analysis—Are We Ready to Go? Once the task description is complete and clear, just one ques-

tion remains: Are we ready to do the job? Here are ways in which the job or the worker may not be ready and the ways to close the gap:

- The inputs are not available. *Close the gap:* Get the inputs.
- The inputs are not good enough. *Close the gap:* Validate the inputs.
- The worker doesn't understand and know how to use the instructions for the technique. *Close the gap:* Provide training or self-training for the worker or get a different worker.
- The worker doesn't know how to use the tools and resources. *Close the gap:* Provide training or self-training for the worker or get a different worker.
- The worker is not comfortable or safe in the work environment. *Close the gap:* Resolve safety issues, give the worker a walk-through, allow time for the worker to become comfortable.
- The worker does not understand the outputs. *Close the gap:* Clarify the definition of the outputs, if possible, with examples.
- The worker does not know where to deliver the outputs or cannot get there. *Close the gap:* Show the worker the delivery location and ensure means of transport and access for the worker.
- The worker does not want to do the job. *Close the gap:* Either work through the motivational issues or get a different worker.

In this section, I'm describing how work is done in incredibly close and simple detail. It may seem like I'm trying to teach you how to tie your shoes, but I hope not. I'm doing this because my 20 years in business have taught me that most problems in offices and on projects come up in this exact area: the very basics of defining a job and giving people the means to do their work. Looking closely, we will be able to see what is not working and make it

Task name	What do we call this job?	
Project name	If this job is part of a larger project, what is the name of the project?	
Worker	Who will do the job?	
Person assigning task	Who is asking that the job be done?	
Output	What is the deliverable?	
Output	How do we make sure the deliverable works and the customer is satisfied?	
Output	Where do we record that the work was done?	
Output	What do we need to clean up when we're done?	
Output location	Where does the deliverable go when the job is done?	
Inputs	What do I need to start this job?	
Process	How do I do this job?	
Process	Are there any interim deliverables or status report times? When are they and what do I need to have ready for each?	
Process	What do I do if I can't get the job done or need help?	
Techniques	What are my instructions for this job? Is there a step-by-step method to follow?	
Tools	What equipment, tools, computer programs, and such do I use for this job?	
Resources	What else do I need to use for this job?	
Resources	How much time will it take to do this job?	
Resources	Is there anything else that costs money going into this job?	
Work environment	Where do I do this job?	
Work environment	What is around me when I do this job?	

TABLE 4-2. Task description template

▼ **SMART THINKING!**

All the Instructions for a Job

Here's an interesting question. What are all the instructions a person needs to do a job? Let's assume that the job requires either no special training or special training that the person has already. What is required so that the person could walk in the first time, read the instructions, and do the job right?

- *A description of the starting point and the end point.* This would be the work request or project plan.
- *Any safety rules and procedures related to the environment and the tools.* Office safety procedures should be in place and equipment safety should be properly posted and included in training.
- *Information that makes the person comfortable and confident.* This is part of job orientation.
- *Step-by-step instructions.* For routine work, this is the SOP. For a project, this is the *work breakdown structure* (WBS) and the activity list.
- *General ground rules, such as when and where to get help and report status.* These can be office

guidelines or guidelines specific to the task.

- *The instructions that come with each tool.* That would include equipment operating instructions, computer program help files, and any useful manuals.
- *Special instructions on how to use the tool for this job in this work environment.* This part is often missed. Some programs—graphics programs such as Adobe PhotoShop® come to mind in particular—can do so many things in so many ways that it pays to have instructions on what part of the program to use in what ways to get particular results. Even in Microsoft Word®, it pays to have instructions in your own office for how to prepare document headers and footers, how to print letterhead, labels, and business cards, and similar tasks.

The lesson: With enough information, almost any willing worker can learn and do a good job. Before we decide the person is the problem, we should make sure he or she has everything needed to get it done right.

work, so that we can get it done right!

Provide Training with Time for Learning. Once the job is clear and the worker says that he or she has all inputs, tools, techniques, resources, and a proper work environment, then we are good to go—if the worker knows how to do the job. What if she or he doesn't?

Then we need to provide training or an opportunity for self-training, including the time necessary. And we need to realize that the quality of work is lower anytime someone does a job at which he or she hasn't become an expert.

To determine if any training or self-training is needed, we ask four questions:

- *Readiness for task.* When we check for readiness, using the list above, we ask the worker, "Can you do this? Picture yourself doing it. Is there anything you don't know how to do?"
- *Business issues.* We make sure the worker understands the business issues—the reasons for the task—and educate him or her about the business value of the job if needed.
- *Project issues.* We make sure the worker understands the project schedule and process issues.
- *Technical issues.* We make sure the worker has the technical skills for the job, including the ability to use the particular tools involved.

Managing Multiple Projects

My administrative assistant will have probably 20 or 30 small projects or special tasks to do at any given time. A few of the tasks are clear and simple, but most have a few irritating details to keep track of, a few dangerous little possibilities for things to go really wrong. Our work changes so fast that I need to be able to hand these to my assistant quickly and count on him to do them right. As a result, he needs to keep track of a lot of things all at once. This is the smallest level of multiple-project management—tracking multiple projects and tasks for self-management.

The next level is tracking multiple projects done by a small team, including where everyone is involved in some projects, but only one person or some people are involved in others.

▼ BOTTOM-LINE BASICS

A Big Project Is Made up of Small Jobs

Successful project management boils down to just three things:

- *Defining a big job clearly.* In the first four chapters, we've learned to do that.
- *Breaking up a big job into small jobs.* We'll cover that in Chapter 5, when we look at work breakdown structuring.
- *Doing each small job right.* In this section, you've learned what you need to do to teach each worker to do each job well.

At the highest level, we might have many projects, each with its own project manager and several—or even hundreds—of full-time people. And we need to keep track of all that work at a high level. That includes things like making sure work on a new project is available for people when their current project is done and making sure that experts can move from one project to another wherever they are needed. In *Project*

▼ BOOST YOUR BUSINESS!

Help Every Team Member Become a Good Self-Manager

Management is really hard when we have to tell other people what to do. Instead, I strive for a coaching style of management. I work to build each team member's skill at self-management. What does that mean? It means that, if you're on my team, you'll get better and better at understanding the job to be done, committing to do it, and getting it done right.

You can do the same for your team. Define jobs clearly. Even better, teach everyone to define his or her own job and write up a manual—a set of standard operating procedures—for his or her job. If any people do lots of different things, teach them to write and use simple project plans. Help people define and close gaps so they can succeed in their work. I've seen how a new worker who, at first, can only do a short, one-hour job alone can become independent and able to take on week-long projects and gets them done right.

The lesson: Learn to be a good coach and everyone does better together.

Management for Small Business, we'll focus on the first two levels.

Multiple-Project Management for Self-Management. The most basic tool here is a simple spreadsheet. You can create a spreadsheet in Microsoft Excel®

▼ FOCUS!

Getting It All Done Right

In a small company, our days may be full of different small tasks and pieces of projects. In a larger company, our team is doing all different things. The art of multiple-project management is keeping track of it all so that every job moves ahead and finishes well on time.

Worker:					
Updated:					
Projects					
Start Date	Due Date	Project	Deliverable	Link/Notes	Status
Small Tasks					
Start Date	Due Date	Task	Deliverable	Link/Notes	Status

TABLE 4-3. Multiple-project tracking template

or a table in Microsoft Word where you list each project on one line. Use Table 4-3 as an example.

To use the multiple-project tracking template (Table 4-3), we need two processes: adding items to the tracking list and updating the tracking list.

Adding items to your multiple-project-management tracking template:

1. The first time you use the template, enter your name at the top.

▼ BOTTOM-LINE BASICS

Get Each Job Done Right

If each team member is good at completing a simple project—as we discussed above, in the section on self-management—then multiple-project management is easy. If workers are not good at managing themselves and team leaders can't track small projects, then you're simply not ready for multiple-project management. Get the basics of good project management in place first. Then come to this section to organize your ever-changing work.

---

2. Each time you use the tracker, put the current date in the Updated field.
3. In the Projects section, use one line for each project, as follows:
   a. Enter the earliest date you can start work in the Start Date field.
   b. Enter the date the work is due in the Due Date field.
   c. Put the project name in the Project field.
   d. Put the major project deliverable in the Deliverable field.
   e. Create a simple project plan and put a link to that document in the Link/ Notes field.
   f. In the Status field, enter READY if you could start the project at any time, HOLD if the project is on hold waiting for some information, or WORKING if you are working on the project.
4. If any information is uncertain or missing, enter "??" (double question mark) next to the information you need to check or add.
5. If you are using Microsoft Excel, you can use

the Comment feature to write up additional information.

6. Enter small tasks in a similar way, but in the Small Tasks section. Generally, you will not need to write a simple project plan for a small task. This entry, possibly with some comments, should be enough.

The status of a project is the current state of the project. See the Key Terms sidebar for a list of all the possible statuses of a project and what they mean.

To update your multiple-project-management tracking template:

1. Gather information about the status of each project you are working on.
2. Tie up any loose ends. Finish anything that is nearly done.
3. Open your multiple-project tracking list.
4. Review each project, looking at the tracking list and also at the simple project plan or any other project documents. If any information is

missing or uncertain, get the information correct and then put it in and remove the double question mark (??).

5. If anything is stuck or on hold, talk with the person who assigned the task and resolve the problem.
6. If you have completed any work, update the project plan and also update the Status field on your multiple-project tracking list.
7. If any new problems have come up, try to resolve them. If you can't, put in an appropriate double question mark (??) or comment.
8. Check the status and due date on any project. Highlight in color any projects that are coming due or are overdue.
9. Review all the information for accuracy.
10. Prioritize the work on your list—and get it done right!

Some people will say that it doesn't pay to get this organized, that it simply takes too long. In my own experience, I've learned differently.

Yes, it is easy to get bogged down when we first start doing this. Yes, it can seem overwhelming. However, with a little practice, keeping this list up to date can take just a few minutes. And it saves hours. What hours? It saves the hours we spend running around looking for lost information, the time lost to anxiety when we make mistakes because we have to do things at the last minute, and the time we spend redoing work that we did poorly or forgot how we did last time. By focusing on keeping organized, we prevent fires; each fire we prevent, each crisis averted, is one mess we don't have to clean up later.

Here are some tips on making the most of your multiple-project-management tracker:

- *Put all of your projects and one-time tasks in the tracker.* Yes, I mean *all.* Even the little ones. Sometimes we do little tasks for big reasons—like buying an airline ticket to get to a

KEY TERMS

Status Current situation: what is happening right now. On a project, status includes a description of what work is done, what work is not yet done, and a description of any risks or problems.

Ready to Start Indicated by READY in our template, means that the job could start at any time.

On Hold Indicated by HOLD in our template, means that the task or job cannot start yet, usually because some information or input is missing.

Working means that the job is in process, being worked on right now, but is not yet due.

Due means that the project is being worked on right now and it is due before the next status meeting.

Overdue means that the project is still being worked on, but it is late, past its due date.

client meeting. Don't let yourself lose track of anything.

- *Use the tracker to diagnose and fix problems.* If you don't know where your time is going, keep track of estimated and actual work time in your tracker. If you lose track of people's names and phone numbers, put the info in the tracker with the task for that person.
- *Use your tracker to plan your work daily.* Going through the tracker and deciding which items are urgent and which ones are important is a great way to start your day or to finish it.
- *Set aside time to clear out the small jobs.* If you see over a dozen jobs piling up, you know it's time to take half a day and get the small stuff off your desk.
- *Sort your tasks.* You can sort your tasks by start date or due date. You can make your own priority field and put the tasks in the order you want to work on. You can also sort tasks by client name, if you add that field. Microsoft Word has a Table Sort feature and Microsoft Excel has a Data Sort feature.

When you can keep track of all of your own projects and tasks, teach your team to do the same thing. If each person works separately, then each can have his or her own list and you can have weekly or daily status meetings to help everyone keep everything on track. If you are working together on projects, you'll need to collaborate using multiple-project management for small teams.

Multiple-Project Management for Small Teams. In tracking multiple-project management for small teams, there are several issues. Some are covered here, some have been covered already, and some are covered a bit further on in this chapter.

- *Effective checking of inputs and outputs adds quality.* As each person completes a task, it will be passed on to someone on the team.

During planning and at various project gates, we should make sure that your output (deliverable) will work as my input so that there are no delays when starting a new step.

- *Work together at gate reviews* to ensure success.
- *Regular status meetings and notifications about project changes* are essential to success.
- *Maintaining shared project files and avoiding document duplication* keeps work going smoothly.
- *Each person should work to become a proactive self-manager,* as described earlier in this chapter.
- *The project manager should practice giving clear work assignments,* as described in the next section.
- *Software for multiple-project management may help.* Simple project-management software packages don't do well for multiple projects. It may be worth investigating and investing in special software tools for teams completing multiple projects together.

Projects run smoothly when everyone does every step well, so the next step can start easily. If your deliverable is my input and you don't finish up in a way that gives me exactly what I need, where and when I need it, then my work will be delayed as I look for it or call you and tell you to fix it. If that happens, I am running around just trying to get my work done, instead of focusing on doing it well. And I may run late or do a poor job for the next person. Many projects deliver poor quality, run late, or even fail exactly because the details of each deliverable are not defined well or not done well. There are two things we can do to prevent this:

- *Plan deliverables as a team, focusing on the inputs.* We get together as a team. You say to me, "My output is your input. That makes you my customer. Describe exactly what you want, what you could get that would make you say, 'Wow! This is exactly what I needed. Now, I can do my job with no problems.' Then, after you describe it to me, make sure I understand it and we've gotten it written down right." If everyone does this for everyone else on the team, it creates a great plan and a great team spirit. This type of team planning ensures that you don't think you know what I want when you don't.

- *Let your team members check your deliverables with you.* As soon as you finish a job, bring the results to any team member who will work with it next. Say, "Here it is. I think I got it right. Could you check it and make sure?"

In Chapter 2, we introduced stages and gates. You may remember that there are always at least three stages on any project, no matter how small— plan, do, and follow through. Set up a gate at the beginning of the project and one at the end of each stage. Here's what the team can do at each gate:

- *Before planning, kick off the project.* Bring all your team members together and make sure you all know the why, what, who, how, when, where, and whether of the project. Discuss goals, work assignments, schedules, quality, and risk.
- *At the end of planning, review the plan together.* This is your team's big chance to prevent problems and save lots of time in the doing stage. Every mistake you miss now will take ten times as long when you run into it while you're doing the work. If you haven't already checked each person's outputs as the next person's inputs, do it now.
- *At the end of doing, go over the details.* This is the last chance for you and your team to find problems and fix them before the customer finds them.
- *At the end of follow-through, celebrate and review.* You're done! That's worth celebrating. And whether you got it done right easily

▼ **SMART THINKING!**

A Review at Every Gate

If the members of your team are practical, success-oriented people who want to do good work and don't get into blame sessions, you can accelerate their learning and get good at doing good work fast. Instead of reviewing each project only when it is over, include a short review at each gate. At the end of planning, ask, "Did anyone learn anything new about planning that we should do next time? Are there any templates to change? Any mistakes to avoid?" Whatever people come up with, update your ways of working and your templates.

And be sure to send me your ideas.

or you barely squeaked through, your project is worth a review. What did you learn that will help you do a better job next time?

In addition to gate reviews, we also need to run status meetings weekly. Even when we follow our original project plan, we need to check status, make sure we're on track, and solve any problems as soon as they appear. If there are changes to the project plan, such as change requests from the customer or a change on the team that requires rescheduling, make sure everyone knows about them.

Last, we need to make sure all team members have the same information all the time. There should be one location for all computer documents related to the project and one file drawer for all paper documents. For paper documents, people need to put things back when they're done, so others can use them. A simple check-in, checkout system—such as a checklist of file folders or documents in the front of the file, where people initial and date the list when they take out an item or put it back—is a big timesaver. Having the checkout system reminds people to put things back. And, if someone forgets, then anyone else can look at the list and know who has the item.

We need a similar system for computer files. If only one person is allowed to change a given file, then things are easy. That person makes changes and everyone else can view, copy, or print the file but not change it. On the other hand, if we want two or more people to be able to change the same file, we have to handle two problems. The first is that it won't work if two people change the same document at the same time—both sets of changes won't end up in the file. Second, we may need to keep track of who made which changes to the file and also who has seen and approved the file at various gates along the way. Fortunately, there are tools for file sharing and collaboration that take care of these problems. If you plan on intensive teamwork, then be sure to get the tools you need.

If your team can manage one project well using the tools we've described, then moving up to multiple-project management is pretty easy. Here are the extra steps:

- At your weekly status meeting, review every project.
- As department head, track the start and end of each project, line up new projects, and make sure everyone has enough work to do.
- Create a "job jar," a list of jobs that any team members can do any time when they're between projects.
- Create a "learning jar," a list of things people can study and learn between projects.
- Delegate small projects to individuals and medium-sized projects to team leaders as soon as they're ready.

Assigning Work

When we're running a project, even a small one, we need to be able to assign work to other people. There's an art to that.

One time, I was teaching project management to a class of computer technical professionals. One of them said to me, "I don't understand how to manage people. I tell two computers to do the same thing and they both do exactly the same thing. But, just recently, I became a project leader. I told two people to do the same thing and they went and did completely different things."

I replied, "Welcome to the human race. People are like that; we're inherently unpredictable."

And that is the challenge of management. Our language—unlike computer languages—means different things to different people. Our memories—unlike computer memories—are not perfect. There is a real plus in each person's unique perspective and talents. But when it comes to assigning work, it can be difficult to make sure each person understands the job to be done.

All of the tools and templates we've introduced so far will help. The tools are even better if you teach people to write them and use them, not just to read them and follow the instructions. In addition, it helps to do these things when delegating work:

- *Let people know you want them to be proactive and self-managed.* You want them to own the work, to take responsibility for making sure it gets done right.
- *Let people know that you want them to stretch—a bit at a time.* Don't hand someone a job twice as big as he or she has ever done before and expect the person to succeed. But do ask everyone to do a good job, learn from mistakes, and get better and better as time goes on.
- *Support people in making mistakes—and learning from them.* You can't expect people to grow without making mistakes. And you can't expect people to make mistakes if they get yelled at, criticized, or warned they could lose their jobs when they do. Yes, mistakes cost a lot, but they are a part of doing busi-

ness. It is our job to make sure that people can't make big mistakes. If we put someone in a position where he or she can make a big mistake, then we've given the wrong job to that person or put the wrong person on the job. We want people to be able to stretch, take risks, and fail sometimes, as long as they learn from those mistakes, do better, and make different mistakes next time.

■ *Make everything clear in writing.* That's the only fair way to check to see if the person did the job right.

■ *Give people training when they need it.* Give people a chance to tell you they don't know how to do something, even if you think they should already know it. Then give them a way to learn it—spend a little time with them, let them do some self-guided study, send them to a training class, or just give them some time to figure it out. One great way to help people learn things is to have them write instructions for themselves. The instructions make the job clear and also give you a training tool for others.

■ *Make sure they tell you that they understand the job.* When giving someone work, have him or her read the job description template (Table 4-2). Or, perhaps even better, tell the person what you want, have him or her write it, and then rewrite it with him or her to fill in the details. Then have the person go over the questions in the template and make sure he or she understands the job in every way. Sure, it takes longer to get the job started. But it takes a lot less time to get it done.

■ *If you give a person several jobs, make sure that the priority and due dates are clear.*

■ *If jobs, priorities, or due dates change, make sure that the worker understands and that the latest instructions are written down.*

If we take these steps, we can delegate more and more work. Team members can become self-managed on larger and larger jobs. Then the whole team becomes more flexible. We solve more problems and everything runs better.

Running a Program Full of Projects

Once you've mastered multiple-project management, you can review the idea of program management and you'll be able to pull a program together. The big challenge in program management is that we're pulling together *many different types of projects,* each of which requires different expertise. We probably don't even know how to do many of the things we want to make sure our team will get done right.

For example, let's say that you're preparing the company for its first big presentation and booth at a trade show. When you come up with your initial plan, you might have a list of projects like this one:

■ Design a booth with displays and banners, and have it built.

■ Develop a computer presentation of your products for the web.

■ Develop a live product demonstration presentation and be able to give it several times a day.

■ Participate on a professional panel, including writing a presentation and improving your public speaking skills.

■ Complete several new products and release them in time for the trade show.

■ Arrange for a reception hosted by your company.

■ Invite customers and potential customers.

A list like this one includes projects that require every skill from computer programming to catering. Some of these projects are essential for success and every one of them adds value—that is, every one increases your chance of getting new business as a result of the trade show. You'll need to be able to work with many people, understand how they think and what they need, and keep it all on track to get it done right.

Team Training in Project Management

We're better off if everyone is self-managed, if everyone thinks in terms of clear tasks and deliverables, of getting it done right. I think that every project team member should have basic project management training. If anyone can lay out a job or a task, keep track of it, and deliver, we get two big advantages:

- Team members manage their own work and deliver clear status reports on time. This frees up the project manager to focus on the customer, on project changes, and on looking ahead at risk to prevent problems and at quality to make the product, service, or results better.
- Team members can step up. If you need to be out of town for a while, one of them can run the project. If a new small project or subproject needs to be done, you can trust them to plan, do, and follow through.

Team training can be beneficial even if members of the team have had project management training before. There are a lot of project management systems out there and they're not all the same. The words change: an *output* in one is a *deliverable* in another; a *risk plan* in this one is a *contingency plan* in that one. Also, many people know project management, but few people know all the parts of it and how to make it all work together. So, if we train everyone in the same method and make the training thorough, the training will pay for itself in the next few projects.

With a focus on self-management and with good training, everyone can run a project—or more than one. Outside of NASA, project management isn't rocket science. It's mostly common

sense. I've found that people can learn to become organized and that they enjoy the feeling of a job well done. That's enough motivation for anyone to learn to succeed.

Tools for Project Management Teams. So far, we've talked about tools and templates that you can use in Microsoft Word or Microsoft Excel. And it is more important to understand project management and have a good plan than it is to use project-management software. But let's talk a little about the software that's out there.

Microsoft Project® is a popular and inexpensive program that will track your projects. Although it is called project-management software, it would probably be more accurate to call it project-tracking software. Microsoft Project won't help you much with defining or planning a project. Once you've got a plan and a detailed schedule—the work breakdown structure that you'll learn about in Chapter 5—it is good for tracking work against that schedule.

Given that Microsoft Project is inexpensive and training is readily available, we need a pretty good reason to use any other program. But, in fact, there are several good reasons. As of this writing, in 2005, these are some limitations with Microsoft Project:

- It doesn't work well for multiple projects. You can set up more than one project, but they become very hard to coordinate once work starts.
- It doesn't easily link into a timesheet program.
- It doesn't work easily for multiple simultaneous users.

What would the ideal small company project management software look like?

- It would be web-based, so everyone could see it at the same time.
- It would have secure access, allowing differ-

ent users the rights to see and change different things.

- It would integrate with at least some system of timesheet data entry.
- It would easily manage multiple projects and show people's schedules across those projects.

Of course, any recommendation regarding software that is in a book is likely to be out of date by the time you read it. But, as of this writing, I've found two companies that offer products worth evaluating for multiple-project management. One is at www.webintellisys.com. It offers a single-user multi-project desktop program and a multi-user web-based program, both at reasonable prices. The other is www.primavera.com, a company that offers top quality, high-end project-management software customized for different industries such as construction and information technology.

Consider using project management software, but your first investment should be in learning and team training. It isn't the fancy tools that make you succeed; it's the ability to plan together, work together, keep track of things, and *get it done right!*

CONCLUSION

We've covered a lot of territory in this chapter. On the big side, we've learned about managing programs and portfolios, strategic planning, and organizing our company to combine projects and production work smoothly with matrix management. We've worked our way down into the crucial details, learning how to describe a small job and how to help every team member be able to manage his or her own work.

In these first four chapters, we've given you the reasons why project management is worth learning and using in a small or medium-sized business. We've also set the context or framework for organizing work into projects, selecting and scheduling projects, and enabling your team members to succeed at doing projects together.

In Chapter 5, Scope: What Are We Making?, we're going to turn to the details of preparing a project plan. You already have all the basic ideas. In the next chapter, you'll learn how to plan larger projects and make sure that your plan is complete and as good as it can be.

The Bigger Picture of Project Management

In Part II, you'll learn all you need to know to get it done right project after project. In project management, planning is the first key to success. So, Part II offers three chapters on planning, followed by two on doing the work and two on following through to success.

Chapter 5, Scope: What Are We Making? focuses on project scope. It includes eliciting user requirements, defining product architecture, and creating the work breakdown structure (WBS). When you finish the processes in Chapter 5:

- *You will have a clear, complete, and detailed picture of the product, service, or solution you are making.* Defining your project is the most important planning step: it goes a long way toward preventing failure.

- *You will have moved from defining what you are doing to defining how you will do it.* Good architecture and a detailed description of our project set us up to describe how we will do the work.

- *You will have all the inputs needed to estimate time and cost.*

In Chapter 6, Time and Money: Estimates, Due Dates, and Budgets, you will learn the art of estimation and how to resolve a gap between the required schedule and budget and the resources needed to complete the project. When you finish Chapter 6, you will know how to build a schedule and budget that will describe what you and your team are going to do each week—or even each day—of the project.

At this point, you have a plan for your project—in a perfect world. This plan is what will happen if no one makes any mistakes, if nothing unexpected interferes, and if everyone understands one another all the time.

Life isn't like that. So, we need to do a bit more planning—planning to bring errors and unexpected events under management and to manage people, communications, contracts, and coordination of the project. All this is covered in Chapter 7, Ensuring Success by Completing the Plan. There you will learn how to plan for quality, risk, human resources, communications, procurement, and project integration.

At last, we are done planning and ready to get to work! Chapter 8, Managing Project Work, provides a clear understanding of project execution, monitoring, and control. After the theory is clear, we get practical in Chapter 9, Keeping the Project on Track. In that chapter, you will learn how to run weekly—or daily—status meetings and lead your team in solving problems so that the work moves smoothly to completion.

Chapter 10, Delivering Customer Delight, focuses on the crucial and difficult final stages of a project and teaches you how to make sure that the customer is happy with you and the results of your project. We wrap up Part II with Chapter 11, Focus on Success, in which we talk about how to take all that you've learned and apply it to small and large projects.

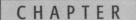
Scope: What Are We Making?

IN THIS CHAPTER

In Chapter 3, we introduced the four questions we needed to answer to define a project and know if it was worth doing. When we answer eight more questions, we have a complete project plan. Here are the 12 questions that we answer when we make a complete project plan, along with the project management terms and areas of knowledge that help us answer those questions. The interrogatives and the project management areas of knowledge are in italics.

- *Why* are we doing this project? Focus on value, benefit, and purpose.
- *What* are we making? Define the *scope* of the project.
- *How* will we make it? This is also included in *project scope management.*
- *When* will we do it? *Project time management.*
- *How much time* will it take? *How much* money will it cost? *Project time management* and *project cost management.*
- *What* makes it good? *Project quality management.*

- *How can we make sure* it gets done? *Project risk management.*
- *Who* will do it? *Project human resources management.*
- *How will we keep in touch and stay on the same page? Project communications management.*
- *What do we need? How will we get it? Project procurement management.*
- *How do we keep it all together? What do we do if things change in the middle? Project integration management.*
- *Whether* we should do the project, or cancel it? Since we've already done our initial simple project plan and decided to start, we answered "yes" to this question at the first gate. However, remember, more gates lie ahead, one at the end of each stage. And, at any gate, we can say, "No, we should stop, we should cancel this project." Of course, we hope that won't happen and we're doing all we can to make the project a "go" and keep it going.

Even so, the possibility of cancellation should always be real. That keeps us on our toes.

Planning our project is so important that we've dedicated three chapters to it. In this chapter, we'll develop the core plan: *what* we're making and *how* we're making it with scope planning. In Chapter 6, we'll cover time and money: *how long* it will take and *when* it will get done with time planning and *how much* it will cost with cost estimation and budgeting. In Chapter 7, we'll complete the project plan by asking the remaining questions and covering the remaining project management areas.

In this chapter, you will learn how to ask and answer all of these questions. You'll complete a project plan that will leave you ready to *get it done right!*

A S I STARTED WRITING THIS BOOK, I GOT A LETter from a former employee. He worked with me when he was a senior in college. He learned project management and became very good at self-management and at doing excellent work on projects up to a week long. When he got his degree in finance, he moved on to a career in banking. A few months later, he sent a letter asking, "What do I do if my boss tells me that planning takes too long and I should just go ahead and do the job?"

Unfortunately, this question is all too common. Few people—I almost want to say, few bosses—understand the value of good planning. But I would say that good planning and honest communication about the situation, problems, and solutions is the key to project success. Even with all the good work that the Project Management Institute, researchers, and project management professionals have done over the past 30 years, project success rates are not much above 50 percent. In small business, we need to do better than that. And we can.

The first step is to define projects clearly and choose projects that are worth doing. We've done that in Chapters 1 through 4. The second step is to plan our projects well. Let's go for it!

▼ Focus!

Making a Plan That Works

Good planning, as we've stated, can reduce project costs by a factor of ten. Good planning can reduce future maintenance costs by a factor of 100 or more. Good planning pays for itself. So, what's the key to good planning? How do we do it?

We look at the plan from every possible perspective. We plan to make it right, we plan to make it good, we plan to keep costs down and get it done on time. We plan for the unexpected, we plan for communications, we plan our team. We look at every resource and issue and problem the project faces and we plan for them, bringing all issues and resources under management.

That makes a robust plan, a plan that can keep going through a world where, no matter how well we plan, people will misunderstand each other, unexpected things will happen, and people will simply make mistakes. Life is like that.

Is there such a thing as too much planning? Yes, but it's a long way before we get there. In the next three chapters, you'll learn all you need to plan a project. And it starts with planning what we're doing.

The lesson: Good planning gets us ready to make the project work. And a good plan starts with the scope.

SCOPE: EXACTLY WHAT AM I DOING?

When we know what we're making, we take it apart. We disassemble it technically and figure out exactly what each part looks like. This disassembly to define product and project components is *work breakdown structuring*. This then allows us to define the *project scope*, which the PMI defines as "the work that must be performed to deliver a product, service or result with the specified features and functions."

Our initial idea, when we say, "Let's do this! Let's solve this problem" or "Let's do this! Let's realize this opportunity," is the beginning of project scope planning. To complete project scope planning, we need to do three things:

- *Use progressive elaboration* to specify the scope, to define more and more precisely what we are making.
- *Use inclusions and exclusions* to define what we are making clearly, distinguishing it from what we are not making.
- *Connect* what we are making (the result) to what we are doing (the work processes) using *work breakdown structuring*.

Since we've already seen that a recipe is a good model for a small project plan with inputs,

▼ Focus!

Scope: First the Big Picture, Then the Parts

In scope definition, we first want the big picture of what we are making: What is it? What will it do? We clarify this with the customers and stakeholders—we get them to tell us what they want through requirements elicitation—and write it up using inclusions and exclusions. When we finish scope definition, we have a statement of *product scope,* which the PMI defines as "the features and functions that characterize a product, service or result" of a project.

▼ Key Terms

Robust Able to survive through change.

Cancellation The ending of a project after it starts, but before it succeeds.

Scope "The sum of the products services and results to be delivered as a project" (formal PMI definition).

Customer The primary recipient and user of the product, service, or work result created by our project, the central stakeholder.

Stakeholder Anyone affected by the project process or results.

Requirements elicitation A dialogue with our customers and stakeholders that leads to a high-quality scope statement.

Inclusion Something to be included in project results, a statement of a planned work result.

Exclusion Something *not* to be included in project results, something that is not a goal of the project.

Work breakdown structuring The planning process that defines the components of what we will produce (work results) and outlines what we will do (work processes).

Work result Work product.

Work product The results of our work, what we're producing in any project, subproject, or task.

Work process The activity we do in our work, the actions we take that result in a work product.

Progressive elaboration Incremental development and refinement of the initial project concept to specify the scope and to define more and more precisely what we are making.

processes, and outputs, our sample project for this chapter will be a party with some good food and entertainment. Since I'm moving in a few months, I'll make it a housewarming party. (I'd invite you, but if this book sells well, all of the readers won't fit into my new place.) Let's start by illustrating each of the three points above as they apply to planning a party.

- *Progressive elaboration.* When we started, the idea was just "Hey, honey, when we get to New Orleans, let's throw a housewarming party." That sets the event—a party—and the location—our new apartment in New Orleans. Progressive elaboration will define the party more exactly—the date, the people who will be invited, the food and entertainment, and anything else we come up with.

- *Inclusions and exclusions.* The clearest way to define anything is to say what we will do and what we won't do. For example, I've already excluded the idea of inviting every reader of this book—as much fun as that would be. I'll be sure to include my wife's colleagues at her new job. Since Kris and I both like to cook, we'll include lots of food and exclude the idea of using a caterer—we'll make the food ourselves.

- *Work breakdown structuring.* The *work breakdown structure* (WBS) is the backbone of our project. It describes everything we will do (work processes) and everything we will make (work results). For example, *home-cooked food* is a work result and the only way to get there is *Kris and I do the cooking.*

In this section, we will learn the following methods:

- *Scope specification,* the process of defining our work results and work processes.
- *Architectural perspective,* seeing the customer and technical views of the project as we develop the scope. Using the architectural perspective includes:

> ▼ **KEY TERM**
>
> **Work breakdown structure (WBS)** A hierarchical, graphical picture of a project that defines the scope and breaks down the work to be executed by the project team to achieve the project objectives and produce the required deliverables; a description of everything we will do (work processes) and everything we will produce (work results).

- *Involving everyone* in project planning, as teamwork in planning gives better results.
- *Working with words and pictures* effectively.
- *Developing multiple views of the product and project* to make sure we've planned scope completely and done a good job.

Scope Specification—Defining What Makes It Good

Technically, the question of scope is "What are we making?" and the question of quality is "What makes it good?" But I have found that an excellent way to get better results at lower cost—to be effective and efficient—is to combine those two questions. When we ask our customers, "What will make this good for you?" then they get interested and tell us more.

Who should answer those questions? Ultimately, everyone involved, every stakeholder. But we begin with the customer. The customer is the central stakeholder, the person or group of people who will use the product, service, or result of the project and who will get the most value out of it. For consumers—individual customers—that value is personal. For business customers, that value is realized when they use project results, work in a new way, and realize value for the business. Usually, that means making more money or

> ### ▼ BOTTOM-LINE BASICS
> ## What We Do and What We Get
>
> There is a universal law that connects what we do to the results we get. As a proverb, it is phrased, "As you sow, so shall you reap." If you want watermelon, spit your watermelon seeds into the garden. If you don't want a mess, don't spit your tobacco on the floor. This very simple connection between what we do and what we get is at the heart of project management—and it often gets lost in the a lot of technical confusion.
>
> We can use scope management to keep in mind this crucial connection between product—*what* we will get from our work—and process—*how* we will work. As we define our product in detail, we are also specifying in equal detail the process that will give us that result.
>
> We should also note that the way we work affects the result. If we work with careful attention, we do quality work, as opposed to sloppy, rushed, or inattentive work. And a high-quality work process leads to high-quality work results.
>
> *The lesson:* First we define *product* scope (features and functions of the result). Then we define *process* scope (the work to be done). Our work process creates our work result, and we want it to be a good piece of work.

spending less money as a result of the project.

Requirements Elicitation: Finding out What the Customer Wants. So, we begin our project scope definition process by going to the customer and saying, "This is what we're doing. Let me explain the basics of what you're getting and then you can tell me what will make it really good, what will give you the best value."

> ### ▼ BOTTOM-LINE BASICS
> ## The Customers Can't Always Tell You What They Want
>
> Life—or at least our projects—would be easy if customers came to us and said, "Here's what I want: it should do this, it should look like that, it would be great if it could also work this way." Very few customers can come to us and lay out what they want like that. As a result, we need to learn how to extract desires and requirements from the customer. The formal name for that is *requirements elicitation*. Here are some of the reasons we need to work to elicit and define customer requirements.
>
> - *Some customers simply don't know what they want until they see it* and don't know what will work for them until they try it out and use it.
> - *Some customers aren't available.* If we are developing a product or service for sale, we don't even know who our customers will be. We need to either let a marketing department be a substitute for our customers or develop some kind of a customer focus group.
> - *Some customers know what they want, but can't define it unless we guide them* through the process of describing the product or service, its functionality, and its value step by step.
>
> *The lesson:* To define project requirements, we're going to have to find the customers and guide them through the process of telling us what will be good for them. In Chapter 14 we'll take a closer look at ways to find and keep customers.

▼ SMART THINKING!

The Project Doesn't Always Begin with the Customer

Although requirements definition always begins with the customer, our projects don't. Sometimes, someone knows something is good for the customer and the customer doesn't know it yet. Maybe we are technical experts who think we've figured out how to build a better mousetrap. Or maybe we know a vendor who has a good idea and our project is to make the connection between that vendor and a customer.

But we need to be careful. Failed business ventures are full of cases where someone thought an idea was good for the customer, but the customer didn't think so. So, if the idea comes from someone other than the customer, then we need to be sure the customer understands, likes, and—above all—sees the value in what we're doing.

The lesson: Good ideas can come from anyone, but a good project has to serve the customer.

▼ KEY TERMS

Scope statement A statement of what we are and are not making during this project, a statement of all work results, clarified by a listing of exclusions.

Scope specification A refined, precise scope statement detailed out through progressive elaboration.

So, let's say we're ready to begin defining customer requirements. We've got the customer, some sample customers, or a surrogate for the customer (such as the marketing group or the producer and the network of a TV series). How do we find out what they want? How do we find out what makes it good and write a product or service specification?

The first question we should ask is "Are we delivering just one product to one customer group, or are we delivering a production system that will make many products that will eventually go to many customers?" Here are some examples of projects that go to just one customer group:

- *We make something on contract for a customer.* For example, we build or renovate a building, we run an event, or we design and deliver a custom piece of equipment or software.
- *We make something to be used by a person or group inside our own company.* For example, we buy and install a computer system, we renovate our offices, or we set up a photography studio.

The other possibility is that our project is creating a system that will bring a product or service—or maybe a whole line of products and services—to market. In that case, our company will eventually have many customers. *But we don't know who those customers are right now.*

In the first case, we know who the customer is and we elicit requirements directly from the customer or customer group. In the second case, we have to work with a surrogate, a substitute for the customer. We can do our best in selecting the surrogate, then hope that the surrogate represents our eventual customers accurately.

Let's say we've arranged all of this. Now, we want to meet with the customer group or surrogate group. (To keep it simple, I'll just say "customers" from now on.) How do we find out what they want in the product or service? First we show it to them or tell them about it. Here are four ways to do that:

- *We show them a mock-up.* We discussed prototypes in Chapter 3. This early in the project, we won't have a working prototype, but we might be able to make a mock-up. If we do, we can let them play with it, watch them, and get their ideas.

- *We show them pictures, diagrams, or plans.* Then we watch their response and ask them what they think.
- *We give them options.* We show them different possibilities and ask what they think.
- *We share the idea in an open-ended way.* This can encourage the customers to define the product more fully.

In general, the items earlier on the above list are better. If possible, we should show the customers a prototype of the product or at least a picture of it. Why? Because then we get to watch how they respond to and interact with the product, rather than just having them interact with us.

When we introduce them to the idea of the product or service, we begin a process of getting information about what they want, a process of *requirements elicitation.* There are several ways to do this:

- *We show the customers the problem and offer to let them design the solution.* If the customers are willing to define the solution with us, rather than respond to our ideas about the solution, then the results can be excellent. This could be an exciting brainstorming session, bringing together the customers' understanding of the business problem and the technical expert's knowledge of possible solutions.
- *We construct a formal survey or questionnaire.* This is a very good idea. If we have a structured set of questions ready, we will get a lot more useful, detailed information from the session.
- *We record the session or have two note-takers* so that we don't lose any information.
- *We use a structured interview technique.* Some fields have special methods, often using

trained experts, to bring the customers and technical sides together to define a product. For example, architecture and engineering use rendering, a technique that creates two images—a visual picture for the customers and an engineering diagram for the technical team. A change to either picture changes the other picture at the same time. Software development uses joint application development (JAD) and rapid application development (RAD) to bring customers and development teams together.

The result of this first meeting is a bunch of notes. We put those together into a revised prototype or picture and a revised product description. Now, we have what *we think* the customers want. But we have to find out if we're right.

▼ Bottom-Line Basics

Never Start Work on a Project Until the Customer Approves Product Design

It would be a big mistake to meet with the customer once, then write up the plan and get to work. Always show your customer the plan. You might have misunderstood something. The customer might have left something out. A careful review of the plan with the customer is essential to project success.

So, what would requirements elicitation look like for our housewarming party? Well, the guests—and we as host and hostess—are the customers. Yes, we are customers of our own project, in this case. Why? Because we want to enjoy the party! Often, in small businesses, we are our own customers on a project. In defining the customer group, we have three options:

- We can say that we are the primary customers. We want to enjoy the party and we hope others will, too, but we'll focus most on what we want.

- We can say our guests are the primary customers, but that we will be surrogates for them. That is, we think we know what a good party for them would be and we decide to make the decisions ourselves, instead of asking them. This option might work for a party, *but it almost always fails for a business project. It is a very bad idea to make what you think customers want without asking them.*

- We can decide that our guests are our primary customers and we need to find out what they think makes for a great party, instead of deciding for them. We'll use this approach, because it's the best way to illustrate requirements elicitation methods.

So, using a housewarming party, here are the four types of samples to show our customers.

- *We show them a mock-up.* We could make some sample dishes and get tapes of the musicians we're thinking of hiring. We invite a few friends over for a small party and ask them what they think of the menu and music for a housewarming. Those friends are surrogates for all the people we will invite to the event.

- *We show them pictures, diagrams, or plans.* We make up a menu and show photos from our last housewarming, along with a floor plan and a schedule. We show these to some of our guests and ask how we can make it better.

- *We give them options.* We ask if we should have a sit-down meal or go buffet style. We ask if we should run all day and have people drop in or if we should bring everyone together for just a couple of hours.

- *We share the idea in an open-ended way.* We call friends and say, "We're having a housewarming party. If you come, what would you hope to see?"

As you can see, these different approaches give the customers more or less input into the design of the event. In general, the more time and money we have, the more input we can allow the customers. If time or money is very restricted, then we will need to limit the options to what is doable and have the customers choose within those limitations.

So, how would we proceed with different requirements elicitation methods for our party?

- *We show the customers the problem and offer to let them design the solution.* This would be more suitable if we were a caterer designing a party for a customer. In that case, we would talk to the customer, hear how he or she wants the party to be, and let him or her know what we can do within the space, the time, and the budget.

- *We construct a formal survey or questionnaire.* We prepare a menu and some schedule options and send them out to all the people on our invitation list, asking them to return the survey or call us to tell us what they would like. That seems a bit odd for a party, but, if you ever sit down with an event planner, that is exactly what they do for weddings, symposium meetings, and so forth.

- *We record the session or have two note-takers* so that we don't lose any information.

- *We use a structured interview technique.* OK, now we're getting really silly. But I suppose we could hire a professional event planner to go interview our guests and come back with a report of what we should do for our housewarming party. And, as I mentioned above, professional event and party planners have structured checklists and some do relatively structured interviews.

After our meeting or survey, we put together a plan for our party. The biggest elements are probably the date, the schedule, the menu, and the

▼ SMART THINKING!

Plan How Many Times to Meet with the Customers

On a small, simple project, in a field where you are expert, one planning meeting with the customers, followed by review and approval of the plan, can be enough. On the other hand, on complicated projects, we may meet with the customers several times, reviewing, improving, and adding detail to the ideas. In some cases, we may work with the customers all the way through the project, developing the plans with them as we go. Usually, though, it is better to have one or a few planning sessions, then lock down the plans in detail before beginning work. That costs a lot less and takes a lot less time than dealing with a constant flow of new ideas from the customers.

▼ THINK FOR YOURSELF!

Plan a Requirements Elicitation for Your Project

It's time to pick up pen and paper and plan your project again. To plan a requirements elicitation for your project, answer these questions:

- *Who are the customers?* If there is more than one group of customers and they have different needs, answer each of the rest of the questions for each customer group.
- *Can you meet the customers?* If not, who are the surrogates?
- *Can you prepare a prototype mock-up?* If not, can you prepare some kind of picture or diagram the customer can respond to?
- *What questions do you want answered?* Prepare a survey questionnaire you can walk through with the customers.
- *How do you want to capture the information and organize it?*
- *How many times will you need to meet with each customer group* so that they have a full picture of what you are doing and so that you have a full picture and detailed description of what they want?

entertainment. We write up those things and show the preliminary plan to our friends and see what they think. One of them reminds us that our party date conflicts with a big public event, so we change the date. A few others, on seeing the final menu, remind us to make some adjustments for other friends with special diets. When we're done, our customers have approved our plan.

Stakeholder Planning Meetings: Including Everyone. A project affects the customers, the team, and a lot of other people. Table 5-1 lists all the terms for the different roles of people on a project.

For our party, let's say that my Dad has offered a housewarming gift: he'll pay for the costs of the party. That makes him the sponsor. My wife and I are the executive managers, as well as the project team. I'll be the project manager and, within the team, we can say that she's the technical lead for the food preparation, that is, the chef. Our guests—and we as host and hostess—are the customers. Vendors include the stores where we buy

food and other supplies and the musicians we hire. Peripheral users are the friends who miss the party, but stop by to gobble up the leftovers, and the folks who look at the party photos on our web page. Other stakeholders include our neighbors, who might not like the music. If the party gets too wild, the police might be stakeholders as well, when they stop by to break things up.

So, how does a project manager work with the sponsor? I'll need to let my Dad know how much money I need and either fit the project within his budget or supplement the budget myself. I'll need

Stakeholder	Role	How Project Manager (PM) Works with Stakeholders
Sponsor	Kicks off the project and provides the money	PM provides regular status reports and reports special problems. Also makes requests for additional funds if needed.
Executive managers	Run the company that is doing the project	PM provides regular status reports and reports special problems. Also goes to them if there are irresolvable problems getting people to work on the project or if there is a conflict between the project and company operations or policy.
Customers	Receive primary benefit from project results	PM elicits requirements during planning. PM manages their expectations and documents changes to the specifications at their request. PM makes sure that they are satisfied with project results at each gate and works with them to define necessary changes to the project or product.
Project manager		PM is responsible for running the project with the team on a daily basis.
Project team members	Work full time or the most time on the project, planning and doing the actual work to create the result	PM leads team members to work together to achieve project goals with high quality on time and under budget. PM meets with them daily or weekly to update project status and address any possible problems or changes to the plan.
Vendors	Provide products or services to the project team	PM defines project needs, negotiates purchase agreements or contracts or has the team do this, and approves the activities.
Peripheral stakeholders	Have some occasional contact with part of the product	PM identifies these people and makes sure that the project plan includes their requirements. PM ensures that they test and approve any components they will use.
Other stakeholders	Anyone else connected to the project	PM identifies additional stakeholders and communicates with them as needed for project success.

TABLE 5-1. Who's who on a project

to let him know of any major changes to the plan, such as a change of date or a need to cancel the party. Of course, Kris and I, as executive managers, would need to know about that, too.

We've already discussed how to plan with the customers. And, obviously, we deliver the party to the customers at the end of the project. On some projects, we keep customers informed all the way through. So, we could have a party page on our web site, where we let customers know when we've booked the band, where we post our menu and

recipes, and where customers can make special requests and suggestions.

Most of the work with the vendors consists of simple shopping, either locally or ordering over the internet. But the musicians are an exception. We'll need to hear the bands play, to meet the musicians or their agents, choose our favorite, negotiate an agreement or contract, and have a backup plan in case our favorite band can't make it at the last minute.

▼ **SMART THINKING!**

Every Stakeholder Matters

When we're delivering a system to customers, every stakeholder matters. The fundamental rules of systems tell us that if one part of the system is broken, the whole thing might not work. So, there could be someone with a small but crucial role. If the product doesn't work for him or her, it doesn't work at all.

For example, let's say we build custom equipment that uses a lot of electrical power. The building maintenance manager at our customer's factory is a peripheral stakeholder. If we don't coordinate with him and meet his spec-ifications, then the electrical power to run our equipment won't connect with it and the whole machine won't work.

Power, environmental issues, standards and regulations, security issues, and logistics (such as making sure what we deliver will fit through the door) are all crucial to project success. Too often, we leave these details to the very end, creating a messy delivery and higher costs, and courting project disaster.

The lesson: Work out the details with every stakeholder for project success.

We'll want to let our neighbors—the peripheral stakeholders—know about the party. In fact, let's invite them. That way, they won't complain about the noise.

Design Specification: Writing up the Results. The complete, clear document that describes what we are making is called a *design specification.* According to the Institute of Electrical and Electronics Engineers, a good specification has these ten qualities. It is:

- *Complete.* The whole scope is there.
- *Consistent.* It doesn't contradict itself.
- *Correct.* It contains no errors and accurately represents user requirements.
- *Feasible.* It can be accomplished within the time, cost, and constraints of the project.
- *Modifiable.* It can be revised without getting scrambled.
- *Necessary.* All the information is needed for the project.
- *Prioritized.* Items are identified as required or, if not required, given an order of priority,

so that if scope has to be reduced, we know which items to cut first.

- *Testable.* The items are defined well enough that the project team and/or the user can look at each of them and say if the product meets the requirement.
- *Traceable.* Each detail of each requirement can be traced to the customer who requested it, to each module and feature necessary for its implementation, to its place(s) in the work breakdown structure, the activity list, project plans, tests, and other records of project activity.
- *Unambiguous.* Each element of the specification has only one reasonable interpretation.

Although the IEEE recommended these specifically for software design specifications (in document 803.1993), I find that it helps to review any specification and every project planning document with these qualities in mind. For links to more support for preparing a good specification, see the CD that comes with this book.

Simple Architecture for Your Project

I mentioned architecture in Chapter 3. Now I'll show you easy ways to apply it in projects for small businesses. To do good architecture, follow these steps:

1. Identify all groups and get everyone involved.
2. Give each group a picture of the project that they will understand and a written description of the project that captures the details important to them.
3. As one group's picture changes, change the pictures for the other groups at the same time.
4. As you write up the plan, make sure that the detailed descriptions for the different groups match up with one another.
5. Confirm the final picture and the final detailed descriptions with each group.
6. Double-check everything before the gate review.

▼ **Focus!**

Architecture for Small Projects

There is a simple way to do good architecture for your project. On a project, there are always at least three groups with different perspectives—the customers, the project manager, and the technical people. Sometimes, there are more groups. The project manager simply has to meet with each of these groups, give them all a picture and a description of the project, and then coordinate the ideas and changes from each group across all the other groups and into the project work plan, budget, and schedule.

Why Architecture Has to Come First. Architecture has to come first, before detailed planning. We can begin architectural work during requirements elicitation and we need to finish it shortly after we know the customer requirements. Why? Because architecture determines the pieces of the project—

the components. After that, work breakdown structuring will name those components.

Here are some examples that illustrate why architecture must come before detailed planning on all types of projects:

- *Architecture* would determine if we're going to renovate a building or tear it down and build a whole new building. We need to decide that before creating our *construction plan,* the *work breakdown structure* that shows the steps of work. The steps for a renovation are totally different from the steps for new construction.
- *Architecture* would determine if we're going to buy a computer program or hire programmers to do a custom job. The *work breakdown structure* would be totally different for purchase, installation, and configuration of software vs. custom coding of software.
- *Architecture* would determine if we're going to run a formal opening for our new store ourselves or hire specialists to do it. In the first case, we would need to define the work breakdown structure ourselves. In the second case, the vendor would do it for us.

Note that, in each of these cases, the architectural choice gives us an approach to the project that leads to significant differences:

- A completely different work plan
- Use of different vendors
- A very different result at a very different cost on a very different schedule

This is what makes good architectural decisions important and why we need to complete architectural planning early. Good architectural decisions lay the foundation for all the work that follows. On a good foundation, effective work can be done that will lead to success. Choose the wrong foundation and you'll get worse results at higher cost or things will fall apart altogether. Even worse—and this happens all too often—if the project manager ignores architectural issues and moves ahead with detailed planning, then the whole project is on very shaky ground. It's like making a movie with no script and no central theme. A lot of film gets shot, but nothing comes together. If we ignore the issue of architecture, the results can be disastrous. Conflicts and project failure are nearly certain and the team and the project may not recover.

Identify the Groups and Involve Everyone. So, our first job is to define all the stakeholder groups on our project. This may sound odd, but even a one-person project has three groups. Let's say that I'm arranging a personal vacation, just for myself. I'm the customer, the project manager, and the technical person. My requirements for my vacation will be different from each perspective.

- *As a customer,* I want the location, environment, and events I will enjoy at the right time and within my budget. I will also have a driver, a priority that provides direction for the project—perhaps as much relaxation as I can afford.
- *As a project manager,* I will focus on process and on risk reduction. I will want to ensure effective and efficient work to meet customer goals. I will want to reduce the chances of problems interfering with relaxation on the vacation.
- *As the technical person,* I will have specific needs. For example, let's say I'm driving to a country cabin. I'll want to make sure the car is fixed up and ready to go, that supplies are all packed so I don't have to leave my retreat to get something I forgot, that I've got a good map, and that I arrive during daylight so I don't get lost.

To find the stakeholder groups for your project, ask these questions:

- Who cares most about the deliverable product?
- Who will make sure the project runs well?
- Who will provide technical expertise?
- Who is required, by job or by law, to check up on or be responsible for project process or results? For example, if our project is a home renovation, then the city inspector may be required to check the electrical work, plumbing, or other issues during or after construction.

Your answers to these questions define your stakeholder groups: the key customer or customers, the project manager, and the different people with different technical expertise. Not every stakeholder is involved in architecture. Some stakeholders have a purely technical function; they do not need to be involved in the architectural process. Only those stakeholders whose perspective is complicated and includes a lot of issues need to be included in the architectural planning. If a stakeholder has just one issue that he or she is responsible for, then we can address it in a later planning stage, after architecture is complete.

Let's make this clear by returning to the plan for our housewarming party. We have two customer groups: my wife and I (as host and hostess) and the guests. If we were planning to invite children, there would be a third group with different needs. I'll be the project manager. Our four technical groups are the cooking team headed by Kris, the menu planning and purchasing team, the music team, and the invitations team.

Some stakeholders and roles are not essential to the architectural process. My Dad is concerned about just one issue—money—and I can track that for him. The vendors at stores are just doing their routine work. And the party cleanup crew has no special needs. (That would be different if we were going to need a toxic waste cleanup team.)

So, we have two customer groups, one project

management group, and four technical groups. Good architecture means communicating well with all these perspectives, especially:

- *For customers:* Ensuring that each group understands the product and its value for them and eliciting their requirements while keeping constraints in mind.
- *For the project manager:* Ensuring that constraints and assumptions are documented and finding ways to structure the overall process and product so that the customers are satisfied, the technical requirements are met, and we are still within our schedule, our budget, and other constraints.
- *For each technical group:* Elicit their expertise to identify issues and potential problems and their solutions. Engage them so that they

think of solutions appropriate to the size, schedule, and budget of the project, key constraints, and the driver of the project.

If we do this architectural work well, translating issues across customer and technical perspectives, we are laying the groundwork for a high-quality project with excellent results.

Words and Pictures. There is a reason that architects use drawings of the house for customers and blueprints for the engineers. Each stakeholder group needs to see a picture of the product. That's the only way we can be sure that they really understand us and we really understand them. There are three reasons that pictures help:

- *A picture really is worth a thousand words.* When we see pictures, we take in a lot more information than we do with words. If you

---

▼ SMART THINKING!
Keeping Constraints and Drivers in Mind

As we plan our meetings with customer and technical groups, we should keep in mind the scope of the project and any special constraints. I've seen projects start off in the wrong direction because the project had a limited budget, but customers were told, "Tell us everything you want." If we want our customers to be reasonable on the budget, we can't elicit their dreams; we should elicit just their requirements.

In addition, if we make constraints clear, it will help customers and technical people focus on the problem and the best solution. If I ask you to plan a great vacation for yourself, you could go anywhere on the map, literally. If I say, "Plan a weekend getaway that's within a three-hour drive," then you can focus on working up a great vacation within those limitations.

Not all constraints are about time and budget. For example, if one person on the vacation is afraid of flying

and another gets carsick easily, we'll probably do something local or take a train.

The project driver comes into play near the end of architectural planning, after we've laid out a basic plan that meets our goals and works within our constraints. In the last meeting, or at the end of the meeting, we say, "When we defined the project, you named this driver. How can we get more of that?" For example, if the driver is maximum enjoyment, we ask, "How can we make the plan even more fun with this basic plan and within our budget?" But if the driver is to keep costs low, we ask, "How can we reduce cost on the plan while still having good fun on this vacation?"

The lesson: In project architecture meetings, begin by using the constraints as a focus and end by maximizing the driver.

▼ **SMART THINKING!**

One Project, Lots of Groups

How many different groups, with different perspectives, might be involved in a project? It could be as few as three, but on complex projects, it can be a lot more. Consider the list a company might have that builds commercial jet aircraft. This is just a sample list of stakeholder groups; it might be done differently in the real world.

Customer-side stakeholders:

- Airlines that will buy the jets
- Pilots
- Passengers
- Maintenance people–to be able to maintain the jets cost-effectively
- Security organizations
- Safety inspectors

Stakeholder groups concerned with project management issues:

- The company's executives
- The program manager
- The portfolio manager
- The project manager

- The strategic planners for the customers, who want to know when orders will be filled, when the jets can be put into operation, and when payment is due

The most important engineering groups:

- Aeronautics
- Engine design
- Materials design for the pressurized hull and weight factors
- Engineering and materials design for strength of joints and landing gear
- Electronics for the controls
- Ergonomics for the pilot's compartment and passenger compartment designs

Since a change in any one of these areas could have a crucial effect on the safety and affordability of the aircraft, the architectural component of a project like this one is extremely significant.

The lesson: Be sure to identify all the key stakeholder groups and include them in your architectural process.

---

want to see this for yourself, pick up any comic strip from the daily paper. Write out, in your own words, all that you see and all that is happening in those three or four little boxes that make up a comic strip. You'll probably fill a page or more.

- *Pictures put us on the same page.* The context, or frame, of a discussion determines meaning. For instance, at a bank a CD is a certificate of deposit. At a music store, it's an album. Similarly, if I ask for something soon, that adverb has very different meanings depending on whether we're planning our day or planning our week. Words are not as good as pictures for setting context.

- *Pictures and words add up to the best communications tool.* Often, neither pictures alone nor words alone will work. But the two put together catch our attention and make everything clear. That's how a one-way sign on a street works.

It takes a lot of time to make pictures, but if we can't make a mock-up, then it's great to make a picture. The time we take to provide a picture is a smart investment to avoid the time, cost, and irritation of clearing a roadblock when we're in the middle of the project.

Multiple Views of the Project and Product. Words and pictures together give a lot more than either

---

▼ **SMART THINKING!**

The "Aha!" Moment: Seeing a Picture Helps

There is an experience so hard to define that psychologists just call it the "aha!" moment. It's that instant when—aha!—we suddenly get it, when everything falls into place, when the picture becomes clear. When coordinating perspectives in architectural planning, we need to do our best to make sure that that happens for each group of customers. One of the best ways to do that is with a mock-up. If we can't do a mock-up, then pictures, analogies, and descriptions of the process—how it will work or how the customer will use it—are best.

One time, my team had gotten really stuck on a technical point about how to set up login for users from home. I drew a giant picture of the login screen the size of the wall. Then I said, "OK. To let a person log in, the network needs three things: the username, the password, and this thing called the context. Now, the user knows his name and his password. The problem is here. The user doesn't know his context. When he's dialing in from home, the network doesn't know it, either. How can we tell the network what the user's context is?"

Seeing the big picture, one of the technicians had an "aha!" moment and told us the solution. Once the problem was clear, the solution was easy to create.

The lesson: Use visual and written aids to make sure your stakeholder groups have an "aha!" moment and get what you are trying to do. Then they'll be able to help with design and reduce project costs.

---

one alone. Generally, pictures provide the frame, the context. They get us on the right page. Then words fill the page, giving us details that we need.

If we're designing the dream house for the family, they'll want to see pictures of it and also the written description that might be used if it were to be sold, with the number of rooms and room dimensions written down. And, of course, they'll want a written estimate of the costs and completion date.

Our technical group—the construction team—will want blueprints, which are pictures with details written in, plus written technical specifications. The engineers will take the blueprint one step further, adding detail to the pictures and specifications to the written material. When the plan is done, it will be a complete set of words and pictures describing what we're going to build.

On any project, we have to create a *work breakdown structure* (WBS)—a hierarchical, graphical picture of the scope of the project that breaks it down into small jobs—and a *WBS dictionary*—a written description of each job to be done. You'll learn how to create a WBS a little later in this chapter.

▼ **KEY TERM**

WBS dictionary A document that describes each component in the work breakdown structure (WBS).

Confirming Your Architecture. When we've met with each stakeholder group, one or more times, and developed a plan that everyone basically agrees on, we're nearly done with architectural design. Now, we pull everything together and check the whole architecture against itself.

What does that mean? It means that we make sure that the different views—the views that make sense to each customer group and each technical group—match one another. If the customer

▼ SMART THINKING!
Changing the Way TV Is Made: From Film to HDTV

A short documentary was made about one TV show's transition from using film movie cameras to using digital movie cameras–high-definition television, or HDTV. It described why and how *The Dead Zone* made the move before the start of its third season. The primary reason for making the change was simple: the show needed to cut costs by about $100,000 per episode. This one change could save almost that much by eliminating the cost of film. If they didn't do that, they'd have to find ways to cut each group's budget by some amount, causing a lot of hassle and possibly reducing the quality of the show. All kinds of soft value statements–HDTV is the wave of the future–could be made. But the bottom line was in hard dollars.

If it would work.

That was co-executive producer Shawn Piller's concern. He knew film. He didn't know HDTV. *The Dead Zone* is full of unusual lighting and special effects. He told the team to create a test–essentially a prototype show–demonstrating that the new cameras would work with the lighting, the sets, and the special effects. The team designed, created, and examined a comparison test of HDTV digital cameras and film cameras.

Why was that worth doing? Because a lot more than $100,000 a week was at risk. That was the potential ben-

efit. But the potential cost was that viewers wouldn't like the show–and that would be a production disaster.

The conclusion of the comparison test: HDTV was *different,* but it was not *worse.* The show could go to HDTV.

After the decision, there were still details to work out. Some of them were hassles. Cameramen weren't used to having cables trailing out behind them. Also, the new cameras were a bit difficult to use for some shooting styles typical of *The Dead Zone.* But there were plusses, as well. The director and producer could watch the filming live on a separate monitor, instead of having to wait until the dailies–the sets of film shots for the day–were processed. They could guide the cameramen in new ways and begin to plan the editing of the film and addition of special effects on the day of the shoot.

HDTV worked for *The Dead Zone.* One change in technology spared budgets. That new technology changed almost everyone's job in a small way and it changed the bottom line in a good way.

The lesson: Good architectural planning and good prototyping pay off when we're changing the way we do our work because one change in one area changes something for everyone. Those changes might be good or bad, but we don't want them to be unexpected.

---

requested higher ceilings on the first floor, then we make sure that change was made, not just in the customer's picture, but also in the blueprints and the cost estimates. If the construction engineer recommended a new type of building material, we make sure that change made its way into the cost estimates and that the customer saw a sample and approved its appearance and value.

We can think of each drawing as a different per-

spective—a picture from a different angle—on the same thing—the product we are planning to make. We have the customer perspective(s), the project management perspective, and the technical perspective(s) and we want to make sure that they are *consistent* with one another, that they match, that they are all pictures of the same thing.

Once we know that all the pictures are consistent, then we need to make sure that the words and numbers—descriptions, technical specifications, and cost figures—match the pictures. When they do, then our whole plan is consistent.

Now, we return to each stakeholder group for approval of our plan. Some groups, perhaps all, will approve with no changes. If they begin to talk about minor design points, you can say, "There are great things to work out, but if you're thinking about those details, then we can say that the architectural design is done. I'll come back for another meeting for the detailed design."

So, let's return to our housewarming party and make the architectural decisions. In this case, the idea of a *housewarming party* locks down a lot of the architecture. It will be a party at our house and it will involve inviting friends and associates. Here are two examples of other types of parties that would require much more architectural planning:

- *A wedding.* As long as the ceremony takes place, almost everything else is open to change. But it is crucial that the key participants be happy. There have been weddings at home, in churches, in reception halls, outdoors, on exotic vacations, in airborne balloons, and even in cyberspace. Some weddings have a sit-down dinner, others only a buffet. Some have hundreds of guests; others are done in secret. All these major decisions are the architecture of a wedding. Equally important are decisions of who will do what. Will we use a wedding planner? A catering service? Laying out the answers to the biggest issues of *what* we are doing and *how* we are doing it is the work of architecture.

- *A fundraiser.* If we wanted to run a fundraising event for a not-for-profit organization, we would make many decisions, including choosing location, entertainment, and publicity. Here, the constraints would be that we want to keep costs low, so that most of the money goes to the organization and not to pay for the event. We also need to make sure that the event will draw lots of people, give them lots of reasons to donate, and leave

---

▼ BOTTOM-LINE BASICS
Architecture or Design

It is crucial to know which parts of a plan are architectural and which are design. The architectural parts are the ones we need to finish first. They are larger, so that a change from one perspective matters a lot to another perspective. Smaller changes—changes or details that have little effect on other areas—are part of design; they can be worked out later in planning or, in some cases, even during the project.

Occasionally, an item that seems small in one perspective is very large in another. Knowing when that might happen requires architectural experience and expertise in the particular field. For example, because my background is in database design, I can tell when a customer request for a new report from the computer is trivial and when it is going to require a database redesign, which is very expensive. Similarly, a construction manager can tell you which house renovations are easy and which ones are complicated and expensive.

The lesson: It is important to know when architecture is over and your basic plan—your pictures and blueprints—is approved. Then everyone can get to work with further planning or with doing the project. Don't extend architecture into detailed design, but have the expertise to know when a small change makes a big difference somewhere else.

them with a good feeling about our organization and us. The architecture—the major design decisions—is likely to determine the success of the event.

Kris and I are moving into a small apartment. That defines an architectural constraint for the party: we simply won't have room for lots of people all at once. Let's take a look at how that one constraint affects several parts of our party plan:

- *We won't have a band.* We'll go with either recorded music or a single musician.
- *We'll probably run the event all afternoon and evening.* Since we don't have enough space to invite all of our friends at once, we'll invite them all to stop by for an hour or two, spread out over time. Architecturally, we're overcoming our limitation on space by expanding the time.

The other big architectural decision has to do with whether we do it ourselves or use vendors. Again, a constraint comes into play—we like to cook for our friends. So most of the food will be our own. We may buy a few prepared things and lay them out, but we're not leaving it all to a caterer. On the other hand, musical talent is not big in our family. If we decide to go for live music, we'll probably want to hire the musician.

There is one more architectural constraint; it isn't obvious, because it isn't about the event itself. It's about the project, not the process. The housewarming party will happen not too long after we move into town. So, we're going to be busy with lots of other things. We'd better plan to either keep it simple or get some help. Thinking this through, we come up with this rough outline—this architectural plan—for our party.

- We will have a housewarming party in October 2006, on a weekend afternoon and evening. We will invite friends to come for a couple of hours over the course of the day.

- We will buy the drinks and some prepared food, so we have time to make fancy dishes ourselves.
- We'll choose a theme for the food: either Tex-Mex to celebrate our arriving from Texas or Cajun/Creole to celebrate the food of our new hometown.
- We'll either have just one musician or play music from our collection.
- We'll ask friends to help with setup and cleanup.

We know the architecture is done because it feels comfortable. When we read it, we feel we have a clear picture and we can base our plans on it. Of course, in planning something bigger, that feeling is important, but we would also have to validate our plans. We might cross-check our menu and the size of our guest list against our budget, for instance.

STEP BY STEP: THE WORK BREAKDOWN STRUCTURE (WBS)

A *work breakdown structure* may sound intimidating, but it isn't. In fact, it's just a big, fancy to-do list. Once architecture is complete, we can prepare the work breakdown structure (WBS), a fully detailed work plan for our project.

The WBS: Key to Successful Planning

From the work plan, the WBS, we can develop time and cost estimates, a risk plan, a quality plan, and other documents that bring all aspects of the project under management.

What does it mean to *bring something under management?* It means that we are aware of the item or issue, we understand it, we've defined it, and we've arranged to get regular information about it. Once we've defined something—usually in a plan—and we can get information about it, then that item can be under management. To keep it under man-

▼ **SMART THINKING!**

Creativity on Projects: Plusses and Problems

As we discussed in Chapter 3, some businesses benefit from creativity more than others. The same can be said of projects. So, it is good to ask early on, "How much creativity is good for this project?"

To ask that question well, we need to talk about different types of creativity, or what some people call *creativity* and *innovation*. Creativity is about doing something new and different. Innovation is about doing something in a new or different way or applying an idea used in one situation to a different situation.

Since every project is unique, there is always some creativity involved, especially in the planning stages.

One type of creativity involves making something more new, more different. For example, instead of just buying a computer program that works for companies in our industry, we design our own computer program—a costly and risky adventure—and make it work exactly for our company.

We can understand this kind of creativity by comparing types of vacations. The most creative vacation might be to buy a one-way ticket to somewhere we've never been, take a map or tour book, and go and see what happens. A middle level of creativity might be a guided adventure, like an exotic safari. Less creative would be a cruise or a tour with hotels booked at every location. Least creative of all would be a vacation where we stay in one hotel and visit a few nearby sites.

Similarly, we can look at a project and ask, "How many different things are we doing? How many are new and different for our team?" The more things, and the more that are new and different for our team, the more creative the project. Note that I said, "new and different *for our team.*" Philosophers will tell you it's creative only

if it's never been done by anyone ever before. But that doesn't matter for business. What matters for a business is how new this is for our team, because, with anything new to our team there is a risk that it will spiral out of control and fail. The risk is the same whether someone else, somewhere else in the world, has done this job before or not.

So, whenever we are thinking of doing something new, we should ask, "Is it worth the cost? Is it worth the risk?" As we work with our customers to define requirements and architecture, we should guide them according to our planned scope, our available resources, and our willingness to risk the costs of making creative ideas work.

With innovation, on the other hand, we are not changing what we are doing. We're not adding extra features, bells, or whistles. We're working smarter. We're finding new ways—often less expensive—to solve our problems. Innovation usually comes from the technical team.

One example that is easy to see is special effects in movies and TV. Ever since the original *Star Wars* series, companies like Industrial Light & Magic have been finding faster, less expensive ways to create special effects. A plane crash on a TV series budget in 2004 looks better than a plane crash on a Hollywood blockbuster budget of 1997. The technical teams in special effects companies—now a kind of cottage industry, thanks to the constantly dropping price of computers—are always outdoing themselves to make images more realistic and more impressive while producing them faster on a lower budget.

This kind of innovation is a real plus for our projects. We can get it in one of two ways:

- Find the best people.

- Create a team of really good people dedicated to getting better and better.

Companies that have these kinds of innovative departments often end up innovating in other, profitable ways. I've seen companies create innovative solutions for their own problems and then become vendors to their own industry, selling the solution to their competi-

tors. Is that kind of innovation right for you?

The lessons:

- Guide customer creativity in the design of the solution to fit your budget and your desired level of risk.
- Support technical creativity or innovation to solve problems in new ways, faster, at lower costs.

▼ THINK FOR YOURSELF!
Plan the Architectural Meetings for Your Projects

Time to pull out your project plan again! Follow these steps to plan architectural meetings:

1. Identify stakeholder, customer, project management, and technical groups.
2. Figure out which of these groups have a complicated set of requirements, so that you need to involve them in architectural planning.
3. Decide what types of mock-ups, pictures, or drawings would be best for each group, most likely to give them an "aha!" moment.
4. Decide what types of written specifications each group needs.
5. Decide how many meetings you think you will need with each group.
6. For each meeting, lay out an agenda. What will you show them? What will you say? What do you want them to say and how will you record what they say?

If appropriate, prepare a questionnaire and be ready to record responses.

7. Hold the meetings.
8. Between meetings, revise the plans and keep revisions of the different pictures consistent as you go, as best you can.
9. If problems come up or if extra work is needed, make the time for additional meetings.
10. When all stakeholder groups seem to be close to agreeing to the plan, write up final plans for each group and make sure all pictures and plans are consistent.
11. Hold a final meeting with each group. Aim for approval of the architecture and note future design issues. If there are any architectural changes at this stage, make sure that each group confirms them.
12. Prepare a final, approved set of architectural plans.

---

agement, we track or monitor it. That is, we look at its current situation, compare that situation with the plan, and decide if we need to do anything to keep on course. We'll talk more about monitoring and control in Chapter 8, Managing Project Work.

For now, let's finish creating our plan. When the

plans are done, we've brought everything under management—which means we've done all we can early on to ensure the success of our project. That's good. Most failures happen because of missed steps or poor choices early in a project. If we've done good planning, our chances of success are high.

▼ SMART THINKING!

Approved by the Producer

Peter Jackson, the director of *The Lord of the Rings* movie trilogy, wanted to have all members of his project team understand the world they were creating and then add their own creativity to the project during the three years it took to make the movies. He also wanted a consistent look and feel to everything that was done. Every item—the storyboards that became the film sequence, the sets, each prop, and each costume—was drawn up first. Where appropriate, scale models—mock-ups—were made. Jackson reviewed every drawing and mock-up. The team created a "seal of approval" to indicate that Jackson had approved a particular drawing or prototype. That way, any of the several hundred artists and technicians could look at an item and—if it carried the "seal of approval"—go into production to create the final version that would be used in the film.

Approving hundreds of different drawings, plans, and prototypes may sound like micromanagement, but it wasn't. In fact, it had the opposite effect. Because they knew that Jackson cared enough to review each idea, to request changes to what he didn't like, team members cared about each detail as well. And knowing that Jackson had approved a drawing or prototype gave each team member the confidence to go ahead and put hours of work making the final product excellent, knowing that it would be included, perhaps with small changes, in the movie. The result was a creative team of hundreds who worked together from the overall plan down to the tiniest detail, putting it all together into three movies, each of which won multiple Academy Awards, with one—*The Return of the King*—winning 11, more than any other movie ever.

The lesson: When we, as project managers, do good architectural work, we provide a foundation for all of the detailed technical work and give confidence to our team members that they are working on solid ground, not wasting time on something that might not be used. Our architectural work lays the groundwork for creative and innovative contributions from the team, adding value to the project.

▼ BOTTOM-LINE BASICS

Make Sure Everyone Understands the WBS

A clear, complete, unambiguous WBS is essential. If everyone understands the WBS in the same way and nothing is left out, then our time and cost estimates will be good. But, if we leave out one part of what we're making, that part of the work will be left out of all of our other plans as well. And if the WBS is unclear, people are likely to make things that don't fit together. Then you'll need to do expensive rework to save the project.

Making the WBS

The best way to create a WBS is to have your team do it with a little help from you. Up until now, most planning has been about coordinating with different groups. You, as project manager, could do most of that yourself. But there are several advantages to working with your team to create the WBS, instead of doing it for them.

- People do better work when they plan work for themselves.
- The WBS requires technical expertise. Some members of your team can do it better than you can.

▼ **Focus!**

The WBS: What We're Making and How We'll Make It

We've completed several important planning steps already:

- We've chosen *which* project we will do.
- We've decided *whether or not* we're going to do it. We'll start and then check again at each gate.
- Through requirements elicitation, we've defined *what* the customer wants. In particular, we've decided *what the product of this project will do for the customer.*
- Through good architecture, we've locked down the big picture of what we're making and how we're going to do it. We've also gotten all stakeholders to agree on the plan by bringing them all onto the same page.

This work lays the foundation for detailed planning. Creating the WBS is the core step of our detailed plan-

ning. The WBS defines *what* we will make in detail and also begins to describe *how* we will make it. The WBS is the crucial link between *work results* and *work process.*

Now, we learn to make the WBS. Once we have a good WBS, we will be ready to create our detailed time and cost estimates and the other plans we will need to succeed.

A WBS is a deliverable-oriented hierarchical decomposition of the work to be executed by the project team to achieve the project objectives and create the required deliverables. It organizes and defines the total scope of the project. Each descending level represents an increasingly detailed definition of the project work. The WBS is decomposed into work packages. The deliverable orientation of the hierarchy includes both internal and external deliverables.

- Team members working together are less likely to make mistakes or leave things out than if they're working alone.
- When the team is done creating the WBS, you know everyone already understands it.

There are two basic approaches to creating a WBS:

- Create the WBS from scratch.
- Copy and improve a WBS from a prior project.

Let's start with the first situation, where you create a WBS from scratch. If you don't have the plans from a similar project, you have to make your WBS this way. Even if you do have plans, this is often a better way to get an accurate WBS. For details, see the sidebar, When Does It Make Sense to Copy a WBS?

Creating a WBS from Scratch. In doing work breakdown structuring, we're actually going to create three documents. The first is the formal work breakdown structure, a graphical representation of the project subcomponents. Then we'll describe each lowest-level component in a WBS dictionary element or work package. From these, we'll going to create a list of milestones. From the list of milestones, we'll create our project to-do list.

Let's get started. Table 5-2 shows the process of creating a graphical work breakdown structure.

Applying these steps to our housewarming party, we get the diagram in Figure 5-1. Read the sidebar, Understanding and Using the Graphical WBS, to get a better handle on the value of these diagrams.

Once the WBS is complete and correct, we can build our WBS dictionary. In this dictionary, we

▼ SMART THINKING!

When Does It Make Sense to Copy a WBS?

Some people try to organize a project by copying the WBS from a prior project. In some cases, that works. For example, if you produce a magazine every month, you can copy the plan from the last month, change the dates, the names of the features, and a few other things, and then work out the details. But that works well only if the current project is very similar to the project whose WBS you are copying.

And what if you think the two projects are similar, but they are not? Then you can get into real trouble. Your plan—the WBS for your project—will look good, but parts will be missing.

If you decide to copy a whole WBS from a prior project, you will need to check every requirement from your requirements specification against the WBS. And that is a tedious, time-consuming job.

In most cases, it is probably easier to make a WBS from scratch, by asking for each requirement, "What do we need to do to meet this user requirement?" That will give you an accurate WBS based on the requirements for this project.

Doing the whole WBS from scratch would take a lot of time. Of course, if we have no other WBS to work with, that's our only choice. And it's better to take a lot

of time in planning than to have a bad plan and take ten times longer trying to get the work done with a bad plan.

But, if we do have some old WBSs from prior projects, there is a way to use them to save time. The key is to copy *parts*.

If one component of what we are making is nearly identical to something made on an earlier project, we copy that part of the WBS from the earlier project. If a component is similar, we copy it carefully and make any changes that are needed.

In this way, we build a new WBS that works for this project and save time by using pieces of old WBS. There are two advantages of this approach:

- We reduce the risk of having a WBS that we think is right, but isn't.
- When we see a part of the project that is new and different, we can get innovative in our work plans. We know we need a new solution and we plan the best one that we can.

The lesson: It is more important to do the WBS right than to do it quickly. Take a shortcut by copying a past WBS only if you can be sure that you are not leaving anything out of your plan.

---

create a work package for each lowest-level component of the WBS. The WBS dictionary should work like this:

- Each lowest-level component is described fully and clearly. If you hand the dictionary item to a worker, he or she should be able to get it done right.
- Each user requirement is in one or more WBS dictionary elements. If we build and

deliver all the WBS dictionary elements, we should have everything the user wants. We ensure this through *requirements tracing* (the process of making sure that all customer and technical requirements are included in the WBS), which we discuss later in this chapter.

Table 5-3 is the blank template for a work package description. Not surprisingly, a work package description is quite similar to the task description

Work environment	• A project being planned in an organization that uses the *Get It Done Right!* method.
Input	• The initial simple project plan or project charter • The requirements specification, which defines the features and functions of the work product • The architectural plan, which defines the major components of the work product
Tools	• A word processing program, a software drawing tool, or a lot of sticky notes
Resources	• Time from the team members who will be doing the work (If the team members doing the work are not available, the project manager can make the WBS, working with other technical experts as needed.) • Time from the project manager
Techniques	• Structured interviewing • Reviewing diagrams and documents

Process	**Make the project WBS.**
	1. At the top of the page, draw a box naming the product, the work result of the project.
	2. List each major project component from the architectural plan
	3. Put the list of major project components on the second row of the diagram.
	4. Look at each major component and break it into subcomponents.
	    4.1 As you create subcomponents, consider the skills of the people on your team and organize the components by skill set, so one person can do each job.
	    4.2 As you create subcomponents, include the features and functions from the requirements specification in the components.
	    4.3 Keep a cross-check list that identifies which subcomponent contains which feature.
	    4.4 If a subcomponent is large, break it down further in the same way.
	    4.5 When each component is a manageable size—perhaps taking 80 hours of work for a large project—the WBS diagram is done.
	The items at the bottom of the diagram are your lowest-level components. Not all parts of the diagram have to be broken out equally far.

Output	• A graphical work breakdown structure for the project

TABLE 5-2. Process for creating a graphical work breakdown structure

we used in Chapter 4, Table 4-2. When we describe work packages—what we are making—we are getting close to describing project tasks—what we are doing.

Table 5-4 gives instructions for defining work packages using the work package template.

Let's get back to planning our party. Table 5-5 contains the WBS dictionary for our housewarming party, with several work package descriptions shown.

Though only part of it is shown, I wrote that entire table with 11 work packages in only 36 minutes. First, I decided that the three gates of a simple project—plan, do, follow through—were enough for our party. Then I put in the party as the project name and copied the template. I wrote each work package description, one at a time, following the instructions in Table 5-4. As I wrote each work package description, I focused on the deliverables:

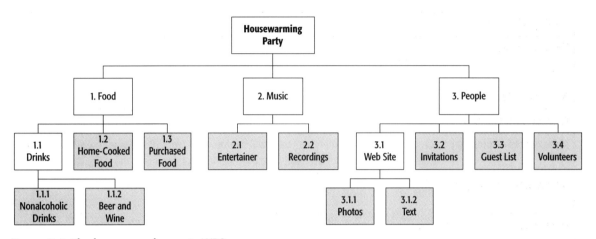

FIGURE 5-1. The housewarming party WBS

> ▼ **BOTTOM-LINE BASICS**
> ## Understanding and Using the Graphical WBS
>
> The WBS has several unusual features that make it useful:
>
> - *The WBS has no horizontal order.* Vertically, bigger items are at the top and components and subcomponents are lower. But, if we wanted to, we could redo the diagram in Figure 5-1 with People as component #1 or put Beer and Wine before Nonalcoholic Drinks, and nothing would change in the diagram except the numbers. The value of that is that it frees up our thinking. Often, the part we think of first or the part we think of as most important shouldn't be done first. By making the WBS graphical, we can play around and figure out the best order for doing the work. One way to do this is to put each box on a sticky note and move them around.
> - *No activities are listed.* In the graphical WBS, we are showing work results, that is, components of the product. So you don't see activities such as *set party date* or *choose entertainer.* Those will come
>
> when we turn our WBS into a project to-do list.
>
> - *Shaded boxes are our lowest-level components.* Each of these components will be a work package in the WBS dictionary. We can use the work packages to define the project milestones.
>
> We need to check the WBS against our architectural plan and user requirements. Do the components in the WBS match the architectural components? Can we find a place in one component or another for each user requirement?
>
> We need to check the WBS for assumptions. For example, someone checking my work and seeing item *2.2 Recordings* might ask, "Aren't you going to need a sound system?" I'd answer, "I've got a great home stereo that will do the job." But I might have said, "Oops, you're right, I didn't think of that." Then I could add an item, *2.3 Sound system.*

Work package number:
Work package name:
Project name:
Account code:
Worker or team lead:
Milestones for planning gate:
Milestones for doing gate:
Milestones for end of project:
Revision date:

TABLE 5-3. Template for a work package description in the WBS dictionary

- What do I need for this to be well planned?
- What do I need for this to be ready for the party?
- What do I need for this to do well at the party and be cleaned up afterwards?

As I answered these questions, I found new items and thought of details that hadn't occurred to me before. For example, when I wrote up 1.1.1 Nonalcoholic Drinks, I added ice and cups. Then I made sure that ice and cups showed up at each gate—on the shopping list, ready for the party, and cleaned up afterwards. I then carried these ideas forward into the wine, beer, and spritzers. The party is getting better during the planning stages. Working out these details now will save lots of hours and hassles on our party. If we didn't work them out now, we couldn't add them later without running into real trouble on our schedule. In fact, if the 1:10:100 rule holds true—as it always does— these 36 minutes saved ten hours—360 minutes— of time on the project. Think what that translates to if you are paying a team member $30 an hour. It's $15 instead of $300, a savings of $285. More

than that, with every project planned this well, people can run multiple projects and get all of their work done.

Now, we have our WBS and WBS dictionary. Table 5-6 gives instructions for validating them.

> ## ▼ SMART THINKING!
> ### Ensure Value with Requirements Tracing
> Requirements tracing is essential on all but the shortest, simplest projects. Why? Because the customer sees things one way and the technical people see things a different way. Requirements tracing makes sure that customer requirements get included in technical work packages and get done. We will also use requirements tracing to design our test plan. That way, we can be sure every requirement is defined, planned for, worked on, tested by the team, and then delivered to the customer for final testing and approval.
>
> *The lesson:* It is much better to trace requirements from the beginning than to face a dissatisfied customer saying, "But it doesn't do what I wanted it to do!"

Work environment	▪ A project being planned in an organization that uses the *Get It Done Right!* method.
Input	▪ The initial simple project plan or project charter ▪ The requirements specification, which defines the features and functions of the work product ▪ The graphical WBS
Tools	▪ A word processing program ▪ The *Get It Done Right!* work package template
Resources	▪ Time from the team members who will be doing the work (If the team members doing the work are not available, the project manager can make the WBS, working with other technical experts as needed.) ▪ Time from the project manager
Techniques	▪ Thinking, writing, and cross-checking
Process	**Make a work package description for each lowest-level component of the WBS** 1. From the project plan, identify the stages and gates of this project. Copy the Work Package Template (Table 5-3) from the *Ultimate Guide to Project Management for Small Business*. Modify the form to add gates if necessary. Fill in the project name. 2. Identify all the lowest-level components from the graphical WBS. 3. For each lowest-level component, do the following steps: 4. Copy the Work Package Template created in Step 1. 4.1. Enter the Work Package number and name from the graphical WBS. 4.2. If you are using financial account codes and have set up the accounting system for this project, enter the account code. If not, this can be done later. 4.3. If you have set up your project team, assign the work to the best team member for the job. If not, this can be done later. 4.4. For each gate, define exactly what deliverable (work result) should be ready for review at the gate for this work package. 4.5. Review the list of user requirements and make sure that every requirement related to this package is included at each gate. 4.6. Enter the current date as the revision date in the last row of the table. If you change the work package description in the future, be sure to update the date.
Output	▪ The WBS dictionary for a project, containing descriptions of all lowest level components as work packages

TABLE 5-4. Process instructions for creating the work package descriptions for the WBS dictionary

Table 5-7 is a sample requirements tracing matrix.

As we mentioned earlier in this section, you might want to create a WBS by copying and revising the WBS from a similar past project. Table 5-8 provides instructions for that.

You now have complete processes for creating a WBS from scratch or by using a past project, for completing the WBS dictionary, and for validating your scope planning. I recommend you use these tools on every project. You'll get better and faster with practice, and you'll be headed for success and satisfied customers.

Work package number: 1.1.1	
Work package name: Nonalcoholic Drinks	
Project name: Sid and Kris's Housewarming Party	
Account code:	
Worker or team lead: Sid	
Milestones for planning gate:	▪ Estimate of total quantity of drinks needed ▪ Decision on whether or not to make blended nonalcoholic iced drinks at home ▪ Shopping list for drinks, with quantities ▪ Quantity of ice planned ▪ Cups or glasses planned ▪ Estimated cost
Milestones for doing gate:	▪ Ingredients for iced drinks purchased ▪ Recipe tested, confirmed delicious ▪ Nonalcoholic drinks purchased and refrigerated ▪ Cups purchased and/or glasses cleaned ▪ Ice in cooler
Milestones for end of project:	▪ Drink-making during the party ▪ Excess nonalcoholic drinks given to helpers and guests ▪ Cups thrown away, glasses cleaned ▪ Blender and counter cleaned, iced drink ingredients put away ▪ Spills cleaned up
Revision date:	
Work package number: 1.1.2	
Work package name: Beer and Wine	
Project name: Sid and Kris's Housewarming Party	
Account code:	
Worker or team lead: Kris	
Milestones for planning gate:	▪ Estimate of amount of beer needed ▪ Estimate of amount of wine needed ▪ Shopping list with brands, quantities, sangria or spritzer ingredients, plastic wine glasses, and alternates if we can't get the brands we want ▪ Estimated cost ▪ Decision about sangria or spritzers ▪ 2 corkscrews found or purchased
Milestones for doing gate:	▪ Wine purchased ▪ White wine cooled ▪ Red wine room temperature and decanted ▪ Beer purchased and cooled ▪ Sangria prepared, if we're having it ▪ Spritzer ingredients lined up at bar, if we're having it

TABLE 5-5. Housewarming party WBS dictionary (continued on next page)

Milestones for end of project:	▪ Extra opened wine given to helpers and guests ▪ Excess beer and wine given away if we don't want it ▪ Spills cleaned up
Revision date:	

Work package number: 1.2	
Work package name: Home-Cooked Food	
Project name: Sid and Kris's Housewarming Party	
Account code:	
Worker or team lead: Sid and Kris	
Milestones for planning gate:	▪ Decision on what one main dish we each want to make, recipe obtained and tested, and shopping list prepared ▪ Decision on what hors d'oeuvres we want to make, recipes obtained and tested, and shopping list prepared ▪ Decision on quantities ▪ Plan for plates, napkins, and utensils ▪ Estimate of budget
Milestones for doing gate:	▪ All ingredients and needed plates, napkins, and utensils purchased ▪ Dishes made and being kept warm or cool ▪ Kitchen cleaned after cooking ▪ Hors d'oeuvres ready to serve
Milestones for end of project:	▪ Food eaten and enjoyed ▪ Excess food given to helpers and guests ▪ Kitchen cleaned after party ▪ Spills cleaned up
Revision date:	

Work package number: 1.3	
Work package name: Purchased Food	
Project name: Sid and Kris's Housewarming Party	
Account code:	
Worker or team lead: Kris	
Milestones for planning gate:	▪ Shopping list for all purchased food and party utensils and items ▪ Estimated budget ▪ List of stores we need to go to ▪ Consolidated shopping list, including lists from other work areas

TABLE 5-5. Housewarming party WBS dictionary (continued)

Milestones for doing gate:	▪ All items purchased ▪ Items chilled if needed ▪ Items heated if needed ▪ Utensils laid out ▪ Items ready to serve ▪ Kitchen cleaned after preparation
Milestones for end of project:	▪ Food eaten ▪ Excess food given to helpers and guests ▪ Food put away ▪ Spills cleaned up ▪ Kitchen cleaned ▪ Garbage thrown out
Revision date:	

Work package number: 2.1
Work package name: Entertainer
Project name: Sid and Kris's Housewarming Party
Account code:
Worker or team lead: Sid

Milestones for planning gate:	▪ Decision between musician or entertainer and on types ▪ List of possible entertainers ▪ Budget
Milestones for doing gate:	▪ Entertainer selected, agreement signed, time decided, or decision not to have entertainer
Milestones for end of project:	▪ Entertainment enjoyed, entertainer paid
Revision date:	

TABLE 5-5. Housewarming party WBS dictionary (continued)

PMI Scope Processes

This is the definition of Project Scope Management from *A Guide to the Project Management Body of Knowledge, 3rd Edition,* Appendix F*:

Project Scope Management includes the processes required to ensure that the project includes all the work required, and only the

work required, to complete the project successfully. Project Scope Management is primarily concerned with defining and controlling what is and is not included in the project. The Project Scope Management processes include:

▪ Scope Planning—creating a project scope management plan that documents how the project scope will be defined, verified, and controlled, and how the work breakdown structure (WBS) will be created and defined.

*Copyright and all rights reserved. All material from this publication in this chapter has been reproduced with the permission of PMI.

▼ **SMART THINKING!**

Good Planning vs. Gold-Plating and Scope Creep

Good planning is the work we do early on to meet and exceed customer requirements and to work out all the details as best we can. If we do this early, we can plan for a very high-quality project with little effort. Good planning prevents two things that can be very bad for a project:

- *Gold-plating.* Gold-plating means adding unnecessary extras late in a project. An extra that adds no value—like gold-plating on a battleship—is a pure waste of money. An extra that could have been valuable if we had agreed on it at the beginning is not worth it if we think of too late, after we're done planning. Why? Because every change after planning takes ten times longer and costs ten times more than it would have if included in the original plan.
- *Scope creep.* Scope creep is where things keep getting added to the project and the project gets bigger and bigger, kind of like the Blob In the old horror movie. If a project is poorly planned or project change is not controlled, people start to add more stuff into it. Customers do this to get more of what they want. Project team members do it either to meet their own needs or to please the customer. Executives may like it at first, especially if they can bill for the extra work. But *scope creep leads to project disaster.* As scope grows, our schedule falls apart, and we use up all of our time and money long before the project is done.

The lesson: Plan all the details of your project well so there will be few changes, and no opportunity for gold-plating or scope creep (the growth of a project beyond the planned design, requirements, objectives, and/or deliverables through changes suggested, requested, or demanded by one or more of the stakeholders).

- Scope Definition—developing a detailed project scope statement as the basis for future project decisions.
- Create WBS—subdividing the major project deliverables and project work into smaller, more manageable components.
- Scope Verification—formalizing acceptance of the completed project deliverables.

CONCLUSION

Congratulations! If you've taken your project all the way through this chapter, you've prevented most of the common causes of project failure. Most complete project failures happen either because no one has a clear sense of the team is to be doing or because some people think one thing and others think something else. If you've written down a clearly defined scope and gotten everyone to agree to it, you're past those pitfalls.

Improving our chances of success and improving the quality of our project work and work product comes with additional planning and then with good tracking of the project. Chapters 6 and 7 focus on planning. Then Chapters 8 and 9 show us how to make sure we follow those plans when we get to work. If you're ready, turn to Chapter 6, Time and Money: Estimates, Due Dates, and Budgets, to learn project time estimation and scheduling and project cost planning and budgeting.

Plan a Project Now

If you've gotten this far, it's time to switch from reading to planning. Return to the prioritized list

Work environment	▪ A project being planned in an organization that uses the *Get It Done Right!* method.
Input	▪ The initial simple project plan or project charter ▪ The requirements specification, which defines the features and functions of the work product ▪ The graphical WBS ▪ The WBS dictionary
Tools	▪ A drawing tool for revising the WBS ▪ A word processing program ▪ The *Get It Done Right!* work package template
Resources	▪ Time from the project manager
Techniques	▪ Thinking, writing, and cross-checking
Process	**First, validate the WBS internally.** 1. Make sure that, if all the work is done on all subcomponents of a component, component will then be complete. 2. Make sure that no extra work was added in any subcomponent if it is not necessary to the larger component. 3. Complete steps one and two for the entire graphical WBS from the bottom up. 4. Check that the work package in the WBS dictionary is complete and clear for each lowest-level component. 5. If a work package is too large or complicated, divide it and revise the WBS. 6. If any work results are missing, add them to a work package if appropriate or add a new work package and revise the WBS. **Second, validate the WBS to the original project plan.** 1. Review your simple project plan or project charter and all other project documents and ask, "If we do this work, is this what we will get?" 2. Revise the WBS and WBS dictionary as needed. **Third, set up a requirements tracing matrix and trace requirements.** 1. Create a table with the WBS packages listed across the top and the requirements listed down the side. 2. Whenever the work for a requirement is included in a work package, mark that box on the table with an X. 3. Where useful, add a short description of the activity, deliverable, or work quality that will fulfill the requirement in the box. 4. Make sure that, if each X on a line is done, the requirement will be met by the final product. 5. Revise the WBS and WBS dictionary as necessary.
Output	▪ WBS and WBS dictionary internally validated ▪ WBS and WBS dictionary validated to project plan ▪ WBS and WBS dictionary validated to customer requirements ▪ Requirements tracing matrix prepared

TABLE 5-6. Process instructions for validating a WBS and WBS dictionary

of projects you defined in Chapters 3 and 4. Pick up one project—small if you're new to this, medium-sized if you have some experience—and do a thorough scope plan for that project. Write it all up, because the outputs of scope planning are the inputs for time and cost estimation. When your project scope plan is ready, you'll be able to create the budget and schedule for your project in the next chapter.

These ideas and tools become real for you when you start using them. So, start planning to *get it done right!*

	1.1.1 Nonalcoholic Drinks	1.1.2 Beer and Wine	1.2 Home-Cooked Food	1.3 Purchased Food	2.1 Entertainer (optional)	2.2 Recordings	3.1.1 Phots on Web Site	3.1.2 Web Site Text	3.2 Invitations	3.3 Guest List	3.4 Volunteers
Enjoyable preparation			Easy-cooking food we like	Most food purchased							Get all the help we need
Lots of guests come							✓	✓	✓	✓	
Guests enjoy the party	✓	✓	✓	✓	✓	✓	✓	✓	✓	✓	✓
Quick cleanup afterwards	✓	✓	✓	✓		✓					✓
Party easy to get to, no hassle							Map	Date and directions posted early	Proofread, sent early	Prepared early	
Within my Dad's budget	✓	✓	✓	✓	✓				✓	Number of people	
Party theme expressed	✓	✓	✓	✓	✓	✓		✓	✓		

TABLE 5-7. Sample requirements tracing matrix for the housewarming party

Work environment	▪ A project being planned in an organization that uses the *Get It Done Right!* method
Input	▪ The initial simple project plan or project charter ▪ The requirements specification, which defines the features and functions of the work product ▪ The architectural plan, which defines the major components of the work product ▪ One or more WBSs from past projects ▪ The project plans or charters and architectural plans from those projects
Tools	▪ A word processing program, a software drawing tool, or a lot of sticky notes
Resources	▪ Time from the team members who will be doing the work (If the team members doing the work are not available, the project manager can make the WBS, working with other technical experts as needed.) ▪ Time from the project manager
Techniques	▪ Structured interviewing ▪ Reviewing diagrams and documents
Process	**Make the project WBS.** 1. Compare the architectural plans of prior projects with this project. 2. Start a new WBS. 3. At the top of the page of the new WBS, draw a box naming the product, the work result of the project. 4. Make a list of each major project component from the architectural plan. 5. Put the list of major project components on the second row of the diagram. 6. From this point forward, compare each component with a similar component from one or more past projects. 7. Find the past component that is most similar to the one in your current project. 8. Revise that component to meet the requirements of this project. 9. If there is no similar component in any past project, create a new component for this project. **Validate the project WBS.** 1. Compare the WBS with the simple project plan, project charter, and architectural plan. Adjust the WBS so that it includes everything that is needed for the current project and no other items. 2. Review the requirements specification for this project. Highlight any requirements that did not exist in past projects. Make sure all requirements for the current project are included in this WBS. Make sure that any work that was done on past projects that is not needed on this project is deleted from the WBS. 3. Review your team for this project. Make sure that the WBS is broken down appropriately for your team.
Output	▪ A graphical work breakdown structure for the project

TABLE 5-8. Process instructions for creating a graphical WBS from a prior WBS

Time and Money: Estimates, Due Dates, and Budgets

IN THIS CHAPTER

In Chapter 6, we complete the core of our project plan. In Chapter 5, we did scope planning, answering the questions "*What* are we making?" and "*How* will we make it?" Now, we can ask about time and money:

- Exactly what activities will we do?
- How long will the project take from beginning to end?
- How much work will we have to do?
- How much money will we need to spend?
- Where will the money go?
- When will we need the money?

We answer these questions by creating good estimates and budgets.

The chapter is organized into three sections:

- Understanding Allocation and Estimation—knowing the difference between the desired due date and cost, on the one hand, and the realistic delivery date and cost on the other, and learning how to make a good estimate
- Time: How Long Will It Take?—time planning, including defining activities and building the schedule
- Money: How Much Will It Cost?—cost planning, including preparing the cost estimate and budget

By the end of Chapter 6, we you will know how to complete the core of a project plan.

THERE IS A PRACTICAL REASON FOR DIVIDing the work of planning into three stages. Scope comes first because, if we don't know what we're making, we'll get lost in the rest of our planning. We have to know what we want before we ask how much it will cost and how much time it will take. Now, in Chapter 6, we will be adding our time and cost estimates—our schedule and our budget—to the plan.

That would have been a complete project plan 30 years ago. But project problems in

> ▼ **Focus!**
>
> ### Honest, Straightforward Planning
>
> Once we've finished scope planning, we have the scope statement, the WBS, and the WBS dictionary. These are the inputs for creating the rest of our core plan. This work is pretty straightforward. Finishing the plan requires three things:
>
> - *Honesty.* All too often, people have the habit of demanding things early, knowing others will delay, or claiming work will take longer than it will. Team planning requires honest attention on the real situation, not politics.
>
> - *Clear understanding.* Pay attention to the definitions and ideas in the rest of this chapter. It's not difficult, but you don't want to miss any steps. Scheduling and budgeting are kind of like driving a car: once you know what each pedal, button, and lever does, it's all pretty easy.
>
> - *Practice.* Take the time to plan well. It pays off on each project, and it gets easier one project after another.

the last three decades have taught us that more planning is needed. We can think of our scope, time, and cost plan as the core plan, or as the ideal plan. If everything goes according to plan, this is what will happen.

Let's finish the core plan now. In Chapter 7, we'll look at the additional planning we need to do make sure everything *does* go according to plan, so that we *get it done right!*

UNDERSTANDING ALLOCATION AND ESTIMATION

Once we have our WBS and WBS dictionary, we've completed scope planning and we're ready to deal with questions of time and money. Before we get into detailed time planning and budgeting, I want to identify some crucial concepts that people often miss. And when we miss these key points, it often means that the plan is no good at all.

All too often, I find that otherwise capable project managers don't prepare good estimates. I've seen several reasons for this:

- They simply don't know how. They learned the theory in class, but never got practice applying it.

- They've never really seen that estimating can work.

- They think it will take too long.

I'm here to say that estimating can work, it does not take that long, and good estimating really pays off. If you run your own small business, you want to be able to count on getting your projects done on time and within budget. If you run a company or department for someone else, you want to look good by delivering on time and within budget. Either way, it all starts with good estimation.

An estimate is a prediction of what we will be able to do. We plan our work. We think about when we can finish and how much it will cost. That's our estimate. Then we do the work and see what happens. See the sidebar, Straight Shooting and Good Estimating to see how to make a good estimate.

The estimation methods in this book have these qualities:

- *They avoid bias* by identifying the major sources of bias and taking steps to prevent it.
- *They are detailed enough to be accurate.*
- *They are easy to learn.*
- *They are written processes that you can ana-*

> ## ▼ BOTTOM-LINE BASICS
> ### Straight Shooting and Good Estimating
>
> When we aim a gun, we're making an estimate. We adjust the angle of the gun barrel until we estimate that our bullet will hit the center of the target. Then we shoot and see what happens.
>
> What could make us miss a target when we're shooting? Either we're aiming off in the wrong direction or we just aren't careful enough. Those two problems we want to avoid are *bias* and *inaccuracy*.
>
> - *Bias* in aiming a gun happens if the sights on the gun barrel were not lined up right: we aim at the target, but our shot is always off in one direction or the other. *Bias in estimating* happens when we do something that makes our estimate come out too high or too low, over and over again.
>
> - *Inaccuracy* in aiming a gun happens if we are distracted, if our hands are shaking, or if we are simply exceeding the range the gun can shoot. To be accurate, we need to check that we're working carefully in small steps to do everything right. *Inaccuracy in estimating* happens if we don't take the time to estimate each small part of the project and to put the estimate together right.
>
> *The lesson:* To estimate well, use methods that avoid bias and ensure accuracy.

lyze, improve, and repeat. After you've estimated a project, you can compare actual results with your estimate. If you followed a written method and your estimate was off, you can figure out what you missed. Then you can improve your process and use the improved process next time.

▼ KEY TERMS

Bias A type of error in estimation that causes a repeated similar difference between the estimate and the actual result, time after time.

Inaccuracy The degree to which an estimate differs from the actual result.

The first thing that leads to bad estimates is confusion about what an estimate is. In each project, we have two statements of time and cost: the allocation and the estimate. Some people have an allocation and think that it is an estimate, but the two are really very different. What's the difference?

- *An allocation comes from outside the project and is about what the customer or company wants.* The allocation comes from the customer or the executive sponsor saying, "This is how much I want to pay" and "This is when I want it done." The allocation is created when that customer or executive looks at his or her budget, the schedule, other things that take money in the business, and other things on the schedule. The allocation says, "For the project to be good for the business, it should be done in this amount of time, for this much money." It doesn't say that it is possible for the project to be done within the allocated time and budget.

- *An estimate is built by looking at what is inside the project and what the project team can do.* There are several estimation methods, but in all of them we look at the work that is inside the project and figure out how much it will cost and how long it will take.

An estimate has nothing to do with the allocation, with what the customer and the boss want to

KEY TERMS

Allocate To give a certain amount of money or a time or due date to a project. An allocation can be considered a project constraint imposed by the customer or sponsor.

Estimate To attempt to figure out what future results will be, particularly how much a project will cost or how much time it will take.

spend or when they want it done. If we want to make a good estimate, we should ignore the allocation. Why? *Because paying attention to the allocation leads to bias.* If we like the boss and want to make him or her happy, we will tend to say, "Sure, I can do this project by your deadline." If we like the customer and want the job or if we want to land the contract in competitive bidding, we say, "Sure, I can do this project on this budget." But those ideas bias the estimate. The same is true if we think our boss is asking us to do the impossible. When we think, "No one could do the project by that date," we'll tend to inflate our estimate unreasonably.

So, the first step in avoiding bias is to ignore the allocation when making the estimate. The second step is to avoid any ordinary, habitual bias. Most people are either optimists or pessimists. If we create an estimate without paying attention to that tendency, our estimate will come out unrealistically low or unrealistically high.

SMART THINKING!
Use the Allocation in Planning, but Not in Estimating

When we start planning a project, we usually have either an explicit allocation of funds or a general sense of the amount and either a specific delivery date or deadline or a general idea. And we should plan with those in mind. Allocations constrain and define the project, but do not alter the estimate.

Here's an example. A manager came to me and said, "My boss asks me to do an audit and only gives me 160 hours to do that job. But it is a much bigger job than that." We brought his question to the boss, who said, "When I allocate 160 hours to a particular audit, I'm sending a message. I'm saying that the subject of the audit is only worth 160 hours of our time, given what else we have to do. It's the audit manager's job to design *some kind of good audit* to fit within that budget." Once the manager understood this, he realized that he could adjust his planning. He could make the scope of the audit small enough to fit the allocated schedule.

So, adjusting our plan to the available time and money—the constraints caused by the allocation—makes sense. But adjusting our estimate would get us into trouble.

Here's an example of why it is dangerous to bias our estimate to match an allocation. We might convince ourselves to estimate this way. We need to land a contract to meet our annual goals. Our company can bid low on a contract and make the money to meet that goal. So, when we estimate, we go as low as we can. As a result, we win the contract, but lose money, because we have to pay hourly workers until the job is done, not just until the time worked reaches the estimate. So we pay out more than we make and lose our shirts through winning the bid.

The lesson: It is right and appropriate to consider allocations as constraints in planning. Just don't let them bias your estimates of how long your plan will take to complete or what it will cost.

▼ **SOMETHING SLIPPED!**

Scotty's Estimation Technique

There is an episode of *Star Trek: The Next Generation* in which Commander Montgomery Scott, the Chief Engineer from the original series, who has managed to survive a few hundred years, gives some advice to the young Chief Engineer of the new show, Geordi LaForge. He says that he always doubles or triples his estimate of how long a job will take when he tells the Captain. That way, in the crunch, he can come out looking like a hero!

The joke is funny, but, unfortunately, all too true. I know many engineers who try to buy more time by pro-viding misleading estimates to managers. I know even more managers who hope to push engineers and technical workers to work harder by giving them phony deadlines. None of this works. When everyone knows that no one is telling the truth, then no one is motivated to good teamwork and good planning.

The lesson: Honest allocation, expressing real business needs, and honest estimation of project effort, giving our best estimate of what it will take to do a job, are essential to teamwork, project success, and business success.

What do we do if our estimates tell us that we can't complete the project within the allocated time and budget? That's a very real problem. By separating allocation from estimation, we're able to see this problem as early and as clearly as possible. When the estimate is done, we compare it with the allocation and the problem is right in front of us. The project costs more than the customer is willing to spend or will arrive later than the acceptable due date. Now, we have to reconcile that gap. Seeing the problem as a gap, we have these four choices:

- *Reduce the scope.* Do less, so we can fit the schedule and budget.
- *Increase the allocation.* Get more time and/or money approved.
- *Work smarter.* Look for more efficient ways to do the job.

▼ **KEY TERM**

Reconciliation The process of deciding how to close the gap between an allocation and an estimate or between an early estimate and a later one.

- *Cancel the project.* Some projects just can't be done affordably. It is better to stop now than to throw away a lot of time and money on something that just won't work.

Of course, deciding to cancel a project is easier if you are running the project for yourself and you can make that decision. It's a lot harder to go to your boss and say, "I just can't make this project work." But sometimes we have to take the problem upstairs. How do we do that well? Try these steps:

- *Educate the boss in advance.* Explain that you'll be planning and estimating. Teach him or her the 1:10:100 rule. Explain that you'd rather bring bad news now, as soon as you're done planning, than not say anything, go ahead, and put time and money into a project that will later fail.
- *Agree on stages and gates.* One of the purposes of gates is that we have several chances to check and make sure the project is doable. Of course, we always hope it is. But we need to be realistic and cancel a project as soon as we discover it's bad.
- *Communicate cooperatively.* Don't just tell the boss, "I can't do this." Be prepared to explain

▼ BOTTOM-LINE BASICS

The Iron Triangle

We can understand scope, time, and cost as a triangle, with one item on each side. There's a rule about triangles–if one side gets longer, then one or both of the other two sides must get longer, too. So, if we increase our scope, the project will need more time, more money, or both (Figure 6-1).

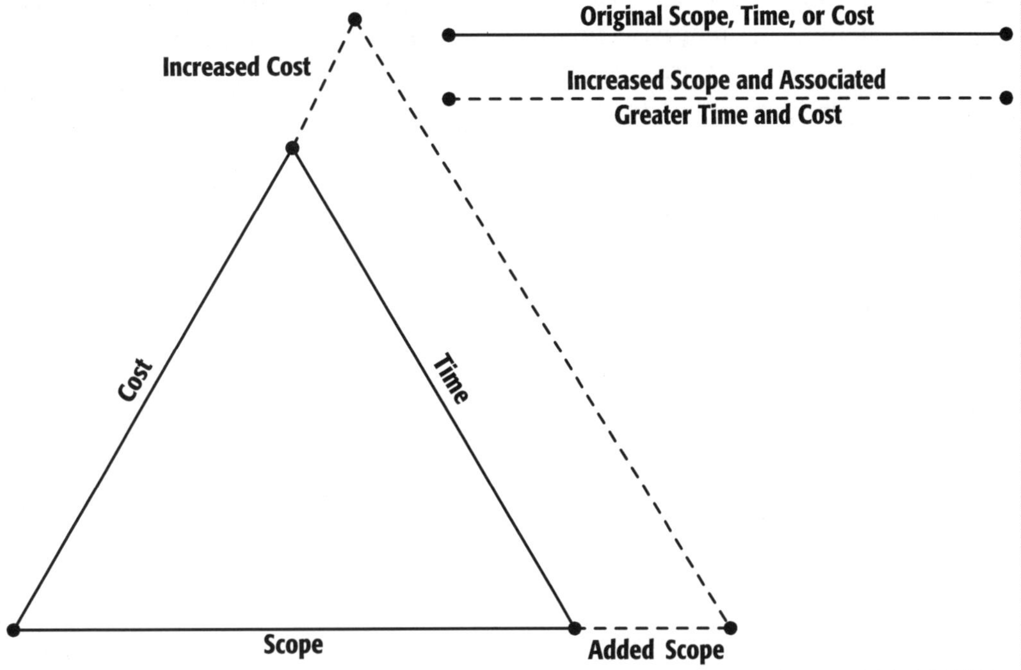

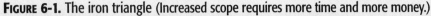

Increased Cost

Original Scope, Time, or Cost

Increased Scope and Associated Greater Time and Cost

Cost

Time

Scope

Added Scope

FIGURE 6-1. The iron triangle (Increased scope requires more time and more money.)

Teaching our boss and our team about the iron triangle is useful. When we are asked to do more with less, we can mention the iron triangle and say, "Unless we find a way to work smarter, we just can't do that."

---

the problem and propose solutions. Say things like "I can do most of what you asked for. Here's what I can do with the budget you gave me and here's what I can't do. But if you allow this much extra time and this much more money, I can do it all."

By separating estimates from allocations, we bring these problems to the forefront during planning. Then we work with our boss and the team to resolve the problems we find.

In the next two sections, you will learn how to estimate the time and money a project will take. The methods will show you how to make an honest estimate, as free as possible from bias and as accurate as possible with the information you have.

TIME: HOW LONG WILL IT TAKE?

Once we've defined our project scope, we are ready to make a really good estimate of how long the work will take. The key is in the details. If we can accurately estimate how long each task will take, we should be able to figure out how long the project will take. In this section, you will learn the core ideas of time management, which we will illustrate with our housewarming party project. A complete project plan and a schedule for the housewarming project are on the CD that comes with this book.

But what do we mean when we ask, "How long?" Suppose I can give five hours a week to a project and the work will take 15 hours. Does that mean that the work will be done in 15 hours or that the project will be delivered in three weeks? The answer is both! We have two different meanings of "how long?"—two definitions of time:

- *Effort* is the amount of work time spent, measured in person-hours or person-days. In the example I gave, I'm putting in 15 hours of effort on the project.
- *Duration* is the time from the beginning of something until the end of something. For this project, the duration is three weeks.

For a single task that we start and do until it is done, we can say that *duration = effort / number of people.* So, a single, divisible task that will take 12 hours can be done by one person in 12 hours, two people in six hours, three people in four hours, four people in three hours, and so on. Not many jobs are really like that. But if we were manually addressing and stuffing envelopes for a mailing list, that equation might work.

Planning time for a project is much more complicated, but it all starts with remembering the difference between effort and duration.

Now that we understand effort and duration, we're ready to build the schedule for the project.

▼ **Focus!**

Take Care in Time Planning

Time planning and estimation is a logical, step-by-step process. Once you understand the ideas, it is pretty easy. In fact, most bad schedules really aren't bad schedules at all. They're bad work breakdown structures. If you've defined all the work to be done, these steps will make sense and come naturally, maybe with the help of some project management software. The key, though, is to understand all the ideas and use them. Otherwise, plugging our project into project management software is kind of like a bad writer using a word processor. A story can look neat on the page and still be a lousy story. A project schedule can look neat on the calendar and milestone charts, but still be full of problems.

The lesson: Learn and apply the details of time management and avoid running late.

These are the main steps:

- *Activity definition.* We start with the WBS dictionary and break up the tasks into even smaller pieces.
- *Activity sequencing.* We put the tasks in order.
- *Activity resource estimating.* We figure out how much work and resources each task will take.
- *Activity duration estimating.* We figure out how long each task will take, beginning to end.
- *Schedule development.* We put all of this onto a real-world calendar.

This may seem like a lot, but actually, each task is quite small. For a small project, you can just sit down and do it all. Even for a large project, it is a pretty straight shot if you use project management software.

▼ SMART THINKING!

Pick the Right-Sized Team for the Job

For most tasks, there is a number of people that is most efficient. We've all seen road crews with two men digging and one more leaning on a shovel. We've probably also been in situations where we had to carry something heavy and it would have gone ten times faster if someone had helped. These are examples of inefficient planning.

Here are some examples of efficient planning of team size:

- For physical labor, such as construction, technical managers know ways to determine how many people to put on a job.
- In some cases, such as medical surgery, the number of people is determined by the expertise needed to complete the job.
- For working with data, teams of two people are often most efficient. Here are two examples of that:
  - In computer programming, a system called buddy programming, where two programmers team up at one computer, has been found to create high-quality program code quickly.

Usually, one writes while the other watches for typos and errors and thinks of new ideas. The buddies switch off, so the programmer who has the better idea of how to do a particular task writes and the other one helps.

- A very smart city auditor faced some budget cuts and layoffs and had to do as much work with only 15 people instead of 20. He decided that all audits would be done by teams of two. His logic was this: one person, working alone, can get bogged down. If there are three people, a team member can avoid a job by saying, "Someone else will do it." But if there are two people, then each person feels, "If I don't do it, my partner will have to do it," and is more responsible.

The lesson: In planning your project, put the right number of people on each task. You'll reduce project effort and cost and prevent delays.

▼ KEY TERMS

Activity definition The process of identifying the specific schedule activities that need to be performed to produce the various project deliverables.

Activity sequencing The process of identifying and documenting dependencies among schedule activities.

Dependency A relationship between two schedule activities or an activity and a milestone, indicating when each activity starts and ends, usually because output from one activity is input for the other.

Activity resource estimating The process of estimating the types and quantities of resources required to complete each schedule activity.

Activity duration estimating The process of estimating the number of work periods that will be needed to complete each schedule activity.

Schedule development The process of analyzing schedule activity sequences, schedule activity durations, resource requirements, and schedule constraints to create the project schedule.

Project schedule The planned dates for performing schedule activities and the planned dates for meeting schedule milestones.

▼ SMART THINKING!

The Right Time for Project Management Software

Up until now, project management software would not have been very useful. However, once the WBS is created, it makes sense to enter it into project management software and use the software to build the schedule. Creating schedules on a calendar is one thing that project management software does better than any other tool.

Instructions for Activity Definition

In activity definition, we finish the shift from *what* we are making—work product—to *how* we will make it—work process. The simplest and easiest way to do it is to set up a to-do list that moves from our starting point to our milestone and then help the team member who will do the work to complete the list.

An activity list starts with inputs, focuses on process, and leads to outputs—that is, to milestones or deliverables. The activity list itself does not list out the resources, tools, and techniques, as they are described elsewhere. A well-written recipe is a good example of a project to-do list or activity list.

Speaking of recipes reminds me of our housewarming party. The box on the next page shows an example of an activity list from the plan for the party.

Normally, as soon as one task ends, the task

▼ SMART THINKING!

A To-Do List Built by Two

There is a very good reason to help team members build their to-do lists. With experience, a person can make a good list by himself or herself. But, until we've practiced it for quite a while, we tend to leave things out. Working in pairs, we can help each other. One person pictures the work he or she will do, while the other person asks questions and writes down the answers. This works well because the best way by far to make a good to-do list is through visualization—actually picturing the work. But it is very hard to visualize—a nonverbal, right-brained activity—and write—a verbal, left-brained activity—at the same time. So, the person who will do the work visualizes and the other person thinks logically, asking questions and writing down the results.

Here is the best way to do this:

1. In advance, set up the to-do list with initial situation, milestones, and room for steps in between.
2. Set up some uninterrupted time.
3. Ask the person to picture doing his or her work.

4. Ask him or her to name one thing he or she will do.
5. For each step named, ask, "If you were starting today, could you do that right now?"
6. If he or she says, "Yes," very clearly, write it at the top of the list. If he or she sounds uncertain, ask what he or she would do first. If he or she says, "No," ask, "What else would you have to do first?"
7. Write down the steps he or she would do first and then the step named.
8. For any big step, ask, "How would you do that?" Then, indented under the big step, write the smaller steps he or she would do to do the big step.
9. Walk through each step from the beginning—the initial situation—to the goal—the milestone. Ask him or her if, doing all those steps, he or she would reach the goal and complete the job. Add anything else that either of you think should be done.

The lesson: Work with team members, or have them work in pairs, to make very accurate to-do lists.

Activity list for 3.2 Preparing the Guest List

- INITIAL SITUATION: We have moved to New Orleans and set up our apartment.
- Decide how many people we can invite.
  - Look at the size of our apartment and see how many people can fit.
  - Consider how long guests are likely to stay and how long the party will run.
  - Consider what percentage of invited guests will not come.
  - Decide how many people we can have at the party and how many to invite.
  - MILESTONE: Number of invitations decided.
- Decide whom to invite from out of town.
  - Look at list of family and old friends.
  - Decide who might come from out of town.
  - Add these people to invitation list.
  - MILESTONE: List of out-of-town guests ready.
- Decide whom to invite from New Orleans.
  - Review Kris's address book, make list.
  - Review Sid's address book, make list.
  - Think about roles in our lives and people we know from those roles, add to list.
  - Review all names on list, think of others.
  - Add these people to invitation list.
  - MILESTONE: List of New Orleans guests ready.
- Compile final list.
  - Count names on list.
  - If total is equal to or less than the number of invitations we've decided to send, list is done.
  - If total is greater than the number of invitations we've decided to send, choose whom to drop from the invitation list and make a final list.
  - MILESTONE: Final guest list prepared.

▼ KEY TERMS

Lag time Amount of time after one activity starts or finishes before the next activity can start or finish, sometimes negative (in which case, synonymous with *lead time*).

Lead time Amount of time required for one activity before another activity can begin.

dependent on it can start. But sometimes we need to adjust the start time with lag time or lead time.

Sometimes, we need to wait for something to happen, even though no task or activity is required. For example, bread can't be sliced as soon as it comes out of the oven. It needs to cool for half an hour or it will just squish under the knife. No work is done during that half hour—the bread just sits there and the cook can work on another task. So, we allow a half hour of lag time before slicing the bread.

Lead time is the opposite of lag time. Here, one task comes after another, but we can get a head start on the second task. Finishing our pasta sauce and our spaghetti is a good example of that. If we want to serve at 6 p.m. and spaghetti takes ten minutes to cook, then the spaghetti goes in at 5:50 p.m. Let's say that our sauce needs 25 minutes to cook. For both to finish at the same time, the sauce should start 15 minutes before the spaghetti starts. We could give them a start-to-start relationship— starting at the same time—and then adjust the sauce with a 15-minute lead time, so it starts 15 minutes earlier than 5:50 p.m., at 5:35 p.m.

We can also characterize dependencies as either *required* or *optional.*

A dependency is required if, logically, the items must go in that order. We have to cook spaghetti before we can serve it. (If you've never tried to eat raw spaghetti, trust me on this one—it won't work.)

On the other hand, sometimes we prefer to do things in a certain order, but it is not essential. I may prefer to make the cold salad before I start cooking, so I put that first. But, if I get a late start, I can make the salad later, while the bread is cooling. If a dependency is not essential, but preferable, we note that it is not required; it's optional and we can adjust the schedule if necessary.

Lastly, we should remember that not all project tasks are done by the team. Sometimes we purchase something from a vendor or engage a consultant to do some work for us. Also, we need approvals from the customer at each gate before we can move on to the next stage of the project. In each of these cases, we are relying on someone outside the team—an *external* agent—to do something for the project. We call the link between an external task and the project an *external dependency.* Since we don't have control over those outsiders, every external dependency is a risk. In Chapter 7, we'll learn how to identify and manage risks.

> ## ▼ KEY TERM
>
> **External dependency** Relationship in which the start or finish of an activity requires input from someone or something outside the project team.

Once we've defined the activities and dependencies, we can build a network diagram of our project. The easiest way to do this is by entering the activities into a project management software program and then linking the activities with the dependencies. The program will automatically draw our network diagram for us.

Figure 6-2 shows a network diagram of the *make a list of guests from New Orleans* activities from the preparations for our housewarming party. In this diagram, our initial situation and final milestone are circles, activities are boxes, and dependencies—or links—are arrows. All of the links are start-to-finish dependencies.

Estimating Resources and Duration

Before we can turn our activity list into a schedule, we need to decide three things:

- How will we do each job?
- Who will do it?
- How long will each job take?

Deciding how we will do the job and who will do it is the detailed level of implementation planning. The PMI calls it estimating resources. When we understand which resources—people and skills—we need for the job and decide how the job will be done, then we can estimate effort and duration for each task. There are several ways of doing this:

- *Bottom-up estimation.* This is the most accurate. We break the tasks into very small pieces, estimate the effort for each one, and add up the estimates.

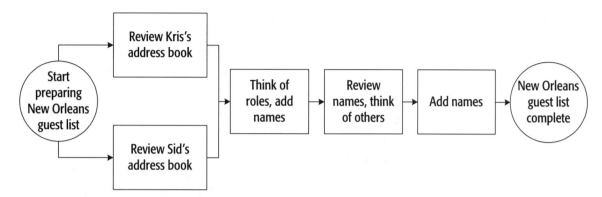

FIGURE 6-2. Sample network diagram: Make a list of guests from New Orleans

- *Parametric modeling.* This method uses a parameter—some unit of measure—and estimates how long it will take to perform the task on that unit. For instance, we may ask, "How long does it take to lay one shingle on a roof?" and then multiply by the number of shingles.
- *Analogous estimation.* This is a comparison with historic records. If we have records of similar work from past projects—especially if it was done by the same people—we can use those for our estimate. It helps to ask in what way the work on this project will be the same or different.
- *Three-point estimation.* We can make our estimates even more accurate by making a pessimistic, average, and optimistic estimate of each task. Then we take an average of the three. This prevents the bias caused by the fact that some people estimate with persistent optimism and others with persistent pessimism.

If we add our effort and duration estimates to our activity and dependency network diagram, we have the basic information for our project schedule.

> ## KEY TERMS
>
> **Bottom-up estimation** Method for estimating the activities at the lowest level of the activity list or WBS, added up to produce a total estimate.
>
> **Parametric modeling** Method for estimating that uses a measurable factor (such as size in feet or a count of the number of units to be produced) times an expected cost or effort per unit to produce the estimate.
>
> **Analogous estimation** Method for estimating based on comparison to past projects or activities. To be accurate, it requires an experienced team and research to determine that the activities of the current project are, in fact, similar to the past activities used in the comparison, or to make an adjustment for the differences.
>
> **Three-point estimation** Method for estimating that uses an analytical technique that takes three cost or duration estimates to represent the optimistic, most likely, and pessimistic scenarios. This technique is applied to improve the accuracy of the estimates of cost or duration when the underlying activity or cost component is uncertain. Three-point estimation can be combined with other estimation methods.

Schedule Development: Making Your Calendar

In addition to our activity list, dependencies, and duration estimates, we will need some other inputs as we prepare the real-world schedule for our project:

- *Calendars* showing when each person is available—and perhaps tools and spaces as well.
- *Constraints,* such as required schedules for meetings.
- *Resource constraints,* such as dates when inputs from external sources—external dependencies—can be delivered.

Putting all of these together, we can create a *baseline schedule* for our project. We know that things will probably change, but the baseline is the

---

▼ BOTTOM-LINE BASICS

Scheduling: When Your Project Hits the Real World

As we build our activity list and sequence, our project looks straightforward. But when we try to put the plan into a real-world calendar, we discover all kinds of little problems, such as the following:

- The person who is best for a job isn't available when the job needs to be done.
- We have to add holidays.
- The key project expert needs a vacation early right in the middle of the project.
- A vendor can't give us an essential component on our schedule.

As always, it is better to discover those problems in planning. Take the time to do detailed planning. Dig into the details and find these problems in advance. It costs less and is a lot easier to solve these problems during planning than if we wait until they happen and then run around trying to put out fires while our project schedule falls apart.

▼ SMART THINKING!

Contingency: How Much Leeway Do We Put into Our Plan?

So far, our project plan has assumed that everything will go well and that no problems will come up. But no one is ever that lucky. Some things will go wrong. When we look at risk planning in Chapter 7, we will ask how much we want to adjust our baseline schedule to include the extra time we will need to get our work done in spite of unexpected barriers, which we call *risk events.*

▼ THINK FOR YOURSELF!

How Do You Estimate?

Think about how you do estimates now. Compare what you do with the methods in this chapter. Would you get better estimates if you added some of the ideas, methods, and tools you see here? If so, take the time to improve! You'll find extra tools to help on the CD.

---

plan we will use when we make status and progress reports. As we do our work, we manage the project by comparing reality with the baseline plan.

PMI Time Processes

This is the definition of *project time management* from *A Guide to the Project Management Body of Knowledge,* 3rd edition, Appendix F:

Project Time Management includes the processes required to accomplish timely completion of the project. The Project Time Management processes include:

- Activity Definition—identifying the specific schedule activities that need to be performed to produce the various project deliverables

- Activity Sequencing—identifying and documenting dependencies among schedule activities
- Activity Resource Estimating—estimating the type and quantities of resources required to perform each schedule activity
- Activity Duration Estimating—estimating the number of work periods that will be needed to complete individual schedule activities
- Schedule Development—analyzing activity sequences, durations, resource requirements, and schedule constraints to create the project schedule
- Schedule Control—controlling changes to the project schedule.

MONEY: HOW MUCH WILL IT COST?

Once we have our WBS, our WBS dictionary, and our schedule, we have all we need to make our cost estimate and budget. The cost estimate is the total of what we will spend; the budget is the schedule indicating when we will spend the money. So the cost estimate is a number or, more likely, a range. It might say, "The project will cost between $80,000 and $100,000." The budget (defined here as a planned schedule for spending money) explains how we will need to spend that money over time.

For example, if we are doing a project that involves doing a lot of planning buying an expensive piece of equipment, and then configuring it and installing it, our budget might look like this:

Month	Cost Budget
1	$5,000
2	$5,000
3	$65,000
4	$15,000
Total	$90,000

In this example, months 1 and 2 are calculated from the cost of the project team doing its work. In

> ## ▼ Focus!
>
> ### Estimating Project Cost
>
> Many people think that cost is a key factor in project management. Actually, though, cost is a result, rather than a cause. We plan our work—our scope and how we will use our time—and our purchasing and the cost plan is a result of those other activities. We monitor cost during the project, but, if we're spending too much, it's not because spending is out of control. No, the excess spending is a symptom. It's our work—our activities—that are out of control. The activities are taking too long and producing too little.
>
> Still, it is valuable to set up a project budget for these reasons:
>
> - We must make sure we can do the project within the allocated budget. If we can't, we should adjust the project, adjust the budget, or cancel the project.
> - During the project, we can track progress against cost. If we see we aren't getting the bang for our buck, we can find out what is going wrong with the work and fix it as soon as possible.
>
> *The lesson:* Estimating our budget is an essential part of project planning. It gives us the *cost baseline* that will be the measuring stick for our project.

month 3, we buy the equipment for $60,000 and also keep working. In month 4, our work expenses go up. Why? Because, as our schedule shows, in addition to the project team doing its work, the customer department has to spend time learning to use the equipment and testing it. Our total budget, $90,000, is the middle of our estimated budget range of $80,000 to $100,000.

For the most part, building a budget and an estimate is a matter of looking at our plan and counting up the costs. As a result, the key to suc-

▼ BOTTOM-LINE BASICS
Do We Count Time as Money?

Many companies don't translate the time spent by their own staff—*internal time*—into money when planning projects. There are several reasons for this:

- The owners figure, "We have to pay these people anyway, so why count the time?"
- It can be hard to turn a salary into an hourly figure. It's also risky, because if employees see one another's hourly wages, they can figure out their salaries, which might either violate company rules or cause other problems.
- It just seems like extra work.

However, in most cases, it is important to count internal time as money. Here are the benefits:

- *The only way to get total cost on most projects* is to count internal time, external time, and purchasing costs as money.
- *We can calculate ROI* on a project only if we know the total cost.
- *We can make clear decisions about using vendors—outsourcing.* If we think of internal time as free, then we don't have an easy way to decide when to use our own people and when to hire help for a project.

We could actually make a project cost more, in total, by not getting the outside expertise we need.

- *We avoid bias against outsourcing.* If we don't count internal time, then two projects that actually have the same cost could look very different. One appears expensive because we use a consultant and another appears cheap because we use only internal labor.

There are some occasions where a company can count internal time without turning it into money. If all projects have very low expenses and use only internal time, then we can compare the value of projects against the hours worked without turning the hours into dollars. Some industries, such as internal audit, are already set up to work this way and it works for them. But even a company in that industry should consider counting internal time as cost if it changes the way it does business and some projects have more expenses due to purchasing or consulting.

The lesson: Take the time to calculate project cost unless all of your projects use only internal time, without significant consulting or purchasing expenses.

---

cessful budgeting is a good work breakdown structure. If we've missed items in the WBS, then our budget can't come out right.

Often, we want a cost estimate before we have a complete work breakdown structure. Why? Because planning—creating the WBS—can be over half the work for some projects. We don't want to get halfway through the project without a cost estimate. We need to know as soon as possible how much a project will cost. So, let's look at some techniques for estimating project cost before we have a complete WBS.

Early Estimation

There are two important things that everyone needs to know about early estimation:

- *Early estimates may be necessary, but they are often inaccurate.* We need to make sure that we, and our bosses, understand that any estimate prior to a complete project plan could be completely wrong. And the more new and different this project is for the team, the more likely we are to be just plain wrong.
- *Early estimates take time.* All too often, bosses say, "I need to know what this project will

cost. Tell me in two hours." That is unrealistic. To do an early estimate, we need time to review whatever project plan we have, gather some data, put on our thinking caps, and add up the numbers.

There are four basic ways to do an early estimate:

- *Create a rough plan and do a bottom-up estimate.* In other words, do a quick version of a WBS and then add up time and cost.
- *Parametric modeling.* For some projects, we can estimate cost based on a parameter, a unit of measure. If we're painting an office, it might be dollars per square foot. We count square feet, multiply by a factor that we know or get from a vendor, and add some contingency for other problems.

- *Compare estimates from vendors.* If we're going to have someone do the work for us, we can get bid estimates and compare them.
- *Analogous estimation—comparison with past projects.* We could try to say, "This project is about like the one we did last year. It should cost the same." This is the fastest technique, but it is kind of quick and dirty. If we're going to compare with past projects, we should clean up the process a bit. Here's how:
  - *Always use past actual figures, not past estimates.*
  - *Estimate piece by piece, if you can.* Instead of using just one past project, compare each part of this project with a part of a similar past project.
  - *Ask what will be different.* Even if the same team is doing the same project, there will be differences in both process and product. For the process, you can consider: Will it cost less because my team has more experience? Will it cost more because we lost one team member with expertise? Will the cost change due to salary increases or changes in price of things we need to buy? For the product, you can ask: Is what we are making simpler or more complex? Is it bigger or smaller? Each time you answer one of these questions, adjust your estimate up or down, as appropriate.

When we put together our early estimate, we should ask two more questions:

- *How accurate do we think the estimate is?* We could present it as a range, even a very large range, such as "between $5,000 and $15,000."
- *What makes the estimate uncertain?* We can list points where we lack knowledge that could improve our estimate. We can also list choices that would change the cost. And we can list risks—potential problems that could increase the cost.

So our final early cost estimate will be a range plus an executive summary explaining the reason for the range and perhaps providing some options. The sidebar, Sample Early Cost Estimate for the Housewarming Party, shows what a good early cost estimate looks like. Note that I used information from the early architectural plan from our party, not the WBS we developed later.

▼ **KEY TERMS**

Cost estimate The expected amount of money a project will take, based on analysis of the project plan.

Early estimate An estimate based on project information before the WBS is complete, validated, and approved.

Late estimate An estimate based on the WBS as well as other project documents (more accurate, as the work plan is complete).

As you can see in the sidebar, if we want to spend only $100, we can have a party for 20 people with no alcohol and no live music. If we have to buy prepared food instead of cooking ourselves, that party would cost $160. If we add people, alcohol, and live music, the party for 40 people with alcohol and a musician would cost $400, or $520 if we have to buy more prepared food.

This illustrates how project costs are based on the choices of what we buy and what we do. A cost plan like this one could actually help us make our decisions. We can lay out the options in a *decision matrix,* like the one you see in Table 6-1.

There are three types of things that will cause the actual cost to vary from our early estimates. We should identify each of these in our summary.

- *Decisions that are not yet made.* These are shown in the decision matrix.
- *Unknown or uncertain information.* I might note that I haven't researched the cost of a

▼ **SMART THINKING!**
Sample Early Cost Estimate for the Housewarming Party

The housewarming party will cost between $100 and $520.

There are several ways we can control the costs of the party. Here are the most important decisions that would change the cost:

- We are thinking of having between 20 and 40 people. We estimate food costs at $5 per person. Inviting fewer people would bring down the food costs.
- Food costs could increase to $8 per person if we do less cooking and buy more prepared foods. We could choose to do this or it could be the result of a risk event—we run out of time to cook.
- Alcohol would cost $50 for 20 people or $100 for 40. We could save $50 to $100 by not serving alcohol, either leaving it out of the party or making the party BYOB—bring your own bottle.
- A professional musician would cost $150. If we just go with our own music collection, music costs would be zero.

musician in New Orleans or that I'm not really familiar with buying alcohol. Here, we might improve the estimate with a bit more research right now, early on.

- *Risk events.* These are things—like not having time to cook—that may or may not happen, that we can't predict.

We should make our early estimate as clear as we can and make sure that everyone understands the estimated cost range and how we can keep costs under management. As you will see in the next section, once we have a work breakdown structure, we can make a much more accurate estimate.

▼ SOMETHING SLIPPED!

This Estimate Was Way Off!

A customer came to the company's information technology (IT) group and asked how much it would cost to prepare a certain new report. The customer wanted an estimate within two hours. It was December, they'd neglected to ask earlier, and they needed to finish the department budget for the new year. A project manager warned them that he couldn't do a good estimate that quickly and that he really needed more information, but the customer pressed him to go ahead. He did and his estimate of $2,000 went into the budget.

Early the next year, the department asked the IT group to create the report and a project manager was assigned. He did a thorough plan and his cost estimate was $170,000. The customer was understandably upset and asked how an initial estimate of $2,000 could change to a later estimate over 80 times higher. Here are the reasons.

- Two hours is simply not enough to do an estimate—or even figure out which questions to ask.
- Without a chance to ask questions, the project manager assumed the data was all on one computer system. It turns out that the data was scattered across six computer systems. Either the customer didn't know that or neglected to tell the estimator.

- The project manager was told to create a report, but the customer did not specify how often the report needed to be run. The project manager assumed that it could be run periodically. The customer wanted constant, real-time data. The architecture for a report from one computer system with inactive data is simple and the company already owned the report-writing tool. That led to the $2,000 estimate. The architecture for real-time data collection across six systems is very different. It required a tool that cost over $100,000 that the company would have to purchase, plus the cost of configuring the tool and setting up the report.
- Essentially, what it sounded like the customer wanted when they were in a hurry and didn't take the time to explain was completely different from what they really wanted. A lot of confusion and anger could have been avoided by timely, clear communication.

The lesson: Estimation is a valuable activity for a business. We should put time and effort into providing proper information and allowing enough time for good estimates to be done.

Detailed Estimation from the WBS

Our best estimate comes when the WBS is complete and approved by the team and the customer. At that point, two of the three reasons for uncertainty are resolved: We've made decisions about what we will do and we've done our research to get information we don't have—or we do it while we make the cost estimate. In addition, with the plan complete in front of us, we will be able to do a much better job defining and managing risk than

we could have earlier in the project.

Cost estimation from the WBS and activity list is simple, if tedious. We simply add up the cost of performing each activity in the project. Each activity has certain inputs. If we have to buy them, we include the purchase cost. Each activity will take a certain amount of effort. We multiply the effort (person-hours) times the cost (dollars per hour) and we know what the task will take. We add up the totals and we're done.

How many people?								
	20 people				40 people			
Food $5/person	$100	$100			$200	$200		
Food $8/person			$160	$160			$320	$320
Alcohol? Yes ___ No ____								
No alcohol	$0		$0		$0		$0	
Alcohol		$50		$50		$100		$100
Musician? Yes ___ No ____								
No musician	$0	$0	$0	$0	$0	$0	$0	$0
Total w/ no musician	$100	$150	$160	$210	$200	$300	$320	$420
Musician	$150	$150	$150	$150	$150	$150	$150	$150
Total w/ musician	$250	$300	$310	$360	$350	$450	$470	$570

TABLE 6-1. Sample decision matrix: Housewarming party cost options

A detailed cost estimate for our housewarming party is on the CD. Table 6-2 shows a summary version of that estimate, based on the following decisions and research:

- We expect 28 people to come.
- We will do the cooking ourselves, so food costs are $5 per person.
- We got an accurate price on wine for sangria and for beer.
- We decided not to hire a musician.

There's something wrong with this project budget—we didn't count the cost of our time! Of course, for a personal event like a housewarming party, we wouldn't charge for our time by the hour. We've worked up that example on the CD that comes with this book.

However, I should show you how to turn an estimated effort—work time planned for the project—into a cost estimate. The key question is "How much is each person's time worth?" There are several ways to calculate this figure:

- For external time—consultants or hired labor—charge the project with the price agreed to in the contract or work agreement.
- For internal staff time, choose one of these options, depending on what information you have and who will see the project budget, so that you don't release salary information if you don't want to.
  - In some medium-sized companies, the payroll department or human resources already has a cost-per-hour figure for each employee or can work one up for you. If that's available, use it.
  - Use an average figure for all employees, so that the project is planned as if all employees have the same salary; salary information remains confidential. This isn't quite

WBS#	Work Package Name	Estimated Cost	Notes
1.1.1	Nonalcoholic drinks	$28	$1/person
1.1.2	Beer and wine	$60	Based on shopping list
1.2	Home-cooked food	$56	$2/person x $28 people
1.3	Purchased food	$56	$2/person x $28 people
2.1	Entertainer	$0	Cancelled
2.2	Recordings	$32	Bought two CDs for party
3.1.1	Photos	$0	Used digital camera
3.1.2	Text	$0	No cost
3.2	Invitations	$10	Postage
3.3	Guest list	$0	No cost
3.4	Volunteers	$0	No cost
Total Party Cost		$242	

TABLE 6-2. Sample detailed cost estimate: Housewarming party for 28 people, purchasing plan

accurate, but, if you do it for all projects, it's good enough to work with.

– Calculate an hourly figure based on annual salary, plus 30 to 50 percent extra for overhead, divided by the number of hours the employee works per year. If an employee makes $40,000 and we add 50 percent for overhead costs, that's $60,000 per year. If the employee works 2,000 hours per year, that's a project cost rate of $30/hour.

We can enter this figure into a spreadsheet program or our project management software. We then calculate the estimated cost of work time per activity on our project and total all activity times for an accurate estimate of the cost of project work. If we add the planned cost of project work and the planned cost of project purchasing, we have our total estimate of project cost. If we look at this in terms of what we will spend each week or month of the project, we have the project budget.

PMI Cost Processes

This is the definition of *project cost management* from *A Guide to the Project Management Body of Knowledge*, 3rd edition, Appendix F:

Project Cost Management includes the processes involved in planning, estimating, budgeting, and controlling costs so that the project can be completed within the approved budget. The Project Cost Management processes include:

■ Cost Estimating—developing an approximation of the costs of the resources needed to complete project activities

■ Cost Budgeting—aggregating the estimated costs of individual activities or work packages to establish a cost baseline

■ Cost Control—influencing the factors that create cost variances and controlling changes to the project budget.

▼ **THINK FOR YOURSELF!**
Does Your Company Allocate and Estimate Well?

Now that you understand good ways to allocate funds and set due dates and good ways to estimate time and cost for projects, you can improve your business by asking how well you do and where you could improve. These questions will help you improve your approach to allocation:

- Do you define projects clearly and then set reasonable budgets and due dates?

- Do you give team members deadlines because those deadlines are really necessary for the project—as opposed to using them to put pressure on team members to get the job done?

- Are you open to hearing that a job can't be done within the time you requested or within your budget?

If the answer to any of these questions is "no," ask yourself, "Would my company be better off if we changed our way of making allocation decisions?" If you want to improve allocation methods, you might reread the beginning of this chapter and write up your own guidelines for yourself.

Here are questions to ask yourself about your approach to estimation:

- Do you distinguish allocation from estimation? Or do you ask, "Can you get this job done for this much money?"

- Do you allow enough time for the estimation process?

- Do you follow a structured, repeatable estimation process that you can use and improve?

- Do you distinguish between early estimates for projects and estimates done after the WBS is complete, which are far more accurate?

- Do you have a way of reconciling estimation and allocation in project planning and decisions of whether to do a project or to continue a project?

If you answered "no" to any of these questions, ask, "Would my company be better off if we adopted the methods in this chapter?" If so, you might read the methods, check out the CD for additional tools and set up a good estimation process for everyone on your team.

CONCLUSION

We have now completed planning the iron triangle for our project—scope, time, and cost. But we aren't done yet. Project success depends on planning *all* aspects of the project. We can do this by coming up with a plan for each of the nine areas of project management knowledge defined by the Project Management Institute. The six additional areas of planning are essential, because they help us make sure our project won't slip out of control. We will bring error and uncertainty under management and plan for communications and coordination of the project plan in Chapter 7, Ensuring Success by Completing the Plan.

Make Estimates for Your Project Now

If you have been developing a project plan as you read this book, you completed the scope statement, requirements specification, and WBS at the end of Chapter 5. Take those and create estimates, a schedule, and a budget for your project. Then compare your allocation and constraints—your budget and your time line—against your estimate and decide if you want to go ahead as planned, make some changes to your plans, or pick a different project.

When you have a project plan ready to do, turn to Chapter 7, Ensuring Success by Completing the Plan, and finish the plan.

Ensuring Success by Completing the Plan

IN THIS CHAPTER

In Chapter 7, we complete our project plan, focusing on bringing everything related to the project under management to ensure success. In terms of the project management knowledge areas of our plan, we covered scope in Chapter 5 and time and cost in Chapter 6. Now, we will plan for the other six areas and prevent these common project problems:

- *Project human resource management* is about getting the right team and closing any gaps between what the team can do and what the team has to do to get it done right.

- *Project procurement management* is about getting what we need—and whom we need, if we're hiring vendors or consultants to work on the project. We make sure we have what we need when we need it and we also coordinate the project plan with good business practices for contracting and purchasing.

- *Project quality management* is how we bring error under management, ensuring that we deliver to specification so that we deliver real value to the customer and meet all requirements.

- *Project risk management* helps us bring uncertainty under management. We work to expect unexpected events and be ready for even the events we don't expect, so that we can succeed through the inevitable challenges that come up.

- Using *project communications management,* we keep everybody on the same page and make sure everyone can keep working and no one drops the ball.

- We use *project integration management* to coordinate all of our plans and prepare for changes to the plan.

This is a lot of planning. But experience shows that it pays off by covering all the bases and ensuring success.

▼ Focus!

Get Ready for Trouble Before It Shows Up

Three certainties of life sure seem to be:

- Unexpected things happen.
- People make mistakes.
- Things change.

Add the facts that we often don't understand one another and we change our minds, and you'll see the reasons for the topics in this chapter. The additional planning we do here takes into account the real world and real people and gets us ready to do really good work with our teams. I don't know that any project plan can be truly bulletproof. After all, if a big meteor comes and wipes out the planet, you probably won't finish your project. (But will it matter?) So, some things will always remain outside of our control. Even so, it makes sense to bring everything we can under management, to be as ready as we can to overcome challenges and succeed.

PROJECT MANAGEMENT IS EASY IF WE ARE WILLing to learn from the mistakes of others. Ensuring success means avoiding the pitfalls and problems that are always all around us. We can do that by learning from the 30 years of business experience that have gone into creating the PMI's *Project Management Body of Knowledge.* It gives us a picture of all of the things others have learned about avoiding problems. And in this book we turn that theory into simple practice.

If you're not willing to learn from the mistakes of others, then you're setting yourself up to learn from your own mistakes—and that's expensive.

Over time, the PMI has found the nine areas of knowledge to be a practical list of all the areas we need to bring under management, all the possible problem areas for a project. So, by preparing a plan that covers all nine areas, we prepare for just about anything. And that preparation ensures success.

Here are the questions we need to answer to complete our plan:

- *Who should do the work?* We need to choose, set up, and improve our team.
- *What inputs or resources do we need to get by contract or by purchasing?* Project procurement management links our plan to contracting and purchasing.
- *How will we prevent and manage error?* Errors during the project are costly—and errors in the product can be fatal.
- *How will we deal with uncertainty?* Are we ready for the project to go worse—or better—than expected?
- *Who do we need to talk to and when?* We build a project communications plan.
- *How do we put it all together and get ready for changes during the project?* We do it with project integration management.

WHO SHOULD DO THE WORK?

One definition of a successful project is *the right people doing the right job.* If that's true—and it often is—then selecting the team for our project is the most important part of planning. If it's the most important part, why didn't we do it sooner? Simply because we can't decide who the right people are for a job until we know what the job is. Scope definition must come first. Then we can put

▼ Focus!

Putting the Team Together

The focus of project human resource management is getting the right people doing the right job. Now, we turn activities into skills and roles, select the people, make sure they're ready, and make them into a team.

▼ **SMART THINKING!**

Planning Can Be Over Half the Project

Planning and design can actually be over half the work required on a project. During planning, we're not just doing the project management work of defining the project plan; we're also doing business work and technical work. On the business level, we're defining what will add value to our business or our customers' business. On the technical level, we're designing the product, service, or result of the project.

For example, in writing computer programs, the most successful methods use 60 percent of the project time and effort in planning and design, where we figure out exactly what the customers want and we design a solution. Only 10 percent of our time is spent in writing program code and 30 percent in testing the code and fixing the problems we find before it goes to the customers.

The lesson: Planning doesn't just mean figuring out the work we will do; it's actually doing the most important part of the work.

---

our team members together and have them work out the detailed WBS. Or we can do the WBS ourselves, complete the time and cost estimates, and then involve the team.

In a small business, when planning our project team, we have two basic options:

- *Get the people ready for the job.* Often, we have to do the work ourselves or work with the people we have. In that case, we shouldn't just plunge ahead. We should perform a gap analysis with the question, "Are we ready for the job?" And then we should close the gap, as described in Chapter 4, in the section called Gap Analysis—Are We Ready to Go? We can meet with experts and get a little advice, we can get some training, or we can take time to study up to be ready for the job.
- *Get the right people for the job.* Sometimes, we're better off paying an expert. In that case, we should define the job clearly and hire the project resources we need.

If we plunge ahead with people who are not prepared for the work, we are headed for trouble. Instead, we should get the people together, plan the work, and ask them what they need to get ready to do the work. Then we provide what they need early

on in the project.

In a small business, people will rarely be working on a project full time. They'll be balancing project work with their regular responsibilities. As we review the project plan, we should think about who needs to work how much time at what point during the project. First, we bring people together early for the planning. Then some of them work on the project steadily, while others come in when the workload is high, when their particular skills are needed, or when they have some time available. It is good to be flexible. In a large organization, this requires a lot of structure and negotiation. In a small business or team, we can just assemble all of the team members every week and make sure that our project or proj-

▼ **BOTTOM-LINE BASICS**

Safety First

Sometimes, working on a project means working with new tools or in a different location. This means we should take a moment to pay attention to safety. Team members should be given safety guidelines, taught how to use and take care of equipment properly, and know any safety rules that apply to the workplace.

▼ **THINK FOR YOURSELF!**

Time? Or Motivation?

If I'm honest with myself, I see that finishing work on time is more about focus and motivation than about time. The same is true for others. When I teach time management classes, business managers always want to know how to stay focused on the job and avoid procrastination. The answer is simple: we need to define clear goals—*what* we are making—and know the value—*why* it matters. And then we need to remind ourselves of those every day.

For projects to succeed in a small business, the owner or manager must coach each person, prioritize his or her work, and help him or her see the reasons why the work is important. When we do that, we minimize procrastination, last-minute rushes, poor-quality work, and conflicts between project responsibilities and regular responsibilities.

The lesson: Help each team member by giving clear goals, priorities, and practical reasons why the work is worth doing. This is the heart of matrix management for a small business.

ects are on track by communicating the priorities. So, in a small business, matrix management is mostly helping people juggle their time.

In this section, we'll look at two topics from the *Project Management Body of Knowledge:*

- *Project human resource management* for building our team.
- *Project procurement management* for contracting experts and workers and for purchasing what we need.

Project Human Resource Management: Building Our Team

This is the definition of *project human resource management* from *A Guide to the Project Management Body of Knowledge,* 3rd edition, Appendix F:

Project Human Resource Management includes the processes that organize and manage the project team. The project team is comprised of the people who have assigned roles and responsibilities for completing the project. While it is common to speak of roles and responsibilities being assigned, team members should be involved in much of the project's planning and decision-making. Early involvement of team members adds expertise during the planning process and strengthens commitment to the project. The type and number of project team members can often change as the project progresses. Project team members can be referred to as the project's staff. Project Human Resource Management processes include:

- Human Resource Planning—Identifying and documenting project roles, responsibilities, and reporting relationships, as well as creating the staffing management plan
- Acquire Project Team—Obtaining the human resources needed to complete the project
- Develop Project Team—Improving the competencies and interaction of team members to enhance project performance
- Manage Project Team—Tracking team member performance, providing feedback, resolving issues, and coordinating changes to enhance project performance.

Let's put the four processes into simple lan-

▼ **SMART THINKING!**

A Little Expertise Goes a Long Way

Most people get locked into thinking that they have to figure everything out and do it themselves or they have to get someone else to do the job. That kind of thinking is bad for projects and bad for business. In reality, a little bit of the right expertise goes a long way to reducing project cost and preventing project disaster.

Projects are unique—they always contain something new. And the only way we can be confident that we know how to do something is if we've done it before, lots of times. So, on a project *there will always be some things the team doesn't know how to do.* The most important thing to do in project human resources management is to identify those things early and close the gap.

Of course, on most projects, the work is familiar. It is similar to what we've done before. It's just not quite the same. And it's those little differences that will trip us up every time.

What can we do about that? Well, think of it this way. An expert is someone who knows his or her way around so well that those little differences don't cause problems. He or she can see them ahead of time.

And there is always an expert available—*always.* We live in the information age. We complain about information overload. Make use of all that information. If you need to know something you don't know, you can count on this: *someone already knows it who probably has a book or a web site or will talk with you on the phone for free or for a small fee.*

Find that expertise. Do it now, during planning. It's a lot easier to find the information and close the gap now than in the middle of the project. That's when you find that the expert you want just went on vacation and his or her book just went out of print.

I'm hoping you'll take this advice. But many people won't. Why not? In a word—ego. Most people are locked into thinking in one of two ways:

- Some think, "I can't do this; I have to hire someone expensive." That's the sign of a weak ego, a person not confident of being able to learn and grow and solve the problems.
- Others think, "I have to do this all myself." That may be a person who overrates himself or herself, thinking no one can do the job, or a defense for a weak ego that needs to prove something by going it alone.

Well, sorry to be blunt, but get over yourself. You and your team can do the job, and yet you'll do it better—at lower cost and with lower risk of project failure—if you get the expert help you need early in the project.

The lesson: Don't let ego get in the way. Identify what your team and you don't know and get some expert help or training early in the project.

---

guage and I'll show you what you need to do in each process to get it done right.

- *Human Resource Planning* starts with defining the roles and skills your team needs. If we define the job clearly—as described in Chapter 4, using Table 4-2, the task description template—and give each person what

he or she needs to do the job, the team can succeed.

- *Acquire Project Team.* If you're the boss of the company, this mostly means making sure that you and your team have time to focus on the project without being overwhelmed by other work. The tools from Chapter 4 for

▼ BOOST YOUR BUSINESS!

Make People into a Team

People don't become a team because you tell them that they have to work together. Hoopla, rah-rah, and a brass band don't work, either. Here are some things that really help people become a team:

- *Getting together and listening to one another about how we want to be treated.* Create a time where each person names one thing he or she wants to give the team and one thing he or she wants to receive from the team. Some items will be general, such as respect. Others will be specific, such as not interrupting one another and showing up on time for meetings. Put them all together into a set of ground rules or a code of conduct beginning with the words, "We will."

- *Working toward a common goal.* Explain to the team what each person brings to the project and how each of you will contribute toward project success and better results for the business.

- *Coaching with praise for small successes.* Simple phrases like "Thank you for listening" and "Good job," offered promptly and frequently, make a real difference.

---

organizing and prioritizing work with program, portfolio, and matrix management will help. If you need to hire outside expertise, begin with gap analysis and gap reconciliation to define exactly the expertise you need. You probably won't hire someone permanent to help out on a project, so acquiring people falls into procurement management, which we will discuss in the next section.

- *Develop Project Team.* This is what we discussed above. Determine through gap analysis the skills the team members need to acquire. Then help them get those skills, through coaching, training, study time, or expert assistance. Developing the project team also includes turning the group into a team. See the sidebar, Make People into a Team, for suggestions.

- *Manage Project Team.* Throughout the project, we need to keep the team focused on the work. We need to know what is going on with our people and then we need to resolve or remove any problems so that they can do their work. Good team management is about cooperation, focusing on the goal, preventing

conflict, and resolving conflict in a straightforward way. See the sidebar, Confront the Problem, Not the People, for tips.

Many owners and managers in small companies think that they can't give incentives because they can't afford big bonuses. Actually, except in certain fields such as sales, where commissions are part of salary, big bonuses aren't that effective, anyway. Here are some tips on project incentives that work:

- *Frequent, prompt praise for small successes* creates the fastest behavior change, according to psychologists.

- *Praise people for doing their job.* At the weekly status meeting, you can say, "Good job, thanks," every time someone says he or she has finished a task.

- *Let people know how their good work helps the business.* When you make the connection between good work and business value, your people can become more committed to your company.

- *Make praise supportive, not competitive.* Don't reward "the best team member of the

---

▼ SMART THINKING!
Confront the Problem, Not the People

This may seem odd, but in human resources management *confrontation* is considered a good technique for solving problems and resolving conflict. That's because the idea is to confront the problem, not the people. It means that we shouldn't sweep the problem under the rug, avoid it, and hope it goes away. Instead, we should bring the team members together, put the problem in front of us—on the whiteboard or the table—and solve it.

That works for technical problems and it works for people problems as well. The key is to focus on the problem—symptom, cause, and solution—without blame. If two people aren't getting along, bring them together or speak to each of them separately. Focus on the needs of the project, on the present and the future. Ask what they can do to solve the problem and work well together. You'll be amazed at what people can do when you expect them to solve problems and do well. We tend to live up to what our boss expects of us.

---

month." Instead, reward each person whenever he or she does a job well or stops doing something that you asked him or her to stop doing.

- *Ask team members what motivates them.* One might want a small cash bonus, another, to be taken to lunch, a third, a plaque or thank-you note. Give them what they want. Consider gift certificates.
- *Let the team members decide when to reward one another.* Asking them to thank and reward one another helps them focus on being helpful and seeing how others help them.

Project Procurement Management: Getting Whom and What We Need

Project procurement management links our project plan to two other areas of specialization—purchasing and contracting. Much of the information in procurement management doesn't apply to most projects in small businesses; procurement practice has a lot do with large government contracts, bidding rules, guidelines for subcontractors, and the Uniform Commercial Code that governs business contracts and purchasing. For some small businesses, such as small subcontractors to government

or military contractors, this expertise is essential. But I'm going to assume that, if that is part of your business, you know what you are doing.

Here are five key guidelines for procurement for small projects:

- *Plan procurement early.* Many purchases and contracts are easy with enough time, but nearly impossible if you wait until you need to use what you are going to procure.
- *Talk with experts.* Talking with vendors is a great chance to learn about their products and how to use them. Their expertise can speed the project along and prevent problems—and it's usually free.

▼ FOCUS!
Getting Whom and What We Need

For small businesses, most of project procurement management is making a shopping list and choosing sources for the items we list. But, when we are hiring people to join the team, we need to know how to do it right. And if there is a contract—or even a purchase order—for materials, we need to make sure that the legal language matches what the project requires.

- *Work with service-oriented people you understand and trust.* Vendors and contractors who care may cost a bit more, but they're worth it. Remember that the whole project is at risk if you get the wrong thing or it doesn't work. Think about value, rather than cost, when choosing vendors and products.
- *Make sure the contract or purchase order matches the project.* It's a big mistake—and a common one—to order something without requiring that it arrives by the time you need it and that it does what you need. Protect yourself by making your needs clear and by including them in purchase agreements and contracts.
- *Know what you're doing.* If you aren't familiar with the terms of a purchase agreement or if you are new to arranging contracts, be sure to get expert advice and even legal counsel. Some types of agreements can lead to complications you would never expect.

Taking good care in the procurement process prevents project pitfalls. As we mentioned in time management, when we are acquiring something for a project, we are dealing with an external dependency—with something we need that is not under our control. Each external dependency is a risk, and early attention to risk items increases our chances of project success.

Here is the description of *project procurement management* from *A Guide to the Project Management Body of Knowledge,* 3rd edition, Appendix F*:

Project Procurement Management includes the processes to purchase or acquire the products, services, or results needed from outside the project team to perform the

*This was developed by the Project Management Institute. Copyright and all rights reserved by PMI. Material from this publication has been reproduced with the permission of PMI. The applies to each citation of this book as they appear in this chapter.

work. This chapter presents two perspectives of procurement. The organization can be either the buyer or seller of the product, service, or results under a contract.

Project Procurement Management includes the contract management and change control processes required to administer contracts or purchase orders issued by authorized project team members. Project Procurement Management also includes administering any contract issued by an outside organization (the buyer) that is acquiring the project from the performing organization (the seller) and administering contractual obligations placed on the project team by the contract. Project Procurement Management processes include:

- Plan Purchases and Acquisitions—determining what to purchase or acquire, and determining when and how
- Plan Contracting—documenting products, services, and results requirements and identifying potential sellers
- Request Seller Responses—obtaining information, quotations, bids, offers, or proposals, as appropriate
- Select Sellers—reviewing offers, choosing from among potential sellers, and negotiating a written contract with a seller
- Contract Administration—managing the contract and the relationship between the buyer and the seller, reviewing and documenting how a seller is performing or has performed to establish required corrective actions and provide a basis for future relationships with the seller, managing contract related changes and, when appropriate, managing the contractual relationship with the outside buyer of the project
- Contract Closure—completing and settling each contract, including the resolution of any open items, and closing each contract.

HOW DO I MAKE SURE IT GETS DONE RIGHT?

Our project plan is nearly complete. We've answered these questions in detail.

- *Why are we doing this project?* We've answered by defining value and purpose.
- *What are we making and how will we make it?* We've answered by defining scope.
- *How long will it take?* We've answered with time planning.
- *How much will it cost?* We've answered with cost planning.
- *Who will do the job?* We've answered with human resources management.
- *What do we need to buy and how will we get it?* We've answered with procurement management.

Now, we ask:

- *How do we make sure it is good?* We answer with project quality management.
- *What if something unexpected happens?* We answer with project risk management.

Project Quality Management: Making It Good

The underlying reason for quality management is that errors are part of life. Auditors have a saying, "Without attention, everything degenerates over time." We pay attention to quality management because we know that errors can always creep in. Since errors will happen, we decide to bring errors under management proactively, in a straightforward way, so that the errors don't occur or, if they do, that we correct them. Quality management pays off because preventing and eliminating errors increases product value while reducing project rework and reducing the risk of project failure.

Here is the formal definition of *project quality management* from *A Guide to the Project Management Body of Knowledge,* 3rd edition, Appendix F:

> Project Quality Management includes the processes and activities of the performing organization that determine the quality policies, objectives, and responsibilities so that the project will satisfy the needs for which it was undertaken. It implements the quality management system through policy and procedures, with continuous process improvement activities conducted throughout, as appropriate. The Project Quality Management processes include:
>
> - Quality Planning—identifying which quality standards are relevant to the project and determining how to satisfy them
> - Perform Quality Assurance—applying the planned, systematic quality activities to ensure that the project employs all processes needed to meet requirements
> - Perform Quality Control—monitoring

▼ **Focus!**

Success Means Preventing Errors and Being Ready for the Unpredictable

We can't just assume that everyone will do a good job and everything will go according to plan. In fact, those are dangerous assumptions that can sink a project. Instead, we want to bring error under management, and we do it with *quality management.* Also, we want to figure that unexpected things will happen—as they always do. Bringing different possible future events under management is the goal of *risk management.*

Quality management is the work we do to make sure we do a good job, where we focus on getting it done *right.* Risk management is the work we do to make sure that we succeed, even when things get in the way. In risk management we focus on getting it *done*—no matter what happens.

specific project results to determine whether they comply with relevant quality standards and identifying ways to eliminate causes of unsatisfactory performance.

Project quality management includes three processes: quality planning, performing quality assurance, and performing quality control. In this chapter, we are focusing on quality planning. We'll look at quality control and quality assurance in Chapters 8, 9, and 10, when we learn how to keep a project on track and deliver customer delight.

It's not enough to have a good plan. We also need to implement it correctly, to prevent errors. Quality management is the work of making sure that our plan is good and that we implement it so that the product meets specifications. That means giving the customers what they want, giving the customers a product or service that works, delighting the customers. Quality adds value. If our project delivers results to a paying customer, quality is what gives us repeat business and referrals. If our project delivers results inside our company, quality is what makes sure that the new system that we use after the project is over works well, delivers lots of value, and is easy to use, inexpensive, and easy to maintain.

Here are the most important things we can do to deliver quality in our project:

- *Design quality in from the beginning.* It is much less expensive to prevent errors than to fix them.
- *Keep the team focused on quality.* If each job is done with quality and each team member strives to make sure that the work he or she delivers is excellent for the person who will use that that output as an input, then all that quality work adds up to a quality product.
- *Design tests before you do the work.* If we design our tests after we start working, we increase the chances of letting errors slip through.

- *Check everything using a buddy system.* No one can see all of his or her own mistakes. Part of human nature is to see things a certain way—to read what we thought we wrote, and to see what we thought we did. Make it a policy—with no blame—that everyone's work gets checked by someone else as the project goes along.
- *Triple-check everything at the gate.* Gate reviews are an excellent way to ensure quality. We catch errors before they move on to the next stage, where they cost ten times as much to fix.
- *Leave enough time for testing, rework, and retesting.* Don't assume that all tests will go well. Allow time to find and fix problems and then to recheck to make sure everything is good before the product goes to the customer.
- *Keep getting better.* During the project, use every gate and every error you discover as a chance to find root causes, implement permanent preventative solutions, and add to your lessons learned.
- *Study quality methods and apply them in your field.* Every industry from construction to software engineering has its own quality best practices. Learn them and apply them.
- *Remember: high quality from the beginning saves money.* Many people think that quality is expensive. The opposite is true: mistakes are expensive. When we focus on quality from the beginning, we can make fewer mistakes, reducing total project cost and shortening the schedule. We deliver better results with less rework, sooner, while spending less money.

Let's take a closer look at the most important of those ideas.

Design Quality in from the Beginning. We design quality in from the beginning by:

- *Doing a good, thorough, clear job at requirements specification,* so we understand what the customers want, why they want it that way, and how they will use it. Then, when we have to make a decision in the middle of the project, we can make the choice that will work best for the customers.
- *Doing a good job in architecture and technical design.* For example, if our product has fewer parts and joints, it is likely to be stronger and last longer.
- *Choosing high-quality vendors and components* and making sure the vendors understand our quality requirements.

Design Tests Early. Test design should come right at the end of planning. The most important input is the requirements traceability matrix. From that, we define the tests we will perform on components and on the final product to ensure quality. We also plan to arrange to create the *test bed,* which is the testing system that lets us make sure things are working. The actual work of building the test bed, test design, testing, and rework is part of the technical work of the project, but planning all the tests, doing them right, and following through on test results and fixing any problems we find are key parts of project quality management.

Setting up the test bed and defining all the tests before project work starts has two advantages. Both of them help ensure better project results by ensuring the independence of testing from building the product.

- When we design tests early, the team members will feel less pressure to rush tests at the end. They will probably be feeling pressure to meet the deadline. You don't want them taking shortcuts by skipping tests. Instead, have the tests ready to roll and easy to do, so that the team can test everything and fix everything before delivery, even under time pressure.

- When we design tests early, we design them from the specification—from what the customers want. If we wait and design tests later, it is very easy to unintentionally design the tests based on our ideas about the product—on our ideas of what the customers want—instead of using our write-up of what the customers really want. If we do that, our product passes all the tests, but they don't prove our product is right for the customers. We may deliver a product with something missing or something not working.

Our test plan should include multiple tests of every customer requirement. We need to make sure that everything gets tested in each component, so that only good components go into the final product. Then we need to test the whole product as a system to make sure it works for the customers. After every test, if rework is needed, we need to make sure that it is done, the product is retested, and we learn whatever lessons will help us avoid similar errors on this project and future projects. We can prepare for this by defining checklists for all of our tests and leaving enough time in the schedule for rework.

Putting Together the Quality Plan. Quality planning should lead to concrete results. For a large project, we should write a full quality plan. For a small project, we should ensure that our activity list includes quality assurance and quality control steps and we should also prepare appropriate checklists and diagrams. For example, we will want to create checklists for each project gate. Our checklists should make sure we do all the review work at the gate thoroughly, answering these questions:

- What documents and components should be reviewed?
- Exactly what should be checked for in each document and component?

If you lay out these checklists during planning,

▼ SOMETHING SLIPPED!
Why Didn't We Know the Mirror Was Bent?

The folks who made the Hubble Space Telescope made a big mistake that ended up costing taxpayers hundreds of millions of dollars. And the mistake occurred, in part, due to a failure of independence in testing.

Telescope mirrors have to have a nearly perfect curve—varying from the ideal shape by a fraction of a wavelength of light—or they give a fuzzy, distorted image. The final shaping of the mirror is guided by a laser; a laser is also used to measure the mirror's curvature in testing.

The laser used to build the Hubble Space Telescope was very expensive. The team decided that they couldn't afford two such precise lasers, so they used the same laser for cutting and for testing. They had a second laser for testing, but it wasn't as precise.

When the test results came in, the test with the more expensive laser said everything was fine. The less expensive laser showed that there might be a problem. The team, instead of finding out why there was a difference, went with the information from the better laser—and forgot to take into account that the better laser had been used to cut the mirror.

The error in cutting was the mirror image of the error in testing. The mirror was the wrong shape, but, when reflected through the wrong-shaped lens of the cutter and tester, it looked right. So the mirror was approved and the telescope went up into space.

When the images came back fuzzy, we knew we had a problem. But it was very expense to build and send a replacement part—a corrective lens—when the service technician had to go up into outer space to deliver the repair!

The lesson: Set up your tests before you get to work and keep testing independent of work. Otherwise, your product can pass all the tests and still not work for the customers—and that will cost you a lot in money and in reputation.

---

checking will be faster, easier, and more reliable during gate reviews and throughout the project.

In planning, don't leave anything unclear. Whenever we are not clear about a process on our project, we should take the time to diagram it. If nothing else, do an informal sketch. If you or someone on your team knows a method like data flow diagramming or flowcharting, that's even better. If we follow the rules when making structured diagrams, they force us to clarify our thinking and find gaps in our process. When we fix the diagram, we're improving our plan at the same time. Here's a tip: we know something is clear when it is clear to everyone on the team; if people see the product differently, then the project is headed for trouble.

A clear quality plan or set of quality checklists gives us the tools we need to ensure quality through every step of the project. To pick just one example, we might improve our party shopping lists by structuring them the way you see in Table 7-1.

Table 7-1 is a quality manager's idea of a shopping list. (If you guessed that I drive my wife a little crazy, you'd be right.) In a business setting, though, detailed descriptions of each relevant feature of each component and a way of checking those at the end of each project task make a lot of sense. We want to be sure that the worker has all the information from the requirements specification. Then he or she can confirm that each item meets requirements. That ensures that the quality of his or her output is good. That output becomes the input for the next stage of the project—the ingredients to

Work Package No.	Work Package Name	Planned Quantity	Quantity Purchased	Item Name	Check	Manufacturer	Check	Planning Notes	Notes During Shopping
1.1.1	Nonalcoholic Drinks								
		1 gallon		Fresh-squeezed orange juice		Whole Foods			
		4 2-quart bottles		Seltzer		Any		For punch and sangria	
		12		Cola					
		12		Ginger ale				We'll use the leftovers	
1.1.2	Beer and Wine								
		2		Red wine		4 Chimneys		For sangria	
		24 bottles		Beer		Samuel Adams, various types			
		4/6		Large/small oranges				Organic if possible for sangria and punch	
1.2	Home-Cooked Food (ingredients, partial list)								
		1 quart		Red beans, dry, bulk		Any		Organic if possible	
		5 lbs		White rice		Lundberg or Arrowhead Mills		Organic if possible, medium or long grain	
1.3	Purchased Food (partial list)								
		1 large bag		Cheddar popcorn				Organic or skip it	
		2 boxes		Whole wheat pretzels		Snyder's			

TABLE 7-1. Sample quality checklist: Shopping for the housewarming party

cook, for instance. If the ingredients are right, the cook can focus on cooking well, instead of running out to the store to fix an earlier mistake. Our quality checklists are really nothing more or less than detailed plans of exactly what we need to get it done right.

Project Risk Management: Making Sure It Gets Done

In quality management, we brought error under control. Now, with risk management, we're going to do the same with uncertainty. If there's one thing that we can be sure of, it is that the future is uncertain. That means things will not always go as planned. In project risk management, we face that uncertainty and deal with it.

We could say that project risk management involves expecting the unexpected, but it is more than that. We need to expect the unexpected, but then we also need to plan for it and then do something about it. And we also need to be ready for events that are unexpected in spite of all of our planning. This gives rise to some basic ideas of risk management:

- About the only thing we can be sure of is that things will not go exactly according to plan.
- We are better off thinking of what might happen and preparing for it than we are being caught off guard.
- We can prepare a risk plan including a list of risks. We can make allowances for risks in the project schedule and budget.
- We can use the risk plan to track the status of risks during the project, check for risk events daily or weekly, and bring risk under control.
- The uncertain future includes possible unexpected good events, called *beneficial* or *positive* risks, as well as *negative* risks, which are problems for our project.

Here are some simple things we can do to manage risk and increase the chances of success:

- *Teach every member of the team to pay attention to risk and to inform you of any risk to project success.* Risks are almost always easier and less expensive to deal with when identified soon. Make sure your team knows to think about risk and talk about risk.
- *List risks and then evaluate each risk and decide what to do about it.* We'll show you the steps in this chapter.
- *When things go wrong ask, "Why? Can it happen again?"* Some of the trickiest risks are small problems that happen over and over again. Looking closely at small problems, we can fix the root cause before small problems pile up into a disaster.
- *Manage risk throughout the project* by making it part of the weekly or daily status meeting.

Here is the formal definition of *project risk management* from *A Guide to the Project Management Body of Knowledge,* 3rd edition, Appendix F:

Project Risk Management includes the processes concerned with conducting risk management planning, identification, analysis, responses, and monitoring and control on a project. The objectives of Project Risk Management are to increase the probability and impact of positive events and decrease the probability and impact of events adverse to project objectives. Project Risk Management processes include:

- Risk Management Planning—deciding how to approach, plan, and execute the risk management activities for a project
- Risk Identification—determining which risks might affect the project and documenting their characteristics
- Qualitative Risk Analysis—prioritizing risks for subsequent further analysis or action by assessing and combining their

probability of occurrence and impact

- Quantitative Risk Analysis—numerically analyzing the effect on overall project objectives of identified risks
- Risk Response Planning—developing options and actions to enhance opportunities and to reduce threats to project objectives
- Risk Monitoring and Control—tracking identified risks, monitoring residual risks, identifying new risks, executing risk response plans, and evaluating their effectiveness throughout the project life cycle.

Although the PMI identifies six processes in risk management, only four of them are relevant for small businesses. Risk management planning is a very small item for small business projects. We don't need to set up a different, elaborate risk system for each project. We can just take the tools in this book and apply them. Quantitative risk analysis doesn't apply to projects in small and medium-sized businesses at all. It requires the application of statistics and goes far beyond what any but the largest companies would need.

So, for small and medium-sized businesses, we need a simple, practical way to do these four processes: risk identification, qualitative risk analysis, risk response planning, and risk monitoring and control. Here is a simple way to manage risk on our projects to make sure that we get it done right!

▼ **BOTTOM-LINE BASICS**

Who Are You Counting On?

One of the most important ideas in project risk management has a fancy name: *external dependency*. But it's a very simple idea. Any time you count on getting anything from anyone outside the team, that person might not get you what you need when you need it. That is a project risk. The key words here are *anyone* and *anything*. There are many external dependencies on every project. Here is a thorough list of stakeholders to consider to get you started.

- *Customers* must provide information for the requirements specification, answers to questions, and review and testing with approvals or specific corrections for each document and component at every review gate. In some cases, customers must make timely payments to launch the project or keep it going.
- The *sponsor* has to provide money on time.
- *Senior executives* have to provide people, answers to questions, and resolutions to conflicts.
- *Vendors* are providing products that must be delivered on time and meet specifications.

- *Consultants* should be included in the project team and their work should be on the project schedule. Until they are fully integrated with the team—if ever—we should still consider their deliverables external dependencies.
- *Regulatory agencies* may need to provide permits to allow work to proceed.

Note that the word *anything* is very broad. A project can be delayed when a customer forgets to call you at the end of a gate review and say, "You're doing a great job, keep going." So, *anything* includes project components, review and approval, answers to questions, money—whatever information, person, or item is needed to do the next jobs on the project schedule.

The lesson: In building a list of external dependencies, don't just look at vendors. Look at everyone, especially the customer, and ask about everything, including answers, permits, and approvals.

Risk Identification: Listing the Risks. We start with knowing that something could go wrong, that something unexpected could happen. We ask, "What could that be?" Then we write down the answer. The best time to hold a major risk-planning meeting is shortly after the activity list is done. We should pay attention to risk before that, but we cannot make a thorough list of risks until we know the project activities. At that point, our goals are clear and we know the details of our work plan. Our focus is positive and we want to keep it that way.

Risk planning means looking at what could go wrong to make sure that things go right. We don't want a doom-and-gloom session; we want a sense that we can handle uncertainty with good planning, attention to risk, and appropriate, timely action.

Here are ways of asking what unexpected events could happen, of asking what could go wrong or unexpectedly right, of expecting the unexpected. Be sure to have someone writing down the answers as your team brainstorms with these questions.

- Review the WBS, the activity list, and the list of items we plan to purchase and ask, "What could keep us from getting what we need and doing a good job?"
- Ask, "What are we getting from outside the team? Who are we depending on outside the team? What would happen if they don't deliver?"
- Ask, "What have we never done before? What areas are difficult for us?"
- Ask, "What has gone wrong on other projects that could happen again here?"
- Finally, ask, "What could go unexpectedly right? What could make the project easier, get it done sooner or at lower cost, give us a better result?" List those positive risks, too.

The result of this meeting is a list of risks, formally called a *risk register*. Of course, anyone can suggest additions to the list of risks at any time and everyone should add anything that may be headed our way. The risk list grows and changes throughout the project.

In our first big risk meeting, once we have our initial risk list, we are ready to do qualitative risk analysis and risk response planning. In fact, we can do all of them in one meeting.

Qualitative Risk Analysis. We now want to describe each risk, so that we will be able to manage it. There are six things we want to do for each risk:

- *Name* the risk.
- Describe the *consequence* of the risk.
- Define the risk *trigger*.
- Determine the *likelihood* of the risk.
- Estimate the *significance* of the risk event.
- Describe *options for managing* the risk.

See the Key Terms sidebar for definitions of these terms.

Likelihood and consequence are independent of one another. For example, rain may be very likely for the day of the housewarming party, but it is of little consequence for an indoor party. On the other hand, it is unlikely that one of us will get sick, but we'd have to cancel the party—the worst possible consequence. We can rate likelihood on a scale of 1 to 3 (low, medium, and high) or 1 to 5 (very low, low, medium, high, and very high). We rate consequence from 0 to 1, with 1 meaning project failure or cancellation and a number between 0 and 1 indicating the increased cost, delay in time, or loss of some scope or quality. Read on for a list of ways to manage each risk event.

Risk Response Planning and Risk Monitoring and Control. Once a risk is on our list, we have to decide what we're going to do about it—our risk management options. By putting it on the list, we've *accepted* the risk under management, that is, we've committed to keeping track of it and doing something about it. *Risk acceptance* is not passive; it is very active. In addition to accepting the risk, we

▼ KEY TERMS

Risk name An identifier for the risk, usually the risk event itself.

Consequence of a risk What will happen if the risk event happens and is not managed. Typically, project failure, increased time and/or cost, and/or loss of scope or quality.

Trigger The event that will let you know a risk is likely to happen or is already happening.

Likelihood An estimate of the chance that the risk event will happen.

Significance The measure of the consequence—cost in dollars, delay in time, or project failure.

Management options for risks Choices we have for dealing with a risk before or when it happens.

▼ BE AN EXPERT!

Good News Can Be Hard to Manage

It's important to prepare for positive risks. Even good news will throw off your schedule and your budget.

Here is an example from some volunteer work I'm doing as I write this book. I'm helping the local chapter of the Project Management Institute (PMI) create a symposium—a day of professional development, including learning and job opportunities. The day had been set for August. Then a major company that provides project management training offered to bring a class to our town and have us co-sponsor the event. That would bring in a lot of money and a lot more people. Good news! But their date was October. We had to reschedule our event and change a whole lot of our plans. The co-sponsorship is a great opportunity, but it required a lot of preparation and planning.

The lesson: Think of what good things might happen, too. Even positive risks require changes to our project plan.

can also do one or more of these:

- We can *mitigate* a risk. That means reducing its likelihood or reducing its consequence. These are two separate actions and we can do both. For example, we can reduce the likelihood of not getting the fresh ingredients we need for our recipe the day before the party by finding two stores that carry what we want and by getting up early to shop. We can reduce the consequence by having an alternate recipe ready if we can't get the ingredients.
- We can *avoid* a risk by changing our plans so that the risk cannot possibly happen at all. For example, if we decide to settle for frozen vegetables instead of fresh and then buy them early and put them in our freezer, we have avoided the risk of not being able to get fresh vegetables.
- We can *transfer* the risk, for example, by getting insurance. Risk transference is not that important for most projects. When we trans-

fer a risk, someone else foots the bill if the risk happens, but the project still gets into trouble or fails. However, risk transference is important in some industries. For example, in the movie business, a production company can transfer risk to an insurance company by getting the movie production *bonded*. This means that the movie is insured for being completed within a certain budget. If it isn't, then the insurance company that offers the bonding will cover the extra costs. In a bonding agreement, insurance companies get to approve the résumés of the key team members, and they want to see that people have a proven track record. So, to work on a bonded movie, producers, directors, and other people on the movie have to

Risk Name	Consequence	Trigger	Likelihood	Significance	Management Option
Illness—Kris or Sid	Cancel party	Feel sick	Low	1.0	Accepted. Mitigate by reducing likelihood—stay healthy, avoid stress.
Farmers' market rained out	Can't get best ingredients	Rain the day before	Low	0.2	Accepted. Mitigate by reducing consequence—have alternate recipes ready.
Find a musician	Positive risk—add live music to the party	Meet a musician we really like	Low	0.3	Accepted. Increase chances by going out to hear live music. If it happens, announce on web site, add to invitation if time, adjust party budget.

Table 7-2. Sample risk list: Some risks for the housewarming party

have a proven track record of working on productions of a similar size and delivering within budget. As a result, bonding transfers the risk away from the production company and also places a constraint on who can be hired to work on the movie. This is a constraint on the team, and it also influences people's careers. If a movie professional is seen as responsible for a project that exceeded its budget, it can be hard to get work later because insurance companies will hesitate to bond a movie when they see the name of that professional.

Table 7-2 is an example of a risk list—or risk register—showing some of the risks for our housewarming party. A complete risk plan for the housewarming party project can be found on the CD that comes with this book.

Table 7-2 shows how the risk list might look at the end of planning. The risk list is a living document. Each week, we add new risks that we think of or encounter, we cross off risks that don't happen, and we implement our mitigation strategies as needed and note that in the plan.

Our plan is getting very solid. We just need to put the final touches to it and we're ready to roll through the project and get it done right!

GETTING READY TO ROLL

Our plan is nearly done. There are just three things left to do.

- *Plan for communications.* The PMI says that 90 percent of a project manager's time is spent communicating: interviewing people and writing up the plans, sending reminder e-mails, holding status meetings, and talking on the phone or meeting in person to take care of problems and keep things moving. A lot of this is informal, but we can do well to organize some of it into a project communications plan.

- *Set up a plan and a system for dealing with project change.* So far, we've been planning as if we're going to follow the plan through the project without any changes. But what if the customer needs something different or if we encounter a technical problem? We need a way to plan for changes to scope, time, cost, and other project elements. Most important, we need a way to see how a change in one area—such as a risk event or a customer change request—creates changes in other areas, delaying the schedule, increasing cost, requiring a change to our procurement plan, causing a reschedule of tasks, and maybe affecting product scope or quality. If we set up an *integrated change control system,* we'll be ready to handle change requests as they come in and adjust the project as needed.

- *Tie the whole plan together and pass the planning review gate.* Just as we tied together the various stakeholder perspectives with architecture and we cross-checked everything, now we need to tie together the entire project plan and make sure it is correct and consistent. When we, our team, and the customer approve the whole plan, we can move ahead and start doing the work of the project.

Project Communications Management: Keeping Everyone on the Same Page

Sometimes, it seems to me that writing a communications plan is overkill. I mean, I've planned everything else—and now I need to plan when and how I'm going to talk to people! It seems like too much, but it isn't. Time and again, experience has shown me that a good communications plan is going to be needed sooner or later. If we do it sooner, it prevents delays and tension. If we skip it, we'll end up putting one together to dig ourselves out of the hole we've dug ourselves into.

If we've brought the team members together to listen to the customers, then during planning we're all on the same page. The communications plan has three goals:

- To make sure that the team members stay on the same page—and stay on the same page

as the customers—all the way through the project.
- To make sure that any information—such as an approval, a correction, or a change of plans—gets to everyone who needs it when he or she needs it, so that the right work can be done at the right time, without delay.
- To manage expectations, so that the customers don't end up expecting more than they specified.

What does it really mean to *be on the same page?* Well, here's one example. One night when I was in second grade, I found I couldn't do my homework. I knew this was stuff we hadn't learned in class. Sure enough, when we checked the next day, we found I had copied down the wrong page number from the blackboard. That's how my parents found out that I needed to wear glasses.

When people are trying to communicate, if they aren't on the same page, nothing makes any sense. For a true funny story of that, see the sidebar, Breakfast Tacos.

A good communications plan describes how we will give each stakeholder the information he or she needs to get work done throughout the project. It also describes how we will keep track of two types of information:

- *Project management information:* information about how the project will be managed, including the project plan, all project changes, schedules, and supporting information.
- *Project technical information,* including technical specifications, requirements documents, survey results, descriptions of the working environment, architecture, and any other information needed to make a good product or service throughout the project.

Here is the PMI's definition of *project communications management* from *A Guide to the Project*

Management Body of Knowledge, 3rd edition, Appendix F:

Project Communications Management includes the processes required to ensure timely and appropriate generation, collection, distribution, storage, retrieval, and ultimate disposition of project information. The Project Communications Management processes provide the critical links among people and information that are necessary for successful communications. Project managers can spend an inordinate amount of time communicating with the project team, stakeholders, customer, and sponsor. Everyone involved in the project should understand how communications affect the project as a whole. Project Communications Management processes include:

- Communications Planning—determining the information and communications needs of the project stakeholders

- Information Distribution—making needed information available to project stakeholders in a timely manner
- Performance Reporting—collecting and distributing performance information, including status reporting, progress measurement, and forecasting
- Manage Stakeholders—managing communications to satisfy the requirements of, and resolve issues with, project stakeholders.

Here' s another basic fact of life: Information can always get lost or confused. We bring information under management with project communications management to increase the chances that the right information and authorizations will reach the right people in time for them to get their work done without delay.

Here are three simple steps to setting up effective project communications:

- Set up a document repository, a central place

▼ Bottom-Line Basics

Breakfast Tacos

A friend of mine in San Antonio–a saleswoman who likes to start her day early–pulled into a strip mall to order breakfast. Now, anyone who knows San Antonio can tell you that breakfast in this town is a breakfast taco. So, that's just what she ordered. She'd pulled into a drive-in–maybe a Taco Bell™, or maybe a Taco Cabana™, or maybe even Bill Miller's Barbecue™. It did not matter: every San Antonio restaurant has breakfast tacos. So she ordered one.

The clerk shot back, "So, what do you really want?" She thought he was trying to give her a hard time, so she shoved a five-dollar bill at him and said, "Like I said–a breakfast taco." He said, "Really, we don't have those here. What do you want?"

They went back and forth like this several more times.

She looked a bit more closely at where she was and was extremely embarrassed. The menu was covered with Happy Meals. She had pulled into the wrong driveway; she was at a McDonald's™–the one place in San Antonio that doesn't sell breakfast tacos.

The lesson: My friend and the drive-in clerk could not understand each other, because my friend was at the wrong store–on the wrong page. If that happens on a project, there is no way to get the message through. We can prevent that problem by creating and following a good communications plan.

▼ BOTTOM-LINE BASICS

Why Do We Need Information?

In a communications plan, we are defining the information needs of project stakeholders. But what does that really mean? Why do we need information? We need information for two purposes:

- As input to decisions
- As input to work we're going to do

All of the work and decisions of the project are listed on our activities list in our project schedule, organized from the work breakdown structure. If we look at these documents, we will see who needs to do what work when and who needs to make what decision when. We build the communications plan by asking, "What information or document does this person need as input for this task or decision?" If we do that for every task and decision on the project, then we know the project won't be delayed by missing or lost information.

where everyone can go to get project information when they need it.

- Prepare guidelines and schedules for status meetings and other routine meetings.
- Prepare a communications plan for gate reviews, customer contact, communication with peripheral stakeholders, vertical communications, and team members and stakeholders with special communications needs.

We'll take a look at status meetings in Chapter 9. Let's look at the other two items now.

Set up a Document Repository. We can simplify the communications plan a great deal by building an *information repository* where we store all project management and project technical documents. For a small project where security is not an issue, this is very easy to do. If everyone is in the same

office, we could simply have a folder on the hard drive of a computer—a network server, if you have a network—and rules for who can change files and who can only look at them. If people are at multiple locations, you can do similar things with a web server. Information repositories become very complex, though, if you can't trust people to handle information well. There are two problems:

- If you have some things that only some people should see and other things that are accessible to everyone, you are going to have to secure documents in different ways. This requires computer or network security, user names, passwords, and file access control.
- If you want to make sure that the only people who change documents are those who are allowed to change them, then you'll need a tool that tracks document version control.

There are special tools to solve those problems called *document management systems*. Primavera's line of project management software (www.primavera.com) has built-in document management.

I run a small company and we don't need any special tools. We're careful about creating clear filenames and putting dates and our initials on each file and things run just fine. The CD contains sample rules for file names for a document repository.

If you create a document repository, then you can make sure that only the most up-to-date version of each document is available and that anyone who needs information can get it whenever it's needed. You can also keep track of which documents have been approved by the project manager, team members, and the appropriate customer representatives.

Preparing the Communications Plan. Table 7-3 provides the process steps for preparing a communications plan that will meet the needs of these four project activities:

- *Gate reviews,* where we need to guide the team

Work environment	▪ A project using the *Get It Done Right!* method, where the WBS and activity list are complete and planning is nearly complete
Input	▪ List of stakeholders ▪ WBS and WBS dictionary ▪ Activity list (or schedule, if it is ready) ▪ List of milestones, stages, and gates ▪ All other project plans
Tools	▪ Word processor
Resources	▪ Project manager's time—under half an hour for a small project, a few hours for a large one
Techniques	▪ Reading, thinking, and writing
Process	**Plan each gate review with these steps.** 1. Identify which project customers should be included in each gate review and which documents or components they need to approve. 2. Review the quality plan to define what constitutes a review of each document or component and ensure that all necessary inputs are available at the gate. 3. Plan to distribute all review documents at the opening of the gate review. 4. Schedule gate review meetings with team and customers. 5. Define all possible outputs of the gate review, including approval, minor and major rework requests, and calls for project cancellation. 6. Inform customers and technical staff of the gate review schedule, including educating them about the time that will be required of them. 7. Schedule the gate review, ensuring all information and people will be available. 8. Repeat steps 1-8 for each gate review and for final product delivery. 9. For final product delivery, add appropriate customer acceptance, project closure, and contract closeout activities. **Plan communications with peripheral stakeholders with these steps.** 10. Identify peripheral stakeholders and the project deliverables that each peripheral stakeholder needs to review and approve. 11. For each stakeholder, prepare a schedule of when he or she will review documents, test components, and perform final tests on the components that concern him or her. 12. Contact each stakeholder and identify his or her preferred forms of oral and written communication. 13. Include time for review and testing and, for each of these reviews and tests, steps for all possible outcomes (approval, change requests, or rejection). For the final test, include final customer acceptance sign-off. **Plan vertical communications with these steps.** 14. Identify the project sponsor, senior executives, and executive customers. 15. Ask each one how often and in what ways he or she wants to receive routine project status reports. 16. Explain project escalation procedures to each one and make sure that each one understands the project's need for prompt response to escalated issues.

TABLE 7-3. Process instructions: Preparing a communications plan (continued on next page)

Process	17. Write up the vertical communications plan.
	18. Identify any other special project communications needs.
	19. Identify project stakeholders and team members in unusual situations, such as working for a vendor, working in a different department from most of the team, working at a different location, or having disabilities requiring special communications tools.
	20. Determine which other team members each of these individuals needs to communicate with.
	21. Contact all these individuals and define appropriate methods of communication.
	22. Identify project team members with special technical needs, such as computer software or equipment that handles specialized data, graphics, or other media.
	23. Prepare a section of the plan covering how all of these methods will be used.
	24. Compile all of this into a project communications plan.
Output	A communications plan, including: • Agendas for gate review • Contact plans for peripheral stakeholders • Other communications guidelines as needed

TABLE 7-3. Process instructions: Preparing a communications plan (continued)

▼ SMART THINKING!

A Communications Plan Saves the Day

I'll admit right upfront that this story starts with a mistake—my mistake. The project is writing this book. Early on, I decided to include case studies by interviewing entrepreneurs from all kinds of businesses—everything from running a coffee shop to developing precision manufacturing test machinery to making TV commercials. I lined up people to talk to.

Then I let the ball drop. My WBS included making a survey and a communications plan, but I got all wrapped up in writing the main text and I kept saying to myself, "I'll do that as soon as I'm back on schedule with writing these other chapters."

Well, I never quite got caught up. And the deadline was looming.

So I sat down and did what I should have done much sooner. I wrote up a mini-project plan for getting the interviews, a communications plan with everyone's name and e-mail address, and a survey form. I started on a Thursday afternoon, with the goal of getting three out of four of the people interviewed as soon as possible. Three days later, I had four interviews completed—including an extra—and the last one scheduled. Writing the communications plan got the roadblock out of the way and got the project rolling. You can see the results in eight case studies in Part III.

The lesson: A good communications plan clears the way for efficient, high-quality work. Don't wait like I did. Write one now!

▼ **THINK FOR YOURSELF!**

Find a Communications Barrier

Think about projects you've worked on that ran into problems. Can you think of one where better communications would have prevented the problem or perhaps solved it quickly? Think out—or even write down—the outline of the communications plan that would have helped in that situation.

▼ **BOOST YOUR BUSINESS!**

Write a Communications Plan Now

If you are doing a project as you work your way through this book, now is the time to follow the instructions in Table 7-3 and write your communications plan.

and customers through a process of ensuring each document and component is satisfactory, make any necessary changes, and resolve problems or consider project cancellation.

- *Component approval by peripheral stakeholders.* Sometimes, approval of a particular project component is needed from just one or a few stakeholders.
- *Vertical communications* to keep the sponsor, senior executives, and executive customers in the loop and escalate issues to them if needed.
- *Other special project communications needs* that may arise.

Build the communications plan cooperatively with those involved and let them know what the plan is. There's no point in building a communications plan and then not communicating it!

For most projects, that's all there is to a communications plan. However, some projects may require additional communications planning. This is especially true if customer surveys or customer

sales are part of the project and the team is not experienced in these areas. For example, for the professional development symposium mentioned earlier in this chapter, we need a special communications plan. Chapter volunteers—who are project managers, not salespeople—will be calling up sponsors and asking them to donate money in return for having a booth at the event.

Project Integration Management: Pulling the Plan Together

You're almost done! Two more small steps and the project plan will be complete.

- *Prepare a change management plan.* So far, everything we've done has been designed to meet the original scope using the original architecture and technical plans. Realistically, though, a change to those plans is a possibility. In some types of projects, change after the plan is laid down is a near certainty. But changing a project in the middle is always expensive and often puts the whole project at risk. So, we need to prepare an integrated change management plan to be ready for change requests, decide what to do, and handle the change well if it happens.
- *Pull the plan together and make sure it works.* So far, we've produced a plan for each of the eight knowledge areas that the PMI defines as essential for project success. Now, we have to look at how one plan affects the other. For example, if our risk plan says this plan is high risk, that means it is likely to take longer and cost more. We should probably add something to our budget and schedule to take that into account, but how much should we add?

These two issues are solved through the planning involved in *project integration management*. Integrating our project plan means tying it all together.

Here is the definition of *project integration management* from *A Guide to the Project Management Body of Knowledge,* 3rd edition, Appendix F:

Project Integration Management includes the processes and activities needed to identify, define, combine, unify and coordinate the various processes and project management activities within the Project Management Process Groups. In the project management context, integration includes the characteristics of unification, consolidation, articulation and integrative actions that are crucial to project completion, successfully meeting customer and stakeholder requirements and managing expectations. The Project Integration Management processes include:

- Develop Project Charter—developing the project charter that formally authorizes a project
- Develop Preliminary Project Scope Statement—developing the preliminary project scope statement that provides a high-level scope narrative
- Develop Project Management Plan—documenting the actions necessary to define, prepare, integrate, and coordinate all subsidiary plans into a project management plan
- Direct and Manage Project Execution—executing the work defined in the project management plan to achieve the project's requirements defined in the project scope statement
- Monitor and Control Project Work—monitoring and controlling the processes required to initiate, plan, execute, and close a project to meet the performance objectives defined in the project management plan
- Integrated Change Control—reviewing all change requests, approving changes,

and controlling changes to the deliverables and organizational process assets
- Close Project—finalizing all activities across all of the Project Process Groups to formally close the project.

We have already discussed creating the project charter and the preliminary scope statement—we called it the *simple project plan.* Now, we will discuss setting up the integrated change management plan and to finishing development of the project management plan. Directing execution, and project monitoring and control will be covered in Chapter 8 and closing the project will be discussed in Chapter 10.

Getting Ready for Changes to the Project. Project change management is crucial to project success. Losing track of a change can mean making a product that simply does not work. Even when it is not that bad, a mismanaged change will do one of these things: reduce product scope (we don't deliver everything the customer wants), reduce product quality and value (the customer gets less from the project, reducing the ROI to below what we promised), or increase project time and cost. Project change management is also complicated because we have to track many project change requests from many stakeholders and decide what to do with each one. Project change management rests squarely on the shoulders of the project manager. Here are the things we should prepare to do.

- *Prevent unnecessary change requests by educating stakeholders.* At the very beginning of the project, we should explain that any feature costs ten times less if it's in the plan than if it is requested later, that adding late changes increases project risk, and that some things that we can include in the beginning simply can't be added later at all. We should encourage stakeholders to participate fully in planning and then let them know that, if they have ideas for changes later, they should definitely tell us, but that we may or may not be able to include them in the project.

- *Set up a system for collecting change requests.* Some people will fill out a change request form; others will expect you to do it for them. Either way, you will need to document change requests in writing. A standard form is available on my web site; the link is on the CD that came with this book.

- *Set up guidelines for processing change requests.* You need to answer questions such as these: Will you only accept truly essential changes or will you allow those that are beneficial and low-risk, even if not essential? Who is involved in the project, customer, and technical aspects of the decision on each request?

- *Create a plan for the following steps.* You will need to gather full information about the change, evaluate it, include others in the evaluation, decide what to do with it, and then, if you approve the change, revise the baseline plan. Evaluating a change request requires looking at the effect of the change on all nine areas of the project: scope, time, risk, quality, procurement, and the rest.

- *Track the status of the baseline plan and all change requests.* At any moment during the project, you should be able to say what changes, if any, have been added to the baseline plan, and also what change requests are under evaluation.

The best thing you can do for yourself is to create a reasonable change management system and use it, project after project.

Creating and Reviewing the Project Plan. It's time to make sure that your plan is a good plan. Bring all of the project planning documents together and, working with at least one member of your team, prepare the plan for the review at the project gate at

> ▼ **KEY TERMS**
>
> **Change request** A request for a change to project scope, time, cost, constraints, or other defining aspects of the project plan or the product we are making. The request maybe initially verbal, but it must then be written down to be managed.
>
> **Project change** An approved change request and all supporting documentation, resulting in a revision of the baseline plan.
>
> **Baseline plan** The project plan we use when we compare status with the project plan.
>
> **Initial baseline plan** The project plan as approved at the end of the planning gate.
>
> **Revised baseline plan** The project plan revised to include one or more approved project changes. From that point forward, the actual work of the project is compared to the revised baseline plan.

the end of planning. Remember: this is your last chance to catch any errors. They'll cost ten times as much later as they cost if you catch them right now!

Have at least two people read everything. Also, be sure to cross-check the plan. Does the activity list match the WBS? Was every activity considered in making the procurement plan, the budget, and the risk plan? Was every component and every document included in the quality plan? Was every stakeholder brought on board in the communications plan?

In addition to this cross-checking, there are some final touches we need to add to our plan:

- *Contingencies.* Contingencies are a way of linking the risk plan back into the cost and schedule baseline. Since we know that some risk events are almost certain to occur—we don't know which ones, but it is very unlikely that no road blocks will get in our way—we can recognize in planning that our project schedule and budget need some leeway.

- *Cross-references.* People need to be able to read the plan and keep track of it. We could make one large document. But it can be better to keep the plans separate and then make a list of all of the documents. Small things like proper footers with revision number, date, and page number are essential. Remember: a plan works only if everyone can stay on the same page!

There is one important thing to note about contingencies. They are not freebies. The money and time are available to be used, but only for a specified reason.

Some project management systems set up two contingencies. One is for project change requests.

It is a pre-approved pot of the customer's money available to pay for extras the customer thinks of later. The second contingency is for project risk events and errors we discover the plan. We draw from this money on two occasions. First, if a risk event occurs and we need extra time or money to deal with it and bring the project back on track. Second, if we were simply wrong about an estimate and work takes longer or costs more than we thought it would.

After we take care of these items, our plan is ready for review at the planning gate.

The Planning Gate Review. When we've thoroughly checked our plan and we think it's ready, it probably is. But what does the team think? What do the customers think? How about the sponsor? Is there anyone who may have just said, "OK" without

---

▼ SMART THINKING!
Rolling-Wave Planning: We Don't Have to Create the Project Plan All at Once

In the last three chapters, we've planned the whole project down to the last detail. But that isn't always possible and, even when it is, it may not be the best choice. There is a way to move the project ahead before we've planned all the details of every part: *rolling-wave planning*. We create our plan—including all nine elements—to a certain level of detail. We might create the WBS and WBS dictionary, but not the full activity list and schedule. Then we take some parts of the plan and work them out in full detail. Other parts, we leave unfinished: we estimate their schedule and cost, define key risks, and figure that we'll plan them as we go along.

In this way, we have a rolling wave of planning. At the planning gate, we approve the plan and then start the work based on the parts of the plan that are complete. Some team members are planning the next part. There's always one part of team doing work and another detailing out the next step of the plan.

Sometimes, we have no choice—we have to do rolling-wave planning. For example, if we have a project that requires particular technical or engineering expertise and the right person for the job isn't available during planning, we may have to leave some areas in the plan unfinished until the right person is available to do the planning.

Rolling-wave planning can be risky, especially because our early estimates might be wrong. But when a team is in a stable environment and doing a type of project that is pretty routine for that team, it can work well most of the time. And it creates a smoother workflow for both the customers and the project team.

The lesson: Rolling wave planning can work with an experienced, stable project team. But if project management is new to you, you're better off nailing down the plan in the beginning.

> ### ▼ SMART THINKING!
> ### Fast-Tracking: A Bit of Risk to Get a Bit Ahead
>
> Sometimes, a gate review can put a whole project on hold. That can be really expensive if you have to keep paying your team. Everyone is sitting around, unable to do more work, while you go chasing an executive who's off on a junket to Alaska or Asia. And what if this is a project that you know is going to go ahead? What are you waiting for?
>
> You can take a risk called *fast-tracking*. You can figure that approval will come and you can get your team working on development while the plan is still in the gate for review. Have team members work on the things that you are most confident are planned well. Then, when the approval comes in, you're on schedule or even a bit ahead.
>
> What if the project gets canceled? Well, that's the risk. Then you started building something no one is going to pay for. So you don't want to fast-track for too long. And you don't want to let a gate review get delayed forever. Focus on getting through the gate before it's too late.
>
> *The lesson:* A little fast-tracking can save you some time at low risk. But don't get too far ahead of the customers' approval.

really reviewing the plan? Is there anyone who maybe just never got onto the same page at all?

The planning gate review is the chance to triple-check all of these things. In addition to reviewing the documents, you should also walk through the schedule with your team members and the major milestones with your customers. In a walk-through, you want everyone to actively picture the work they will do, the documents they will write or edit, and the product components they will create and test. In *The Seven Habits of Highly Effective People,* Stephen Covey says, "Everything is created twice, first in the mind." The clearer the first creation is, the easier and faster the second creation will be. In our project, the plan is the creation of the mind. When it's done, you're ready to bring your product into reality. It's time to do the project.

CONCLUSION: READY FOR LAUNCH

In Chapters 5, 6, and 7, you've learned how to make a really good complete project plan. Work up a plan for yourself or, even better, work up a plan with your team. Then you're ready to launch the second stage of the project—after planning comes doing.

In Chapter 8, Managing Project Work, you'll learn about execution, monitoring, and control. That means implementing the plan, building the product, and making sure you stay on course even as unexpected things happen and people make mistakes. In Chapter 9, Keeping the Project on Track, we'll get into the nuts and bolts of running a status meeting, adjusting tasks to get back on schedule, and rebaselining the project when changes are approved. You're on your way!

It's Time: Put the Plan Together

If you're building a project as you read this book—and that's a really good idea, because the only way to learn project management is by doing it—then it's time to pull your plan together with project integration management and get it through the planning gate.

As soon as you're through the gate, you're ready to do the project and *get it done right!*

Managing
Project Work

IN THIS CHAPTER

In Chapter 8, you will learn all about how to manage project work, staying on schedule and on budget to get the job done right. Specifically, we will cover the following areas:

- *Manage the plan with feedback.* Many people talk about feedback, but very few know how to use it well. You'll learn how to get feedback, use it, and correct your course effectively and efficiently.

- *Understand feedback, monitoring, and control* so that you know how to apply them to managing project work and ensuring project success.

- *Learn the status-reporting process* so that we know how to keep the project on track with our team, step by step.

- *Understand the five process groups and know*

how to use them. The PMI has organized our work into five groups of processes. We'll learn why and how to make use of this idea as we get work done.

- *Choose and improve your life cycle.* Learn how to set up the best series of stages and gates for your project. If you get this right, you prevent the project from running off the road and crashing before you know it.

- *Get clear about the difference between project life cycles stages and project management process groups.* These are two valuable ideas that often get confused. We'll keep them clear for you.

By the end of Chapter 8, all the ideas you need to manage project work will be yours.

PROJECT SUCCESS—AS YOU REMEMBER from Part I—relies on managing the business aspect of the project, the project management aspect, and the technical aspect. After planning, as we begin to do the actual project work. Here's how we keep all three of those on track:

- The *business level* will take care of itself

▼ Focus!

Keep Steering Toward Your Goal

The plan is done, reviewed, and approved. Now, it is time to get to work. But how do we keep the work on track? That's what this chapter is about—the art of navigating. It's just like driving or sailing. Every week or even every day, we check our course with these steps—and correct our direction if we have to.

- Ask where we are and get an answer to that question.
- Look to the plan to see where we want to be.
- See if there is a difference.
- If there is a difference, decide what to do about it.
- Do whatever it takes to get back on course.

In this chapter, we'll get clear on all the ideas about how to stay on course to success. Then, in Chapter 9, we'll put those ideas into practice.

if the project goes well and there are no big changes to the company. During the doing stage of the project, what matters to the business is that the project delivers good results on time and under budget. We make sure that happens by managing the other two levels of the project. But we do need to keep alert for certain problems on the business level, which we need to bring under management:

- *Is the project in trouble?* If the project might fail, then you need to tell the people upstairs—the sponsor, the senior executives, and the customer—so that they won't be surprised if it needs to be canceled.
- *Does the project need something from the company or customer?* Sometimes we need something—money, people, information, decisions, or approvals—from the company or the customer to keep the project moving.

- *Are the project and the company getting along with each other?* Sometimes we hit resistance. Maybe a department manager won't return calls to solve problems about getting people onto the project or getting a specification correct. If this persists, you have to work it through so the project can continue.
- *Is the company changing?* Sometimes a change to the company can require a change to the project plan or even cancellation of the project.

- The *project level* we manage during the doing phase through execution, monitoring and control, and revising our plan as needed. Specifically:
  - *Execution* means directing that specific tasks be done by specific people each day or week.
  - *Monitoring* means gathering status information so you know where the project is and what the risks are.
  - *Control* means evaluating the status and taking corrective action, if necessary.
  - *Revising the plan* happens at four levels.
    - *Corrective action.* We adjust for small things—such as falling a day behind on one task—by arranging for corrective action without changing the baseline plan.
    - *Rebaselining.* Big changes to the schedule or budget require a change to the baseline plan.
    - *Managing risk.* We watch for uncertain and unexpected events that might change the course of the project. We take action to deal with these events. Depending on how much impact an event has on the project, our action may be small (corrective action) or large (rebaselining or change management).

- *Change management.* A change to the scope or a change to the budget or delivery date beyond approved limits requires project change management.

■ The *technical level* of the project is managed through the project life cycle. We have the team do the work and deliver outputs—milestones—to the gate for review. In addition, we use the project communications technique called *escalation.* If a technical problem is found that isn't easy to solve—that creates a risk of delay on the project, blowing the budget, or project failure—then the team reports this to the project manager, who addresses it right away, supporting the team in solving the problem. If the architecture and technical planning are done well and the team is skilled, this is not too likely to happen. But we need to make sure that our team members know that they can tell us—in fact, we encourage it—if there is a problem in the project.

In the 1920s, a bright fellow at Bell Labs named Walter A. Shewhart, one of the founders of quality management, defined a simple approach to doing better work—*plan, do, check, act* (PDCA). About 20 years later Gregory Bateson, a brilliant thinker—one of the inventors of the computer, who also contributed to philosophy, anthropology, and psychology—came up with an idea called *feedback,* which describes how PDCA works. If we understand these ideas, we will know how to keep our projects on track.

We've continued to come up with more good ideas about how to get it done right. Over the last 40 years, a lot of bright people have thought about how to organize projects. Some of that work grew up in specific industries. For example, the first project management life cycle—the System Development Life Cycle (SDLC)—was a solution to delays in developing computer systems. We will use life cycles to organize the technical work of the project so we can keep it under management.

The Project Management Institute (PMI) was founded in 1969 and began to work on defining project management that is independent of any specific type of business and useful for all. The PMI defined the nine knowledge areas we discussed in Part II; I like to think of them as all the bases we have to cover in planning and doing our project. The PMI also defined five process groups. We will use the process groups to organize how we do the project management of the project.

When you know how PDCA, feedback, the life cycle, and the process groups work together, you're you'll know all you need to know to make your project work during the doing stage. We'll get practical and show you how to use what you've learned in Chapter 9, Keeping the Project on Track.

MANAGING TO THE PLAN WITH FEEDBACK

If you want to get the idea of this section quickly, start by forgetting everything you've heard about feedback. First of all, I'm not talking about that horrible squeal that you hear when a microphone is turned up too loud near a speaker. Second, if you have any ideas about "positive" feedback being good and "negative" feedback being bad, forget them now. After I explain what Bateson was really talking about when he invented the idea, we'll explain how so many people have misunderstood the idea of feedback for almost 50 years.

Back in Chapter 6, I compared estimating and delivering a project to aiming and firing a gun. Now, I'm going to change that a bit. Once you fire a gun, there is no way to get the bullet to change course; it's too late. But a project is more like a guided missile than a bullet. We can guide the missile—make it change course—to increase the chances of hitting the target. Once a bullet leaves the gun, it is out of our control; it is unmanageable. But a guided missile is under our control; it is under management. And our project is under management as well.

Because I'm a peaceful fellow, I'm going to use two other analogies. Instead of talking about guided missiles, I'm going to talk about sailboats and cars. All four things—guided missiles, sailboats, cars, and projects—can be managed the same way—with feedback.

What Is Feedback?

Feedback is information we receive that tells us whether we need to change direction to meet our goal, which way, and how much. Bateson defined the idea when working on creating radar-controlled gunnery; the idea was later applied to guided missiles and a lot of other things. What Bateson did was to explain how we do something we've always done. When we take a walk, drive a car, or sail a boat, we use feedback to make sure we get where we want to go.

Before you go any further, read the two sidebars, Navigating a Sailboat and Keeping a Car on the Road, and review the definitions in the Key Terms sidebar.

The example of the sailboat, where we check our location once an hour, is an example of periodic feedback. In driving the car, we are working with continuous feedback: we get information about the car's position in the lane all the time and use it to stay on course, moment by moment. Many other systems work with continuous feedback. A common one is the thermostat that controls the heating and air conditioning in your house. The thermometer constantly—continuously—measures the temperature of the house. The moment the temperature is a few degrees higher or lower than the temperature setting, the thermostat adjusts the heater or air conditioner to turn off or turn on to keep the temperature steady.

Status, Goal, and Situation. When we get status information, it can describe where we are in rela-

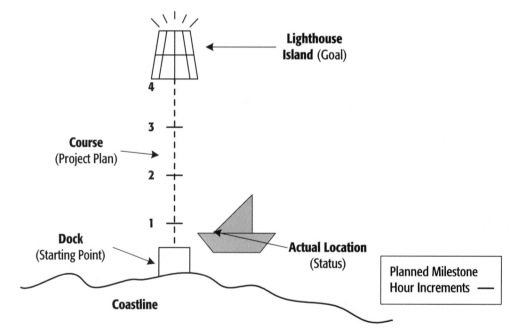

FIGURE 8-1. Navigating a sailboat

▼ BOTTOM-LINE BASICS

Navigating a Sailboat

Figure 8-1 shows how to navigate a sailboat—or keep a project on track. Our journey begins at the dock, on a point jutting out from the coastline. If we follow our plan, we will travel straight up the map, following the dotted arrow to Lighthouse Island and the trip will take four hours.

Let's compare this four-hour sailing trip to a project with a four-week doing stage. We plan our trip or project before we start. Creating the project plan is like plotting our course on the map. We define our starting point and our goal, plan the course from the former to the latter, and set milestones along the way. When we're confident the plan is good, we prepare the sailboat. When we've planned and prepared, we check our plans and preparations. That's the planning review gate. Coming out of that gate, we're ready to launch the sailboat, to set sail toward our destination, or to launch the project, to get to work. Of course, on a sailing trip, we don't want to just sail for four hours and hope we reach the island. Instead, we want to do a reality check once every hour and find out where we are. If we're off course, we'll want to do something about it. The same is true on our project. Once a week, we check the status of the work—find out where the project is—and figure out if we're off course. Here are the steps:

- We find out where we are.
- We compare where we are with where the plan says we should be.
- If there's no difference, if we're right where we planned to be, we just keep going, because we're doing fine.
- If there's a difference, we ask if it's big enough to matter. (If we're running two minutes behind after an hour, we're probably just not going to worry about it.)
- If the difference is big enough to matter, then we need to solve this problem. We'll have to use the techniques for defining and solving a problem that we learned in Chapter 3. Once we do that, we'll know what changes to make to get back on course.
- We execute those changes, taking *corrective action.*

This comparison between a project and sailing defines the process of a *status report.* We'll do more with that later in this section. For now, the key notion is feedback—information we need to know to decide whether to change course and, if so, which way to go.

The lesson: Feedback is a comparison of our current location and our planned location, through a process of analysis called *status reporting.*

tion to our goal. It can also describe where we are in reality, so we can plot our position on a map. If our map of reality is correct, then the results of the two approaches are just about the same. But if our map of reality is wrong or incomplete, then plotting to our destination without paying attention to reality can be very dangerous. Read the sidebar, Knowing Where We Really Are, and then come back to the text to see how this applies to your projects.

As you can see, status reporting on a project is more than just knowing where we are on the plan, where we are in relation to our goal. We also need to know how the team is doing, if the boat has sprung a leak, and whether a hurricane is coming our way. And—this is very important—if our original plan was wrong, then we have a bad map. We'll need to be able to check and see if our plan was realistic or if we misestimated our work or didn't know about a hidden reef.

▼ BOTTOM-LINE BASICS

Keeping a Car on the Road

I hope you've never tried to drive a car with your eyes closed. There's a good reason not to. When we're driving, every few seconds we check our status on the road. If we're between the painted lines that mark the lane and not drifting, then we don't change what we're doing. But if we are drifting to the right or left, we take corrective action, steering the car back into the center of the lane. Let's take a close look at this process:

- We monitor the location of the car in the lane.
- If the car stays in the center lane, everything is fine and we make no changes.
- If the car is drifting, we make a small adjustment to stay on course.
- If the car goes out of the lane, we make a bigger adjustment faster to get back on course.
- As we drive, we are continually monitoring our status—where the car is—and comparing it with the plan—to stay in the lane, marked by painted lines. Many times every minute, we're making a decision to keep driving the way we were or to make a small change.

If we get distracted or we're tired, we don't check as often. Very quickly, we realize that our car is drifting out of the lane. This points out a key issue in monitoring project status—the more often we check, the sooner we can correct our course. We can use that idea on our project in two ways:

- At critical points in the project, we may check status three times a week or even daily, instead of once a week.
- If we train our team members to track their own work, then they keep close control of their tasks. If they drift out of the lane between status reports, they let us know. Our team can help us keep the project under control the same way the raised rumble strips on the painted lines do—by making noise if we're drifting off course.

The lesson: Monitoring a project is like keeping a car in the lane. The sooner we see we're off course, the sooner we can fix it and the more likely we'll make it to our destination.

▼ KEY TERMS

Feedback Information returned to a system that allows the system to adjust its functions to stay stable or reach a desired goal.

Status Current situation, what is happening now. On a project, status includes a description of what work is done, what work is not yet done, and a description of any risks or problems.

Periodic feedback Information gathered at regular intervals, such as hourly or weekly, typical of status reporting.

Continuous feedback Information gathered and used constantly to keep a system in balance or on course.

Status reporting Process of gathering feedback and status information, analyzing it, and deciding what corrective action to take.

Corrective action An adjustment to our plans and actions that will keep us on course and get us to our goal.

▼ SMART THINKING!

Knowing Where We Really Are

Let's say that we're taking our sailboat trip on a clear night. When it comes to the hour and we want to gather status information, we can locate ourselves in relation to the stars. That tells us where we are in the real world. But on a cloudy night, we have to rely on the beacon from the lighthouse. That tells us the direction to take to our destination. If there's another lighthouse in sight, we can see the angle toward both lighthouses and know exactly where we are—which direction is toward the lighthouse and also how far it is to the lighthouse.

So, we can get information about where we are by checking with reality or by checking with signs toward our destination. Checking with signs toward our destination is called *homing in,* as in a homing pigeon—a pigeon that always returns home—or a homing device on a guided missile.

Once we know where we are, we check our position against a map. Why? Because it isn't enough just to know how to get to our destination. We also have to know how to avoid trouble on the way. We need a map that will show reefs and sandbars, so that we can make sure our adjusted course isn't going to run us aground. We need more than a map, too. A look at the weather would be nice; if a hurricane is coming our way, we may want to change our plans.

There are some tragic cases where homing in on a goal without paying attention to reality has created real trouble. For example, a plane landing in stormy weather was receiving a homing signal from the airport. The pilots knew they were lined up to the runway, less than a mile away, and 300 feet above the ground. What they didn't know was that there was a 400-foot hill between them and the airport. The homing signal looked just fine, but, as the plane approached, it crashed into the hill.

Other things can create trouble on our trip. If we are flying or driving a motorboat, we could run out of fuel before we reach our destination. If the airport or dock at our destination closes at a certain time, we have to be able to arrive before that time. If our boat springs a leak, we could sink before we reach the dock.

To safely make it to our destination, we need:

- An accurate, up-to-date map of reality
- A view or picture of reality to see what is going on right now, such as weather conditions
- A plan—a plotted course on the map—that works in reality
- Our location in reality and on the map, based on checking our location in reality or on homing
- Enough resources—fuel—to reach our destination
- To know where we are in time and to be able to reach our destination on schedule
- A ship—or project team—that is functioning and able to stay afloat, keep moving, and be steered in the right direction

The lesson: All of the problems a ship or plane might encounter also apply to a project. If you understand everything that could go wrong, you'll see how to navigate to success.

We'll put that all together a little later in this chapter, when we look at the *status-reporting process.* Before we do that, let's learn about positive and negative feedback, learn how to use the plan, do, check, act (PDCA) system, and then clarify the ideas of feedback in monitoring and control.

Positive and Negative Feedback and Staying in Control.
Let's go back to our example of steering a car to keep it in the lane. If we're drifting to the right, we

steer left. If we're drifting to the left, we steer right. In landing a plane, if we're too high, we go down, and if we're too low, we go up. Course correction is always the opposite—the negative—of the direction that we are going relative to our goal.

This is what makes negative feedback so great. Yup, I want lots of negative feedback. If I'm too high, tell me to come down. If I'm too slow, tell me to speed up. Negative feedback keeps me on course to my destination. Negative feedback keeps me in the lane when I'm driving. Negative feedback keeps me *under control,* instead of going *out of control.*

Suppose you're trying to give me feedback and I misunderstand you. I'm driving with you beside me. You see I'm drifting to the right and you say, perhaps a bit alarmed, "Sid, you're drifting to the right." But I'm not listening well and I hear, "Sid, go right." I'm drifting right and I turn to the wheel right. Suddenly I'm out of the lane and the car might crash. The message I receive is "Turn right," but I'm already turning to the right. That message is positive feedback. *Positive feedback* takes us very quickly *out of control.*

Remember that the horrible squeal you hear when a microphone is put too near a speaker? That's positive feedback, as well. If a microphone picks up the sound from the speaker, then some of the sound is fed back into the amplifier, boosted, and put back out the speaker. The louder sound immediately goes into the microphone, gets boosted again, and comes out. The squeal gets louder and louder—pure distorted noise. That's another example of positive feedback: the system keeps doing more of what it's doing.

"But wait," you say. "I always thought that positive feedback was praise, and that's a good thing, and that negative feedback was criticism, and that's a bad thing. Are you telling me it's the other way around?"

Yup, I am. Don't feel bad that you've got it wrong. Psychologists, human resource managers,

and business people have been making that mistake since the 1950s, when they misunderstood Gregory Bateson's ideas. Bateson's ideas apply with people and animals as well as with machinery. But there's a difference: a car doesn't care how you make a course correction, but people are very sensitive and they do care. Most people don't like to hear that there are problems. They want to hear that everything is OK, that things are just fine: they want reassurance, positive feelings rather than negative. So the term *positive feedback* was misunderstood to mean *reassurance* and *negative feedback* was misunderstood to be *criticism.*

Let's clear all that up. *Negative feedback* isn't criticism; it's course correction. Back in Chapter 1, I said that I like plain, straightforward language. If there's a problem, I'll schedule a solution. If I'm off course, I'll steer in the opposite direction and get on course. To really help me out, give me a reality check. Let me know I'm off course and I'll steer back on. Negative feedback is exactly what I need to stay on course. Positive feedback would be bad, because it's a direction that says, "Keep doing more of the same."

▼ KEY TERMS

Negative feedback Information that directs a system to do the opposite of something it is doing. When applied to a measurement of error, negative feedback can be used by the system to reduce the error and remain on course and under control.

Positive feedback Information that sends a message, "Keep doing more of the same." When used by the system in relation to an error measurement, it increases the error, so the system heads out of control.

Under control Close enough to the plan or path that we can stay on track.

Out of control So far off the plan or path that we can't get back on track and reach our goal.

Negative feedback keeps us on course or under control, which is pretty much the same as under management. That's a good thing. In contrast, if we follow positive feedback about an error, we add to the error. If we're too slow, we slow down until we grind to a halt. If we're too fast, we speed up until we crash. If we're going up and down, we go wildly out of control, up and down more and more, until things blow apart.

Are there any good uses of positive feedback? Yes. It isn't what you want to stay on course by correcting an error, but it does have other uses, as we'll see in the next section.

The Four Levels of Staying on Course. Now we're going to put together all we've learned about feedback. If you understand this section, you'll have all you need to know to use feedback well in four ways to manage your project.

Here are the four levels of staying on course, from the lowest level—most detailed—to the highest level—most general.

1. *Staying on track and on time.* At the lowest level, we stay on course by following the plan at the detailed level. We want feedback continuously or at least very frequently. On a project, a capable, self-managed worker does this himself or herself. If every team member works to deliver on schedule and lets you know when he or she can't, then the project is staying on track at the detailed level and going at the right speed—fast enough to meet our deadline and not so fast that we crash or burn out.

2. *Meeting milestones.* If our plan is good and we're staying on track and going the right speed, then we will meet each milestone on time. At each weekly status meeting, the project manager should be tracking deliverables toward the milestone. If someone needs to work faster or work slower and be more careful, the manager provides negative feedback to help the team member correct course. If

someone is delivering each deliverable in good quality on time and on budget, then the manager can offer positive feedback by saying, "Good job, do it again."

3. *Finding out that the plan or the map is wrong.* What if everyone is working right on schedule, but you check status and realize you won't meet your milestone on time? In that case, you've just discovered that your project plan is wrong. Perhaps something was left out of your WBS and there is more work to do than you expected. In that case, you've discovered that your plan doesn't work in reality and you need to adjust your baseline plan, to *rebaseline*. Sometimes, though, the plan is right, but the map is wrong or incomplete. It doesn't show the reef or the hurricane—the unsolved technical problem or the corporate budget cut. These are managed with *project risk management*, where we keep an eye on uncertain events in reality and adjust our map and plan to get to our destination, even if our course is blocked. This is illustrated in Figure 8-2.

4. *We change our plan and our destination.* Sometimes, we start on a trip to one place and then decide to go somewhere else. This is illustrated a bit later in the chapter, in Figure 8-4. In this case, there is nothing wrong with our old map or our old plan; we just decide on a new destination, so we need a different plan. So we plot a course and stay on track by the new course. In project management, this is called *scope change control:* we manage changes in scope and adjust the plan to reach the new goal.

When things are going well, these four levels are separate from one another and we handle each one separately. The team stays on track and the members let us know if they are getting off track. We do status reporting to see if we're going to make our milestones. We use positive and negative

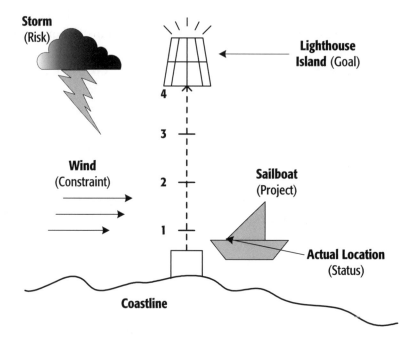

FIGURE 8-2. Risky sailing

feedback to perform appropriate corrective action to reach those milestones. If unexpected events happen, we use risk management. If the customer wants something extra, we do scope change control. Let's return to our sailing trip to see how this lays out on the map.

Figure 8-2 illustrates some of these issues. Reality contains a thunderstorm. That's a risk. If our plan had a risk item, "thunderstorm," then our plan matches reality. In that case, we might be a bit more prepared: we'll be looking out for the storm and we might have some useful gear in the boat. If it wasn't on our risk plan, then our plan didn't match reality as well. Either way, we have to deal with the thunderstorm. Reality also includes wind. Sailboats need wind. But the direction and force of the wind limits our course and our speed. We can't change what the wind is doing, so it's a constraint we have to take into account. Right now, that wind is making our trip more difficult. It's blowing toward the right and we're already too far to the

right, so we're going to have to sail more into the wind to get where we want to go. That will be harder. It will take more effort and be slower than racing downwind. But that's the way we have to go to get to our goal.

On a project, a threatened cut to the budget or the loss of a vendor's services might be like the storm cloud. A rule saying that our team has to drop the project to take care of customer problems would be a constraint, like the wind. As we seek to make the project work, we have to take these aspects of reality into account, whether they are in our plan or not.

So far, we've been talking about the situation as we find it, about managing in the present. It also pays to look ahead. Given the way the wind is blowing, the storm is probably moving straight toward Lighthouse Island, our destination. This means that the storm is going to get worse for us—be a bigger risk. That kind of thinking is called a *risk forecast.*

On a project, if we know that team members must be pulled off to take care of problems and we know that a busy season in sales is coming up, we can make a risk forecast that there will be more interruptions during busy season. The constraint—workers are pulled to take care of customers—plus the risk—busy season—combine to make our risk forecast say, "more interruptions." We could ask, "If we know that there is a busy season, why is it a risk?" Well, it's true that the event is not completely uncertain. But we cannot predict how big it will be and how much it will affect the project. That unpredictability makes it a risk event.

There are other kinds of forecasts besides risk forecasts. And forecasting—looking ahead—is a very good thing for a project manager to do. So let's look at forecasting in Figure 8-3.

In Figure 8-3, we can see the process of navigation, which is status reporting for a sailing trip. After one hour of sailing, we plot our current location. We put that on a map next to our planned course and we can see that we are off course. From this information, we can identify a number of other crucial elements. In project management, we call putting all this information together *status reporting*. By comparing our current status information with our plan, we can figure out these things:

- *Our progress,* what we've done so far, represented by the line from the dock to the boat.
- *A forecast,* the answer to the question, "What will happen if we keep going the way we are going?"—the long diagonal line, showing where we will be after two, three, and four hours and making it clear that we're not going to reach our destination unless we do something.
- *A corrective action,* a change in our course so that we are headed for the island.
- *A corrected course,* our new plan from here forward to our destination

It's a good thing we checked our course after an hour. If we had waited until we'd been sailing for

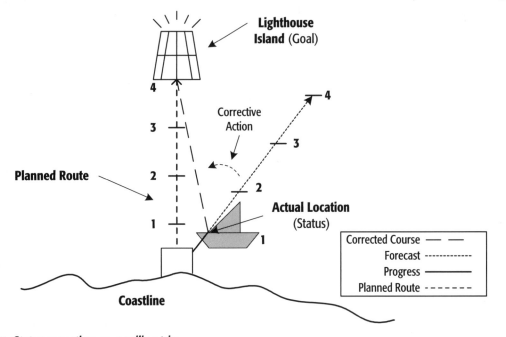

FIGURE 8-3. Status reporting on a sailing trip

> ## ▼ KEY TERMS
>
> **Status information** Any information about where we are and what is going on that is input to status reporting.
>
> **Progress** What we have accomplished from our starting point to our current status.
>
> **Forecast** A prediction of what will happen. Our first forecast is a prediction of what will happen if we keep doing the same things. We can also forecast the results of corrective action, risk events, and other things.
>
> **Corrected course** The new plan from here forward that, we hope, will get us to our destination.
>
> **Rebaseline** To change the plan we are using as input to the status-reporting process.

three hours, our trip would have been a lot longer. This is why regular, frequent status reports are important. Equally important is prompt corrective action. We need to understand the problem, choose the best solution, and implement it promptly to keep our project on track.

Following our new course, we will reach our destination. But we will have deviated from the original plan. If the deviation is small, we can consider that we followed the baseline plan, with some adjustments. If the deviation is large, then we need to rebaseline the plan—to come up with a new plan. There are two signs that a change is large enough to rebaseline.

- *If we will fail to meet milestones.* Since we report milestones to the sponsor, upper managers, and the customer, we need to let them know if we are rescheduling delivery of our milestones.
- *If we exceed our contingencies.* In planning—particularly due to risk planning—we added

contingencies, extra time and money beyond what the plan absolutely needed. As long as we are using our planned contingencies, we are close enough to our baseline plan to keep going with the original plan. If we have to go upstairs to ask for more time or a later delivery date, then we have to revise—rebaseline—our plan.

If we rebaseline a plan, we set aside the original plan and the new plan becomes our new *baseline plan.* For the rest of the project, we compare our status information with this new plan. If we have to rebaseline again, then we always use the most recent plan as the current baseline plan in our status reporting. Of course, when we rebaseline, we have to make sure that everyone—the team members and all stakeholders—knows that we're on a new plan. And we have to tell them significant points about schedule, delivery date, budget, and risk.

Note that when we rebaseline the plan we're still heading for our original destination. All we're doing is correcting our course and plotting a new course—a new plan. In our analogy to project management, we're working with time and cost, but we're not dealing with scope change, where we change our destination.

So far, we've assumed that our basic goal on the project has not changed and that we are planning to reach our goal—get to the island. If we're really late or it's costing a lot more, we've rebaselined, we've changed the plan, but we haven't changed the goal.

What do we do if the goal changes? That's illustrated in Figure 8-4, where we see what happens to our project when someone comes up with a better idea when we're almost to our goal. Someone rolls out a bigger map and says, "Gee, Paradise Island is only a little farther away. That sounds like a lot more fun than Lighthouse Island. Let's go there!"

On a project, that someone could be a customer

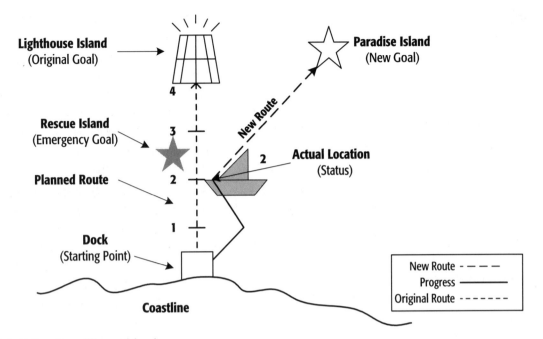

FIGURE 8-4. Sailing to a different island

with a requested addition to scope, or a technical person with a bright idea, or a collaboration— accidental or intentional— between a project team member and a customer, that causes us, in the interest of wanting to offer more, to end up gold-plating and putting the project at risk.

Why is it risky to set a new destination—to add to scope? There are several reasons:

- *We planned for only a four-hour trip.* It's a good thing we're in a sailboat. In a power-boat, we'd run out of gas. On a project, adding to scope can mean out running out of time and money.
- *We don't have a map or a plan.* Did I mention that Paradise Island is surrounded by poi-sonous coral reefs full of killer sharks? Of course not; I didn't think you were planning to go there. We haven't analyzed and brought under control any component that is new to the scope, that was not part of our plan. As a result, there will be unknown risk, quality, time, and cost issues.

There are two ways we can change scope. One is by adding to it—going to Paradise Island. The other is by reducing it—delivering less than we originally planned, which would be going to Rescue Island in Figure 8-4. In the latter case, something has gone wrong—the wind is against us, the boat is damaged, or a sailor got sick. We can't do all that we planned, so we'll do something less, but at least we won't be lost at sea. We reduce scope so that we can deliver something of value, even when we can't deliver all that we contracted to do for the customer. Usually, scope reduction is one possible corrective action for poor planning or for major risk events. If we're running behind, we still have to live with the iron triangle. If we can't take more time and spend more money, we may have to deliver less scope.

Status Reporting: How Often? In Figures 8-2, 8-3, and 8-4, we've shown how we work with the four uses of feedback on a sailing trip—or on a project. It would be nice if the four uses of feedback stayed distinct and separate from one another, but sometimes things get messy.

Let's use a road trip as an example. If we run out of gas or make a mistake and get lost, we've failed to stay in our lane and on time. Once we straighten that out, we may find that we can't reach the hotel where we have reservations—our milestone—before we're too tired to continue driving. So a problem at level one—a failure to stay on course—requires a solution at level three—risk management. We find a closer hotel and stay there that night. But we were too late to cancel our first reservation and the closer hotel is more expensive, so now our trip is over budget. Maybe we can cover this with our contingency fund. But, if we can't, we'll have to save money. Maybe we can do that by spending one day less at the amusement park during our vacation. In that case, we've made a level-four change—a reduction in scope, due to a level-three change—risk management—that came from a level-one change—a failure to stay on course. This is a case of a cascade failure, where

one small error snowballs into a big problem, leading to a real loss of value.

How do we prevent cascade failure? The stronger, the more robust, our team and our plan are, the more likely we can handle the inevitable shocks on the road and stay on course. The key to being robust is making good use of information. This is illustrated in Figure 8-5.

In the sailing trip illustrated in Figure 8-5, we can't follow the plan exactly because the wind is coming straight down our path and a sailboat can't head straight into the wind. The solution is called *tacking*. We sail close to the wind, but a bit to the right, then correct by sailing close to the wind, but a bit to the left. The key question is "How often should we tack? How many times should we change course?"

In Figure 8-5, we see that there is a right frequency to feedback and corrective action. We will never follow the plan perfectly: we will always be making some adjustments. The key is in knowing how often we should receive status information,

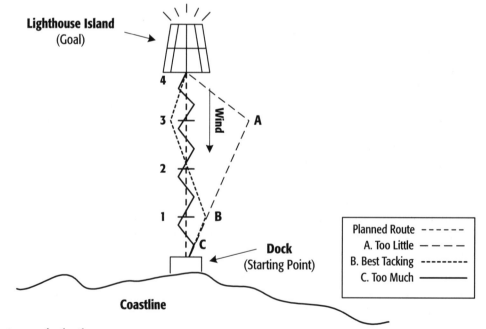

FIGURE 8-5. Tacking to our destination

do status reporting, and take corrective action. Course A shows what happens if we tack too few times: we go the wrong direction for too long, our whole course is longer, and we are inefficient. Course B shows what happens if we tack the right amount. We stay close to the course with few course changes, so we have optimal efficiency. Course C shows what happens if we tack too often—if we over-manage. Every time we tack, we lose speed in changing course. If we tack way too often, then we go so slowly that we are worse off.

The question in project management that is similar to tacking is "How often do we do status reporting?" If we wait too long, the project can go out of control. If we do it too frequently, we wear down the team because we're over-managing, we're always asking them how they are doing and making little changes.

On most projects, we do status reporting and take corrective action on a weekly basis. That fits well with a WBS component size where the lowest-level components are 80 hours of effort—two weeks of work for one person. So, if we've got a project a few weeks long, the team is good, and the risk is low, then weekly status reports are probably good enough. We should feel free to change that general rule and do what is best for the project. If we've got a project that is very new to the team, that has a high risk, or where the team is still learning self-management, then we probably want to run a status meeting twice a week. For truly critical projects, we will want to check status daily. We can also change the frequency of status meetings during the course of the project. If we see a storm coming or we have just changed course to a new destination—that is, if project risks or scope change issues have come up—we can meet with the team or with certain team members more often until things return to normal.

You now know all you need to know about how to use feedback to make a project succeed. The process of status reporting doesn't use feedback alone; it also uses the plan, do, check, act (PDCA) technique. Let's learn PDCA, which is a great way you and your team members can use feedback and be more self-managed so that they stay on track and on time. After you learn PDCA, we'll put feedback and PDCA together into a step-by-step procedure for status reporting and corrective action.

Plan, Do, Check, Act (PDCA)

PDCA was originally a method for engineers, workers, and teams to improve quality in industrial and electronics production. As mentioned earlier, it was developed by Walter A. Shewhart of Bell Labs in the 1920s. He published the idea in the 1930s and went on to develop the field we now call quality control. W. Edwards Deming, the founder of the Total Quality Management methodology, promoted PDCA. The goal of PDCA was to apply the attitude and process of the scientific method to problems of process and engineering in business.

The basic idea of PDCA is that an engineer, seeing a problem, can follow these four steps:

- *Plan.* Design an experiment, a change that he or she thinks will solve the problem.
- *Do.* Create a situation where the test can be performed and results can be gathered as measurements comparing the results of the new approach and the results of doing things the old way.
- *Check.* See if the new method achieved the desired improvement.
- *Act.* Take appropriate action. For example:
  - If the improvement was achieved, implement the change permanently.
  - If some improvement was achieved, but not enough, alter the experiment and try again.
  - If nothing changed or if things got worse, analyze the results and design a new experiment.

PDCA was originally designed for manufacturing and assumed that work environment. Important assumptions included that there was ongoing production, that there was an output specification for the product, that PDCA would be applied iteratively to production problems where the output was not meeting the specification, and that what was being changed was the technical or engineering work process.

Deming promoted PDCA as a core component of Total Quality Management (TQM). In fact, many people think he invented it, though actually he learned it from Shewhart. In TQM, PDCA grew in several ways:

- The Japanese developed a teamwork model for quality management, and so PDCA was used by teams, not just by individual engineers. With several experts proposing different causes for the defect, the teams planned, did, checked, and acted upon better experimental solutions, leading to faster improvement.
- PDCA expanded across the supplier-input-process-output-customer (SIPOC) chain. If a team of engineers eliminated all significant problems caused within their own processes, the next step of improvement was to improve the inputs they received from their suppliers. They did this by requiring higher standards and, at the same time, teaching PDCA and other TQM methods to their vendors.
- PDCA was used to examine all processes, including management processes, not only technical work processes. As a result, work was managed more effectively and costs, delays, and time to problem resolution all decreased.
- PDCA was linked to the later notion of feedback. Understanding how feedback works allowed PDCA to be generalized beyond manufacturing to a larger context of other industries and businesses.
- Most recently, PDCA was expanded by Six Sigma quality engineers to DMAIC—Define, Measure, Analyze, Improve, Control. That level of quality engineering is really beyond this book; I mention it so that, if you know Six Sigma or DMAIC, now you know where they came from and you can see how to apply them on projects.

All of this is good, but how to we take PDCA out of the production world and apply it to our projects?

1. We replace the product specification from production with the requirements specification of our product.
2. We realize that we are trying to deliver a unique product just once. As a result, our goal is not a change to improve production. Instead, it is a change to the product: we experiment and refine what we're making until it meets the requirements specification.
3. We allow enough time in our project schedule to plan, do, check, and act repeatedly until we get the results the customer requires by including PDCA activities as project quality management activities and project technical quality work activities in our schedule.
4. We document the changes that result from PDCA into the project plan and the technical product plan. If the changes are within our baseline plan and allow us to meet specifications, we're done. If the changes require extra time or money, then we are dealing with project risk management by applying our contingency funds or time to the project. If the changes give us a reason to recommend a change to the scope, then we escalate the issue to get customer approval through project change management, more formally called *integrated change control.*

The neat thing about PDCA is that it is easy to learn and implement. You can have everyone on

▼ SMART THINKING!

No Gold-Plating!

PDCA is great, but, for some engineers and technical folks, it can become a runaway train, especially if they are perfectionists. Each PDCA cycle leads to an improvement and also to ideas for more improvements. Before you know it, the product has bells, whistles, and gold-plating the customer never asked for. The engineers think it is great, but the customer didn't ask for something ten times better ten weeks late at ten times the price.

How do we set a limit to prevent this? We teach our team: "Use PDCA to meet the customer requirements. The moment you meet them, bring me a list of your other good ideas—plan them (P), but don't do them (D). Before you do them, I'll check them (C) against the project baseline plan, schedule, and budget, and I'll also find out if the customer wants them. If we can fit them into the plan or if the customer approves the change, I'll give you the green light."

If we don't do this kind of tracking, we are allowing scope creep. It really doesn't matter if the ideas for bells and whistles come from the team or from the customer. Either way, new ideas during the production (doing) stage of the project add ten times as much to the cost as they would if they were put off to the planning stage of a later project.

The lesson: Don't let any cycle become a positive feedback loop. Even a team trying to do a better and better job can take your project out of control.

---

your team checking their work and fixing it as they go. Here are some advantages to that:

- If each person checks his or her own deliverables before the gate, the odds are that there will be less rework at the gate review.
- If people get used to the idea that everything gets checked, then they won't take it as personally when their work is reviewed.
- If you can set up a team or buddy approach where people check each other's work, then you get the team members focused on helping each other do high-quality work. This leads to a better work environment—more supportive and less critical—as well as to better project results.

While our teams are doing PDCA to deliver better technical results, we can apply PDCA to solve project management problems. If we see that we are running persistently behind schedule or over budget or that we are failing to keep track of what a vendor is doing, we can do something about that

problem with PDCA. Our planning (P) would probably use the techniques for defining a problem, defining multiple causes, and defining a root cause from Chapter 3, Solving the Right Problem. In fact, once you define the problem, you'll probably find a solution worth trying right here in this book! Then you do it (D), and check (C) if it works. If it does, then you make sure you keep using that improved way of managing the project; that's your action (A).

In summary, PDCA is a simple, effective tool for improving both project technical work and project management processes.

Understanding Feedback in Monitoring and Control. Have you read this section on feedback and PDCA closely? Check that closely. If you didn't, go back and play with the ideas a little more before you go on to the two sections.

In the next section, on the *status-reporting process*, you will learn a step-by-step process for receiving status information and using it to take corrective action, keep the project on track, and manage the project with all four of the levels of feedback we introduced above. After that, you'll learn about the five PMI process groups and you'll see how we include feedback to ensure and improve project effectiveness and efficiency all the way through the doing stage of the project.

THE STATUS-REPORTING PROCESS

Picture yourself and your team in the middle of the project. A week ago, you passed the planning gate, assigned all the members, and got them started. One week has gone by. What's going on? Have people gotten things done? Have they gotten stuck and not told you? Have they decided on a better way to do things and gone off in a totally different direction? Did they misunderstand you when you assigned the work, so that they aren't doing it yet or are doing something other than what you want? Or—and this is typical of a project in a small business—have they gotten caught up with routine work or customer requests or other problems and not done any work on the project at all? Remember the principle auditors follow: "Without attention, everything degenerates over time." All of the things I mentioned come up routinely. And the solution is to prepare, do, and follow through on the weekly planning meeting.

Here are the steps of gathering and using status information. Note that the weekly planning meeting—usually called a *status meeting*—is in the middle, covering steps 9 to 17.

1. Get *status information from every team member on every assigned task.* Get the status of each assigned task, including hours worked, percent complete, and any problems from each person working on the project. Also ask about the status of any risks related to their work and any new risks they see. You can gather this via a conversation, an e-mail inter-

> ## SOMETHING SLIPPED!
> ### The Status Meeting Is Really a Planning Meeting
> If you go back about 20 years, before project management tools were well known and before we were all connected by computers, status meetings really were about gathering status information. Now, we can be much more efficient. Although we still call them status meetings, the meetings really should be *weekly project-planning meetings.* We should get the status *before* the meeting, prepare the status report, and then meet to decide what to do—what corrective action to take—based on the status report. As one project manager I was talking to recently put it, "If you launch a meeting by asking people for status, you've already missed the boat."

office memo, or data entered directly into a project management or timesheet information system. The time you collect this information is the *status date.*

2. *Enter the status information into your project management information system.* You may be working with Microsoft Project® or another package or simply using Word and Excel tables. Whatever your system, mark off the items that are complete, count up the hours, and update the project records of actual work done, actual time spent, and actual money spent.

3. *Define project status.* Know what is done and what is not, how much time has been spent, and how much money has been spent. This is the equivalent to being able to map your location when you are sailing so you can say, "We are here."

4. *Compare your status with your goal for the week.* Where did you plan to be at this point? Check the plan and see if each activity that was

to be done by the status date has been done. Were any other activities done, indicating you are ahead of schedule? Have you spent more or less money and time than planned? Each difference between the plan and the actual situation is a *variance.*

5. *Evaluate each variance to see if it is significant.* Small variances—such as someone being one hour behind on a ten-hour job or an item budgeted for $100 costing $105.23—are just not worth worrying about. If you paid attention to them, you'd be micromanaging. That would hurt team morale and not be worth the time, energy, and headaches. So do something about only problems that are big enough to matter. A difference between planned WBS items (work) completed and actual work completed is a *scope variance,* a difference in effort (hours worked) is a *time variance,* and a difference in money spent is a *cost variance.* As you review the plan, also check the status of risk events and look for signs of new risks.

6. *Sort the significant variances into groups according to what you are going to do next.* Here are the groups:
   - *Items that involve just one team member and don't change scope, project, or schedule significantly.* If a person reported a problem and asked you for help or is repeatedly running late or doing poor-quality work, then resolve that with the person one on one before the staff meeting.
   - *Small but significant variances in scope, time, cost, or quality.* For these, propose a solution to the worker or get a proposal from the worker and then put the item on the agenda for the status meeting.
   - *Significant variances in work done, time, cost, or quality.* For these, you are going to have to pull the team together, evaluate the problem, and develop a solution.

   - *New risks.* Identify any new risks, update the risk plan, and prepare it for discussion at the weekly planning meeting.
   - *Proposed or approved changes to product scope.* Identify all issues that would actually change what you are making and prepare them for the project change management process.
   - *Other issues.* Review all nine project management areas and any other communication or conversations you've had and add them to the meeting agenda. On the agenda, specify whether you just want to be aware of this issue, you want someone to plan action, or you are going to take action yourself.

7. *Help team members stay on track and on schedule.* Check each item of the types in the first two bullets under step six and address them with the team member before the weekly planning meeting.

8. *Prepare the agenda for the weekly planning meeting, including all items from step six.* For items from the first bullet, you can say something like "Joe is running a bit behind, but he'll take care of it." For each other item, define the gap and determine whether the team needs to monitor it or to take some action. If action is needed, put planning and assigning that action onto the meeting agenda.

9. *Hold the weekly planning meeting.* Cover all items on the agenda. Get everyone on the same page. Spend less time on smaller items and items with a clear solution. Spend more time on items that could really change the project plan. Make time for brainstorming on complex issues to define the problem clearly and come up with proposed solutions.

10. *Discuss scope issues.* Is work getting done on time? If not, why not and what can be done? Remember that there is no such thing as

"almost done" and that when a person says a job is done, someone else can use that deliverable as input without needing an explanation or a fix.

11. *Discuss time and cost issues.* If the project, in general, is using more effort than expected or running behind schedule or spending too much money, bring that up with the team.

12. *Discuss quality issues.* If things are getting done, but not well, work will jam up at the review gate.

13. *Review the risk plan.* Check status on every risk. Introduce the new risks that were reported or that you learned about. Have the team suggest any possible new risks—a little proactive worry is good for a project. Cross off any risks you have gotten past and make sure that someone is watching or working on every current risk.

14. *Review other issues as needed.* If there are any issues of human resources, procurement, or anything else, now is the time to bring them up.

15. *Discuss whether the plan needs to be rebaselined.* If the project is running so far behind or over budget that it will not meet the gates, then you need a major revision to the schedule—a rebaselining. If you do, let the team know and expect to spend some time during the week figuring out the best way to make the plan work.

16. *Discuss whether the scope or the whole project needs to be changed.* Work through the status of change requests and decide what needs to be done.

17. *Close the weekly status meeting.* Make sure that every item is assigned to someone on the team for some further monitoring, planning, or work.

18. *Follow up on routine items to keep on course with the baseline plan.* Take care of things and help any team members who need or want help.

19. *Keep monitoring and managing risks.*

20. *Follow up on rebaselining, if needed.* This will involve some time developing a new plan and

schedule and some time meeting with people to figure out the best new plan and to come up with a permanent preventative solution for the root cause of the problem that forced a rebaselining.

21. *Follow up on project change management.* Approve or reject changes, inform people of the decisions, and rebaseline if needed.

That's a lot! Now you know why a project needs a manager! But it may not be as much as it seems. If you've planned the project well using the method in Chapters 5, 6, and 7 and you've been very clear in defining work and helping your team as we discussed in Chapter 4, then many of these items won't come up at all. The team members will manage the small items themselves and our good work in product specification and project planning minimizes the likelihood that major delays, scope changes, or risks will throw us off our original plan.

Remember that, although I called this a weekly meeting, you may choose to track all of these items twice a week or daily if the project needs particularly close monitoring due to high risk or other complications.

▼ SMART THINKING!

A Status Meeting for a Team of One

Of course, in small businesses, we often do small projects. The project might be short—a few hours of work over a few days. And the team might be small—you may be the only person on the project, a team of one.

You should still gather status information, do status reporting, and take corrective action. When you are working alone, it is easy to keep going and think you're doing well when actually you've lost track of something or you're running behind and you don't know it. Sitting down and going through the 21 steps of status reporting and corrective action is as important for a team of one as it is for a team of 20.

USING THE FIVE PROCESS GROUPS

The Project Management Institute organizes its 44 standard processes for project management into five process groups. (It also organizes them into nine knowledge areas, which we covered in Chapters 5, 6, and 7.) Now, we'll see how to use process groups to organize management of the project and ensure success of the whole project and of each stage.

Here is the definition of a process group and also the definitions of the five process groups from the glossary of the Project Management Institute's *A Guide to the Project Management Body of Knowledge (PMBOK® Guide)—Third Edition*, Project Management Institute, Inc., 2004.*

- *Project Management Process Group.* A logical grouping of the project management processes described in the PMBOK® Guide. The project management process groups are *initiating processes, planning processes, executing processes, monitoring and controlling processes*, and *closing processes*. Collectively, these five groups are required for any project, have clear internal dependencies, and must be performed in the same sequence on each project, independent of the application area or the specifics of the applied project life cycle. Project management process groups are not project phases.

- *Initiating Processes.* Those processes performed to authorize and define the scope of a new phase or project or that can result in the continuation of halted project work. A large number of the initiating processes are typically done outside the project's scope of control by the organization, program, or portfolio

*This was developed by the Project Management Institute. Copyright and all rights reserved by PMI. Material from this publication has been reproduced with the permission of PMI. The applies to each citation of this book as they appear in this chapter.

processes and those processes provide input to the project's initiating processes group.

- *Planning Processes.* Those processes performed to define and mature the project scope, develop the project management plan, and identify and schedule the project activities that occur within the project.

- *Executing Processes.* Those processes performed to complete the work defined in the project management plan to accomplish the project's objectives defined in the project scope statement.

- *Monitoring and Controlling Processes.* Those processes performed to measure and monitor project execution so that corrective action can be taken when necessary to control the execution of the phase or project.

- *Closing Processes.* Those processes performed to formally terminate all activities of a project or phase and transfer the completed product to others or close a canceled project.

Figure 8-6 illustrates the cycle of initiating, planning, executing, monitoring and controlling execution, replanning as needed, and closing a project or a stage of a project. Each process group is represented by a box and the flow of information and work is shown by the arrows.

The PMI process group model relates to an entire project and also to each stage of a project. (That's progressive iteration again.) Since we're talking about the doing stage—the production stage—of our project, let's see how we use the five process groups as the team does the work of the project.

- When we exit the *planning* gate, we *initiate* the doing stage.

- In assigning tasks, telling team members to start working, and allocating time and money for the work, we are getting the team to *execute* the project.

- To make sure that the team is executing in the right direction, we gather status infor-

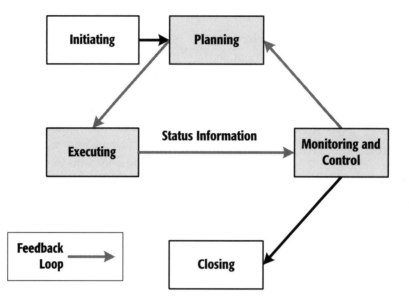

FIGURE 8-6. PMI's process groups shown as a feedback cycle

mation. The status information feeds into our *monitoring and controlling* processes, such as scope change control, risk monitoring and control, and quality control. We tie all of those together with integrated change control.

- If our analysis in the controlling processes indicates a significant variance, we need to do some *planning* work. We've gone around in a feedback loop and we're back to planning. What happens next depends on the size and significance of the variance.
  - If the change is small, the planning work is just a decision on what corrective action to take. We assign that corrective action to a team member to *execute*.
  - If the change is about a risk issue, we manage it with risk monitoring and control and use our contingencies to allocate the time and money while *executing* a *contingency plan*.
  - If the change is large enough that we will miss milestones, miss delivery, or go over

budget, we do more planning so that we can *rebaseline* the project.
  - If the change involves a change of scope— if we're going to increase, decrease, or change what we are delivering—then we *plan* and *execute* project change control. In project change control, we are likely to rebaseline the project.

We've now finished a very thorough look at how to use feedback, PDCA, and the five process groups—particularly monitoring and control—to keep our project on track during the doing stage. Now, let's see if we can improve our use of the project life cycle, stages and gate reviews.

CHOOSING AND IMPROVING YOUR LIFE CYCLE

This discussion builds on the rather thorough introduction to life cycles in Chapter 2, Why Businesses Need Successful Projects. Let's recap the main points about project life cycles from Chapter 2:

- Life cycles are the best way to keep a

medium-sized or large project organized, because the project is too big to think about as a whole.

- Life cycles break a project up into stages. At the end of each stage, we have a gate, where we review the work of the stage and decide whether to proceed as planned, to change course, or to cancel the project.
- The simplest life cycle has three stages: plan, do, and follow through. These three stages are based on the 1:10:100 rule, which shows that, in all industries, fixing a mistake in planning has the lowest cost, fixing a mistake while doing the project work (building the product, service, or solution) costs ten times as much, and fixing the mistake near the end or after the project costs 100 times as much or more.
- To use the principle of the 1:10:100 rule, good project management puts a heavy emphasis on planning and then on making sure the plan is correct at the planning gate review.
- All life cycles are modeled after the biological life cycle, with a very long history across all types of plants and animals.

In this section, we'll look at two things we can do to help ensure project success while also making project management more efficient, which will reduce the cost of the project. First, we'll look at how to do good gate reviews. Second, we'll go into a bit more depth about how to choose or improve the project life cycle that you use.

Improving Gate Reviews

There are two essential things to remember about a gate review:

- *A gate review is a process.* Processes take time, so include enough time for them in the project plan. And be sure that the work of each stage is done well. The output of a stage is the

milestone package—the input to the gate review. And every process does better if it gets good inputs.

- *A gate review involves decisions.* If someone asks, "What will you do after the gate review?" the only answer is "That depends on what we find during the review." In the gate review, you will find things that will lead you to choose to move ahead, to take corrective action, to address risks and project change, to rebaseline, and maybe to cancel the project.

The best way to have a good gate review is to be doing good work on the project. Then, conduct a thorough, objective review and take action appropriate to what you find. The worst thing you can do is to allow bad work on the project and then let that bad work slip through the gate. In the next stage, it will cost ten times as much to fix it.

Here are some steps for helping your team members make sure they do good work on the project:

- *Define jobs and deliverables clearly* using the tools in Chapter 4.
- *Build a plan with a lot of small deliverables.* That way, you can know when each piece of work is done. It also allows you to tell each team member, "Good job, do it again" several times a week. That's effective positive feedback.
- *Involve the team.* Team members who understand the value of the project will want to do good work and they will focus on quality and deliver.
- *Teach your team that there's no such thing as "almost done."* For some people, this is a hard lesson to learn. It involves changing a lot of habits. Constantly encourage each team member to complete every task, to check with other team members who will use his or her deliverables, and to follow through on every task.

- *Implement buddy checking or team checking of small deliverables.* Say to your team, "There are always errors. The only question is 'Do you want us to find them or do you want your customer to find them?'" An independent check increases the chances of catching errors. Allow your team members to check your work and then offer to do the same for them.
- *Lock down good deliverables at the weekly planning meeting.* When a job is well done, make sure the final version is saved to include in the package for gate review.
- *As you get close to the gate review, focus on checking and fixing.* Make it clear to your team that you don't just want everything done for the gate review; you want everything done *right*.

If you follow these steps, your milestone package—all of the input for the review—will be in really great shape. When the work is done well, you will either approve the end of the stage and move on or, at most, require one or two small corrective actions. That is good. It really slows down a project when a major problem or several big and small problems show up at the gate review, so that a lot of rework is required. If you have to do a lot of rework, then you'll have to rebaseline your plan. That increases time and cost, perhaps delaying project delivery and certainly reducing ROI. It also increases project risk. If a milestone package fails gate review and requires extensive rework, then the final delivery may have to be reduced in scope, may contain errors, or may fail altogether.

If you followed the steps listed above, then your milestone package—the collection of deliverables

▼ SMART THINKING!
Four Reasons to Blow a Gate Review

A gate review is actually pretty simple and obvious. We check our work. If it's good, we go ahead. If it's not good, we fix it before we go ahead and adjust the plan to include the extra work. If it's really bad, we call it quits on the project.

If it's so simple, then why am I spending time explaining how to do it well? Because—often without realizing it—we are pressured to do a bad gate review. Here are four common reasons for a bad gate review, with replies to each one.

1. *I promised I'd get it done.* Reply: Thinking like that focuses only on time, not on quality. If you deliver lousy results on time, the next stage will go badly and the customer will be dissatisfied. Better to review it and rework it now than to lose the customer or have to rework later, after you've lost the customer's trust.

2. *I'm sure we're doing a good job.* Reply: Remember the audit rule—trust but verify. A gate review makes sure that everything works *together* and that nothing is missing. Without the review, the milestone package can look good, but be rotten on the inside.

3. *We're already running behind.* Reply: Yup—and if you let a mess slip through the gate, you'll be a lot worse off. It's best to get on top of the whole problem now.

4. *I've never done a review and things usually go OK.* Reply: If "usually OK and occasionally rotten" is good enough for you, then I would not want to do any business with you.

The lesson: Be aware of pressure to skip or skimp on gate reviews. Resist at all costs! Success of your project depends on good gate reviews.

that result from all the work in this stage and earlier stages—is in good shape for the review. That will make your work easier. But, whether the deliverables are all ready or not, you still want to do a good gate review.

A gate review has a different focus from our weekly planning—status—meeting. The weekly meeting focuses mostly on work process. We're asking how the work is going and making sure it is going well through corrective action. We pay attention to results, but the focus is on process. In a gate review, we're not concerned about process. Our whole attention is on the quality of the product. We would do the same gate review of a product whether it was done by our team, done by an outsider, or dropped off by a UFO from Mars. The process that produced the milestone package doesn't matter any more. All that matters is whether the package is good.

Here are the steps of a gate review:

- Inspect the milestone package.
- Decide on appropriate action, execute it, and adjust the project plan.
- Review and revise the plan for the next stage.
- Launch—initiate—the next stage.

Here are the key questions to answer when you inspect the milestone package:

- *Is the package complete?* Are all milestone deliverables from this stage and previous stages here in their most recent (final or current) form?
- *Is each package good?* Does each package meet or exceed specifications and quality standards?
- *Do all the packages align and work together?* Do the pieces of the whole product, service, or result work as a system? Is our deliverable what we planned to deliver? What are the differences?
- *For each variance, how much does it matter?* If something is missing, what will it take to get it? If something is unfinished or untested, what will it take to finish it, test it, and make sure it works? If something isn't up to specification or standard, what will it take to fix it, test it, and ensure conformance and quality?
- *How does the project plan look?* Although the focus is on deliverables, we also look at the plan, because the plan is a deliverable of the project. If we see, for instance, that the results are good, but only because a lot of overtime is being used, then we may want to correct that. We review the plan according to the appropriate practices in all nine knowledge areas and we can recommend changes to the way we are running the project, as well as require changes to the results.

Here are several key qualities of a good gate review:

- *A good gate review is independent.* We want to look at the delivered work packages as objectively as possible. It doesn't matter who did the work. It doesn't matter if we all thought it was great a week ago at the last planning meeting. We're here to inspect the package and make sure it is good.
- *A good gate review is comprehensive.* We look at all deliverables of this stage and prior stages.
- *A good gate review ensures quality.* We don't just want it done or even done to specification; we want it done thoroughly to specification and to meet customer expectations with quality. We want it done *right*.
- *A good gate review ensures consistency.* Our weekly planning meetings focus on current work. A gate review is a chance to look at the bigger picture. Do all the parts work together? Do the parts and the documentation match?
- *A good gate review involves stakeholders where appropriate.* If at all possible, we want to get customer approval on completed compo-

nents and deliverable documentation. If we don't, we may think that we're doing a good job, but we could be wrong. The gate review is a chance to make sure we are meeting customer needs and expectations.

After reviewing the milestone package, we direct appropriate action and update the project plan to include this action. Here are the actions we might direct from the gate review concerning the milestone package and project work to date:

- *Plan for corrective action* to fix any part of any work package.
- *Call for rebaselining* if the review indicates that the project schedule or budget needs to be changed.
- *Plan for changes to project scope.* Any outstanding change requests should be clarified and, if possible, resolved during the review. New change requests may be initiated.
- *Call for a project review.* A project review is even more in depth than a gate review. A small project review may focus on one area that is going out of control, such as cost or risk. A full project review is called if it appears that the whole project is at risk or going out of control. In the language we introduced earlier when we talked about feedback, we call for a project review if we discover that our project plan is not a good map of reality.

In addition to reviewing the past, the gate review process also looks ahead and makes decisions about the future, about the next stage. You should review the plan for the next stage to ensure a high chance of success. In the review, change the plan as needed. Then, you are ready for the last step of the review—deciding whether and how to initiate the next stage. Here are the options:

- *Initiate the next stage now.* If there is no corrective action needed or if corrective actions

are small, we can initiate the next stage at the end of the review.
- *Delay initiating the next stage until corrective action or rework is done and milestone deliverables are reviewed again.* We do this if the changes are large enough that the team has to focus on rework, not new work.
- *Split the project into subprojects.* If we can separate activities in the new stage, we can move ahead with items that are ready while other items are being reworked. As explained in Chapter 7, this technique, fast-tracking, adds to project risk.
- *Withhold approval for initiating the next stage.* If there are serious problems on the project, we may withhold approval until rework is complete and we are sure the project can be completed.
- *Cancel the project.* If we see that there is no way to make the project work or if the customer no longer needs the project done, it is better to stop now than it is to throw good money after bad.

With all these decisions made and plans laid, the stage review is complete. One note: it's really better than it looks. In laying out all of the possibilities, I end up giving equal time to success, problems, and failure. In fact, in this chapter, I probably spend more time discussing problems and what to do about them and failure and how to cancel a project than I do talking about success and moving ahead. There's good reason for that—this chapter is about how to resolve small problems and stay on course. But, as you read it, it can begin to seem like you're lost in a thicket. When you use plans and manage well, it isn't like that. It's just the opposite—there's a clear path with an occasional bramble or fallen branch and sometimes a choice to make at a fork in the road. On a well-run project, a gate review is like a pit stop. You take a quick break, make sure everything is OK, fuel up, and get back into the race.

Adding Stages to Your Life Cycle

Every project should have a life cycle of at least three stages: plan, do, follow through. I mean that. Even a two-hour project will go better if you get clear on what you are going to do, do it, and then make sure you deliver well.

For example, an old friend and client asked me to review a new marketing piece and wanted to pay me for two hours of my time to do it. Before I agreed, we had two phone meetings. In those meetings, I shared my ideas about how marketing worked and interviewed him about how he would use the piece, who would see it, and what he hoped they would do when they saw it. Once I had answers to those questions, I knew what kind of comments he wanted from me and I was ready to get to work. He sent me the brochure and I did the two hours of work, adding my notes. Then I followed through by delivering it via e-mail, calling him to make sure he got it, and sending him a bill. He thanked me for the work, but forgot to pay the bill before he left on vacation, so I had to do a bit more follow-through to finish the job.

The point is, anything we do isn't just work. If we don't plan, we won't do good work. If we don't follow through, someone will not get what he or she wanted and be disappointed. Our work plan will be a lot more accurate if we always include planning and following through as well as working. If each work plan is accurate, it will be much easier to make an affordable program plan and business plan.

Most projects in a small business can be completed using just the three simple stages—plan, do, follow through—and a gate for review before the project and after each stage, as discussed in Chapter 2. However, sometimes, we should add another stage. Or, to be more precise, we should split one of our stages into two. Let's look at the reasons for splitting up each stage.

Reasons for splitting the planning stage:

- *We do a lot of experimental projects—research and development (R&D).* One of the ideas of R&D is to come up with lots of bright ideas, many of which turn out to be bad ideas or impossible projects. In that case, we might want to have a short initial *concept stage*, where we take a quick look at an idea, work up a quick and dirty plan, and decide if the project is workable and the ROI makes it worth

---

▼ Bottom-Line Basics
Recheck the Rework

There is a sloppy mistake some people make at gate reviews that we need to avoid. If we assign corrective action or rework, we can't assume it will get done and get done right. We must schedule an additional review to check the work package after the corrective action or rework is complete. We can keep this review small by checking only the changed package and then checking that the changed package works with the whole system, but we must ensure that the check is done.

If we don't, we're almost sure to include errors in the final product. Some studies have shown that, in writing computer software, for every five bugs fixed, one new one is added. It's essential to check corrected and reworked packages thoroughly, both to ensure that the problem we found is fixed and to make sure that no new problems have crept in.

The lesson: Corrective action and rework assigned at a gate review must be checked thoroughly. We can't just assume the fix was done right and let it go through.

▼ SMART THINKING!

Technical, Project, and Business Reviews

As we've mentioned, a project needs to be managed at three levels: technical work, project management, and business issues. I've reversed the list here for a reason. I'm going from the bottom up because a gate review is mostly a technical review. But it is good to touch on all three levels:

- In the technical review, we make sure that all the work packages—components—are working well and working together.

- In the project review, we adjust the plan to make sure that everything gets done.

- In the business review, we check with the customer to make sure that we know about anything that would make us rethink the product we are delivering or the project work and resources.

The lesson: A gate review is primarily a review of the technical work of the project, but we should also include a review of the project management and business levels.

▼ SMART THINKING!

Why Do Experts Charge So Much?

People thinking about going into business often see that they can do work as good as—or better than—an expert who charges an arm and a leg. Often, that's true. But they also think that they can charge less and be happy. Many try—and find out quite quickly that the problem is that experts can't charge for all the time they spend working. They charge for the doing stage. But the planning stage is mostly done during negotiations and while writing proposals, which is before billing starts. And the follow-through is mostly after the billing is done. And we experts can't charge for our overhead time at all. Most people who start out charging less than others find out pretty fast that, to cover planning, follow-through, and overhead, they have to charge the same arm and leg that every other expert charges.

The lesson: A lot of dollars per hour doesn't add up to a lot of dollars per year, because there is a lot of essential work time we can't bill for.

---

doing, expecting that we will *actually cancel most projects at the end of the concept stage.*

- *We need to plan for the customer, but also plan the technical work.* Sometimes, we have to ask the customer, "What do you want?" and then ask the technical team, "How will we do this?" Formally, the first is called *analysis* and the second is *design.* (Architecture falls in between, starting in analysis and maybe finishing there or maybe finishing in design.) So we split planning into two stages, analysis and design.

- *We need to plan, but we also need to prepare.* Sometimes, in planning, we see gaps we have to close before we're ready to do a project. If we lack knowledge, we need to get some training. If our project involves travel, we need to get everything together and pack. In both these cases, we may want to add a *preparation* stage, so that we plan, prepare, do, and follow through.

As you can see, we might split up the planning stage for any of three reasons: to add some creativity and innovation at the beginning with a concept stage (but make sure it doesn't go too far by closing the concept stage with a review that might well recommend cancellation), to plan what we are doing with the customer and how we will do it with the team, and to make sure we both plan and prepare before we move on to doing.

If we use our case study of a housewarming party, here are the extra stages:

- In the concept stage, we would ask, "Do we really want to do this? Can we handle a party so soon after we move?"
- We would separate analysis from design if we first spent a lot of time asking people what they wanted the party to be like and then took separate time to figure out how we wanted to get everything ready. A wedding planner will do this—first meeting with the families to find out what kind of wedding they want, then calling his or her people to prepare a plan for the customers' approval.
- We might add a preparation stage if we decided to learn Creole and Cajun cooking before buying and cooking for the party.

Similarly, we can split the doing stage if there is a good reason to do so:

- If the doing involves a change of work environment, such as travel, we might want to prepare for the trip and then do the trip. Travel is not the only issue. In Part III, there is a case study about making TV commercials. The costs of the shooting day are very high, so there is an early doing stage called preproduction, where everything is arranged, purchased, and prepared to make production days as efficient as possible.
- Sometimes, the doing consists of activities done by experts who have to work one after the other. In movie making, postproduction follows shooting the film. In construction, one team will do ground prep—digging holes for the buildings, landscaping, putting in roads

and sidewalks. Then another team puts up the buildings. After that, a third team might finish the interiors, decorate, and furnish.

If we have this kind of sequential work in the doing stage, we can break it up into stages. If we do, these stages usually have technical names related to the industry, such as filming and post-production or ground prep, construction, and interior design. If we split up the doing stage of our housewarming party, we might have an advanced prep stage for all the things we could do days before the party, a prep stage starting the day before the party, including shopping for and preparing the fresh food, and a hosting stage, where we enjoy the party with our guests and make them feel welcome.

We should note that, on many projects, we have multiple deliverables during the doing stage that we can work on simultaneously. For example, while one group is building the hardware of a new machine, another is developing the software and a third is writing documentation. These are not separate stages, because they are all occurring at the same time. Instead, they are separate activities, grouped by the deliverables of the WBS. We may want to do all of them in a stage called "building the components" and then put the components together in a stage called "product integration and testing."

We can also split up the follow-through stage of a project. Here are some reasons for doing that:

- If the follow-through requires different kinds of technical expertise, such as delivery, installation, and training, we might break it up into stages.
- If the project involves a big public event, we might organize follow-through into stages such as final preparation, the event, and follow-up.
- If the follow-through is broken up according

to time, we might break it into time periods, such as delivery and six-month follow-up.

For our housewarming party, we might break up the follow-through into two periods by type of work and time: first, clean up and send everyone home, and second, eat leftovers and write thank-you notes.

Three final comments will complete this section on creating a life cycle with more stages:

- There may be industry-standard life cycles in your industry. Feel free to use them. But review them against the pattern of the biological life cycle and the 1:10:100 cost-ratio rule for plan, do, follow through. There are some bad life cycles out there that skip steps or divide work poorly.
- Make sure all work is in one stage or another. Two common mistakes are leaving out architecture altogether and creating a stage for testing, without leaving a time for reworking and retesting to make sure the product actually works before delivery.
- In Chapter 2, I suggested that all projects at your company should follow the same life cycle. I'm going to make a slight change to that now. Your medium-sized or large projects may need a life cycle with four, five, or six stages, but you can use a simpler life cycle for smaller, simpler projects with fewer customers, smaller teams, and less risk. The key is to know why you have the extra stages. Then you can leave them out when the extra management and review time involved in having an extra stage doesn't add value.

Add a stage only if the extra management and review reduces cost, improves quality, or helps ensure the success of your project.

LIFE CYCLES AND PROCESS GROUPS: WHAT'S THE DIFFERENCE?

By now, you should have a pretty thorough understanding of life cycles and process groups. In fact, you may well be sick of them and want to put down the book and finish your project! Let's clear up one common misunderstanding and then we'll close this chapter and move on to Chapter 9, where we get practical. What's the difference between the life cycles and the process groups?

Life cycles are about organizing the *work* of the project over time. That is, they focus on managing the *technical* level. First we plan the work, then we do the work, and finally we follow through to deliver the work to the customer. At each stage, we do an extra gate review to make sure that the technical work has not gone out of control

Process groups are very different from life cycle stages. Process groups organize how we *manage* the project, not how we *work* on the project.

Do you remember *progressive iteration?* That's the idea we introduced earlier that we can use the same tool over and over, at different levels of detail. We used it with the idea of input-process-output (IPO), by showing that a whole project has inputs, processes, and outputs; that each stage of the project has inputs, processes, and outputs; and that each task has inputs, processes, and outputs. Well, the same is true with the five process groups. We can apply them to manage the whole project and then to manage each stage, as well, at a level of greater detail. In this chapter, we focused on how we apply initiating, planning, executing, monitoring and controlling, and closing activities in the doing stage. We can do that in the planning and follow-through stages and for the whole project as well.

CONCLUSION

Now you know the theory of how to keep project work on track. You can teach the members of your team to be aware of activity deliverables and deadlines so that they stay on track and on schedule. You can work with your team so that you set good milestones for gate review. You can perform appropriate planning meetings and gate reviews, leading to effective corrective action and rework. You can manage project risk and change. You can apply the feedback cycle of the five process groups and teach your whole team to do PDCA. And your project will succeed.

If you want to streamline project management to get more value, you can define the best life cycle for projects at your company. All of this sounds like a lot, but really, you're just keeping the infor-

Keeping the Project on Track

IN THIS CHAPTER

Planning was about asking all the right questions and coming up with good answers. Doing is about rolling along–keeping things moving–getting work done and staying on track. The grease on the gears of the project is good communication and motivation is the gas in the engine. So your job is to make sure the gears don't jam by listening well and speaking clearly and then energizing your team members by showing them how to fill up their tanks and hit the road. In Chapter 9, you'll see how to do just that. We'll open with keys to communication and motivation and then show you how to manage all three levels of the project in the doing stage, keeping the technical level, the project level, and the business level of the project on track until all the doing is done.

- In the section on communication, you'll learn about the two levels of feedback in communication and project work and about listening to your team and stakeholders and telling them what they need to know.

- *The technical level* is managed by instructing the team to execute the work–or executing it yourself–and monitoring work status so that you can keep the work under control, ensuring successful delivery of high-quality work packages for the milestones.

- *The project level* is managed by implementing your project plan through controlling your project with reference to all nine knowledge areas.

- *The business level* is managed by managing expectations, changes, and conflict.

Are you as ready to roll as I am? Let's get started!

CHAPTER 8 WAS SORT OF LIKE SITTING through the classroom part of driver's ed—necessary, but not as much fun as driving a car. As you read Chapter 9, you'll have a chance to get beyond understanding and into doing. Dust off your project plan, pull together your team, and use Chapter 9 day by day and

▼ FOCUS!

Making It Happen

In this chapter, you'll learn how to guide your team, working with them and supporting them as they get work done. And, when you have to, you'll be giving them some direction to get back on track. When things go well, you'll feel the joy of knowing that you're getting the right work done and heading toward delivering a good product on time and under budget. In a well-planned project, corrective actions are small, risks and changes are few, and really bad news rarely comes up. Of course, you may discover that you're in the middle of a project that's planned poorly, in spite of all your efforts. Or you may hit one of those major risk events or major changes that happen sometimes, really throwing the project for a loop. Don't worry! With this chapter in hand, you'll be ready to get the doing done right!

▼ BOTTOM-LINE BASICS

Be Ready to Manage Work and People

Keeping a project on track is easy—if you're ready. If you've really used this book and learned what it's saying, then you are. But let's do a quick check before we leave the gate. Before you manage the doing stage of the project, be sure that you:

- Understand how to bring problems under management, define them, and guide your team in solving them with the tools from Chapter 3.
- Understand how to define work clearly and assign work well using the techniques in Chapter 4 and teaching your team members to use them.
- Have a good solid work plan for your project, built following the methods in Chapters 5, 6, and 7.
- Understand the ideas of feedback, control, and corrective action from Chapter 8.

If you're not confident about any of these ideas, go back to those chapters for a quick review. If your plan isn't complete, then work to finish it before or, if necessary, while you get the project going into the doing stage.

week by week as you take your project from a plan all the way to a reality.

COMMUNICATION IS A TWO-WAY STREET

Even though this is the doing stage, where people are getting work done, the key to success is communications. It takes good communications to deliver a work assignment clearly and be sure the team member got it right, to understand status correctly so you can do status reporting and check the work against the plan, to work on risk and quality issues as a team, and to understand and respond to change requests. Your team's job is to do the work and your job is to communicate and make decisions about the work.

I'm getting into one of those difficult areas where I'm going to say really simple things that make sense. The problem is, again, our childhood

habits. We learn to talk early, but it seems like some of us never learn to listen at all! Actually, we all listen, but .... Do we hear what we're told? Do we really understand what to do? Do we let people know we get it and will do what needs doing? Do we write down a plan and then deliver as promised? Some people do, and I enjoy working on projects with them. Really good listeners are easy to be around and good workers keep things going and deliver success, which is exciting.

Maybe you're already like that. I hope so. If so, then this section might help you teach your team members to be the same way. If not, if you sometimes have a hard time getting the message across or you don't always really understand what others are saying or manage to keep track of everything you promised to do, then this section should help you out. But remember: after learning the ideas, you'll have to practice. And you might have to unwire some habits learned when you were still eating milk and cookies and taking naps.

When I say that communication is a two-way street, I mean several things:

- *Communication goes two ways, obviously.* When you have information for me, you talk and I listen. When I have information for you, I talk and you listen. On a project, the project manager receives status information and gives directions to do work and take corrective action.

- *Even when we want to send a message in just one direction, we still need two-way communication.* Have you ever been on the phone and you couldn't hear the other person? You tell him or her some news and then you don't know if he or she got it. You ask, "Are you there?" Maybe you even repeat everything you said. Sooner or later, you hang up and call again. Then, when you can hear the other person, he or she tells you, "I heard everything just fine. In fact, I heard it all twice. I guess you couldn't hear me." Well, that makes it clear: to be sure someone got our message,

we have to be able to hear him or her.

- *Communication has to move into action.* Saying, "I heard you" is just the first step. If I agree to do the work, then I need to take action and deliver the results I committed to.

Figure 9-1 illustrates the second and third points above. In this figure, person 1 is making a request for person 2 to do some work for him. For the work to get done right, two things have to be communicated and confirmed—there has to be two levels of feedback.

The first level is called *feedback communications;* it is a message from the receiver to the sender saying, "I hear you. Do I have it right?" It's not enough for the receiver just to say, "I hear you." All that means is that the receiver heard something, but did he or she hear and understand the right thing? The only way you can be sure is if the receiver repeats it back to you and asks if he or she got it right. Then you can either deliver positive feedback—such as "Yes, you got that right, go with it"—or negative feedback—course correction, such as "No, that's not what I meant. This is what I want: ...." When correct communication is ensured through feedback, the request is delivered and communications feedback—level one—is complete.

To finish the job, person 2 has to do level-two feedback—turning communication into action.

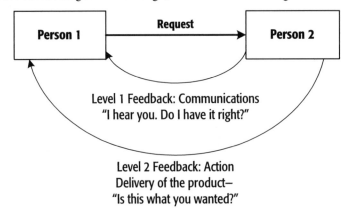

FIGURE 9-1. The two levels of communications

He received the signal, but will he change course? Will he do what he agreed to do? If so, he'll deliver and ask, "Is this what you wanted?" If it is, then person 1 is satisfied. This is *feedback action*. If you want to satisfy your customers and work well with your team members, you need to listen well and deliver what they want.

This may seem like a lot of detail, but consider these two all-too-common problems:

- If someone doesn't get what you're asking for, if the person tunes out and doesn't hear you or doesn't hear you right, don't you think of that person as a poor listener? How do you feel when a team member is like that a lot?
- If someone understands what you want and agrees to do it, but then doesn't do it, how do you feel? Do you think that person is unreliable or lacks integrity? How do you feel about having someone like that on your team?

Learn and share the two levels of feedback—communications and checking, doing and delivering—with your team. A team of good listeners and reliable workers is a good team for your project and your company. When team members learn to communicate well and follow through with action, it makes a world of difference. We need to work at communications with feedback because there are so many things that interfere with messages getting through and work getting done right:

- The sender can fail to put the right information into the message.
- The message can get lost on the way to the receiver.
- The message can get drowned out by noise or interference—other things coming in and overwhelming the receiver.
- The message can get distorted and misunderstood.

Level-one feedback gives us a chance to correct those errors. Then, if we know the message got through, these things can interfere with getting the job done:

- We can forget to do it.
- We can remember to do it, but lose some crucial information, such as where to deliver it or when it is due.
- We can remember it wrong and end up doing the wrong thing or doing the right thing wrong.

These mistakes have to be corrected with level-two feedback, when you deliver the results and ask, "Is this what you wanted?" For big jobs, that would be too late. That's what makes status reports important: we can check that people are doing the right job in the right way and getting it done on time before it is done, so that we can deliver

---

▼ SOMETHING SLIPPED!
Lost at the Restaurant

When I go to a Chinese restaurant, I expect that there might be communication problems. After all, I can't order in the waiter's native Cantonese and he wasn't born speaking English. So I was very pleased when I ordered appetizer #6 and he replied, "The chicken wrapped in lettuce?" I said, "Yes, that's right." He had just done excellent communications feedback by repeating what I wanted back to me in a different way. Now, we both knew that he was going to get me appetizer #6, the chicken wrapped in lettuce.

Dinner came. The appetizer never showed up. I flagged down the waiter and asked him. His face lit up in apologetic surprise and he told me that he had forgotten to put the order in to the kitchen. I got my appetizer for dessert and learned that, if we want to do a good job, we need to deliver twice—first in communications, then in action.

▼ **SMART THINKING!**

Write It Down

My friend Jim Rooney—who wrote the foreword to this book—has a practical tip. Keep a day planner or memo pad with you all the time. If you agree to do something, anything—make a phone call, schedule an appointment, do some work, or deliver some information—write it down. The human memory isn't perfect. You never know what will come up suddenly and interrupt you. Write down what you're going to do—your action items—then check your notes to do and follow through—and be known as a person who *gets it done right!*

instructions for corrective action soon enough to save the project schedule from disaster.

On a project, confirmation of the two levels of feedback should be written down. If we create a project management information system—a document repository as we discussed in Chapter 7—this is easy. People can check their work assignments at any time and easily let you know when they get started, if they have questions about a job, and when they deliver.

Now, let's turn to the first point in the above bullets: a project requires information going in both directions. Let's put listening before speaking, because, if everyone did that, the world would be a quieter place with a lot fewer problems. As project managers, we need to listen well. More than that, we need to work actively and listen actively to receive good information. After we look at receiving information, we'll look at delivering information and motivation.

Getting Good Information

The first step in status reporting is receiving status information. That has to come from your team. To

get good status information, you need to do the following:

- Make sure your team collects and delivers the information you need.
- Clear all incoming communications channels so that you hear the message.
- Reinforce the behavior of delivering good status reports by responding to them with thanks and appreciation for the information.

When we receive status information, we want one thing: the truth. We want the truth about where the project is, what is done, what is not done, and what's going on. Unfortunately, this is not as easy as it sounds. From childhood, we often got yelled at or shamed for speaking the truth as we saw it. We learned to hide things, to shade things, to be polite, to avoid topics that might upset people. We also may not have learned how to keep track of things, organize things, and be clear about facts and situations. So, one way or another, most of us have a lot to learn to be able to deliver good status information clearly.

Remember that when you ask for status from your team. If they're like most people, they're not used to being clear about things and communicating clearly. And they may very much be habitually attuned to thinking that bosses only want to hear good news. It takes patience and persistence to help people retrain themselves to deliver the truth.

To prepare the team, make sure you've established a no-blame environment. Then explain to them what you're going to do with the information you give them. Teach them corrective action and PDCA. At that point, they will understand why you want clear, detailed, complete information.

Next, introduce the team to whatever form you use for status information and make sure they know how to deliver written status reports when appropriate. You can use project management software, develop your own templates, or use the tools on the CD that comes with this book.

You will also want to receive spoken status reports. For that, you need to make sure that you are listening well. Set aside any other jobs or worries and don't take phone calls or allow interruptions unless you must. Also, make sure that you are not expecting bad news or good news from this particular person. Don't let the past bias you. If you take care of these things, you've taken care of item #2 above: you've cleared the incoming communications channels.

Now you are ready to receive status information and reinforce good status reporting, effective communications, and good self-management. When a team member delivers a status report on a piece of work, receive it with a thank-you. Even if the news is bad news, you can say thank you. You're not thanking him or her for what is happening. You're not thanking him or her for making the huge mistake he or she made. Thank the person for letting you know what is going on. Thank the person for delivering the message. Then stop—and let that sink in. Only after that do you respond to the content of the message.

The content of the message is the status of work on a work package. You can categorize the content of a status report on a work package into one of these four levels. The four levels can be thought of as the four levels of self-management capability, from best self-management to the least ability at self-management:

- *"No problem," "It's done,"* or *"It's on schedule."* You respond by saying, "Thank you for doing such good work." Then, since the person can handle all that he or she has, you ask if his or her schedule is full up, or if he or she is ready to take on more responsibility. Note that this person probably ran into problems—but then owned the work and solved the problems.
- *"I have a problem and here's how I want to solve it."* You respond by thanking the person

for thinking through the problem to a solution. If the solution is a good one, you ask, "Could you have gone ahead with that solution, instead of waiting to check with me?" You help someone at this level—identifying solutions—to get to the next level—applying solutions to problems and moving ahead.

- *"I have a problem."* You respond by saying, "Thank you for telling me about the problem." After a pause, you ask, "How would you solve it?" This conveys the message that you want people to think for themselves and to come to you with solutions. When a person learns this, he or she moves from level two of self-management up to level three.
- *"Help! I'm lost. I don't even know what the problem is."* You respond by saying, "Thank you. It must have been hard for you to tell me that." After a pause, you help the person step up to level two by asking, "What's the problem?"

If you do this really consistently, you will find that, one step at a time, people move up from being stuck to being able to describe problems, to being able propose solutions, to being able to define problems and implement solutions on their own. Most people grow—or shrink—to meet their boss's expectations. In this way, as we do projects together, your team members get better at technical work, in their general professionalism, and in their skills of self-management, team leadership, and eventually project management. And the more self-managed each team member is, the easier your job as boss or project manager is going to be.

Note that people's levels will vary. Someone may be very well self-managed—operating at level one or two—on a job he or she is familiar with, but lower on a job in a new environment, or when under stress, or for other reasons.

Keep this up and status reporting becomes easy and routine. If you want to take it further, ask your team members to keep their eyes and ears open for problems. Ask them what risks they see and what challenges they face in doing quality work. If team members interact directly with customers or other stakeholders outside the team, ask them what they think those stakeholders feel about the project. Teach your team to be the eyes and ears of the project and then, when you get together for a status meeting, you will have synergy—the expertise of several people being more valuable than what you can get with each person working alone.

▼ SMART THINKING!

Many Small Steps

Most of us can't jump up six feet to get to a higher floor or platform. But we could jump up six one-foot steps. Or, if you couldn't do that, you could jump up 12 six-inch steps. Big changes are difficult. People make a lot more progress by taking many small steps than by trying to make one big leap. When you learn to encourage your team to take small steps in the right direction and you keep it up steadily, you're learning a tool that psychologists call *shaping*—one of the most effective training tools we have.

Also, when each job is small, there are many opportunities to say, "Great job, do it again," which is both positive feedback and encouragement.

Motivating the Team

Now that you've learned how to help the team members be clear and deliver honest, accurate status reports, we can apply the same approach to motivating them to do good work.

First of all, when a team member isn't doing good work, partner with him or her and coach. Make sure you are following all the steps of defining jobs from Chapter 4. Then share the techniques for defining and solving problems from Chapter 3. Come up with a plan to resolve the problem and have the team member try it out. If it works, have him or her keep doing it. If it doesn't, try something else. This should sound familiar—treating a problem as a gap and working to close the gap with PDCA.

If the work is clear, then the next step is to help the team member have energy for the job. Energy for work is motivation and motivation comes from emotion. To motivate is to evoke motion, to call forth motion, work, or action. To evoke motivation is to emote. How do we help our team members focus their emotions, get involved, and get excited about contributing to a project?

There are four simple things we can do:

- *Care about the project ourselves—steadily.* Our attention, commitment, and enthusiasm are contagious.
- *Bring the purpose to the team.* We began planning by answering the question, "*Why* are we doing this project?" That answer, that reason *why*, is strategy, but it is also motivation. As people, when we know why we are doing a job, we are moved to do it, we start to care about it. We know why the job matters, so then it matters to us. When it matters to us, we want to *get it done right.*
- *Make sure that what's good for the project is good for the team member.* Very few people will do something because it's good for the company, for the boss, or for the customer. People are much more easily motivated to do what is good for themselves, at least in the workplace. And that's only fair. After all, if I'm going to make you—my boss—better off, shouldn't I be better off, too? Use praise, appreciation, and other incentives so that good project work is rewarded fairly and promptly.

- *Keep everything small, simple, and prompt.* A pot of gold at the end of the rainbow is nowhere near as rewarding as a dime at the end of the day. Give small, persistent praise and appreciation for each day's work, each week's deliverables. Let everyone wake up in the morning being able to remember something you said the day before that is a reason he or she will want to see you and come to work for you.

I believe in rewarding people for good work, rather than just saying, "It's part of the job." That doesn't mean that everyone should receive a bonus. Big annual bonuses are unrealistic for small businesses and ineffective for motivation. Instead, we should find small, unique ways of saying, "Thank you" and "Good job!" each week and each month. In a small team, you can even ask what kind of reward each person likes. Also, don't make rewards competitive. If everyone does a good job, everyone gets rewarded.

Oddly enough, if you make small rewards a habit, you are teaching people to do good work on the project. You are letting them know that project success is what really matters. And once they come to believe that, the external rewards—the gifts or bonuses—won't matter as much. Even thank-yous will matter less, though you should never stop giving them. Eventually, what will matter to your team is what matters to you—the success of the project and the company.

Now it is time to turn away from the personal side of the project—communication and relationships—and on to the management of the technical work of the project.

MANAGING THE TECHNICAL LEVEL

The focus of the doing stage is the technical work that delivers completed work packages—complete, tested, working components of the product, serv-ice, or solution we are delivering at the end of the project. We want to deliver each scope component—each WBS package—on time, within budget, and with quality. We can do this by having our team execute the work, then monitoring it and controlling it with the weekly planning meeting or status meeting.

Executing the Work

If the project plan is clear and complete, then work packages and activities are defined, scheduled, and ready to be assigned week by week. To execute the projects, we assign these tasks and go over the week's schedule with each team member. Allow each team member to define his or her own way and order of working up to capacity. If people are less well self-managed or doing a type of work they've never done before, make the assignments smaller and be more explicit about the order of completion. In cases like that, you may want to ask to see some work packages during the week, before the next planning meeting. You can discuss these issues openly with the team, so that no one feels micromanaged, but no one gets lost, either.

In reviewing the plan, there are some problems you may run into. Here are the most common problems and how to take care of them:

- *Lack of clear definition.* If you find that some work is unclear, then treat that as a problem to be resolved by you or someone on your team. Delegate it if you can: give it to the team member with the most appropriate technical expertise.
- *Small items left out.* If you or your team find small things that simply got left off the plan, slot them into the schedule, but also take a closer look at the rest of the plan. If omissions happened throughout the plan, then you're going to need to figure out what work is missing and rebaseline—better sooner than later.

- *A large item left out.* If you find that a large job was left out, you will have to draw from your contingencies—the time and cost budget set aside for risk events—to schedule a project change.
- *A really large item left out or a change in scope.* If the item is really large or if you have to redefine a WBS deliverable, you will have to initiate a change control process.

Once the work is assigned for execution, the team members do the work and we focus on monitoring and control.

Monitoring the Work

Monitoring the work includes the status-reporting process described in Chapter 8 and other things. If our goal at the technical level is to make sure the team delivers high-quality components to the milestone packages on time and within budget, we can break this into two parts:

- Scope, time and cost issues: getting the right work done.
- Quality issues: getting the work done right.

Get the Right Work Done: Monitoring Scope, Time, and Cost. Getting the right work done requires managing in an interlocking series of tasks, with deliverables from each task being used as input for later tasks, so that later tasks depend on earlier ones. Each task has its IPO (input, process, and output); uses resources, tools, skills, and methods; and occurs in a work environment, as described in Chapter 4. Monitoring means keeping an eye on those things. The status-reporting process shows us what's happening with the tasks that are scheduled for this week, but we also need to watch out for problematic trends and warning signs and look ahead at what's coming up.

Here are some trends and warning signs to watch for so that we can make sure the right work gets done on time and within the budget:

- *Repeated weaknesses in the plan,* as mentioned above, require review and revision of the plan.
- *Repeated difficulty in delivering quality* by any team member means that he or she needs training or support.
- *Repeated unavailability of a team member on the project* means that something else—routine work, crises, or projects or illness or some other personal problem—is a risk to project work that you need to manage with the team member.
- *Repeated difficult in delivering packages on time* by any team member means that he or she needs training or support.
- *Persistent problems getting work done* may indicate a problem with the work environment or some other risk or distraction.
- *Continuing delays* are an indication of possible poor tools, understaffing, lack of some other resource, or insufficient training or skill.
- *Confusion or lack of clarity about the work* is a sign of a gap between the worker's skill and the skills needed on the project.
- *Haphazard work done one way one time and another way another time* is a sign of a lack of technical methodology or process, which will create both quality problems and inefficiency.

Any of these problems should be addressed promptly. Things like this come up now and then and taking care of them is a part of life and work on any project. But when they are not addressed—brought under management and fixed so that the gap is closed—then the small inefficiencies add up and the project ends up in hot water—behind schedule, over budget, failing to deliver to specification or with quality. Don't let problems and delays pile up. Use the problem-definition tools in Chapter 3 to define and solve problems, cut to the root cause, and implement a permanent preventative solution.

When we've taken care of the present, it's time to take care of the future. Here is how to look ahead at problems in technical work that might be coming your way:

- *Review the schedule* to identify the tasks that will be coming up in the next two weeks.
- *Look at each task.* If it is not clear to you, sit down with the team member who will do the work and have him or her explain it. Be sure to have the person walk through the work with care and not just glance at the name of the job. If neither of you understands the job, then there's a problem. Work to clarify the plan and add anything that is missing *before* you assign the task, so that it won't be delayed when it is due to start.
- *Look at dependencies.* Determine which tasks may be delayed if current work doesn't get done. Check with the folks on the current work and make sure they let you know if they think they won't make their due date.
- *Look at work assignments.* If someone is assigned too much work, make adjustments. If someone is taking on a new job that requires skills that he or she hasn't used before, check to see if the person is ready. If a new person is joining the team, make sure he or she is available.
- *If a gate review is coming up soon, reinforce the focus on checking and testing*—on quality control of the product—and work to resolve any open problems so that the milestone package is ready and in good shape.

Any issue that comes up in monitoring scope, time, and cost—whether as part of the status reporting process or from some other source—should be documented and brought under control.

Get the Work Done Right: Monitoring Quality.
Monitoring quality on the technical level of the project centers on testing. During planning, we prepared the requirements matrix, the test plan, and the test bed. Now, in the doing stage, we test each component to make sure it delivers satisfactory results on all specifications linked to that component.

Many people have a hard time distinguishing between the technical issues of testing for quality and the project management processes of quality assurance (QA) and quality control (QC). QA and QC were defined in a production manufacturing environment, where new products coming off an assembly line need to be tested, so the same tests are run over and over. The translation of the ideas of testing, QA, and QC to the project world has been difficult. We will discuss QA and QC later in this chapter, when we look at the issues of managing the project level of the doing stage.

For now, at the technical level, let's focus on testing. Testing is very specific to each industry: computer code is tested one way, electrical wiring another way, and an advertising campaign yet another way. But we can make sense of testing in general, starting by identifying three things we can test: the process, the product, and the value.

- *Testing the process.* Here, we are asking if the process that was followed conforms to the specified process. For example, if we have a cake recipe that says, "Preheat the oven and bake the cake for one hour at 400 degrees," then we check records—such as a time log or an electrical recording of oven temperatures—to make sure that the actual process followed the plan for that process.
- *Testing the product.* Here, we measure and evaluate the inputs, the components of the product, and the final product. If our cake is to be made with unbleached white flour, we read the label on the bag before mixing the batter. If the cake is to be a four-pound, yellow, three-layer cake with chocolate icing, then we make sure we get three yellow layers

out of the oven and we put them all into the final cake. Then, looking at and testing, the final product, we make sure it weighs four pounds and is covered with chocolate icing. It's essential to test inputs and components as we go along. It would be very hard to look at a finished cake and be sure that the right kind of flour was used, that the right flavor of layer was produced, or that there was chocolate icing between the layers. Doing that would involve a *destruct test,* ruining our product to see if it was any good. In manufacturing we can afford destruct tests—destroying a certain percentage of a production batch to make sure the rest of the identical items are good—but in project management, where items are unique, we generally need to ensure good process and avoid the need for destructive testing.

■ *Testing the value of the product, service, or result.* The whole point of conforming to specifications and ensuring quality is to add value in the final use of the product, service, or other results of the project. If we can test the actual value, then we can prove that the project results will be worth the investment. The basic way to do that is with a pilot test or a pilot project. A pilot test for a wedding cake would be that the family buys a small cake with the identical recipe, tastes it, and shares it with friends before selecting that recipe for the wedding. A pilot project related to a wedding cake might be if caterer tests a new recipe by letting a few couples try the new cake at their weddings. The caterer might have just one chef trained to make the cake. They don't advertise it, but they mention it to customers. After they try the new recipe at a few weddings, if it is doing well, they train the rest of their chefs, add it to their menu, and launch an advertising campaign centered

around the new, better cake. The small pilot project—a few weddings—demonstrates the value of going ahead with the full project of putting the new recipe into production and promoting it with a marketing project.

In designing and scheduling our technical test plan, we should define tests of process, product, and value for the process of procurement, component development, and final product assembly. Table 9-1 shows examples of these nine tests for each of three types of projects: computer software, electrical work, and an advertising campaign.

Of course, Table 9-1 is not a complete test plan for any one of those projects. A complete test plan will arrange for testing or intentionally not testing every input, every component, and the entire final product to all specifications. In designing the test plan, we have to keep testing reasonable and affordable. In some cases, one type of test can replace another. If the work is done by a certified electrician, that process test may be sufficient, so some product tests can be skipped. If we know the cake was in the oven at the right temperature for the right time, we don't have to taste a slice. Or, if we make a small sample of the cake and test it, we don't need to check the oven temperature. Generally, we want to choose the least expensive test that will ensure that the input, component, or product meets specifications.

A look at five important issues will close our discussion of managing quality at the technical level through testing:

■ *Test components before assembly.* Problems are much harder to find and fix later. Just remember the image of looking at a cake with icing and asking, "Is that the type of cake I ordered?" There's no easy way to tell.

■ *Testing and testing standards are industry-specific.* We may need an expert to let us know the technical requirements we have to meet or the affordable way to do sufficient testing.

Type of Test	Writing Computer Software	Electrical Work	Advertising Campaign
Test of an Input			
Input item to test	*Software specification: English-language description of code to be written*	*Light switch*	*Concepts on storyboard from potential vendors*
Process test	Was pseudocode written according to defined methodology?	Was light switch manufactured to specification by an approved vendor?	Did vendor prepare concept presentation on time?
Product test	Is pseudocode clear and complete? Does it meet IEEE specification 803-1993, the requirements specification for a software specification?	Hook up switch to circuit. Does it work?	Evaluation of concept by customer.
Value test	n/a	Does customer like style, look, and feel?	Test-run of concept with focus group.
Test of a Component			
Component to test	*Software module*	*One room wired and installed*	*One print ad*
Process test	Was software written and were internal tests performed according to project software development methodology?	Was wiring done by a certified electrician following proper procedures?	Was proper color correction used on photograph? Are print colors those specified by customer?
Product test	Does component pass all tests for all features and tests with other components that are now ready?	Do the installed circuits work?	Does the ad work for entire team and all internal customers?
Value test	Does the customer like the look, feel, and functionality of this component?	Does customer like using the switch and seeing the light come on? Is the room lighting what the customer wants?	Test ad in focus group or in limited campaign (such as a pilot test in one city).
Test of Product			
Product to test	*Software application with documentation*	*Wiring of entire house*	*Entire ad campaign*
Process test	Was software written and were internal tests performed according to projects software development methodology?	Was all work done according to proper procedures by a certified electrician?	Were final edited text copies and approved images used in all ads? Were proper methods used in photography, layout, and printing?
Product test	Does program meet all requirements when tested?	Do all circuits and switches work? Are all loads working when tested to appropriate capacity?	Does every team member and internal customer like the whole campaign?
Value test	Does the program work as expected and benefit the customer as expected in the production environment?	Does the customer like location and operation of all switches and lighting and electrical functionality throughout building?	Run entire campaign in a pilot test city, measure response, and modify campaign before national release, if necessary.

TABLE 9-1. The nine types of tests in three types of projects

For example, construction codes differ from city to city.

- *Meeting one requirement may necessitate testing several components individually and together.* For example, meeting a requirement that a new building meets the local code for fire prevention will involve checking sprinklers, fire extinguishers, emergency exit doors, building materials, and more. In software development, a single user function—such as printing a document—is likely to require the combined proper operation of several modules, including the user interface, the file system, and the print driver.

- *Allow time for testing, problem identification, rework, and retesting.* Otherwise, your project will fall behind schedule.

All issues found as a result of testing should be resolved. They should also be reviewed to see if they require additional attention at the level of project quality management. For each problem, we want to ask, "Does this one error indicate a bigger or repeating potential problem that could be addressed through quality assurance, root cause analysis, and permanent preventative action?"

Controlling the Work

Methods for controlling the work—staying on course and on schedule with corrective action, ensuring delivery of milestones, risk management, and change control—were explained in Chapter 8. On a practical level, what we need to do is to match the level of the response to the level of the problem.

We can understand this with an analogy to driving. If I get distracted for a moment and the car starts to drift out of the lane, I should correct the problem and move on. Anything more would be overkill—too much management of a small problem. But if the distraction is going to repeat—say that my pet cat got out of her carrier and is jumping around the car—I had better pull over and take

care of the problem. Or if I've become too tired to drive and I'm constantly drifting out of the lane, I should stop for the night, even if it means not making my appointment that evening. So, whenever we need to make an adjustment, we need to ask, "Is this just something I should let the worker take care of with a corrective action item or is it something larger, riskier, or recurrent?"

- *If the problem is a one-time thing,* assign it as an action item, but make sure that the item can be checked off when it is done.

- *If the problem is small and recurring,* ask the worker if he or she can handle it. If so, then delegate it to him or her and include checking status on it as part of weekly risk management.

- *If the problem is larger, riskier, or recurring,* then bring it under control with risk management or change control, as appropriate.

- *If the problem is unfamiliar or specialized,* get expert advice so you can know what is best to do.

Now, let's learn how to manage, monitor, and control the project at the project level, by making sure that our plan keeps on track in all nine areas of project management.

MANAGING THE PROJECT LEVEL

As we've said, we want to deliver each scope component—each WBS package—on time, within budget, and with quality. We take care of most of that at the technical level. But we also want to keep risk events from getting in the way of that delivery. We want to close any gaps in human resources, procurement, or communications that would slow us down. And we want to tie all of that together so that we see the effects in all areas of a change in one area or of a decision. For these, we need monitoring and control at the project level, across all of the nine areas.

Scope

Scope management issues fall into two categories:

- *Delivering work packages to meet scope requirements* was mostly covered in the previous section, as that is a technical issue on the project. However, when the customer is involved in approving those work packages, we use the process called *scope verification.*

- *Managing requests to change in scope* is the main work of project *scope control* in the doing stage.

In the PMI's 44 processes, there are no scope processes in the executing process group and there are two scope processes in the monitoring and controlling process group: scope verification and scope control. Let's take a look at each of these in turn.

All definitions of process groups are taken from the glossary of The Project Management Institute, *A Guide to the Project Management Body of Knowledge (PMBOK® Guide)—Third Edition,* Project Management Institute, Inc., 2004.*

Scope Verification. The PMI defines scope verification as the process of formalizing acceptance of the completed project deliverables. Acceptance here refers to acceptance by the customer. Using the original scope specification and the WBS, the customer inspects the component and decides whether or not to accept it. Technically, this is separate from quality control, where we make sure that the component meets requirements, that it works right. But we really don't want a customer accepting a component that doesn't work, so the best approach is to do internal quality control—checking each item ourselves to make sure it works—and then combine the customer's inspection and testing for quality control with the customer's inspection for acceptance of the component in scope verification. That is, we make sure we did it right and the customer then makes sure that they got what they wanted and that it does what they want it to do. When the customer tells us that the component is acceptable, we record their acceptance and scope verification for that component is complete.

What if the component isn't acceptable? That leads to requests for changes to the component, then corrective action. If the corrective action or rework is small, we fit it in. If not, then we may need to rebaseline the project plan. At that point, scope, time, cost, and the other six areas of project management are needed to evaluate the change to the plan. That moves this item into *integrated change control,* which we will discuss later in this chapter.

There is one very important note. If a customer

*Copyright and all rights reserved by PMI. Material from this publication has been reproduced with the permission of PMI. The applies to each citation of this book as they appear in this chapter.

rejects a component and requests changes, this is *not* a scope change request. The scope of the project has not changed. The original scope is exactly as originally defined, but the work product doesn't meet the scope requirements. This change is a request for a fix. We're being asked to get the work done right according to the original plan. We're not being asked to do anything new. The corrective action is required to meet original project requirements. To see why that matters, read the sidebar, I Fix, You Pay.

Scope Control. The Project Management Institute defines scope control as the process of controlling changes to the project scope. Here, we are not concerned with the work done to deliver a product that meets the scope specification. We are concerned with anything that could change the scope specification, that could change what we are mak-

ing. Any scope change will show up as a change in the work breakdown structure or the WBS dictionary. For each work package—lowest-level item in the WBS—there are four possibilities:

- A work package can be added.
- A work package can be dropped.
- A work package description—WBS dictionary entry—can be changed.
- A work package can be split into smaller packages, with or without changes to the final product being delivered.

Almost all scope changes must be escalated to integrated change control, because we will have to adjust the project schedule and budget to go with that. Only very small items can be added or dropped without triggering integrated change control and probable rebaselining of the project plan.

▼ SOMETHING SLIPPED!

I Fix, You Pay

There is a major information technology consulting firm—I won't name names—with a reputation for the following practice. They make a lot of money with this technique, but it causes a lot of bad feelings. I think it's downright unethical.

The company works with the customer to come up with a scope specification and a contract. The contract has a fixed price for delivering to the scope and then an extra hourly fee for changes requested by the customer. So far, that's good project management and good business practice.

In scope verification and quality control, when the customer tests something and it doesn't work, the project manager says something like, "We'll be happy to fix that for you, but, to make sure we get it in right, we'll need the issue in writing. Please put in a change request."

Writing up the exact change needed is certainly reasonable and the customer does as asked.

Then, with the bill comes a surprise. This vendor charges for every change request—including the ones that are required to fix problems made by the vendor.

The vendor makes mistakes, the customer catches them, and then the customer gets billed for the time the vendor spends fixing the mistakes. So, the more mistakes the vendor makes, the more they get paid—until they get caught.

The lesson: Distinguish between changes arising from scope verification, which are required to make the product meet the original specification, where the cost should be borne by the vendor, and changes to the project scope, which are added items that the customer should pay for.

Repeated additions to scope are called *scope creep*. As explained in Chapter 5, scope creep is possibly the biggest cause of project failure. See the sidebar, Stop Scope Creep, to learn how to deal with it.

There are two advanced approaches to keeping scope creep under control. Both of them work by designing the project to create a place for the work needed to do change requests:

- *Create a contingency for scope change requests.* We tell the customer, "We know you're going to want extras and changes when you see how this works. Our baseline plan has us deliver the product *as originally specified* on this date, for this much money. But that doesn't take changes into account. So,

instead, let's add up to a month of time and extra money. If you don't request changes, we won't use that time or money. But, upfront, you agree that, if you do request changes, we can deliver later and use some of that money." Then, every time a change request comes in, you give the customer an invoice, saying, "If you really want this change, here's the extra cost and the new delivery date." If they want the change, they accept the *overage*—the billing adjustment—and you add the item to the schedule and budget. You can do this for as many changes as the customer requests, until time or money runs out. Of course, if a change isn't feasible—if it isn't technically possible or it puts the project at

▼ SMART THINKING!

Stop Scope Creep

There are things we can do in planning and controlling a project to prevent scope creep and keep scope changes to a minimum. In planning:

- Define scope clearly and get approval from every stakeholder.
- Define scope in detail, including all requirements.
- Make sure everyone is on the same page with the same picture and that the picture is supported by precise written specifications.
- Teach the 1:10:100 rule to encourage a complete plan and few changes afterwards.

During the doing phase, through scope control:

- *Educate all team members* about the change control process and show them how to submit change requests. Ask that all requests include a justification.
- *Manage sources of change.* When a change request comes in, evaluate its cause. Does it indicate incomplete planning? A team member with a

bright idea? A customer who thinks he or she can just ask for more? A customer who wants more and a too-customer-oriented team member? If the cause is any of these, then, aside from what you do with the one change request, bring the *source of change requests* under management.

- *Manage expectations by keeping in touch with the customers.* Keep the customers posted on progress, so that they stay focused in reality and don't start dreaming up new things for you to do for them.
- *Discuss scope change with your team members,* so they can help you keep it under control.
- *Bring every change request into the scope control process.* Don't miss anything and never ignore anyone. Respond to every change, even if your response is a firm, clear "No."

The lesson: Scope creep can kill a project. Prevent it and keep it under control with proactive planning, education, and control.

risk of failure—then you reject the change and let the customer know.

- *Plan for a second project upfront.* Sometimes, we can be pretty sure a customer is going to want changes. We may know from experience that, when a customer sees the first version of our new system, they're going to want more. In a case like this, we can say to the customer, "Let's plan on two projects. The first will give you the basic system and we'll accept scope changes only if they are essential to making the project work. As we move ahead, we'll receive all of your good ideas for improvements. I'll evaluate them. After we deliver the first version of the product, we'll do a second small project, giving you all the extras you want." In terms of scope and time, this is two projects. But the customer can budget it all as one project with two delivery dates, which may make it easier for them to accept.

Time and Cost

We control time and cost mostly through the status-reporting process. Most of our work on time and cost was done in planning. There are no executing processes related to time or cost. Each has one process in the monitoring and controlling process group. They are appropriately called *schedule control* and *cost control*. The Project Management Institute defines these processes as follows in the glossary of *A Guide to the Project Management Body of Knowledge (PMBOK® Guide)—Third Edition*, Project Management Institute, Inc., 2004. Copyright and all rights reserved. Material from this publication has been reproduced with the permission of PMI.

- *Schedule control* is the process of controlling changes to the project schedule.
- *Cost control* is the process of influencing the factors that create variances, and controlling

changes to the project budget.

Both of these activities rely on *performance reporting*, which the PMI includes in project communications management. Performance reporting is a more advanced, structured approach to the status-reporting process you learned in Chapter 8. The process is pretty much the same. What's new is a system of calculating progress against the schedule and cost called *earned value analysis* (EVA). EVA has been around for about 20 years and it's taught in the *PMBOK Guide* and in plenty of other books. It's also calculated automatically by project management software. It's pretty dry stuff, so I'm not going to teach it all here, but I'll give you the basic idea.

Earned value analysis compares completed scope against time and cost and then gives us a way to forecast when the project will actually finish and how much it will actually cost. It is the mathematics behind the discussion in Chapter 8 around Figure 8-3. Let's see how it works, first with time and then with cost.

If we can show how far we've actually gone (scope delivered) in how much time, then we can estimate how long it will take to finish. With that, we can adjust project duration and calculate a new completion date.

Suppose our project has 200 equal-sized components. Each workweek—five days—we plan to finish 10 of them. At that rate, we'll finish the 200 in 20 weeks. However, at the end of week 2, we find we've finished 16, instead of 20. Clearly, at this rate, we won't finish on time in 20 weeks. In 20 weeks, we'll have done only 160 (eight components per week times 20 weeks). But when will we finish? The answer is calculated like this. We have 200 components to finish and we're doing eight per week. Two hundred divided by eight is 25, so we'll finish in 25 weeks, five weeks late.

We can do the same thing with cost. Let's say we planned each component to cost $200, so the cost of all components will be 200 times $20, or $40,000. We look at our costs after two weeks and find that we've spent $3,000 to create 16 components. We've actually spent only $3,000 / 16 or $187.50 per component. At this rate, 200 components will cost $37,500 instead of $40,000.

At this rate, we'll deliver five weeks late and $2,500 under budget. We can use these figures to propose a new plan. If the customer accepts the plan, then we create a new baseline plan and keep going.

That is the simplest form of earned value analysis. It is the first of three approaches:

- *Earned value assuming cost and time variances will continue.* This is illustrated by the above example. We forecast the future based on the actual cost and time to complete each component to date.
- *Earned value assuming that the extra costs will not continue.* We can use this approach if the reason for the cost increase won't repeat. Perhaps we had greater expenses than expected while the team was learning the job, but now we expect the team to work at the original scheduled rate. In that case, we treat the variance as one-time event and estimate cost to completion and scheduled completion based on the original rate of work.
- *Earned value using re-estimation.* If we want, we can re-estimate the rest of the project, then add that estimate to actual time and cost spent to date and use that as our new plan.

This gives you the basic concept of earned value analysis and the three basic ways of calculating EVA and estimating the time and cost to complete the project. For schedule analysis, we are comparing actual work completed against time spent, seeing the variance from the plan, and forecasting a new plan. For cost analysis, we are comparing actual work completed against money spent, seeing the variance from the plan, and forecasting a new plan.

The very simple calculation of EVA—in which every component is the same size and cost—is not a realistic picture of a project. But, if we have our duration and cost estimates recorded per task in the project plan, we can do the calculations and use EVA to re-estimate the delivery date and total cost of the project.

One way of thinking of EVA is that it shows us how much we have to resize the iron triangle of scope, time, and cost. If the scope is taking more time costing more money to complete, EVA tells us how much more. The results of EVA tell us how it will work out if we keep going the way we are. If they are not acceptable—to us or to the customer—we can also look at revising the project plan. If a project is taking longer and costing more than we planned, our options include:

- *Working longer and paying more* to get the original scope of work done. If the delayed delivery is acceptable to the customer and we can agree on who pays for the extra cost, this approach works.
- *Dropping items from the scope* to deliver on time and on budget, if that is acceptable to the customer.
- *Working harder*—adding people and money to the team or asking people to work overtime, to deliver on time at higher cost. However, this doesn't always work. Adding people to a team can actually slow a project down, rather than speeding it up.
- *Working smarter.* If we can identify the inefficiencies in our process, we can correct them through quality management. See the sidebar, Quality: The Golden Fix for the Iron Triangle, for details.

Quality

Quality management in the doing stage consists of performing quality assurance—an executing

▼ **SMART THINKING!**

Quality: The Golden Fix for the Iron Triangle

The iron triangle says that a given scope requires a given time and cost. By that logic, if we find that the work is taking longer or costing more than we thought, we will have to add time or money to the project to complete all the work. But the iron triangle assumes that we are doing the work a certain way, as planned. If that way of working is the best way we can find and learn for this project, we're stuck with spending more time and money to get the work done. But what if we find a smarter way of working?

Odds are we won't be able to come up with a huge change in our work methods in this process. That would

require too much planning; it would really be a whole new project. But if we can make several small improvements that add up, we may be able to get back on budget and on schedule. The best way to do that is with techniques of *continuous improvement* from quality management. We and our team define inefficiencies in time and/or cost as problems, then analyze them using the techniques from Chapter 3 on problem definition, multiple cause analysis, root cause analysis, and permanent preventative solutions. As we implement the permanent preventative solutions, our rate of scope completion per workday and per dollar increases and we come closer to being back on course.

process—and performing quality control—a controlling process. Here are the definitions from the glossary of the Project Management Institute's *A Guide to the Project Management Body of Knowledge (PMBOK® Guide)—Third Edition*, Project Management Institute, Inc., 2004. Copyright and all rights reserved. Material from this publication has been reproduced with the permission of PMI.

- *Perform Quality Control (QC).* The process of monitoring specific project results to determine whether they comply with relevant quality standards and identifying ways to eliminate causes of unsatisfactory performance.
- *Perform Quality Assurance (QA).* The process of applying the planned, systematic quality activities (such as audits or peer reviews) to ensure that the project employs all processes needed to meet requirements.

There are two big differences between QC and QA.

- QC focuses on project results, such as com-

ponents, and compares them with standards. QA is more general, applying to processes as well as results and ensuring that *all* requirements (not just standards) are met.
- QC is a controlling process, an evaluation of project results against the plan, leading primarily to corrective action. QA is a more general executing process that can review anything at all and can lead to all kinds of changes to process or to management.

QC and QA apply at both the technical level and the project level. We discussed the technical level above. There, QC makes sure that the product—component by component—meets requirements and standards. QA can be used to ensure the team is doing good work.

Because QC focuses on specific project results, it is easy to think that it applies only to the product—the technical level. That is not entirely true. For example, on a large project, we need to be sure that everyone is entering the time and money spent properly to each component of the WBS, because we bill according to WBS items. The billing report is a project result; we can do quality control to check that everyone enters his or her timesheet correctly. The same is true for use of checklists, status information provided, and other results used in the project management process. If this data is gathered accurately and consistently, we have better control of the project. We also have better records at the end of the project. PMI calls the collected project records *historical information.* Accurate historical information is very valuable for the planning, estimation, and risk management of future projects.

Quality assurance at the project management level is a very broad term. Especially in small business, there are many things we can do to ensure the quality of project management and also to improve it. QA for project management can include things like the following:

- Rereading the whole project plan or part of it and making sure we're doing what we said we would do.
- Following up on a part of the project or with a team member who has had trouble and making sure things are OK.
- Brainstorming about quality issues with the team.
- Performing problem definition and resolution on any problem or gap that appears during the project.
- Encouraging the team to focus on quality as a gate review approaches or if there have been quality problems.
- Making sure that all technical testing, rework, and retesting are performed properly and recorded, through audits or other reviews.

When it comes to quality, at a simple level, the most important thing is not to drop the ball. If you have a good plan, you can deliver quality. Will the team do it?

Risk

Risk management during the doing stage is just one process: risk monitoring and control. The PMI defines risk monitoring and control as the process of tracking identified risks, monitoring residual risks, identifying new risks, executing risk response plans, and evaluating their effectiveness throughout the project life cycle, in the glossary of the Project Management Institute's *A Guide to the Project Management Body of Knowledge (PMBOK® Guide)—Third Edition*, Project Management Institute, Inc., 2004.

To put it simply, we have our risk list and now we have to take care of those risks and keep the list up to date. These are the most important practical activities:

- *Have the team members watch out for triggers.* A trigger is an indicator that a risk event is about to happen or is starting to happen and that action is required. Review the triggers with the team and ask them to tell you what they see.
- *Delegate management of risks.* Have different team members take responsibility for keeping different risks under management. That doesn't mean that a team member has to take care of the problem all alone. It just means that he or she has to take care of it—or holler for help if necessary.
- *Track risks against the schedule.* Some risks are linked to certain deliverables, dates, or events. If the work is done and the danger of the risk is past, then we should cross it off the list.
- *Manage risks.* If a risk event happen, manage it or have someone on the team manage it. Do whatever kind of mitigation is appropriate, following a contingency plan or creating one as you go.
- *Check the status of every risk every week* as part of the weekly planning meeting.

- *Identify new risks* as early as possible. If someone thinks something might be a risk, he or she should mention it and you should look into it yourself or with your team.

Keep this going throughout the doing period until you've sailed through the storm and reached your destination.

Communications, Human Resources, and Procurement

In this section, we look at three additional processes as we work on them in the doing stage: communications, human resources, and procurement.

Communications. As we look at communications management in the doing stage, we begin to repeat things that have already been said. In the *PMBOK Guide®*, the PMI focuses on managing the project management level. In this book I've split up the work into three levels—technical, project, and business. Much of the work of communications has been covered in the opening of this chapter and in our discussions of the technical level and earned value analysis. The PMI's description of project communications management in the doing stage consists of three processes:

- *Information distribution* is a process in the executing process group that includes the material covered in Chapter 4 on thorough definition of job assignments, the issues of feedback in communications discussed in Chapter 8, and the team motivation issues we talked about at the beginning of this chapter.
- *Performance reporting* is a controlling process that includes status reporting and earned value analysis, which we have already discussed extensively.
- *Manage stakeholders* is a controlling process that we cover in two parts. We have already looked at how to manage the team. In the

final section of this chapter, on managing the business level of the project, we will discuss how to manage the customer and other stakeholders during the doing stage.

Here are the formal definitions of these three processes from the glossary of the Project Management Institute's *A Guide to the Project Management Body of Knowledge (PMBOK® Guide)—Third Edition.*

- *Information distribution,* the process of making needed information available to project stakeholders in a timely manner.
- *Performance reporting,* the process of collecting and distributing performance information. This includes status reporting, progress measurement, and forecasting.
- *Manage stakeholders,* the process of managing communications to satisfy the requirements of, and resolve issues with, project stakeholders.

Human Resources. The *PMBOK Guide®* organizes the work of project human resources management into one planning process, two executing processes, and one controlling process, as follows. The definitions are from the glossary of the Project Management Institute's *A Guide to the Project Management Body of Knowledge (PMBOK® Guide)—Third Edition.*

- *Human resource planning,* the process of identifying and documenting project roles, responsibilities and reporting relationships, as well as creating the staffing management plan.
- *Acquire project team,* an executing process defined as the process of obtaining the human resources needed to complete the project.
- *Develop project team,* another executing process defined as the process of improving the competencies and interaction of team members to enhance project performance.

■ *Manage project team,* a monitoring and controlling process defined as the process of tracking team member performance, providing feedback, resolving issues, and coordinating changes to enhance project performance.

In focusing on projects for small business, we've discussed all of these activities, but organized them a bit differently. We included human resource planning in activity definition and activity duration estimation, because the best way to plan project work is to have the person who will do the work come up with the plan. That way, the worker's skills and expertise benefit the project during the planning stage and the workers are more self-managed in the doing stage, because they are executing their own plans, instead of doing what someone else planned and told them to do.

Of course, if we want workers to do the planning, we have to acquire the project team earlier, during the planning stage. This makes sense in that the planning stage is really planning and preparation, as we discussed in Chapter 8. Bringing the team on board is preparation in life cycle terms and execution in process group terms. Since the PMI says that each process group occurs during all project stages, this works. We've simply moved much of the activity of one executing process—acquiring the team—into an earlier stage—planning.

We discussed project team development extensively in Chapters 4 and 8 and in the beginning of this chapter. When we define jobs clearly, teach the team to do PDCA, provide feedback, and motivate the team, this is all team development. The PMI's definition adds an interesting point, that there are two parts to developing a team:

■ We can make a team of workers better *workers* by teaching each person to do a better job.
■ We can make a team of workers a better *team*

▼ SMART THINKING!

A Good Team

One very smart project manager I met felt that projects got much better work done with a good team of workers than with a team of good workers. A good team works well together. But a team of good workers can be geniuses or prima donnas who don't necessarily deliver the best results, because they can't develop the synergy that comes from listening and deciding together and serving one another on the team to produce the best results.

This project manager was coordinating a very large project with teams at manufacturing plants all across the country. She had very little influence over what each team did. Her best opportunity to guide teams came up once every six months, when the teams presented their results at a national meeting.

At the first of those meetings, she gave the good team—the group that worked together well—the prestige of presenting first. In her opening remarks, she emphasized how they had developed the solution together and were working together to implement it.

The team of bright people was offended. At first, they felt snubbed, because, after all, they knew they were smarter than the other team and they felt they deserved top billing. But they were smart as well as being full of themselves. They listened to the project manager and learned a lesson. Over the next six months, with a little encouragement from her, they became a good team of good people—working together, deciding together, and helping each other to produce stellar results.

The lesson: With a little bit of guidance, we can make any team a good team of people. And that's what matters for project success.

by teaching all of them how to listen better, express themselves more clearly, make decisions together, and do good work for and with each other.

In our life cycle, we acquired the team members in the planning stage and all along we've been developing them or helping them develop themselves. We've also been managing them through clear definition, assignment, and management of the technical work of the project. That may be all we need to do. However, there are five other circumstances we may need to address for good human resource management during the doing stage:

- *A team member becomes unavailable and we have to replace him or her.* In this case, we do extra work to plan a solution and acquire a team member.
- *New people join the team to do new work.* In some projects there are stages or parts of the doing stage that require different technical expertise. For example, if we're running an advertising campaign, we may need a creative team early on to develop the campaign and a media buyer later on to place the ads.
- *A team member is having difficulty in doing the work.* We focus extra effort in team development for that person, helping him or her get past the roadblock so he or she can contribute to the project. The issues may be technical—not understanding the job or not having the right skills—or they may be about general ability and professionalism. Either way, we can define the gap and help the team close the gap.
- *A team member runs into trouble with conflicting responsibilities or a dual reporting problem with two bosses.* These are structural human resource issues, not personal ones. We need to adjust workloads and resolve conflicts in responsibilities and reporting so

the project team can focus on project work. We should pay particular attention to including outside consultants and vendors as effective parts of the team and making sure their companies are not pulling them away from our project to do other things.

- *Team members get into conflict.* We can use brainstorming techniques that we will discuss in Chapter 11 to prevent and resolve conflicts on the team.

If we take care of these issues promptly if they come up, we keep the team focused on the project and the project rolling along until we get it done right.

Project Procurement Management. Although procurement technically includes all purchasing as well as legal contracting, the PMI's processes tend to describe the process of arranging contracts with a vendor to do the project or to perform subprojects. As I've said, these issues are not relevant to most projects in small business, where we do it ourselves or use our own team to get it done right. If you work by performing contracts for your customers or if you routinely require contracted services, you are probably familiar with how to do that in your own industry. The issues covered in the *PMBOK Guide®* are most significant for large military, government, and business contracts where there are extensive regulations governing contracting and the project is so big that coordinating the project and the contract can be a full-time job.

Here are some recommendations in case contracting or purchasing looks like it might be a challenge in making your project work:

- *Make sure that project plans and contract plans match.* For example, if you subcontract part of a project, then specify in the contract's *statement of work* (SOW) or *statement of objectives* (SOO) that the work specified in the contractor's part of the WBS is completed.

- *Contract for value and results, not just for work or products.* If the contract says that certain work must be done and then it is done, you will have to pay for it *even if it does not meet specifications.* Instead, make sure that each contract requires results that conform to specifications and deliver value as defined.
- *If you are the contractor, providing a project as a service to the customer,* make sure that you plan well and that the contract matches the project plan. Also, consider acceptable solutions to all project outcomes. Make sure you define what the customer must do and deliver—such as clear requirements specifications—so that you can deliver your work. Include *on-time* delivery of those items—external dependencies, deliverables to you from the customer—as terms of the contract. This can be as simple as saying, "If we receive a complete, correct specification by the first of the month, we will deliver by the 30th."
- *You might need special contracting work for just one project.* For example, you might need a construction crew to renovate a new office or build a building for you and you've never, or rarely, done anything like that before. The key is simple: *take time to learn your way around.* Find a friendly professional contractor who will show you the ropes. Check references and, when you do, talk extensively with the vendor's past customers about successes, headaches, and problems. Even if you like the first contractor you meet, talk with at least two others. Whomever you choose, you'll feel more confident if you've done your research and you know your way around the issues. See the case study, Storefront Success, in Part III to learn from Paul Manning, a real expert at growing a business by learning new things that interest him.

- *Don't be quick and sloppy.* We can get ourselves into a lot of hot water by signing contracts and purchase agreements without paying attention to what they say. Make sure you can deliver what you are agreeing to deliver and that you are getting what you want.
- *Consider all the possibilities of what might happen.* Most legal conflicts come up around business contracts because something happens that no one had anticipated. Then, as you deal with the unexpected, you realize how much people can differ in what they feel is fair. Consider every possible cause of a major problem—from each party and from the outside. Also consider the range of possible results, from total failure to extreme success, and discuss what you will do in each case.
- *Take care of the people.* On longer projects, do good stakeholder management to make sure that everyone involved in every agreement and contract is happy with what is happening.

The PMI defines two procurement processes in the executing group: one in the controlling group and one in the closing group. Here are the definitions from the glossary of the Project Management Institute's *A Guide to the Project Management Body of Knowledge (PMBOK® Guide)—Third Edition.*

- *Request seller responses*—the process of obtaining information, quotations, bids, offers, or proposals, as appropriate.
- *Select sellers*—the process of reviewing offers, choosing from among potential sellers, and negotiating a written contract with a seller.
- *Contract administration*—the process of managing the contract and the relationship between the buyer and seller, reviewing and documenting how a seller is performing or has performed to establish required corrective actions and provide a basis for future relationships with the seller, managing con-

tract related changes and, when appropriate, managing the contractual relationship with the outside buyer of the project.

- *Contract closure*—the process of completing and settling the contract, including resolution of any open items and closing each contract.

Integration

We're in the home stretch! Integration is the last of the nine knowledge areas from the PMI and the one it uses to tie everything together. In the *PMBOK Guide®*, it comes first and it's used to organize all project work. That makes sense, but, in introducing this material, I put it last, because that makes it quick and easy. To integrate means to pull things together and it is a lot easier to explain integration when people know about all the pieces of the puzzle. Now that you understand how to manage scope, time, cost, quality, risk, your team, and other issues that can come up in the doing stage, it will be easy to pull it all together.

We need project integration management for one very simple reason: a project is a system and a change in one part of the project can affect all of the other parts of the project. In medicine, one tiny little thing, like an allergic reaction, can make the whole body sick. In computer systems, one small bug can crash the whole system. When the Hubble Space Telescope went up into space with a misshapen mirror—a tiny defect measured in fractions of a wavelength of light—the project to repair the telescope cost hundreds of millions—and the repair didn't even fix the mirror, but just installed a correcting lens.

Of course, not all errors create such dramatic crises as these. The key point is that *we don't know what the effects of a change will be unless we think in terms of the system.* Integrated change control—the key integration process of the doing stage—is designed to make sure that we look very closely at the effects of any change in one area on all the other areas.

The PMI describes the work of project integration management in the doing and follow-through stages in four processes: one for executing the project, two controlling processes, and one closing process. Here are the definitions of those processes from the glossary of the Project Management Institute's *A Guide to the Project Management Body of Knowledge (PMBOK® Guide)—Third Edition.*

▼ SOMETHING SLIPPED!
Success Can Attract Trouble

In *Jackpot,* Jim Fixx, the author of the bestseller *The Complete Book of Running,* shares a story of how writing a bestselling book almost got him sued. In *The Complete Book of Running,* he quotes extensively from a running magazine and highlights the editor of the magazine, who gave him a lot of useful information and tips. When the book became a success, the magazine's publisher threatened to sue, saying that Jim had quoted a great deal of information from the magazine without permission and that he wanted a share of the proceeds from the book.

Fixx dug through his files and found a letter signed by the publisher saying Fixx could use anything he wanted from the magazine. That nipped the lawsuit in the bud. But later, the publisher told Jim that he had wanted to sue not for the money and not because of the long quotes from his magazine, but because he felt hurt that he had barely been mentioned in the book, while the editor had received a lot of attention.

The lesson: Communication and working to maintain good relationships are the best ways to prevent expensive and difficult conflicts.

- *Direct and manage project execution*—the process of executing the work defined in the project management plan to achieve the project's requirements defined in the project scope statement.
- *Monitor and control project work*—the process of monitoring and controlling the processes required to initiate, plan, execute, and close a project to meet the performance objectives defined in the project management plan and project scope statement.
- *Integrated change control*—the process of reviewing all change requests, approving changes and controlling changes to deliverables and organizational process assets.
- *Close project*—the process of finalizing all activities across all of the project process groups to formally close the project or phase.

The PMI's integration processes correspond closely to the four levels of the use of feedback that you learned in Chapter 8, as shown in Table 9-2.

Level one was covered in the section at the beginning of the chapter on managing the technical level of the project. Level two has been covered in this section, especially in the subsections on scope and quality. Level four was discussed at the beginning of this section on project integration management in the doing stage.

That leaves level three. We defined this issue in Chapter 8 as discovering either that our map didn't match reality or that the path on our map was wrong. Now, let's take a look at what that means in practical project terms:

- *A single error in the map* will usually show up as an unexpected risk event. It's the equivalent of discovering a sandbar or a reef on your sailing trip. If you see it ahead of time, you steer around it and lose a little time. If you don't, you're in for bigger trouble.
- *A single error in the plan* will usually show up as a failed or missing WBS component. You will need to fix or add the component. The effect on the project schedule and budget will depend on how early you see the problem, how big the problem is, and whether you can get the right expertise on time. In the case of component failure, we can consider scope reduction—dropping the component out of the plan if it is not truly needed.
- *Having the wrong map altogether* is a problem that's more difficult to see and solve. It will probably show up as a lot of risk events that weren't in your plan. It means that you and your team are all on the wrong page. If things seem to be way off course, then you could have the wrong map—major architectural errors or insufficient understanding of project technical issues. You may need to get some expert help, either in project management or in the technical field of the project.

Feedback Level for Staying on Course	Equivalent PMI Process
Staying on track and on time	Direct and manage project execution
Meeting project milestones	Monitor and control project work
Finding out that the plan or the map is wrong	No exact match, but all of the control processes, especially risk monitoring and control, are useful
Changing the plan and destination	Integrated change control

TABLE 9-2. Four levels of feedback compared with PMI process

- *An error in the planning process, leading to multiple errors in the plan,* will appear in one of two ways. If you were weak in one area of planning, you will see the same type of problem over and over. If you were weak in risk planning, lots of unexpected events will come up. If you were weak in quality planning, many components will fail in testing or in gate reviews. If you were weak in time or cost estimation, each project component will come in steadily late or over budget. If any one area of the plan is consistently wrong or insufficient, go back and improve that plan. The second possibility is that you made an error in architectural planning and that your technical model is not the best one for the project. This will create problems throughout the project or, worse, long-term maintenance problems. You will probably need some expert advice to find the best solution or work-around.

- *Having the wrong map and the wrong plan* is a problem that happens to all of us sometimes. We just go about doing something in completely the wrong way. The usual symptom is massive confusion. If this happens, step back from the situation until you can see the big picture. Talk with people—friends and experts—until you see what the problem is. Then decide whether to cancel the project or restart from the beginning. Don't think it's the end of the world; life brings us these challenges. Projects like these will give you either a bad name or a sense of humor.

We have now looked at the process of integrating project work from many perspectives. Let's close this section with a closer look at integrated change control.

Integrated Change Control. We need a form and a process for integrated change control. I've pro-

vided one on my web site, which you can get through the CD that comes with this book. (I couldn't put it directly on the CD because I'd already published it elsewhere.) Here, let's look at the most some general guidelines, including an overview of the process:

- *Be proactive.* Prevent the need for change with good planning, talk with people to keep expectations under control, and educate people to minimize change requests.

- *Distinguish corrections to meet the plan from changes to the plan.* There is a crucial difference between a request for rework to meet requirements and a change in the requirements. In the first case, the plan isn't changing: you just need to do better work to meet the plan. That may lead to changes in time and budget, but it is not a scope change request. In the second case, the plan is changing and you will need to change the scope plan as well as other parts of the project management plan.

- *Receive all changes in writing or write them down.* That is the only way to keep track of changes. If you don't do this, you're headed for all kinds of troubles. People will think you've agreed to changes you've dropped. Worse, half of the project team will be building one thing and the other half will be building something else, and you'll get something that doesn't work at all.

- *Analyze the change, applying all nine areas, and decide what to do.* Each change *might* affect any of the nine areas of project management and you have to figure out what the effects will actually be. Based on your analysis, you have to decide whether or not to make the change.

- *Be conservative—include only changes that are essential or of high value.* If the project can succeed without the change, then rejecting the change is usually the best choice, especially if you are near the end of the project.

- *Include team members in the decision process* if they have expertise that will help.
- *Follow through.* Update all plans, inform the team and all stakeholders, and get everyone on the same page with the new plan.

We have now looked at the managing project management level of the project in the doing stage from every perspective. Let's turn our attention to managing the business level of the project.

MANAGING THE BUSINESS LEVEL

In this final section of Chapter 9, Keeping the Project on Track, we will look at managing the business level of the project in the doing stage. For small, clearly defined projects, there may be little or nothing that you need to do. That's especially true if you are doing the project for your own company. But if you have a customer outside the team or outside your company, or if the project is going to run for a long time, there are two things you should do. First, you should keep in occasional contact with all stakeholders. Keep them reminded of the project and its value, so that they don't just slip away and lose interest. At the same time, ask them what's going on—and listen. As you'll see, there are a number of issues that can come up for the customer, for your own company, in the market, or with vendors that could challenge your project. As always, the sooner you know about change, the easier it is to manage. In fact, that is particularly true when looking at larger, outside issues that affect a project. Why? Because your project has already been started and money has been spent. If you say that you need information or support to finish it, you'll usually get it because people want to get results from a project once they've invested effort and paid for some of it. As long as you raise the issue early enough and work

cooperatively, people will work to resolve the conflict and make sure your project can succeed.

With this general perspective of knowing what's going on and keeping others informed, you will be able to deal with these issues:

- Managing customer and stakeholder expectations
- Watching for changes outside the project that affect the project and then bringing them under management
- Communicating to customers and executives about changes inside the project
- Preventing and resolving conflict among the project, the company, and the customer

We should be alert for these issues and deal with them promptly if they arise. Let's look at each one in turn.

Managing Expectations

People tend to "remember" that they're going to get everything they want, even if they didn't ask for it. We also tend to dream of more things and somehow expect those to happen, as if by magic. While the customer's expectations are expanding, inflated by hopes and dreams, the specification isn't changing and actual results may even be drifting downwards. While the customer is dreaming, the team is working, running into problems, and maybe dropping the ball here and there. Work quality results are likely to go down if we don't do anything to manage them. If we are not careful, this leads to a large gap, as illustrated in Figure 9-2, where the customer expects more than the specification and the team delivers less.

The solution is gate reviews that bring the project up to specification while bringing the customer back down to earth, as shown in Figure 9-3.

In Figure 9-3, we show the two benefits of gate reviews. We use the gate to identify gaps between the specification and the work results. We then

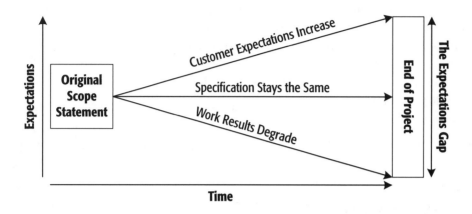

FIGURE 9-2. A project without gates allows an expectations gap

have the team improve the work results to meet the specification. At the same time, we bring the client to the gate review to get project status and see the product under development.

In the first gate in Figure 9-3, the client had some expectations that we understood as change requests, but rejected, bringing their expectations down to the specification. We also brought the work results up to the specification. At the second gate, the client understood what kind of change request mattered. They made a request—an increased expectation—and we approved the change request—increasing the specification to match their expectation. At the same time, we had the team do the work so that the results matched the new, higher specification. We then told the client that we couldn't afford any late changes to

the project, so their expectations stayed level to the end of the project. The work results dropped a little from the specification, but we fixed that in closing the project. As a result, we delivered not only to specification, but also to expectations.

When we create gate reviews that include the customers, we must define the review to be appropriate. You don't want to overload customers with technical jargon until their eyes glaze over and they say, "OK, OK," just to escape. At the same time, you don't want to do a superficial job. Sort through the review milestones and decide which of the stakeholders should see what. You can refer to the communications plan, where you associated stakeholders with using—and therefore checking—different work packages. In addition, you should prepare appropriate presentations, which

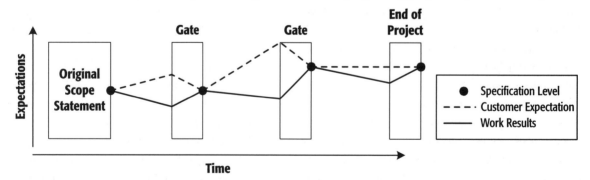

FIGURE 9-3. Managing expectations with gate reviews

may include visuals or even physical prototypes for evaluation or testing.

I can't tell you how important it is to meet expectations. You can do the best job in the world, but if the customers don't get what they expect, they will be disappointed. And each disappointed customer is one step toward a bad reputation—which is the last thing that a small business wants.

> ▼ **SOMETHING SLIPPED!**
>
> ### A New System and No One to Run It
>
> I installed a project management system for an executive team at a large medical school. We did a good job with specification, implementation, and training. Unfortunately, just as we finished, the director who requested the project got a promotion to another institution. Some of his team went with him and others went on to other jobs. Two months after the project was over, the department did not have a single one of the managers there who had requested the new system and very few of the staff who learned how to use it. It was a great system, but it never got used.
>
> *The lesson:* Changes with the customer can reduce the value realized from a project.

Changes Outside the Project

If you are doing a project for your company or your customers, you can deliver to specification, but it can turn out that changes outside the project mean that the value of the project is reduced or can't be realized at all. Large changes—like the customer going out of business before you finish the project—are pretty obvious. But smaller changes to the customer environment or your company environment can matter, as well. Keep in touch with your customer and find out if anything is happening that makes a difference to your project.

Here are some common changes outside the project:

- *A new customer manager or executive comes in* and doesn't understand the value of the project or just doesn't want it.
- *The customer changes the way it works,* using new tools or delivering a new type of work, and the results of your project are no longer exactly what it needs.
- *People on the customer team leave.* At the end of the project, either there aren't enough people to use the system or the new people don't know how to use it.
- *The customer simply loses interest in the project before it is done.* If we catch this change soon enough, we can show the value the project will offer and rekindle interest.

If any of these changes are happening, discuss the project with the customer. Determine if a change of scope, a change of schedule, or even project cancellation is appropriate.

The issues of customer change apply equally when the customer is internal, within your company—and even when the customer is you! If you are changing what you are doing, check periodically to see if you still need the results of the projects you are doing or if some changes to project plans are in order.

In addition to changes with the customer, we may also have to deal with changes in the company or with vendors. Here are some more things to watch for:

- The company has an increase in other business or another major project, so this project becomes a lower priority and workers are pulled away.
- The company has a change of direction and the kind of work done on this project is not a good fit with the company any more.

- Something outside the company—a loss or gain of customers or a major change or crisis in the industry—pulls the company's attention away from the project.
- Vendors the project relies on prove unreliable or become unavailable.
- The company simply loses interest in the project.

In all of these cases, the change is a risk to the resources the project needs to succeed. Since no one likes to waste money by canceling a project that can be saved, you can manage most of these changes if you are aware of them early enough to discuss their effect on the project. If you know what's going on—and that can simply be a matter of asking—you can work early on to ensure the resources you need to finish the project. Or, if the project is truly no longer of value to the company, you can work to get a clear decision to close the project before more money and time are wasted.

Keep in mind that most crises didn't need to be crises. If people communicate well and keep aware of what is happening, most events can be foreseen—at least as possibilities, if not as certainties—and we can shape our plans to the ever-changing situation smoothly.

Changes Inside the Project

Sometimes, we need to inform stakeholders of changes inside the project. In general, if we're not changing scope, due date, or budget beyond approved limits, we can just send routine status reports. We don't need to tell the sponsor, executives, or customers about each WBS package completed or each risk successfully navigated; that's simply too much information. Actually, there are three types of information we do need to deliver to senior managers and key stakeholders:

- *Project status at the level of major milestones,* as we discussed above

- *Routine accounting or timesheet information,* to be tracked for accounting and payroll purposes
- *All changes to the project,* as we discuss below

When we communicate about project change, communication is a two-way street. This means:

- *We receive change requests from stakeholders.* We even need to listen and recognize a request for a change when the stakeholder doesn't know that is what he or she is saying. If an executive says, "There are going to be budget cuts," we need to respond by recognizing a change request, "Can you do this project for less money?" Make sure that any thoughts floating around about the project or product are clarified: either they become change requests or they are noted as exclusions and left out of the project.
- *We discuss changes with stakeholders.* Whoever suggested a change, we look at the effect on executives, customers, and stakeholders. In some cases, we should make the decision. If approving a change request would put the whole project at risk, we should reject it. In other cases, we should give a choice to the customer: "If you want this change, it will cost this much money and delay the project by this much. What do you want to do?"
- *We inform stakeholders about project changes and provide them with updated plans, budgets, and schedules.*
- *We discuss specific changes with specific stakeholders, as appropriate.* Sometimes, one customer or stakeholder will come to us with a change. We see that the change will affect only that one person—maybe it's a change to a report that only he or she sees or a component that only he or she uses. We see that it is low risk and it can fit within the project

schedule and budget. However, we still discuss the change in detail with that customer. We need to be sure to correctly change the revised specification, identifying all work packages being changed, all points in the requirements tracing matrix, and all production and testing activities. Once the change request is technically correct, we can approve it and simply let other stakeholders know. We don't need to discuss it with others, as it does not affect them.

Following those steps, we should be able to keep everyone on the same page, so that we deliver a consistent product that conforms to specifications—we *get it done right* with no surprises.

We should address project changes promptly. Change management should be ongoing, not simply a periodic activity included in the review gate. Take charge of change requests, be decisive, and communicate. Also, if you find that the project might be going over budget or be delivered late, don't wait for the gate—escalate. Tell the sponsor, executives, and the customer about the problem, propose solutions, and work it through with them. And make sure they get the message. Typically, I send an e-mail and also leave a phone message asking the person to look at the e-mail. E-mail alone or a phone message alone is likely to get lost in information overload. In your messages, calls, and meetings, ask for confirmation that the person got the message and understands what is going on.

We introduced the idea of vertical communication and escalation in Chapter 7. Above, we defined when you need to talk with the folks upstairs about project change. Let's take a moment to discuss how to deliver bad news—such as a delay in delivery or a need for more money—to a sponsor, executive, or customer:

- *Take responsibility.* You are responsible for project success, so, wherever the source of the problem was, it was your job to manage it. You did your best, but you didn't succeed. Don't point any fingers; simply own the problem and work toward a solution.
- *Work with your team to prepare solutions in advance.* Don't isolate yourself thinking it is only your problem. Develop solutions and alternatives.
- *Whenever possible, meet face to face.* Unless the executive is far away, don't deliver bad news over the phone.
- *Focus on the present situation and future solutions.* Steer the conversation away from the past and two steps away from blame.
- *Give an executive time to think and decide, but set a time for getting the decision.* If you're asking for more money, it must come from somewhere. If you are delaying a delivery date, it must be checked against schedules. It makes sense that the executive would need to manage these issues and decide what to do. However, for the project to keep going smoothly, you need a decision soon. So be sure to lock down a time for a follow-up meeting or phone call.

Following these steps, you'll find that, as uncomfortable as it can be, dealing with bad news is a lot better than *not* dealing with bad news. Most of the time, you'll get the support you need for your solution or get an even better alternative from the man or woman upstairs.

Conflict

Where people and issues come together, there is always a possibility for conflict. In this section, I'm talking about structural conflict—real disagreements in which what is good for one group or organization is bad for another group and for which a good solution is needed. Let's set aside the issues of how to prevent and manage conflict—we'll cover that in Chapter 11, where we discuss brainstorming, conflict prevention, and conflict resolution. For now, let's focus on what can get the project out of joint with the company or the customer.

Let's consider three cases:

- A project done by your company for a customer
- A project done to launch a new product for your company
- Some other kind of internal project that makes changes in the way your company works

In each of these cases, we need to manage and resolve conflict that may come up between any of two of these three: the project, the company, and the customer.

A Project for a Customer. In this case, you are serving a paying customer outside your company. Of course, you want to do a good job, satisfy the customer, and make money. Conflict between the project and the customer gets in the way of a win/win project contract. Here are some typical issues:

- The customer is not putting enough attention onto the project, particularly not defining requirements clearly or not testing components in a timely fashion.
- The customer has expectations that do not match with what the team can do or what you are willing to do. Some customers agree to a contract and then waste time haggling over every nickel and dime. Others expect lots of extra work for free. Others want shoddy work cheap, when you want to deliver quality, or want a perfect job, when you took the contract with an understanding that they wanted a low price. These conflicts are all about project drivers. Set up a meeting about constraints and drivers and see if you can make the project workable.
- In some cases, the customer asks you do to something illegal or unethical. Don't do it.

Walk away before you land in hot water.
- Sometimes, the issue may not be that clear. The customer may not be just one person. You may work well with a customer manager, but not with the senior management of the company, or vice versa. Or the customer may be short-staffed, so they just can't keep up with their work on the project, even though they want to. Identify the issues and talk things out with people, starting with the people you communicate with well and then including the others, and go for a resolution everyone can live with.

Sometimes, things are going great with the customer, but you are having trouble with your own company. Typically, your company might have gotten a new, big contract with a prime customer and the senior managers want you to start working on the new job before you finish the job you've committed to finish. Or, maybe they are doing the same with your team members—pulling them off to other projects. Go to a senior executive—usually your sponsor. Lay out the issue clearly. Advocate for commitment to completing your project with steady work using the resources assigned. If that is not possible, come up with a workable solution satisfactory to everyone. Often, these issues are managed poorly because people don't define the problem and bring it to the table for a solution.

Last, we can have a situation where the project is getting along great with both customer and company, but our company gets into a separate conflict with the customer. Of course, our company usually likes paying customers. So the typical problem is that the customer isn't paying on time—either for this project or for something else your company has done for them. You may have to stop work until the customer can pay. These are difficult situations. I suggest you identify the problem and then set a clear and reasonable payment requirement from your own company. At that point, you or someone from your company should arrange a meeting with the customer of your project and the executive who signs the checks and find out what they want to do. You don't want to abandon a client in the middle of a temporary cash flow crisis. You also don't want to rack up a huge bill with a client who may never pay. Work these situations out promptly. Even better, set a policy in advance, put it into the project contract, and explain it when you set up work with the client. Then you can say, "This may never apply to you, but here is our company's payment policy. If you think you have any trouble with these terms, please let me know."

A Project to Launch a New Product. In this case, we are developing a new product that the company will produce and sell. If this is the first product in a new line, that is a major event for a small company. If this product is a modification or update of a past product, the project might be essential to keep up with the market, it might be a small new revenue stream, or it might be a major opportunity.

In any case, if the company is behind the product and the marketing team did good research and is getting ready to launch, there shouldn't be any problem. Conflicts arise when these things are not in alignment.

If the company doesn't want to launch the new product, then developing it is a waste of time and money. So, if it seems like the company doesn't want to launch the new product or there is conflict around that, then you need to address that issue immediately. That is really a program management issue larger than the project. The program should be clarified and supported or it should be canceled. If it is canceled, then your project, as part of the program, should also be canceled. If the program is clarified and supported, then the project will get the support it needs.

The success of new product development depends on us doing a good job, but it also depends on the marketing team doing a good job.

In a sense, the marketing team is our customer. They defined the goal of the project through market research and they will have to pick it up and sell it to external customers when we're done. This leads to two possible problems:

- *If the market research was not good,* then we develop the product to specifications, but it won't sell. If this is discovered during the project, we can expect change requests to make the product meet new specifications. At the beginning of a product development project, you should work with the marketers to get clear about how confident they are in their product specification and how detailed it is. If they are uncertain or details are not yet set, design a project with several prototypes and coordinate your development project with their test marketing project.

- *If the market changes,* perhaps due to a new product from a competitor, you may get a change request either to deliver the product sooner or to change it. If the marketers are doing a good job, they got this information to you as soon as possible. Since revenue comes over the long term from getting your best product possible to the market at the right time, you'll want to accept these schedule or scope changes if it is possible to do so.

A Project Changing Internal Operations. The third type of project is one for a customer inside our own company, but we're not creating a new or updated product. Instead, we're changing the way production work is being done. We may be developing or installing new computer software for any department, installing new machinery in a shop, or renovating an office.

In a situation like this, conflict with the customer usually comes up for three reasons:

- *Customers don't see the value of the new way of doing things.* Prevent this conflict or bring it under management by including a promotional effort to explain project value and providing training to ensure easy transition to the new way of working. Include all levels of the customer's employees in designing the solution, so that no one feels a new way of working is being imposed by the boss or by you.

■ *Customers resist changing the way that they work.* Find the reason for the resistance. Help them make the connection between the benefit of the new way of working and the work needed to learn the system and be able to do it. Also, if the customer says the old way is better, listen. He or she might just be right; if so, a project change request is in order.

■ *Customers don't have the time or won't take the time for good specification at the beginning or thorough testing and training at the end.*

▼ SMART THINKING!

Training the Sales Team

A company wanted to have all of its salespeople use a new customer relations management (CRM) software tool to track all sales contacts and orders. It was better for the company, because it would get better information that would help maintain the right inventory and plan future marketing. But the salespeople didn't want to learn the new system. Salespeople generally avoid training because they are rewarded for face time with the customer and for closing deals—especially if they are paid on commission. On a training day, salespeople earn only their base and no commission, which is a big loss. Sometimes, a good new system will fail because salespeople refuse to learn it and then say it doesn't work and wastes their time.

This company was aware of these problems and wanted to prevent them. So, as it developed the software, it launched a promotional campaign to its own salespeople to get them to see the value of the new system, learn it, and use it well. The promotion included:

■ Testimonials from salespeople already on the system about how, after the training, their face time with customers increased because the new system made things easier and their sales and commissions went up.

■ Design of a one-day, no-nonsense training that taught the salespeople how to do their own job on the system.

■ A company commitment to pay each salesperson base pay *plus his or her own average commission* for the training day, so that no salesperson would lose any money by taking the training.

This promotional campaign did two things. First, it removed the barrier to receiving the training: the salespeople wouldn't lose money by losing time with the clients. Second, it convinced the salespeople—in terms of what mattered to them—that this new way of working was worth it. The salespeople believed the new system would work for them, showed up for the training, and made it work.

Some project managers would think that making sure the customer likes and uses the product is beyond what a PM should do, that a PM should just deliver the new product, service, or system. I disagree. The goal of projects is to change the way we work, solving problems, realizing opportunities, and adding value. Whatever it takes to include the customers is worth doing.

The lesson: Motivate the customers to be part of the project from the very beginning to help ensure acceptance and have the company realize the value from your project results.

The customers have their own production work to do—serving their own customers, balancing the books, or whatever. Design specification, testing, and training put them behind in their work. Realize this upfront and have the senior executive of the customer department—their boss or their boss's boss—emphasize the importance of the project. Then, get their commitment and handle any schedule conflicts that come up.

We should be aware of these problems at the beginning of any project that asks people to change the way that they work and we should work it through with all customers and stakeholders.

CONCLUSION

Now you know how to keep your team on track. You help the members manage themselves so that they do good work, you guide them to deliver all results with high quality at the milestones, and you take care of risk and change. And you also know how to keep an eye on everything outside the project team—customers, sponsors, executives, stakeholders, the company, and the customers' company—so that you can watch for signs of trouble and take care of molehills before they become mountains.

If you apply what you've learned so far, you'll be able to complete a product and be almost ready to deliver it to the customer. If we use a golfing metaphor, you've learned to hold the club, set your stance, aim your shot, and do your downswing.

In Chapter 10, you'll learn how to follow through to customer delight, hitting the ball—delivering the product—and following through—ensuring complete customer satisfaction and taking care of all the details, so that the customer and your company realize the full value of your project.

CHAPTER 10

Delivering Customer Delight

IN THIS CHAPTER

In Chapter 10, you will learn to follow through, completing the third and final stage of the project, delivering the product and delighting the customer. First, we'll see why the final stage of our project—where the customer gets the results—is where, all too often, the stuff hits the fan. After looking at the challenges of following through on all types of projects, we'll examine the follow-through stage at the three levels on which we manage on a project:

- *Technical follow-through,* which includes getting it done and getting it right.
- *Project management follow-through,* which includes coordinating with everyone, keeping track of everything, being ready for anything, and writing down what we've learned.
- *Business follow-through,* which includes the steps we take to ensure that the product is supported well and used well, so that value is realized, and then evaluating that value by comparing actual return on investment (ROI) with the ROI as we planned for and used to justify the project at the beginning.

At the end of Chapter 10, you'll know how to follow through and deliver delight.

OUR GOAL IN PROJECT MANAGEMENT and in small business is more than customer satisfaction; it's customer delight. Satisfied customer like what they get and walk away—and might never come back. The keys to success in small business are customer retention—that is, repeat business—and employee retention—that is, keeping our team for the long term.

When we achieve customer delight in our projects, we get both.

What is customer delight? We achieve customer delight when a customer says, "The product exceeded my expectations. More than that, I was delighted by every interaction I had with every person who works for the company."

▼ Focus!

It's All About Customer Value

Our one-time, unique process is about to deliver a product, service, or result. If the specification was good and the customer uses the results well, then value will be realized. If we did good project work, then we are delivering good results on time and within the budget. But now is the time to make sure we're fully ready, we deliver and ensure product acceptance and valuable future use, and then we tie up all the loose ends to complete the project.

It doesn't work to deliver the product and run. Just like a golfer, batter, or tennis player, a project manager succeeds by focusing on what happens after the ball is hit, after the product is delivered. This is the secret of following through: focus on the customer, on delivering solutions and value, not just results and products, and the value will be realized.

That's what it really means to *get it done right!*

Can you think of a company that delights you, that has done such excellent customer service that it's made you into a loyal customer? If so, then you know what I mean. If not, imagine how easy it would be to run your company if customers kept coming back, asking for more. When you learn the art of delivering customer delight from this chapter, you'll know how to make that happen, project after project, customer after customer.

How does customer delight help with repeat business and staff retention? Let's answer that in terms of the three types of projects: a project for a customer, a project to develop a new product, and a project to improve internal operations.

- *A project for a customer.* When we deliver customer delight along with results, customers get exactly what they wanted. If it is a practi-

cal item—a business solution or a custom personal practical product—they know how to use it and realize value. If it is an item of beauty, they see its value. In addition, you gave them no hassles throughout the project. So, they'd be happy to use you again or refer you to their associates and friends. When a team delivers delight to customers, the members have reason to be happy. Being part of project success and working for appreciative customers is a good reason to stay right where you are, instead of leaving for another job.

- *A project to develop a new product.* If we develop a new product that delivers customer delight, our company could be rolling in gold. We now have a product that will keep customers coming back. It's up to the production team to keep up the quality and the marketing and sales team to move the product, but we've made their jobs easy by giving them something that they can sell based on value. If they follow through, then the company's success will mean repeat customers and the production and marketing teams will have profitable, steady work. The project team can be rewarded through bonuses when the product exceeds expectations, as well as appreciation from the head of the company and the whole company.

- *A project to improve internal operations.* If our project gives our employees a better way of working, then customer delight means that the people in affected departments are doing their jobs more easily and getting better results. If it's a profit center, then profits increase as their work gets easier, they have better information, and they can focus more on delighting *their* customers. If it's a cost center, then costs go down, corporate information improves, and profit margins go up. Employees are doing better jobs with less hassle, so they stay with the company. The company is paying more attention to the customers, so customers stay with the company.

So, now we know our goal. But it isn't easy to get there. If it was, then every company would do it and our country would be full of happy customers and employees working on good business systems without any hassle. Heck, we'd probably be down to a three-day workweek. We'd be so efficient that we could work less and enjoy life more with all those delightful products!

Well, life isn't like that—and there's a reason. Customers are people and people are unpredictable. They always want something new and different. Delighting them over and over is a real challenge. It means being able to deliver unique work and get it done right the first time. It also means getting better at what we do, project after project. If you want to keep getting better, set your sights on customer delight and read on to see what challenges you face and how to master them.

THE CHALLENGES OF FOLLOWING THROUGH

What makes follow-through so difficult? Systems theory proposes an answer to that. When we look at processes that occur in time, we can see two types.

One is the unfolding of a plan in a known environment. Most of project work is like that. Once we have our scope statement and architecture laid out, we are working down into the details of planning, changing only very small things. The more we plan, the more our environment is set. When the plan is complete, we roll along a course we've set. We've even—as best we could—thought through the things that could take us off the path. In this way, following a plan and doing the work to make the plan unfold, we are doing our best to keep the unpredictable at bay. In systems terms, we've defined the project in its work environment

as a system and we're trying not to interact with any new systems, but just let the work unfold.

All of that changes when we get to the follow-through stage. When we deliver the product, it encounters the customer. The product is one system and the customer is another. When two systems meet, they form a new system—and anything can happen. This is the second type of process that occurs in time: two systems meeting with unpredictable results. We see it all the time in art and in life: two people fall in love, but are they meant for each other? Will they keep delighting in each other? That's the basis of many romances, from *The Taming of the Shrew* to *Sleepless in Seattle*. What makes it so much fun is that it's unpredictable.

Well, we encounter that same situation at the end of a project, when the customer meets the product. Even if the customers got what they wanted, will it delight them? Will they use it, realize value, and come back for more? The problem is that what is exciting in drama is nerve-racking in reality, especially when the results of weeks or months of work depend on that unpredictable event. What if it doesn't work for the customers?

In formal project management life cycles, the follow-through stage is called *transition to production.* One of my clients has an informal name for it—*the storm period.* The client is an IT development group delivering new computer systems to internal customers. The members of that group know from experience that they will be overwhelmed with lots of unpredictable problems during transition to production—like being caught out in a storm in a small sailboat. In this chapter, you'll learn how to bring your project through the storm and safely to port.

So, when two systems meet for the first time, unpredictable things happen. The first thing we can learn from this is that the issues that come up in follow-through are fundamentally different from the issues that come up at any other time during the project. The second thing is that, if we think through the nature of the systems, we can probably identify the most common problems. Let's do that now, looking at the follow-through stage for projects for a customer, projects that develop a new product, and projects that change internal operations:

- *A project for a customer.* First, we have to distinguish between two types of value the customer is expecting: useful value and enjoyment. In each case, the potential problems are different.

  - *If the customer expects useful value,* then the unpredictable element will usually arise from one of two areas. The first is barriers to effective, efficient use. If the system doesn't work right when the customer gets it, that's one cause of trouble. If the customer resists learning it or has trouble learning it well, that's another. Worst is when both of those are happening—the system isn't working and the people resist learning. In those cases, the product and the customer just don't come together in a useful way. We may have to do a full restart on delivery and training to make the project succeed. To prevent these problems, we should focus our attention on ensuring the system works right at the customer location before the customers see it and on designing, promoting, and implementing an effective training program. The second set of storms comes if the customer is not integrated, that is, if the customer groups are divided, disagreeing about details of the goal. Here are some examples. If some users like it and others don't, we get partial acceptance, which can lead to little or no value. If the executives like it but the users don't, then we get paid but the customer realizes little value and doesn't come back. If the users like it but the executives don't, we might not get paid. If the customer can't support it and keep it running, then there is less value and the customer won't come back. We can work to prevent all of these problems by maintaining good communications with all stakeholders, resolving all open issues, and then making sure that satisfaction from any one group of customers is reported to all the other groups.

  - *If the customer expects enjoyment,* then the key is that the customer likes or loves the product or service *and doesn't feel irritated by any part of it at all.* A long wait at an excellent restaurant leaves a memory of a long wait—and a lost customer. A bus tour of an exotic location with wonderful sights and events and no air conditioning on the bus is a miserable vacation. As a result, the key is to focus on the customer's experience of the product or service down to the last detail. In addition, we have to ensure that we are ready for anything, that we can respond effectively to any reasonable customer request. This requires contingency planning and a good support team.

- *A project that develops a new product* can experience a storm period that's relatively mild if we work closely with the teams that will produce, support, and sell the new product after the project is over. These are your first customers. All these people are within our company, so we can have good access to them. The biggest challenges arise when a company is so compartmentalized or those people are so busy that you don't get to work with them throughout the project—or at least in planning and a lot near the end, as well. If they can tell you their concerns, then you can plan for and prevent many problems. When you do, you are designing quality into the product from the very beginning. Products that are easy to produce, have low maintenance costs, and are easy to market have large profit margins. Our best approach here is, from the beginning of our project, to define quality as that which delivers the product with the best features and fewest hassles to the production, marketing, and maintenance teams of our company.

- *A project that changes internal operations.* We looked at the most important issues for this type of project at the end of Chapter 9, including the example, Training the Sales Team. Key issues are a lack of customer involvement in design specification, so that the system is not easy to use; customer resistance to learning and using the new system; a technical failure of the new system in the production environment; and a conflict between learning the new system and doing regular work. Our best approach is to work cooperatively with the internal customer team. We work to include the customers from the beginning, promote the new system's value, listen to the resistance, and deal with any genuine issues. We make sure the system works in the production environment before the customers see it. We define the priority of training in effective and efficient use of the new system for the actual work and we schedule time for it.

Now that we have an outline of the issues for each type of project, let's look at the work of the follow-through stage in managing the technical level, the project level, and the business level of the project as we deliver the product and make sure we *get it done right!*

TECHNICAL FOLLOW-THROUGH

Technical follow-through is very simple:

- We complete scope, getting it ready.
- We ensure quality, getting it right.

There are two things we can do to make this a success. First, we can do extra work to ensure that the specification really delivers what the customer wants. Second, we can do extra work and testing to ensure that the product meets its specifications and performs as required.

Ensuring a Good Specification

In ensuring a good specification, we must address two issues: ensuring a good customer specification, so that the customer can use the product well, and ensuring a good fit of the product into the production environment.

There are two approaches to ensuring a good customer specification. We covered one of them in Chapters 3 and 5, where you learned about prototypes and learned how to do requirements elicitation by sharing a picture or sample of the product, getting feedback, and creating the document specification. This is a good approach, but when the customer is going to use the product and that use requires that they really understand it well, we may need to do more. For those situations, our best solution is to continue prototyping and testing the prototype with the customer throughout the project. This way, some of the customer users—maybe all of them—get to interact with and improve the product. By the end of the project, they like it because they've made it work for themselves. We can adjust our project plan to include customer prototype testing and feedback in one of two ways. One approach is to insert more gate reviews that include the customer. The other is to have a customer worker assigned to the team either part time or full time to keep testing and using each component as the team develops it. Both of these methods are commonly used in software development when a custom system is being built to improve the way a department works.

The second issue is to make sure that the product will work in the customer environment. The key here is to get to know the environment really well from all architectural and engineering perspectives. Here are samples of questions we should ask:

- What are the environmental factors, such as temperature and humidity, that might cause the product to fail?
- What resources are we assuming the customer has, such as space for the product, electricity, and so forth? Do they meet the specific requirements of our product? I've seen new air conditioners and refrigerators purchased that couldn't be plugged in because the outlet was the wrong voltage or the appliances constantly tripped the circuit breaker.
- Have we identified every user? Do we know how each one will use the new product and what he or she expects?
- Have we identified every type of maintenance, support, and training related to the new system, now and in the future? Does everyone responsible for maintaining and supporting the system and for learning or teaching know how to do their work, so that the system will work effectively and efficiently for its intended purpose throughout its production life? Have we ensured that they will be able to do that for the life of the product?
- Have we identified every stakeholder and kept in touch with them all, so that we know what each expects?
- Have we asked stakeholders to triple-check that the environment and environmental requirements have not changed since they were specified during project planning?

Using these questions will be very different for different types of products, services, and solutions with different types of customers. Within our own industry, we should develop effective checklists to make sure we *get it done right!*

Ensuring We Meet the Specification

If our specification is good, our next step is to ensure that the product conforms to all specifications—the work of quality engineering. We have already discussed this at length in Chapter 9. Tracing all requirements through architecture to components and through the test plan, test design, testing, and confirmation of corrective action and retesting is essential. A project full of checklists will succeed—if they are used with a focus on quality. We need to make sure the team is not so pressured to get it done on time that it doesn't get it done right.

As we approach the final gate, additional tests are required. All of the different types of tests for all different industries would fill a book larger than this one. But we want to make sure that the product will work into the future, not just when we deliver it.

Test design is difficult. How can we say that, because a product passed a test, it will work in the real world? Here are some questions we should consider when designing tests.

- Can we design a test where the system is working in the real production environment, as close as possible, doing what it is intended to do?
- Can we include customers in our tests?
- Can we design stress tests that test the system at capacity and over?
- Can we design aging tests that show how the system will work in the future?
- Can we test how the system will work after it receives routine maintenance? After a failure, emergency shutdown, and restart?

- Can we test maintenance and emergency procedures performed by the customer support team?

This list could go on and on. It's a tough world out there and we need to do a lot to make sure our product will keep producing long after we deliver it.

Testing, Testing: Going Around in Circles. As we discussed in Chapter 9, we must allow time for testing, rework, and retesting to ensure that each module and the whole product pass all tests. The closer we get to our delivery date, the harder this is to do. Just as we're running out of time, we have more and more completed components to test.

We have to assume that some components will fail in testing and that the product will fail some tests, too. Of course, we don't know which ones will fail; if we did, we'd fix them before they failed. If we don't know what the failures will be, how do we know how much time to leave for the tests? There is a rule of thumb that might help. Calculate the time that it will take—in hours of effort—to test everything and verify it as if it will pass all tests. Then multiply by 3.2. So, if testing will take 10 hours if nothing goes wrong, allow 32 hours for that test series. Until you develop a record, that is a good place to start.

We've now completed our guide to managing the technical level during follow-through to make sure the specification is right and the product meets the specification. The product is as ready as it can be. Are we? Is the team? Is the customer? We'll face those challenges in the next section.

PROJECT FOLLOW-THROUGH

In this section, we look at how to do good project management in the follow-through stage. We want to prepare as much as we can for the unpredictable as:

- The product, service, or solution starts to operate in the real world.

- The customer learns to use and starts using the product, service, or solution.
- The customer starts to maintain and support the product.
- The customer executives react to the end of the project and receipt of the product.

As our team is finishing up and testing the product, getting it ready for delivery, we should turn our attention to these activities:

- Coordinate with everyone.
- Keep track of everything.
- Be ready for anything.

If we do all of that, we will be as ready as we can be to do good follow-through. Let's look at each in turn.

Coordinate with Everyone

I hope you haven't thrown your communications plan into a drawer and forgotten about it. If you did, get it out and dust it off well before your delivery date.

Now is the time to triple-check everything with everyone. Review your list of stakeholders and their concerns. Call up or meet with each one and make sure that they are all satisfied with all that they have heard and seen. Ask what you need to do to make delivery day a success for them and for everyone involved with the customer.

Then follow through. Every time a stakeholder requests something, write it down and make sure you or a team member takes care of it and lets them know it was done. If you need a stakeholder to do something for you, ask, then put it in writing, and keep bugging him or her until you get what you need. You want good communications feedback and good action feedback on everything the project needs. Your team is probably used to that by now. But your customers aren't. So, ask for what you need—and keep asking until you get it. I'm assuring you, and you should assure them, that the only way to ensure successful product delivery is if everyone triple-checks the completion of every little detail.

Keep Track of Everything

It's not enough just to talk with everyone; we also have to keep track of everything. On my web site—accessible through the CD—is a tool I call the Open Issues template. It covers all the different types of information we have to track to get through any project in the follow-through stage. It's also good for any project in crisis. Here are the lists of the types of issues you need to track—and what can happen if you don't:

- *Decisions to be made.* If we leave a decision unmade, someone will be disappointed. For example, if a change request came in and we lose track of it, someone will expect to be getting something, but it won't be in the specification.
- *Recently resolved decisions.* We keep these on the list because we need to tell everyone what the decision was. If someone isn't told, then he or she won't be on the same page. Have you ever missed a meeting because no one told you that the location had changed?
- *Work to be done.* These are the simple, straightforward items. If a piece of work isn't done, then some part of the product won't be delivered. Wrap up the loose ends and deliver to avoid customer dissatisfaction.
- *Problems to be solved.* These are more complicated than work to be done. With work, we know what has to be done and how long it will take. But when we discover a problem, we know only the symptom. We still need to diagnose and define the problem, then work on a solution, and finally retest. Unresolved problems near the end of a project are crucial. They require attention from us and from our team. Make sure each one is assigned to someone and resolved.

- *Documents to be changed.* Have you ever bought a consumer electronics item or tool for your workshop and found that the picture of the tool in the instructions doesn't match what you bought? That happens when instructions or other project documentation isn't updated with the changes to the product. Track all needed changes to all documents within the project and all deliverable documents.
- *Information to be gathered.* Here, someone knows something, but someone else needs to know it. We find the information and deliver it to the person who needs it, so the job can get done. Imagine blowing an installation day because you or someone on your team gets lost on the way to the customer's office. Define everything anyone needs to know and get the information to each person well in advance.

If we've taken care of this situation, all of the issues are named. That leaves two problems. We have to resolve the issues. We also have to be ready for the issues that we haven't heard about—and maybe never even imagined.

Be Ready for Anything

Can you imagine the afternoon sun ruining your day? For a TV producer, that's quite possible. Matt Williams, a TV producer who provided two of the case studies in Part III, tells a story that illustrates what it means to be ready for anything on a project.

A crew was shooting a scene indoors. It was running a bit behind, but it wasn't too bad. The current scene had to be finished before 1:30 p.m., because at that point the sun would come through the window, the lighting would change, and the scene would look totally different. The person responsible for lighting had two options. He could either count on the scene being done on time or ask the props crew to build a big wooden overhang to put outside to shade the window. It was a very busy day with a lot of things going on, he was counting on the crew not to fall further behind, and he didn't ask the props team to prepare the device to darken the window.

He was wrong. Just before 1:30, the person responsible for lighting said that they'd need to stop shooting until a shade could be built. The producer was mad, because it pushed the day closer and closer to very expensive overtime. The props team was mad because they were doing it at the last minute, when they could have had it ready and kept the day moving. One poor decision on a shooting day threw everyone off and could have been very expensive.

Project delivery days are like shooting days, so we should learn from folks who make films. Matt tells me that the key to success in the TV and movie industry is to have four or five solutions for every problem that might happen and to be ready to decide which one is best in under 30 seconds and then turn everything upside down to make it work. Folks in the film industry get a lot of practice thinking and working that way. In one sense, project management is even harder. We don't have to work that way very often. Most of the time, most of the project is under our control. But, at the crucial moment, delivery day, all that changes. We have to be ready for anything—and all the work we did up to that point may depend on what we do in that one critical moment.

Project delivery takes many different forms, so our preparation has to take many forms, as well.

- *We ship a product to a customer.* Will they be able to install it, understand it, and use it without us?
- *We install the product for them and leave them to use it.* Will they be able to understand it and use it without us?
- *We provide installation, training, and support.* Will everything go well during installation and training? Will all the people involved work well together? Will they come to the training and be able to use the solution productively?
- *We deliver to many different locations, either for one customer or for many customers.* In this case, we need to make sure that each delivery, with appropriate installation and training, is a well-planned mini-project.
- *We provide a service, supporting a one-time event.* Here, all the value is at the delivery time. There is no second chance. A wedding planner can't say, "I'm sorry I forgot the cake and flowers. Could you get married again next week?"
- *We provide a solution and the customer isn't even there.* We might be fixing a broken pipe while the customer is away. We have to do good work with little guidance and then follow up with the customer.
- *We work directly with the customer's customer.* Here, we represent the customer: if our team makes a mistake it makes the customer look bad. For example, we might be doing an advertising mailing for the customer. We have to more than triple-check the quality of everything we do, ensure successful delivery, and follow up with the customer.

What is your situation? Whatever it is, here are the keys to successful follow-through:

- Know your field. Many of the situations described above are routine for professionals in a specific field.
- Plan delivery day as a subproject. Make a detailed plan and timeline of activities to prepare, do, and follow through on delivery day. Check scope, time, cost, quality, risk, the team, and all the other areas. Then check them again. Then be ready for problems you never even imagined.

If we prepare well, delivery day is exciting. It's a chance to see all of our work pay off. If we don't get fully ready, then we'll have a really lousy time and we and our customer will pay a steep price. Either we'll need to do a lot of rework and follow-up or return on investment for the whole project will be reduced or lost altogether.

What Have We Learned?

When we've delivered and done all we can for the customer, there is one more job to do for our own company. Every project is a unique chance to learn. We can turn expertise into experience by taking information from the project and developing two documents for future use:

- *Historical information,* including the project plan in all its stages and records of actual results, is useful for planning future projects. If we capture this information in an organized way and make it available, we are building our *organizational process assets*—our knowledge about how to do good projects.
- *Lessons learned* is a document that we can create at the end of any stage and also at the end of a project, saying what we have learned about how to get it done right. We can establish new guidelines, improve templates and tools, and define how we can become better project managers.

For a lessons learned survey, see the CD that comes with this book.

BUSINESS FOLLOW-THROUGH

In the last section of this chapter on delivering customer delight, we look at business follow-through. To follow through at the business level, we need to be attentive to customer needs, to take care of loose ends for the customer, the team, and our own company, and to check the project results against the original goal that we defined at the beginning when we defined the value of doing the project and the estimated return on investment (ROI).

Is the Customer Delighted?

How do we know if the customer is delighted? We ask. And, in asking, either we increase their delight by showing, once more, that we care, or we have a chance to make up for any problems that may have happened. And, if we are given that chance, we should use it to the fullest. Be sure to take care of any final commitments that you make.

If you are the customer, you need to talk to yourself. Are you delighted with the results of the project? Are you using the new product, service, or solution you created? Are you realizing value? If not, why not? In a small business, it is all too easy to get caught up with the next thing and the next and not use the good work we've done. But what we don't use has no value for us.

If we have a single customer or customer group—inside our company or external—we should meet with them to hear whatever they need to get closure and ensure project success and lasting value. You might prepare a questionnaire or meeting agenda based on the original project plan, asking your customers if they are getting what they need. If they are external, that is also a good time to ask about the possibility of repeat business or to get a reference or a referral.

If we delivered results to many customers, then we should include some kind of survey or evaluation in our project plan so that we can know what they thought of our work and our service. When distributing surveys widely, it pays to provide some kind of incentive or bonus for replies, so that we get lots of feedback.

However we ask the customers if they were delighted, we should follow through on the answer:

- *If customers are delighted, approach them appropriately about the possibility of repeat business, references, and referrals.* If you are not comfortable doing this, check out books on networking as a marketing technique—it can really build your business.

- *If customers are generally appreciative but have some concerns, listen and follow through.* For those that cannot be resolved, show the customers that you understand the problem and promise that you will make a change to do better next time. Do that even if you expect never to work with those customers again. That promise is really a promise to yourself as a professional—a promise to learn lessons and get better at what you do. If you can address the customers' problems, do so. At the end of a project, it pays to go the extra mile to create lasting appreciation and repeat business.

- *If customers have a major complaint, work out a fair resolution.* Do what you can within reason to come to a good resolution. Don't give away the store, but if there is some reasonable extra or discount you can offer, then do so. Showing customers that you are very concerned to deliver satisfaction even when you can't goes a long way to building a relationship. It also is an excellent way to prevent bad publicity and even more unfortunate circumstances, such as legal action.

Know where you stand on delivering customer delight. Keep learning until you are doing it project after project. There is no more delightful path to small business success than a long line of delighted customers.

Are All the Loose Ends Tied Up?

The Project Management Institute has two processes in the closing process group: lose Project and Contract Closure.

Close Project is a very general instruction to close all activities in all processes from all process groups. We can do this by reviewing our project plan. We check with everyone that each task is done and we double-check with the customers to see that they got everything they wanted. Then we review the project, walking through all nine of the knowledge areas, and we tie up any loose ends.

Contract Closure is an additional step whenever there was a contract as part of the project work. This includes both contracts where we are the performing party and we delivered something to a customer and contracts where we received something from a vendor or consultant. We make sure that the final invoice is sent, received, and paid. We also send any appropriate legal documents that sign off on the fact that the contract is complete, giving the date and stating whether all terms were met or if anything still needs to be resolved. If anything does need to be resolved, we schedule or delegate appropriate action.

Last, we should look at unresolved issues outside the project. What work has fallen behind while we were busy getting this project done? What will our team do next? What do we want to do to thank our team, our vendors, our customers, and other stakeholders? How do we want to celebrate?

Is ROI Realized?

At the end, we should look back to where we started. We began this project with a purpose, a reason *why* we were doing this project. We defined value, defined what we would need to deliver, and how it would need to be used to receive that value. We may have even gone all the way and defined value over cost in terms of ROI.

We now need to return to the original project charter or initial plan and ask, "Did we do what we said we were going to do? Did we solve that problem or realize that opportunity? Was it as successful as we had hoped it would be? Did we hit our target?"

In some cases, we can answer those questions shortly after the project is over. Here are some examples:

- We delivered a project for a customer. We succeeded if they paid the bill, expressed satisfaction or delight, and came back with repeat business or provided references or referrals.

- We ran a one-time event, such as a presentation and booth at an annual industry conference. We defined certain goals in advance, such as getting a certain number of inquiries and selling a certain dollar value in products. We can compare our actual results with our goals. If we didn't reach them, we may be able to define some follow-up actions that will help close the gap.

On some projects it will take some time to see if we are going to achieve our ROI. The day the project delivers may be the beginning of receiving ROI, but it may take years to realize the full value. In that case, we should arrange for a follow-up analysis at an appropriate time. Here are two examples of that type of project:

- *We bring a new product to market.* It will take time to see if the product meets the expectations of our sales forecasts for its product life cycle and if its production and maintenance costs will be as low as we expected.

- *We launch an advertising campaign.* It will take some time to see if it brings us new business.

At the appropriate time, we measure actual ROI. How do we do that? The formula is the same as the one presented in Chapter 3. We should use the same methods for defining value and calculating the ROI number. The only difference is that now we use actual figures, instead of estimates or forecasts.

- If we've realized all the value we're going to get—as is the case when we deliver a project to a customer or attend a trade show—we divide the actual value realized, adjusted for time, by the actual project cost, for our ROI.

- If we're going to continue to realize value over the life of the product or advertising campaign or other result, then the top line is the value actually realized to date, plus a forecast of the value for the future of the product or service. We divide that by actual project costs for our ROI. We can also calculate by the calendar and determine the date when the value gained (adjusted for time) will earn back the cost of the project. After that date, our net revenue will be pure profit.

These ROI calculations are important. First of all, they remind us how important it is to get it done right.

- If the project is over budget, then the ROI ratio is lower.

- If the project is late, then the date we start to get any ROI is later.

- If the project fails to deliver the full scope with quality, then value is lost and ROI is lower.

Second, when we do the actual calculation, we can determine:

- *How good we are, as a business, at picking the right project.* If the project is delivered on time and on budget, but value was lower than expected, then we did good project work, but we overestimated the value of doing the project.

- *How good we are, as project managers, at early estimation.* If the project cost more and took longer than originally planned, we should learn something from that. If project work was good, we can become better estimators so we estimate future projects more accurately. If project work was weak—as we can see in our lessons learned—then we can do better so that we deliver on time and on budget in the future. And if we are in a risky industry where projects are likely to exceed expected costs, we can seek projects with higher ROI.

- *We can do better at coordinating projects with our business.* The ROI ratio points at a crucial business metric—how much money do we have for overhead expenses as a result of project work? A high ROI on customer projects means that we can afford to spend more time and money on marketing if necessary. A high ROI on projects that launch a product means good production revenue at low start-up costs. If we want to launch another project line, it will be easier to convince investors or to put more money into marketing. A high ROI on internal projects usually means that we found an efficient way to save money, reducing overhead costs, or we've improved our ability to make money through marketing, sales, or other business activities.

Use ROI calculations to revisit program and portfolio management. After all, with this project done, you need to figure out what you're going to do next.

CONCLUSION

Customer delight is a delightful goal. The journey toward it can be long, but the value lies in the journey. Each finished project, each satisfied customer, and even each lesson learned from a mistake or a failure is a step in the right direction. Learn the lessons of good follow-through and you do more than master project management: you master good customer service and excel at growing your business.

If you've been reading this book from the beginning, you're probably in total overload by now. That's why I prepared Chapter 11, Focus on Success. It summarizes the most important tools and techniques you need to know to *get it done right!*

Focus on Success

IN THIS CHAPTER

We open with the top 20 list, the 20 most important things to do to make a project succeed. After that, we explore a simple idea that is the key to success on a project of any size—slicing up the project into workable pieces and looking at it from many perspectives. Then we talk about skills for bringing a team together, brainstorming, and preventing and resolving conflict. By the end of this chapter, you'll be ready to make any project work. If you're already skilled at project management, you'll be able to define your next steps to preventing problems and taking on even bigger challenges, confident that you will be able to *get it done right.*

NOW THAT YOU HAVE LEARNED A tremendous amount about good project management, it makes sense to focus on the most important points. We start with the top 20 list of points to make a project succeed. Then we move on to key tools to build your team through successful meetings, brainstorming, conflict prevention, and conflict resolution. By the end of this chapter, you'll not only know how to *get it done right,* but also know how to avoid the pitfalls that keep you from getting the project done at all.

THE TOP 20 LIST

Twenty items may seem like a lot, but I've grouped them in six short lists: one for planning the project, one for preparing your team, one for applying the nine knowledge areas, one for doing, one for using stages and gates, and one for following through.

Four key planning points:

1. *Do the right project.* Using cost-benefit analysis or ROI and considering opportunity cost, look at the project that gives you the biggest value for your effort and is most aligned with your company's

> ## ▼ Focus!
>
> ### Keys to Success
>
> The first ten chapters have given all you need to know to do any type of project in any small or medium-sized business. And that is way too much information. That's why we close Part II by looking at the most important things you need to succeed. I've also included a few other valuable items that didn't fit anywhere else.
>
> Read on for a quick guide to project success.

strategy, moving you in the direction you want to go.

2. *Define scope clearly and precisely.*
3. *Plan the whole project.* Make a plan for each of the nine areas.
4. *Do good architecture.* Work with words and pictures to bring people with different perspectives onto the same page, contributing to and committed to the project.

Prepare your team in just two steps:

5. *Get the right team.* Using the WBS, define the skills needed and get people with those skills. Be honest about gaps and close them by taking time to learn to get it done right.
6. *Get the expertise you need.* Know that being expert in one area means not being expert in other areas—sometimes closely related disciplines. Recognize that projects, being unique work, require learning from and collaborating with experts. Remember: hiring experts you can work with is less expensive than *not* hiring experts you can work with.

Cover all the bases with the nine knowledge areas:

7. *Scope.* Define scope clearly. Teach the cost of changes, in order to reduce change requests.

Then, manage all changes, adding to the project only when it is essential.

8. *Time and cost.* Use unbiased, accurate estimation techniques. Set up systems to gather, track, and analyze time and cost information, so you can keep time and cost under control.
9. *Quality.* Focus on quality at all three levels to ensure value. At the technical level, trace requirements and design checking and testing throughout the project to reduce errors. Then design a test bed and implement the tests. At the project level, work to prevent error; then find and eliminate any errors that slipped through. Do as much testing as you can as early as you can. Allow time for rework and retesting to ensure you've eliminated errors without letting new ones creep in. At the business level, include customers in testing and remember that the goals are customer delight and added value.
10. *Risk.* Plan for uncertainty; prepare for the unexpected. Perform risk management with your team every week of the project.
11. *Human resources.* Help each team member step up in self-management and technical expertise. Teach them all PDCA so that they can improve. Then teach them to work together, until you have a great team of great people.
12. *Procurement.* Get the supplies and resources you need. If your project involves contracts, be sure to keep the contracts in alignment with project value and specifications, not just generally associated with goals and work.
13. *Communications.* Make a communications plan and then follow it so that you are in touch with all stakeholders throughout the project. Make sure that all of them know what they need to know to make decisions and get work done. Analyze status information to create status reports. Be prompt and decisive.

14. *Integration.* Constantly direct corrective action. Evaluate all events that could change the project schedule and all scope change requests. Review the effects of any change on all nine areas before making a decision. Then implement a revised plan with rebaselining.

Keep the project on track with stages and gates:

15. *Use a life cycle.* At a minimum, put a gate at the beginning to clearly launch the project and then a gate after planning, a gate after doing, and a gate after following through.
16. *Make every gate a real evaluation.* Bring every deliverable—parts of the product, product documentation, technical documents, and the project plan and supporting documents—up to specification. If a project can't deliver value, be willing to cancel it.

Use feedback with your team and focus on scope and quality in the doing stage:

17. *Use feedback at all four levels.* Teach workers to stay on track and on schedule, ensure delivery of milestones, manage project risk, and manage project change. Watch out for continuing problems that indicate a serious planning error, such as lack of attention to one of the nine areas or a poor architectural decision.
18. *Focus on scope and quality.* Get it all done and get each piece done right.

Follow through to success:

19. *Deliver customer delight.* Seek to exceed customer expectations while leaving customers delighted with every encounter with your team. Use every success and every error as a chance to learn to do a better job.
20. *Remember ROI and lessons learned.* Compare actual ROI against planned ROI, so you can be honest about the degree of your success. Compile project historical information and lessons learned to make future projects easier.

FIVE WAYS TO PROJECT DISASTER

Success is a matter of moving ahead and steering clear of failure. Here are five fast tracks to failure, so that you can avoid them.

Five ways to *get it done wrong or not at all!*

1. *Scope-less is hopeless.* Don't decide what you are doing—just throw money at a problem.
2. *Focus on time and cost, not quality.* Get it done yesterday. Never let anyone spend money. Don't waste time checking anything—just get it done.
3. *Know the right thing to do.* Don't analyze problems. Don't listen to experts. And—absolutely, above all, whatever you do—be sure to ignore the customer. You wouldn't launch a project if you didn't know everything. What does anyone else know?
4. *Don't thank the team; just push them harder.* Don't waste time with planning. People ought to know what to do. Just tell the team to get it done now—or else.
5. *Avoid big problems.* All of our projects fail. And we've got no time for them, either—we're too busy putting out fires.

Is that a list of how to fail at projects? Or is it also a description of how all too many companies are run these days?

USING PRACTICAL TOOLS AND TEMPLATES

The quick and easy way to learn a new system is with tools and templates. Templates are forms that make sure you ask all the right questions, check everything, and keep things moving throughout the project. There are more templates on the CD and even more on the web site. Open the CD and follow the link to the web site to see all the free templates my company has to offer.

DIVIDE, CONNECT, AND CONQUER

The title of this section refers to several processes that make it easy to complete any project, even a large or complicated one:

- *Decomposition.* Decomposition is the formal term for breaking something down into its component pieces. Work breakdown structuring is decomposition of the project scope and activity definition is further decomposition of the work packages. When we slice work into small pieces, we can manage it better and more easily motivate ourselves to do the work, one piece at a time. We just need to make sure that all the pieces add up to the whole that we want—nothing more and nothing less.

- *Architecture.* Architecture is another kind of dividing and combining. Here, we divide our perspective. In architecture, we look at the project and product from every angle—from every customer group's view and from every technical view. It's kind of like checking a diamond for a flaw. If we can't see a flaw in any of the facets, then the diamond is perfect. But if we see a flaw in one facet, even if we can't see it from another one, we can know the diamond is flawed and, ultimately, won't look good from any angle. Just so, using architecture, we can make sure that the project will look good at every face—every interface with a customer or system and internally as well.

- *Manage all nine areas.* The nine knowledge areas are another way of dividing up the activities of project management—dividing them so we can ensure success in each area. When each area is managed well, nothing can sneak in to cause trouble. The most obvious areas—scope, time, and cost—show

symptoms, but they don't show the causes of project problems. We spend too much money or take too long because of risks that weren't managed, poor communications, lack of attention to quality, or not having the right team. If we take care of all nine areas, we bulletproof our project.

- *Plan, do, follow through at every level.* Progressive elaboration—using the same technique at finer and finer levels of detail—works with the simple life cycle: plan, do, follow through. We can plan, do, and follow through on breaking a book into chapters, and then on breaking a chapter down into sections, and then on writing a section or a paragraph. We can plan, do, and follow through on writing, rewriting, editing, and revising a book for quality. When all that is done, we can deliver a book for publication, or any project to any customer.

Make your big problems small. Then tackle them one by one. Or, take a big opportunity and take advantage of it step by step. Many things that seem larger than we can manage are doable one step at a time.

EFFECTIVE MEETINGS FOR PROJECT SUCCESS

Successful meetings are essential to project success. Here is the text of a paper I wrote and presented at the Project Management Institute's Southeast Regional Conference (Region 14) in Atlanta, Georgia on June 28, 2005. I've included the entire text because it gives a succinct explanation of why meetings matter so much to project success, teaches you how to run a good meeting, and introduces all of the types of meetings needed for project success.

Effective meetings lead to high-quality planning and better control of projects, helping to ensure success. This talk delivers practical tools along with effective meeting and leadership concepts, so that you will be immediately able to improve project effectiveness and efficiency. All types of meetings essential to projects are covered, including stakeholder meetings, status meetings, gate reviews, escalation meetings to sponsors and executives, and post-project reviews.

Introduction: Meetings Matter

There is a lot of evidence that well-run meetings are crucial to project success in all businesses.

Meetings and Project Success. Meetings are essential to project success, and project meetings need to be run so that they are well organized, so that they focus on an agenda with topics essential to project success, and so that they encourage everyone to participate.

Solid Correlation Between Effective Meetings and Increased Productivity. I have taught project management to over 2,000 students in over 60 classes nationwide. I teach the methods presented here and then I ask, "Has anyone ever gone from not using structured meetings to using structured meetings similar to what I recommend?" Usually, one or two people will raise their hands. I ask them, "When you made that change, what happened to productivity on your project?" In every case, without exception, the project managers have reported increased project productivity when effective meeting methods were introduced. I've also heard a few cases where effective meetings stopped happening, and projects ran into difficulty or failed as a result.

One example came from NEC Corporation. In the mid-1990s, NEC had a reputation for producing excellent microcomputers. It was bought out by a *Fortune* 100 company and everybody expected great things. Instead, the product was poor quality and the division soon failed. A former NEC employee was in one of my classes a few years later. I asked him what happened, and he said, very simply, "When we worked for NEC, we had really good, structured meetings. After we were bought out, the new corporation told us we couldn't use those meeting methods any more. Everything fell apart, and the company failed."

I have heard many people tell me, "We had weekly status meetings when we started the project. Then we got too busy, and we stopped having them." But no one—not once—has ever said to me, "And that one hour a week we saved from not going to the meeting gave us the time to get our work done and save the project." On the other hand, I've heard of many projects that ran into trouble, and the team used meetings to solve their problems as a team.

Meetings in a Demanding Environment. Another piece of evidence that meetings are crucial to success comes to us when we see how highly effective teams working in demanding, time-constrained environments rely heavily on meetings for project success. One such environment is the set of a high-quality weekly TV series where each show needs to be filmed in just one week. The creators of *The Dead Zone* (*The Dead Zone DVD*, Season 2, Disk 3) have this to say about their weekly production meetings:

The production meeting is the moment in time when everyone has done all their work, but now it's time for everybody to be sitting in one room—up to 40 people—and each person represents a particular job that they have to do for that production. We make sure everybody is—literally—on the same page. They all express themselves in a constructive way, and everybody in the room works to be helpful to that particular person or particular department. It takes a village to make a television series. We make sure everyone knows that the director is ready, that everyone knows the concerns from the network or studio. We ensure safety. This is everyone's chance to raise last concerns, final concerns. There's no bullshit or friction; everyone wants what they want, but they're all working for the common good of the show. And that's a great position for everybody. We've removed the politics and even the agendas. People can get down and administrate and put all that effort towards developing a good show.

The Meeting Has Got to Be Good. On the other hand, many meetings are a waste of time. Having been to my share of poorly run meetings, I understand why people avoid them. Here, you will see how to create meetings that have none of the time-wasting and uncomfortable problems we've all seen. And the good news is, it's easy. Any project manager can learn to run good meetings and start doing it in just a few hours.

Meetings and Culture. A culture of respect where there is little blame and people want to get good work done is the best environment for effective project meetings. What if you are in a culture that isn't like that? Good news: as long as you run the meeting, you can create a micro-culture for your team and for the meeting. And, as you do, you create a team culture that can be a lot more productive—and a lot more fun—than the corporate culture.

Making Meetings Effective

There are three steps to making excellent meetings for highly productive teams:

- Create a good team culture and effective meeting ground rules with your team.
- Each meeting is a mini-project—plan, run, and close it using your PM skills.
- Have the team share responsibility for meeting success.

Create a Good Team Culture and Effective Meeting Ground Rules with Your Team. Every organization's culture is unique. You will need to assess your culture and decide what needs to be changed. Choose words that work for you and your team. It is the ideas and principles—and putting those principles into practice—that matter. Although I'm going to lay out a method here, please do not forget the three crucial words *with your team.* We cultivate good qualities such as respect and trust, by evoking what each team member wants for himself or herself and for the team.

The key cultural elements for effective meetings and productive work are contained in what I call *the no-blame environment* (*Perfect Solutions for Difficult Employee Situations*, pp. 18-20). As you will see in the next section, this is an environment created and sustained by the team, where the focus is on respect and the desire to do good work, instead of on personal credit or blame. Here is how we create it.

Six Steps to the No-Blame Environment. Taking these steps, you will transform your company or department into a productive no-blame work environment.

1. Recognize that blame exists. We create it together, and we can work to eliminate it together.
2. Recognize that blame adds nothing to the bottom line. Blame is like static—it interferes with communication, slowing things down and cutting into productivity.
3. Commit to a team environment based on respect and based on the idea that everyone is an adult who wants to do a good job.
4. Work structurally using Table 11-1 to create and maintain a no-blame environment.
5. Set up regular, effective meetings for status reports, to set direction, and to clear the air.
6. Receive status reports with appreciation for learning the truth, even if the news is bad news.

Reality-Based	Personality-Based
Responsibility for actions and their consequences	Blame for failure
Accountability for results	Personal praise Politics (in the negative sense of the term)
Supported and balanced by . . .	Avoidance of responsibility Micromanagement
Clear job definition	Denial
Authority	Manipulation
Empowerment	Anger
Ability	Criticism
Skills and tools	Excuses
Knowledge, information, and methods	

Resources, including
    People
    Money
    Information systems
    Information, including status and
       technical specifications	

TABLE 11-1. Views of the work environment

A little further on, you will learn how to run meetings to lead the team in creating its own culture and ground rules. But, before we do that, let's take a look at what makes a good meeting.

Each Meeting Is a Mini-Project—Plan It Using Your PM Skills. According to *A Guide to the Project Management Body of Knowledge, Third Edition,* Appendix F, a project is "a temporary endeavor undertaken to create a unique product, service, or result," so a meeting, which has a beginning and an end and exists to provide specific information and solve specific problems, is a project. A one-hour or half-day meeting is a very small project, but I find that if we take care of the details that happen over and over, our projects tend to succeed. And meetings are part of those details.

Meetings—a Project Perspective

So, let's look at the five process groups and see how to make a good meeting:

- *Initiation.* Define a clear purpose and set of objectives for each meeting and either run it or delegate running it to an appropriate person.
- *Planning.* Create a meeting agenda. Include only the people who need to be there. Make sure the agenda (the meeting plan) includes only items necessary to reach the objective and all those items.
- *Execution* and *control.* Cover the items on the agenda, keep track of time, and have a method for handling unexpected events such as new topics, extended discussions, missing information, and interruptions.

- *Close.* Be sure to review decisions, action items, and open issues (the parking lot) and plan a date for the next meeting.

Now, let's take a look at how to apply the nine areas of knowledge:

- *Scope* is defined in the agenda and should be clear. Cover only what is pertinent and requires a meeting.
- *Time.* Assign time to each item on the agenda. As a group, commit to arrive on time, limit or prevent interruptions, and finish on time.
- *Cost.* Usually, dollar cost is not a big issue for meetings. Where appropriate, have a way to pay for location or refreshments. More importantly, calculate the cost of the salaries of all the people present and let people know how much it costs—per minute—when any one person arrives late. In some cultures, it can be appropriate to arrange for penalties or incentives around the issue of arrival time.
- The *quality* of the meeting can be enhanced by managing—or better, delegating— responsibility to create a good environment and by giving people what they need to be comfortable and work together well.
- *Human resources* are managed by making sure that all the right people, and only the right people, are at the meeting. For example, if you need to meet with Joe and Suki and then with Suki and Ted, don't have one four-person meeting. Have two back-to-back meetings, one with yourself, Joe, and Suki. Then Joe leaves and Ted comes in for the second meeting.
- *Communication.* We manage communication about the meeting by delivering the agenda in advance, with a note that says, "If you're not sure why you're invited to this meeting, please give me a call." That way, if someone calls,

maybe you'll learn he shouldn't be there. Or, maybe you'll be able to let her know why she matters and get greater participation. We also improve communication by following the agenda and providing appropriate materials, so everyone can both see and hear the meeting content. This is particularly important in telemeetings. Last, we follow up by delivering written meeting notes.

- *Risk.* Perhaps most meetings don't need a formal risk plan, but risk should always be considered and discussed. First of all, everyone should know the consequences—for themselves, for others, and for the project— of missing a meeting. We can also reduce risk by sending reminders. During a meeting, we can manage risk by watching the progress on the agenda and the mood of the group.
- *Procurement.* Someone should be responsible for making sure facilities and, if appropriate, refreshments and other items are taken care of.
- *Integration* is handled if we take care of the other eight areas in a collaborative, cooperative manner, communicating well and sharing responsibility for a successful meeting.

The Structure of an Effective Meeting. If we look at a good meeting, in time, we see these steps:

- *Prepare the agenda.* Decide the purpose and goal of the meeting and who should come. Set up each item in order and assign a time for each. An agenda includes:
  - *Who* will be at the meeting
  - *Why* the meeting is being held
  - *When* the meeting is being held
  - *Where* the meeting is being held
  - *How* the meeting will be run, including reminders to arrange to be present for the whole meeting, to not to be interrupted, and to turn off cell phones

- *What* is being discussed, including:
  - An overall *objective*
  - A *schedule* for the next meeting or meetings
  - *Information items,* which are things everyone needs to know, but that do not require discussion (about two minutes each)
  - *Work items,* including brainstorming items, topics for discussion, and topics for decision
  - *Educational items* when appropriate
- *Invite everyone* and confirm that they are coming.
- *Hold the meeting.* People can help by fulfilling these roles:
  - A *host* makes sure that the room is available and set up, and provides refreshments when appropriate.
  - A *facilitator* opens each topic and keeps the meeting moving. You can be the facilitator unless you are one of the major presenters.
  - *Presenters* provide content on each item.
  - A *timekeeper* gives a warning as each item comes close to its time for completion.
  - One or two *note-takers* capture decisions and action items.
  - A *parking lot manager* captures new and unfinished items and items that need discussion, but not by everyone at the meeting.
  - *Observers* can be used at meetings where there is tension or politics. They can interject if things get too tense or off balance. An observer might say, "I notice that just two people have been going back and forth for a while. Maybe we can get some other participation."
- *Keep the meeting moving.* Move through items steadily. Ask side conversations to stop

promptly. Avoid interruptions. If an item is taking too long, if a new item comes up, or if an item comes up that needs to be discussed by some people, but not all, then move that item to the parking lot and return to the agenda.

- *Close the meeting.* About ten minutes before the meeting is due to end, stop working on individual items. Read out all decisions twice; make sure everyone agrees on the wording and understand the decisions. List all action items and make sure people write them down. Have the parking lot manager read each item and assign items to other meetings, phone calls, individuals, or the next meeting agenda. Remind everyone of the next meeting date and location. Thank them for coming.
- *Follow up with meeting notes.* People do not need meeting minutes—descriptions of what happened every minute of the meeting. Short *meeting notes* are much more effective. They include:
  - *The time and date of the next meeting*
  - *Decisions* that were made at this meeting
  - *Action items,* with a person assigned to do the work, a delivery date, and a description of the item to be delivered

Tools for an Effective Meeting. Meeting management can be very quick and efficient if you make yourself a few simple templates in a word processing program:

- *An agenda template*
- *A parking lot,* which is simply a place to list open issues
- *A meeting notes template* with space for meeting schedule, decisions, and action items

Have the Team Share Responsibility for Making Meetings a Success. Make good meetings a shared responsibility. Instead of doing all the work yourself, teach others and let them grow through hosting, timekeeping, note-taking, managing the parking lot, and even facilitating. You can also delegate content and ask people to prepare presentations. You can even ask people to take opposing viewpoints, arguing against their own ideas as well as for them. Most important, you can create a brainstorming meeting to create good meeting ground rules and team culture, as shown in the next section.

Many Types of Meetings

Let's look at the types of meetings:

- brainstorming
- decision-making, including gate reviews
- kickoff meetings for project stakeholders
- requirements elicitation
- status meetings
- escalation meetings
- post-project review

Brainstorming. When we mix flour and water, we get library paste. When we add salt, sugar, and baking powder, we get something much better—biscuits. Similar things happen when we mix people and issues. People and issues alone usually create an argument, adding little value to our project. But, if we add time, space, and focus, we get an effective brainstorming session.

By bringing issues to the team in a good physical meeting location, protected from interruptions, with enough time to deal with the issue, and focusing on the issue (instead of on conflicting opinions), we can move from disagreements to creative solutions. Brainstorming and conflict resolution are large topics, for which there are excellent resources available from *The Harvard Negotiation Project,* including the book *Getting to Yes* (Fisher, Ury, and Patton).

Now that we have the right ingredients, what is the recipe? We can do it in four steps, with a break between steps.

- *Let every voice be heard.* We ensure everyone is included and respected as we gather ideas.
- *Clarification and organization of ideas.* We make sure everyone understand each idea and we group similar ideas together.
- *Prioritization.* We choose which ideas to work on.
- *Assignment.* We assign action items for the development of the best ideas.

A good brainstorming session does not end with just one idea. It ends with several ideas, each worth further development.

Creating Team Ground Rules: A Sample Brainstorming Session. Set the context for a brainstorming session for your whole team. Then ask each of these questions, one at a time. Let each person answer, with everyone listening and you writing down each answer.

- Remember one time when someone on the team did something you really appreciated. What did he or she do?
- Remember one time you did something in a team environment that felt really good, that you would want to do all the time. What did you do?
- Remember one time a team member or superior did something really painful. What was that?
- Remember one time you did something in a team environment that you regretted. What was that?

Ask people to give general answers, not stories. For example, someone may remember getting angry at a colleague. The person doesn't need to tell the story. He or she can just say, "Got angry."

Edit your list. At the beginning of the items from the first two rounds, add two magic words, "We will." For the items from the last two rounds, also insert the word "not." Put it all in the future tense, also insert first person plural. For example:

We will:

- Respect one another
- Listen to one another
- Not interrupt each other

And we will respectfully support one another in doing our best to keep these ground rules.

When you finish this meeting, you have a draft set of ground rules, a draft code of conduct for your team. You can do a similar process to create guidelines for meeting attendance and participation. This process will have your team agreeing on how to be a team.

Decision-Making, Including Gate Reviews. Meetings for making decisions come after brainstorming meetings, when options are prepared for discussion. We now have one idea to decide on, yes or no. Or, we have a few ideas and we want to choose one option. Before the meeting, decide whether you make the decision, the decision is by a vote, or the decision is by consensus. Then, at the meeting, make sure the benefits, costs, and risks of each idea are presented. Follow this with discussion, then the decision.

Kickoff Meetings for Project Stakeholders. A kickoff meeting with the project sponsor as keynote speaker is a big boost for project success. The sponsor needs to state his or her commitment to the project and to ensure funds and resources. The sponsor should ask everyone involved (customers, project team, and stakeholders) to make their part of the project work a priority. The sponsor can then commit to being available to resolve conflicts. Then each worker will know that his or her boss's boss wants this done. If other priorities get in the way later, we all know the project sponsor will be there to help work things out.

After this, the project sponsor doesn't have to stay. The project manager should then convey his or her vision of the project and how people will be working together. Methods and tools should be introduced so they are familiar and resources about them should be provided. The meeting could be brief, with information items only, or it could be used as a chance for team members to get to know one another, develop a project team culture, or work on some key project issues.

Requirements Elicitation. Finding out what the customer wants is not easy. We can ask, "What are your requirements?" But the most likely response will be a wide-eyed look, like from a deer caught in the headlights. There are many structured methods, such as JAD (joint application development) and RAD (rapid application development), to structure communication between the customers and the team. What they all have in common is:

- Sufficient time, space, and focus
- Pictures or prototypes, to get everyone on the same page
- Words, to provide detailed information
- Elicitation, recording, and review, iteratively, to improve the specification
- A standard, such as IEEE Std 830-1998, *IEEE Recommended Practice for Software Requirements Specifications*, that the specification must meet, and iterative improvement until it is met

Status Meetings. The most important piece of information we want in a status meeting is the truth—the truth about scope, time, and cost, but also about risk, quality, and factors from any other areas of project management. From status (current location), we can calculate progress (how we got here) and generate a forecast (where we will end up and what problems lie ahead). From those, we can retune or revise our plans and define the details of our next work period.

The no-blame environment is the key to a successful status meeting. For efficiency, the information can actually be delivered in advance, in a standardized format, perhaps in an automated system. That allows the team to look ahead, instead of spending time figuring out where we are.

Escalation Meetings. Sometimes, we have to go upstairs to report bad news or to ask for help. This is an information meeting or perhaps a brainstorming session, but with political overtones. If we have been up-to-date and forthright with status information, the executive will not be blindsided. That helps a lot. Then we arrive with a clear picture of the problem, take full responsibility for it, take the heat if we have to, and offer solutions, asking the executive to select from possible solutions or improve the solution and authorize it. Understand that the executive may need to take more time or gather more information. Do be sure to leave with a date for a firm meeting or phone call to follow up, so that your team is not left hanging with nothing to do.

Post-Project Review. In a no-blame environment, a post-project review can be rewarding. I'll focus on the project aspect of the review, rather than the business aspect. Our goal is to help everyone in the organization become better project managers. Whether we did well or made many mistakes, even whether the project succeeded or failed, we have learned something that we can add to the knowledge of the company. For every problem, see the root cause and how the problem could have been prevented or detected as early as possible and how it can be solved if it happens again. From each success, tell us how you did it. Even if the project simply followed prescribed methods, pass on the good news: this stuff works!

Conclusion: Meeting Success = Project Success

Meeting management is not difficult to master. Simply apply your talents as a project manager to a mini-project—the meeting. Built a respectful culture and hold effective meetings that meet clear objectives. When you do, you will see problems that used to spiral into conflict or delay become manageable or simply disappear.

References

Fisher, Roger, William Ury, and Bruce Patton. *Getting to Yes: Negotiating Agreement Without Giving in* (second edition). New York: Penguin, 1991.

Software Engineering Standards Committee of the Institute of Electrical and Electronics Engineers. IEEE Std 830-1998, *IEEE Recommended Practice for Software Requirements Specifications.* New York: IEEE, 1993.

Kemp, Sid. *Perfect Solutions for Difficult Employee Situations.* New York: McGraw-Hill, 2005.

Project Management Institute. *A Guide to the Project Management Body of Knowledge (PMBOK$^®$)* (2004 edition). Newtown Square, PA: Project Management Institute, 2004.

CONFLICT PREVENTION AND CONFLICT RESOLUTION

I prefer conflict prevention to conflict resolution. Just as quality costs less if we can prevent error, good teamwork costs less and is easier to maintain if we can prevent conflict. So let's look at conflict prevention first and then at conflict resolution.

Conflict Prevention: Add the Right Ingredients

As we've said, a project is either a problem scheduled for solution or an opportunity scheduled for realization. And once we have defined a project, each step is a small project—a small problem— and each gap or unexpected event is another small problem.

So a project manager's life is full of problems. And that creates a challenge, because people get frustrated when we have problems. People also get frustrated when we have an opportunity and we aren't sure we will get what we want.

So, projects ought to be full of frustrated people. And frustrated people don't do good work. So, to succeed at projects, we're going to have to change that recipe—people plus problems equals frustration. How can we do that?

As mentioned earlier, if we mix flour and water, we get library paste. It's great for sticking book pages together, but it tastes terrible. On the other hand, if we have flour and water and then we add salt, sugar, and baking powder, we have biscuits, pancakes, and all kinds of good stuff. Sometimes, we can make something good out of something bad by adding extra ingredients.

Projects will always have people and problems. If we took either one away, we wouldn't have a project. So, to prevent frustration, we need to add something. Consider these two equations:

- People plus problems equals frustration
- People plus problems, plus time, space, and focus equals good brainstorming

Frustration is what we have when there are problems, but no time and space to create a solution. If we make enough time and space and we focus on the problem—instead of focusing on disagreeing with one another—we can brainstorm together and solve the problem. As a team, when we put a problem in front of ourselves, we become the solution.

With this in mind, let's try these seven steps to creating and maintaining a conflict-free environment.

1. *Accept that conflict is inevitable.* Realize that wherever there are people and problems, there will be conflict.
2. *Realize that conflict isn't a bad thing.* Conflict about problems and solutions isn't a bad thing. There is nothing wrong with people dis-

agreeing with one another. I think something is a problem; you think it isn't. You think a problem has one cause; I see it differently. Our views are in conflict, but we're not, and there is no problem.

3. *The problem comes up when people are in conflict with one another, instead of having the conflict be about the problem, its definition, and its solution.* If people stay on the same side and put the problem in front of them, then the conflict is about the problem and the people are getting along.
4. *A team can commit to work together to define and solve problems by staying on the same side.* If we commit to this, and practice it, we can get good at preventing conflicts between people.
5. *If we do get into a conflict, we can always stop and restart.* When we restart, we focus on working together and facing the problem.
6. *We don't have to agree in order to respect one another.* Make respect primary. If we respect one another, then we have room to disagree. In that space, we take time to focus on the problem.
7. *We can replace conflicts between us with brainstorming and good work toward solutions.*

When people want to work together, we can build a no-blame environment, agree on ground rules for the team, and then make room for brainstorming to replace conflicts between us. We will rarely need conflict resolution, because conflicts won't start.

Conflict Resolution

If a conflict does arise—between me as project manager and anyone on the project, between two team members, or between a team member and a stakeholder or two stakeholders—then that is a barrier to project success. It is then my responsibility to resolve that conflict, removing that barrier so that the team can move toward success.

The approach I take to conflict resolution has four levels. I try the first level and then, if that level doesn't work, work my way up. I rarely have to use the third or fourth levels of conflict resolution.

Level One: Meet, Listen, and Clear the Air. Nine times out of ten, what sounds like a disagreement really isn't a disagreement at all. Instead, it's two people not listening to one another. When people don't feel listened to, they get loud and interrupt one another. So, with no listening, an argument starts. If we start listening, we almost always discover that we didn't have a disagreement in the first place. At the first level of the conflict resolution, we need to listen to one another.

Five times out of ten, the two people think that they are talking about the same thing, but they're really not on the same page. They're talking about two different problems, so of course their solutions are different. Of the remaining five times, where they are talking about the same problem, most of the time they actually agree. They're just describing the same solution in different words. Other times, they have different solutions, but, once they understand each other, they agree on which solution is better. It's only about one time in ten that people have a real difference of opinion. And, when we do, we can turn to problem definition, diagnosis, PDCA, and fact-based decision making, and decide what is best for the project.

Level Two: Slow Down. When people are unwilling to listen to one another, we need to escalate to level-two conflict resolution. Here, I slow the process down. I step in and listen to each of them. Then, with their permission, I share what each said with the other person. And, almost always, they don't disagree. Once they see that, they are usually willing to try again. We establish ground rules of listening with respect, and then people can get together and learn to listen, to share ideas, and to solve problems together.

Level Three: Rebalance. If slowing down isn't enough, we need to rebalance. We can each take time aside. We can try writing down our ideas. If we each write down our own view of the problem, its causes, symptoms, and solutions, we can begin to separate the issue from our feelings. To deal with my feelings, I keep a journal, or I have some good friends I can talk to, without naming names. After that, I can meet with the person again and work through the issue in a no-blame environment. We can realize that working together is more important than whatever is upsetting us and we make ourselves into a team, simply because that is the most important thing to do.

Level Four: Get Help. At the fourth level, we realize that we can't solve this alone. If our best efforts at getting along aren't working, then something deeper is going on. Any two adults who choose to respect one another can work together if both commit to respect and honesty and commit to project success. So, if two people can't work on a project together, then one of those ingredients is lacking:

- Perhaps one of the two people is not behaving like an adult. In that case, coaching or psychological counseling may help.
- If one person does not want to be respectful or honest, then that person should be asked to leave the project, because projects rely on teamwork and fact-based decision making, and those require respect and honesty.
- If one of the people does not care if the project succeeds or wants it to fail, then that person should say so and the issue should be worked out.

As I say, I rarely reach the fourth level of conflict resolution. When I do, it usually indicates that someone is very off balance. I should take care of myself and check closely to see if it is me. Maybe all the stress is getting to me. Or maybe the other person is off balance, but that got to me. Once I am balanced and clear, I am ready to do what is best for the project. Occasionally, unfortunately, that can mean asking someone to leave the team. When it does, the person is usually better off, because he or she didn't want to be there anyway. And the rest of the team is relieved, because the conflict is over and we can regroup, turn to the project, get to work, and get it done right.

CONCLUSION

Last night, as I was finishing writing this book, I had a dream in which I had one of those miniature basketball hoops and a miniature basketball. I was able to reach up and drop the ball in, making one basket after another. Just two points, and another two, and another two.

Yes, nearly half of all projects fail. But I don't think it has to be that way. Most fail due to lack of good management—lack of time, effort, and clear thinking to define problems and pick a good solution. Most all of our problems have been solved by somebody, sometime. All we have to do is define the problem clearly, learn from an expert, and do the work it takes. And if we make the job small enough by slicing it into pieces, then each piece is a small project that can be done.

And all the small projects, done right, add up to success on the big ones.

And success on the big problems means we've realized opportunities and solved the problems that stand in our way. We've kept our business going and growing in a changing world.

That gives us a chance to succeed, to serve, and to take the opportunity to share each person's unique gifts with the world.

Real-World Projects

I n Part III, Real-World Projects, we will get real with project management by looking at all different types of projects in all different types of businesses. Each case study tells a true story of a successful project. Some of the projects were easy; some were quite difficult. Most were managed well, but some were managed poorly. When mistakes were made, the teams gave themselves problems to solve on the way to success. The successes and the mistakes are illustrated with lessons, a half a dozen or more lessons in each case study.

Chapter 12, Storefront Success, tells the story of Paul Manning, co-owner of The Front Porch Café. Paul is a natural project manager who has opened four successful businesses in six years.

Chapter 13, What It Takes to Make a Movie, introduces Matt Williams, a producer who makes TV commercials. Matt's take on making a movie will open your eyes to the value of risk management. You'll learn about the movie business and about how good project management can ensure customer satisfaction and keep your business growing.

Chapter 14, Alignment to Our Customers, shows how research into what our customers like and what they want can guide us in reshaping our business for success.

Chapter 15, A Consulting Firm Launches Its First Product, shows how an engineering firm can change from offering consulting to selling equipment, and some of the challenges it faces in that transition.

Chapter 16, 17 Years of Growth at Kirbo's, shows how four examples of the same type of project—opening a store in a new city—can have a different purpose and face different challenges each time. It also illustrates how good planning and the right people are the most important factors in project success.

Chapter 17, Annual Strategic Planning at QTI, shows an executive project and illustrates the value of reviewing our successes and mistakes and laying out a program for the years to come.

Chapter 18, A Customer Problem Opens a New Business, shows how strategic thinking can lead to entrepreneurial success.

Chapter 19, Even a Kid Can Learn Project Management, shows how a program designed to teach high school students how to make movies also gives them life skills. We see how becoming excited about a project can help anyone—a teenager or an adult—improve professional skills and learn to succeed.

I want you to be able to find case studies for projects in businesses similar to yours and also find projects that are similar to your projects by the part of the company to which the project delivers or by the type of program of which the project is a part. Specifically, each case study falls into one place within each of these three categories:

- type of business
- type of program
- area served within the business

The following three tables will help you select the projects most similar to yours.

Table 1 shows the case studies by type of business. Types of businesses include retail storefronts that serve customers (Retail), business-to-business services (B-B Service), businesses to business products (B-B Product), and manufacturing (Mfg).

Chapter	Title	Retail	B-B Service	B-B Product	Mfg
12	Storefront Success	✔			
13	What It Takes to Make a Movie		✔		
14	Alignment to Our Customers			✔	
15	A Consulting Firm Launches Its First Product		✔	✔	✔
16	17 Years of Growth at Kirbo's		✔	✔	
17	Annual Strategic Planning at QTI		✔	✔	

TABLE 1. Case studies by type of business (continued on next page)

Chapter	Title	Retail	B-B Service	B-B Product	Mfg
18	A Customer Problem Opens a New Business		✔		
19	Even a Kid Can Learn Project Management				

TABLE 1. Case studies by type of business (continued)

In this book we've defined three types of programs: programs that make money by providing project services to customers, programs that develop a new product for sale, and programs that improve internal operations. As you plan your programs and projects, you may want to read case studies that fit into the same type of program. For example, in Chapter 12, Storefront Success, you'll learn what it takes for a small business to make a big decision when The Front Porch Café's owners decide to start roasting their own coffee. In Chapter 14, Alignment to Our Customers, you'll see how to design and implement a program that increases sales by retuning a whole company to better serve its customers. Table 2 shows the list of case studies by type of program.

Chapter	Title	Project for Customer	Develop New Product	Internal Improvement
12	Storefront Success		✔	
13	What It Takes to Make a Movie	✔		
14	Alignment to Our Customers			✔
15	A Consulting Firm Launches Its First Product	✔	✔	
16	17 Years of Growth at Kirbo's			✔
17	Annual Strategic Planning at QTI			✔
18	A Customer Problem Opens a New Business		✔	
19	Even a Kid Can Learn Project Management		✔	

TABLE 2. Case studies by type of program

In Chapter 4, we introduced the idea of looking at a business as a flow of products and information and, in that, suggested that a business could be described as having functional areas. If you are designing a project that will develop or change one of these nine functional areas, you may want to look at a case study that worked in the same area of a different business. Here is a list of the functional areas of a business, with some of the more interesting case studies for each one:

- *Marketing* projects are illustrated in Chapter 18, A Customer Problem Opens a New Business, which shows how a clear and detailed understanding of customer needs can steer an entrepreneur through opening and growing a business, and Chapter 14, Alignment to Our Customers, which shows how a longstanding business can increase profit by paying better attention to its customers.

- *Sales* is needed to land a deal when we sell project services to a customer. Learn how a producer of TV commercials closes a deal with a client and ensures a profit margin in Chapter 13, What It Takes to Make a Movie.

- *Client services* are illustrated in almost all the case studies, but if you want to see an example of a business focused on delighting its customers, read Chapter 12, Storefront Success.

- The *financial* aspect of a small business is changed by any large project, but one that completely changed the way a company makes its money is in Chapter 15, A Consulting Firm Launches Its First Product.

- Many projects involve *research,* but two illustrate it particularly well. In Chapter 12, Storefront Success, you'll see how Paul Manning learned all about a new way of producing his product, and in Chapter 14, Alignment to Our Customers, you'll see how interviews plus statistical research give a company the leverage it needs to boost the bottom line.

- *Analysis* of information is common to most projects. For a look at an in-depth analysis of how an executive can evaluate his own company, see Chapter 17, Annual Strategic Planning at QTI.

- *Executive* decision making at an annual retreat can be a project, as you'll see in Chapter 17, Annual Strategic Planning at QTI. It's an excellent example of how, by treating a meeting as a project, you can achieve your objectives.

- *Product and service development* both play a big part in Chapter 15, A Consulting Firm Launches Its First Product.

- *Infrastructure* changes include everything from acquiring equipment to building a new building, as you can see in Chapter 12, Storefront Success, and Chapter 16, 17 Years of Growth at Kirbo's.

- *Human resources*—finding the right people—is crucial to project success, as you'll see in Chapter 15, A Consulting Firm Launches Its First Product. Also, we can use a project to solve a persistent human resource problem, such as finding new talent, as you'll see in Chapter 12, Storefront Success.

Table 3 shows the functional areas of the business affected by the project in each of the case studies.

Chapter	Title	Marketing	Sales	Client Services	Financial	Research
12	Storefront Success			✔	✔	✔
13	What It Takes to Make a Movie	✔	✔	✔	✔	✔
14	Alignment to Our Customers	✔	✔	✔		✔
15	A Consulting Firm Launches Its First Product			✔	✔	✔
16	17 Years of Growth at Kirbo's	✔		✔	✔	
17	Annual Strategic Planning at QTI					
18	A Customer Problem Opens a New Business	✔	✔	✔	✔	
19	Even a Kid Can Learn Project Management					

Chapter	Title	Analysis	Executive	Development	Infrastructure	HR
12	Storefront Success	✔	✔	✔	✔	✔
13	What It Takes to Make a Movie	✔	✔			
14	Alignment to Our Customers	✔		✔		
15	A Consulting Firm Launches Its First Product	✔	✔	✔		✔
16	17 Years of Growth at Kirbo's	✔	✔		✔	✔
17	Annual Strategic Planning at QTI		✔			
18	A Customer Problem Opens a New Business	✔	✔	✔		
19	Even a Kid Can Learn Project Management					

TABLE 3. Case studies by functional area

Read the case studies in Part III to see how projects work for all parts of all businesses, to see how project management tools were applied in a project similar to your next one, for enjoyment, and to be inspired to *get it done right!*

CHAPTER 12

Storefront Success: Know What You Want, Plan, and Go for It

THIS CASE STUDY IS THE STORY OF A NATural project manager. Paul Manning has never studied project management. I'm not sure he even knew it was a separate field of business expertise until I dropped by for a cappuccino at The Front Porch Café in Kill Devil Hills on North Carolina's Outer Banks and we got to talking. When I met him, he and his wife Susannah Sakal had already opened three successful stores right next to each other— The Front Porch Café, home of "the best coffee on the Outer Banks" for three years running according to readers of *The Coast* magazine; Glazin' Go Nuts, a paint-your-own pottery store; and the Garden of Beadin', a bead shop. In the last six months, they've opened The Front Porch Café Nags Head, five miles away.

Paul took his time planning and preparing to launch his new businesses. That preparation paid off, as all four stores are doing well. More important:

- Paul and Susannah are realizing their dreams, growing and learning.
- They are providing opportunities for their staff to learn and grow.
- The café is a vibrant part of the local community.

Paul has not done everything right, it hasn't always been easy, and he'll be the first to tell you that it's been a lot of work. But, because he did the important things right— having a clear concept, values, and goal, and doing good planning and architecture—the years have been enjoyable instead of overly stressful. Let's take a look at what he's done and, more important, how he did it.

A LONG TIME COMING: OPENING THE FIRST STORE

Paul and Susannah took the first step of turning their dream into a reality in 1993,

This case study is courtesy of Paul Manning, co-owner of The Front Porch Café in Kill Devil Hills and Nags Head, on the Outer Banks of the North Carolina coast, and at www.frontporchcafe.net.

when they wrote a business plan for The Front Porch Café. In 1996, they took the next step by moving to the Outer Banks, the region of the North Carolina shore where they wanted their new store. They had saved up some money to launch the business and were getting to know the local community and changing their lifestyle to be ready to open the store. The opportunity came when the national company Paul worked for was sold and Paul didn't see eye to eye with the new owners. They wanted to boost the stock value and sell the company, instead of continuing to invest in long-term value. Paul decided it was time to make the big jump from employee to self-employed business owner.

Then he and Susannah spent over six months scouting for the right location. As Paul says about a storefront consumer business, "You have to find the right location. That's where you put your nest egg."

Lesson #1: Start-up success is about careful planning that lets us feel the right moment when it comes and know that it's time to take the leap

The Front Porch Café is guided by two simple principles:

- *Exceptional customer service.* The folks at Front Porch try to know every customer by name and know his or her regular drink. One time, a regular parked his car right out front and Susannah saw him and prepared his coffee the way he liked it, a latte with two sugars and whole milk. He was chatting on the cell phone, so she brought it out to him. He told his friend, "You won't believe this. I'm sitting in front of The Front Porch Café, and they brought me my coffee before I even got out of the car."
- *High-quality coffee, teas, and other items.* As you'll see, Paul has paid a great deal of attention to making sure that he serves consistently excellent beverages and food to his

customers.

Paul points out that the coffee shop experience can vary widely. Some places focus on fast service, low price, a neighborhood feel, or a wide selection of items. Any of these could work—as long as they work for the entrepreneur.

Lesson #2: For entrepreneurial success, define what makes you unique and express that in your business.

In the first four or five months, either Paul or Susannah was always there. During that time, they developed their team. When team members were showing the same attentive customer service that the owners had, it was time to let them take over some shifts. Over time, people who have stayed on year-round have moved up into management, opening the door for Paul and Susannah to focus on other parts of the business.

Lesson #3: Nothing can replace your own time and attention to your store. It is essential.

Lesson #4: Find good people who want a career with you and help them grow.

TRAINING, GAINING, AND RETAINING STAFF

Like most owners of customer-service oriented business, Paul finds that getting and keeping the right people is one of the toughest ongoing challenges to the business. In addition, his business is seasonal, so he needs to pick up new employees every summer.

Paul is lucky in that he gets enough applicants. Students come in to apply for jobs as summer approaches. Paul says that, most of the time, he can decide if the person is a good fit within the first ten minutes. If applicants seem friendly and outgoing, attentive to others, and willing to learn, help, and get along, then they are good candidates. He generally hires on the spot. He does take references and sometimes checks them, but that rarely reverses his decision. New employees are told that they need to show that they are doing well after the first week and that a final decision will be made at the end of the first month.

New employees are paired with experienced employees, doing the same job on the same schedule in an informal mentoring program. They learn the job by osmosis, supported by formal training. In addition, there is an employee manual that includes not only the rules, but also the spirit and attitude of the Café. One of the rules, for instance, is that the customer always comes first. At the Café, if your boss just asked you to do something and then you see a customer, you set aside the job you were given and take care of the customer first.

New employees are given feedback and guidance. For instance, one young woman seemed very outgoing during the interview, but once she started work, it was as if she was a different person. She was quiet and didn't step up to help people. Paul let her know that that would need to change. When it didn't, she was let go at the end of the month.

Paul's decision to make the trial period one month long is based on several ideas. One is that a person can learn the job in a week, but it takes about a month to see if he or she is fitting in with the job, the team, the Café, and the customers. Another reason for deciding at the end of the first month is that, if you let a person go after only a month, you are generally not liable for unemployment. If you want to terminate someone after three or four months, you will probably be liable for some unemployment unless the person is clearly breaking the rules—stealing or not showing up for work. So Paul has decided that it is best to make a clear decision at the end of the first month.

Paul says that the team is very good at seeing if a person fits in and he checks with the other team members at the end of an employee's first month

to see if they think he or she should stay or leave. Including the long-term team members in these decisions also builds their confidence in being part of the store's community and not just employees.

Almost all employees work full time. Paul says it takes 40 hours or so for an employee to catch on to the job, longer if they are part time. The initial cost of training an employee is about $300 in their time and his time and other small expenses. A part-time employee would never work out for the summer: the season would be over as he or she was just getting to know how to do the job. So the only part-time employees at the Café are exceptional locals who are in for the long term and have something special to offer.

Lesson #5: Make clear, consistent decisions about hiring and staffing. Make sure those decisions work for your company in all ways: meeting workflow demands, increasing retention, meeting quality requirements, reducing cost, meeting regulatory requirements, and more. Put those decisions into a policy manual and make sure that a practical, thorough up-to-date employee manual is available to all staff at all times.

Paul needs to hire extra people for the summer tourist season. At first, this was a real challenge. Then Giedre, an exchange student from Eastern Europe, found Paul's store on the web and asked for a job. The schedule of exchange students worked better for the store than American students' schedules. Paul needs to keep extra people all the way into early September and most American students need to leave at the beginning of August. In addition, he found that the exchange students were very willing to learn and to work hard. Part of that is certainly economics—one of them earned as much money in a summer as her father earns in a year back home—but it is also a cultural attitude. Paul has had such good success with employees from Eastern Europe that he asked one of them to interview people back home and recommend them to him. As a result, he is getting a steady supply of good workers each summer.

In contrast, when he hired one local high school student, he told her that, as she learned various jobs around the Café, she would be able to get more responsibility. She didn't focus on learning and so she did a lot of scrubbing. After a month, she quit—via a text message, "I quit—I'm tired of cleaning up all the time." Paul says it's the first time he every had an employee quit by text message. But she had created the situation she didn't like by not trying to learn more of the job and then left the situation, missing out on the opportunity the Café was offering.

Hiring foreign students does create a problem with the language barrier. Paul hires only people who know English well enough to serve customers. Still, they sometimes stumble when learning new jobs. Paul solved this by having some come before the busy season and then help with training others in their native language. However, Paul is careful to ask them not to chat with one another in their own language in the store. That could disturb customers. And it is also better for the exchange students—it keeps them practicing their English.

Some of the people Paul hires as permanent employees leave because, after a time, they find that they are just not cut out for this kind of work. Others stay for a while and then grow on to other careers. The last six months have been particularly challenging. Paul and Susannah had a child last November and also wanted to focus more on planning for the store than working behind the counter, so they decided to share just one job slot. Then they opened their new store, so they needed twice as many employees. And a manager who had been with them for quite a while announced that she had gotten a job opportunity in her new career—but stayed on for two months more out of loyalty, to see that Front Porch Two got onto its feet before she left. Paul says, "It feels like, as soon as I hire one per-son, another one leaves. Actually, though, it's worked out OK, and we're ready for the summer."

Lesson #6: Finding good people is an ongoing challenge for any small business, especially one that is growing. Look for innovative ways—such as using the World Wide Web—to cultivate sources of good employees. Find good ways to find good people and keep doing it.

Some of the staff who stay have a chance to grow. Some grow in their technical ability, becoming *barristas*—expert makers of high-quality coffee drinks. This requires a lot of practice—and may involve staying up late after you've tasted too many samples. Paul and Susannah have to be sure of an employee's ability to produce excellent beverages consistently before he or she can run the shop and serve as *barrista*. There are also management opportunities, such as running one of the cafés when Paul and Susannah are not there. In fact, creating a chance for employees to grow was one of the reasons for creating the second café.

Lesson #7: If you want your company to grow, plan for your employees to grow with you.

IMPROVEMENTS—ROASTING AND GOING NUTS!

From 1999 through 2004, The Front Porch Café innovated and grew in a number of ways. One of the most critical and challenging changes was the decision Paul and Susannah made to roast their own coffee beans—*artisan roasting*, as it is called. The change was motivated out of the desire to be able to provide consistently high-quality coffee. In purchasing roasted coffee from wholesalers, a café is limited in its ability to ensure consistent quality. Wholesalers may lump together coffee from different plantations in a single roasting batch and the quality will vary by source and time of year. Also, one of the best roasters available is in Seattle and the coffee takes ten days to arrive. If it rains in Kill

Devil Hills, the store can run out of coffee while waiting for more beans. And a regional roaster Paul used was not as consistent in quality.

However, Paul's main concern about doing his own roasting was also quality. If manufacturers couldn't always roast well, could he? Could he really become a true artisan of roasting? Answering that question took a lot of time and research. Here are some of the questions he sought answers for by talking to vendors and to other cafés that roasted their own:

- What roasting equipment is reliable and produces high-quality coffee?
- Can a small shop do its own roasting and make a consistent top-quality product?
- What are the critical success factors for artisan roasting?
- How much time and effort would it take to learn?
- How much would it cost to do it?

Over time, talking to many people, Paul gained confidence that artisan roasting was the way to go and that he could do it well. He learned from the successes of other stores, and their failures as well. For example, one store had a manager who took on the task of roasting and did very well. But, when he left, the roaster sat in the corner, unused.

Early on, he had a chance to buy a used roaster from a local company that was going out of business and save some money. But he looked at it, saw it was ancient, and figured that it would probably be very hard to maintain. Instead, he let go of the quick opportunity, and began to do real research into the best way to do it, instead of the cheapest.

So Paul chose an excellent roaster and became the chief artisan. He wrote a manual on using the roaster for their café. When Ashley, a staff member, expressed interest, Paul trained her to roast, as well. She added to the manual as they worked and then added roasting recipes for each coffee that they make. Now, Paul takes over when his roaster

is away on vacation. He is considering training another apprentice. Also, the roaster recently went from operating about 20 hours a week—enough for the first café—to about 35 hours a week, supporting both cafés.

Lesson #7: If you are going to change the way you produce your product, do a lot of research and learn all you need to know to be confident in the new process. Also make sure you make the right investment and take the time to do it well.

Lesson #8: Make sure the knowledge on how to run a business stays with the business. A business should never rely on the skill of just one employee—not even yourself. Make sure that each process is fully documented as we described in Chapter 4, so that, if a person leaves, someone with appropriate skills can be trained to do the job in a reasonable amount of time.

Becoming an artisan roaster brought some additional benefits to Paul and Susannah. Some were expected; others were not:

- The coffee is consistently fresh.
- They can sell the coffee in bags locally and over the Internet, which gives them some extra income.
- They are able to select coffees by plantation and season, knowing where the coffee came from by what was printed on the bag, rather than selecting by nation and having to trust that the roaster delivered the right product.
- They have come to know more about coffee growers, organic coffee, and fair trade.

Lesson #9: Becoming an expert has the advantage of offering new value, greater quality, and ways of keeping the business interesting, improving profit, and reducing cost.

Other new growth and changes at The Front Porch Café were easier and less fraught with risk than the decision to roast their own. When the storefront next door became available, they felt it was better to lease it than let it go to someone else. A friend in Michigan had a successful paint-your-own-pottery store running on a simple business model. Paul took the lease, set up the store, and had another money-maker plus some room to grow. An unexpected side benefit was that employees who were good with customers but not with coffee could run the pottery-painting studio, Glazin' Go Nuts, very well. And, of course, mothers watching their children paint pottery would probably want a cup of coffee. And when the coffee shop got crowded, which it does every morning, the overflow could use the seating in Glazin' Go Nuts. At this point, Paul's stores were serving families with children—up into the early grade school years—with pottery and adults with coffee. He added the Garden of Beadin' as another creative outlet to draw customers—particularly teenagers—into the store. At first, it cost little and was just run as a store-within-a-store inside the pottery shop. When the third store in the strip mall became available, Paul took that over and made the bead shop full-sized. Now, people of any age have a reason to stop by his stores on a rainy day.

Lesson #10: Expansion isn't for everyone, but if you see a simple opportunity with several advantages and you're sure you can handle it, grab it.

FRONT PORCH TWO: A DREAM COMING TRUE

For many people, opening one store is success enough. But Susannah likes to realize creative visions and Paul likes to face the challenges of growing. Once The Front Porch Café and its two sister stores were running well, they began to dream of a new café: The Front Porch Nags Head, only 12 minutes away. This dream was backed by sound business ideas:

- They could serve more customers. Having learned the local community, they knew that there were plenty of people who would stop by the new location who weren't coming to the first café.

- They could reduce overhead percentages. Management costs and fixed costs for everything from marketing to bookkeeping to roasting coffee would go up, but would not double, increasing the ratio of revenue to cost.

In addition to the dream and the hard-dollar value, there were several reasons that fell into soft-dollar value:

- They could provide an opportunity for their managers to grow more independent.
- They could express a new level of creativity in the design of the new store.
- They could step back to run the businesses and let managers take care of the stores.

The new store was being built to their specifications, so they had a chance to design, do architecture, and make it what they truly wanted it to be. They made the most of that opportunity, spending a lot of time at other stores and restaurants, learning what works and envisioning what they wanted. Ultimately, the new store was created with a global coffee theme from the world map etched into the concrete floor to the hand-painted coffee-bag national flags of coffee-producing nations hanging from the ceiling. The coffee roaster now sits inside an enclosed glass room at the entry to the store, drawing in customers, but with its noise and heat shielded from the shop, so it can run while the store is open.

Paul did make one mistake that, fortunately, didn't create too much trouble—though it might have. His architect asked him for a plan for the store. Paul knew what he wanted and drew a quick sketch. The architect failed to tell him that whatever he drew was going to be literally set in concrete and couldn't be changed. Paul didn't know how exactly things were being locked down. As a result, overall, Paul had what he wanted, but there were a few inches too little here and there. That may sound minor, until you are trying to fit a 48-inch bakery case into a 45-inch space, and they don't make 45-inch cases. It took Paul a fair bit of hunting and some extra expense to get the appropriate kitchen equipment to squeeze into some of the spaces.

Lesson #11: Pay attention to architecture and work it out in more detail than you might think you need to.

The other challenge Paul ran into was construction delays. Some of those were caused by rain and storms, some by tradespeople who didn't want work Christmas week or when it got too cold, and some by delays in getting permits from the local government. Paul had hoped to open in February, in time to be ready for the Spring Break rush, but the store didn't open until the end of March. They lost some money there, but they had scheduled the opening well ahead of May, so that, even with delays, they were ready for busy season.

Lesson #12: Expect delays, especially when you are relying on a number of vendors, on getting permits, or on experts and dependent tasks. If you have a crucial opening date, aim to be up and running quite a bit earlier.

Paul made one other choice in planning the opening of the new store—one that seems to run against good project management practice but, in this case, was the right thing to do. He opened the new store with a new point-of-sale system, instead of duplicating the cash register at the old store. The new system is better—easier to use, which makes it easier to train new employees—but there was a pretty steep learning curve involved in setting it up, learning to use it, and being ready to teach others.

What Paul realized is that, if he prepared well, the best time to use the new system was at the new store when it first opened. Business would be very light because no one knew it was open; people weren't used to dropping in for coffee on that corner. Business was much lighter at the new store in the first few weeks than at the first store even during the slowest time of the year. So Paul was actually able to set up, learn, and test his new cash register more easily at the new store than at any time at the old store. He prepared well and the new store is running well with the new point-of-sale system. He'll upgrade the old register at the first store after the summer, when business slows down.

Lesson #12: If you really know your business, you can combine projects for optimal results.

TIPS FOR THOSE STARTING A BUSINESS

As I write Paul's story, I'm concerned that it all sounds too easy. The first six years of Paul's business—including moving into artisan coffee and opening up three additional businesses—have been easy enough to be enjoyable for Paul. But he is an exceptional person. Our point is that starting your own business *can* be this easy and fun, but it often *won't* be. Paul has seen a number of stores and restaurants open and fail. To Paul, it was clear that many were headed for trouble before they even got started. Most new businesses fail within the first three years. Paul has some good ideas about why and some thoughts about whether it might be right for you and how to do it well.

- *Starting a business means spending your nest egg to buy yourself a job, then getting to work.* Paul has seen a number of people start restaurants thinking, "Wow! I'll get other people to work for me and I'll have a fun place to hang out with my friends." They usually go out of business quite fast. An owner who doesn't love to work isn't going to make much money. To put it another way, if you don't want to work, don't work for yourself.
- *The manager's salary will be your only income for quite a while.* If you hire a manager to do

things for you, you won't make any money.

- *Really know and plan your business.* Only by really knowing your business can you know all the types of expertise you will need to run the business, succeed, and grow if you want to. Learn from experts and hire expertise where you aren't good enough to do it yourself. But you have to be expert in something and do that yourself or you won't be able to afford to make the business work. If you don't want to bring in your own expertise, take on challenges, and work hard, don't start a business.

- *Know what skills you will need.* Have those skills, be willing to learn them, or be willing to hire someone who can do them, in that order.

- *Be ready to be decisive.* Paul says, "Opening a new store is 1,000 decisions. You have to get efficient at them. The decisions have to be done to open the store. You can't vacillate. You make it and move on."

- *Know the real cost of your business.* This means being ready for expenses. It also means not being hoodwinked by someone who offers to do all your bookkeeping for $5,000 a year when you can get it done well for $300. There are plenty of people who will take your money and not deliver much in return.

- *Trust people, but verify their work anyway.* "Trust but verify" is the auditor's motto and it's a good one for the small businessperson as well. Paul cites a very successful, wealthy local restaurant owner who still closes out the cash register at each restaurant every night at 2 a.m. He has learned from experience that even trusted employees will be tempted to toss in cash from sales without ringing it up and then take it home at the end of the evening.

- *Be there.* At the beginning, be at the store day in and day out. Learn everything there is to know in your own experience. As you hire committed staff, write down what you know—or have them write it up as they learn it—and create efficient ways of transferring your skills to the company and your team.

Starting a business—or growing one from one store to two or in other ways—is fun and exciting. Planning before you do and following through with your team can really make it pay off.

CONCLUSION

When Paul and I finished talking, I asked him what he was thinking of doing next. Not surprisingly, he had his eyes open for new possibilities. Equally expected, he's being cautious.

There's a new mall complex going up about an hour away and the owner wants him to open a café. His research shows that the location is active only during the summer, so Paul would have to earn a full year's rent in three months. To make that work, the new location has to work for breakfast, lunch, and dinner. It might need to be a light restaurant with some good reason for people to come by and stay, not just a coffee shop. He's playing around with ideas, but he's not sure about the one-hour commute. He enjoys being able to go to all of his stores every day.

As usual, Paul is looking at every opportunity from every angle. I'm not sure what he'll do. But I'm sure he'll be up to something new the next time I get to the Outer Banks. If you can't stop by the beach, check out his café at www.frontporch-cafe.net.

CHAPTER 13

What It Takes to Make a Movie

ORKING IN FILM REQUIRES REALLY knowing your business and being confident and decisive. Matt Williams worked making TV commercials in New York City for 18 years. He started out as a grip, working with lights. He watched, learned, and worked his way up to being a gaffer—a lighting expert—and then a cinematographer. A cinematographer directs the photography, that is the look of the project, but also does more—a cinematographer keeps track of everything the cameras and all the camera operators are doing. Matt was looking to make the big step up, from cinematographer to director and producer.

HOW TO BECOME A PRODUCER

Matt got his chance when a pharmaceutical company that really liked his work as a cinematographer asked him to produce and direct close-up shots to be inserted into a commercial he had filmed. Inserts—inserting newly filmed footage into an old commercial—save money. The commercial was already highly successful, but the product labels had changed and the company wanted the new product showing in the old commercial without having to reshoot the whole commercial, which would cost about $250,000.

Lesson #1: In a well-organized business, projects are defined to give a good solution to a problem at the lowest possible cost.

I learned a lot listening to Matt. For one thing, the world of TV and film production is incredibly specialized. Matt likes to specialize in tabletops—that's right, he's a specialist in making movies of products on tables. For another, inserts can be added into a commercial, but it takes a lot of precision with the lighting and the color correction. For a third, making any kind of movie requires a lot of precision about *everything*.

This case study is courtesy of Matt Williams, President of Swanky Pictures, Inc. You can reach Matt by e-mail at ammediate@hotmail.com.

When Matt got the call from the pharmaceutical company, he knew it was his big chance. If he got the contract, he'd be a producer and the work would probably repeat once a month. If they didn't like his proposal, they'd just slip the work into their next big job and he'd lose the opportunity. So his first big challenge was to come up with a workable and convincing proposal in three days, after a short phone call that gave him a brief sketch of what the client wanted.

Lesson #2: Sometimes we have to come up with a project plan with very little information from the customer. If everyone is a technical expert and speaks the same language, this is very efficient. It can also be very risky.

There is a lot of money in TV advertising, but that doesn't mean there's money to blow. In fact, margins are very tight, everything is tracked closely, and a small mistake—especially something that adds extra time—quickly adds hundreds or thousands of dollars to the cost.

Coming up with a bid is very complicated. The producer has to figure out everything and everyone he or she is going to need, then get an hourly or daily price. People's time comes at one of two rates—for either a ten-hour or a 12-hour day, with a slight discount on the last two hours of a 12-hour day. Some studios come equipped with all the lighting you'll need; at others, rental for lighting and equipment is an added cost. In addition, almost everything has two costs: a standard price—the book rate—and the real price you get because you've made a friend or someone is hungry for the work. A producer stays in business on the gap between those two.

Every item a producer misses in planning costs money out of his or her own pocket on production day. Every discount a producer can negotiate stays in his or her pocket. On top of that, the industry standard rate allows a producer to add a 22-percent markup on top of costs. That markup has to cover business operating expenses—the costs of running an office, rent, insurance, advertising, and everything else. So a producer needs to plan well to make money on each shoot and also negotiate well and do excellent work in order to get enough jobs to stay in business.

Lesson #3: Every decision has an effect on time, cost, quality, risk, and the other project factors. Planning needs to take every effect of every decision into account.

MAKING THE PLAN

One part of getting ready to negotiate is preparing to show that your way of doing the work is really the best way—the way that will give enough quality at an acceptable cost. And a key factor in that is the cost of time. The moment a producer goes over a standard day, he or she is paying overtime for everyone and everything. If a shoot takes two days instead of one, the cost of everything doubles. A producer's job is to compress the schedule into as few days as possible, have everything needed, and make that day work no matter what happens.

This requires a lot of expertise. So producers have to listen, as well. If anyone—from a grip to a gaffer to an actor—has a better way of doing something, the producer needs to listen and decide. Is it the better quality at the same cost? If it takes more time, can we afford it? If it saves money, will it work? On a good crew, each person will be able to make clear suggestions and the producer will be able to make lightning-fast decisions—usually in 30 seconds or less. At the same time, someone is always there representing the customer. The customer may make requests or suggestions. If so, the producer has to be able to say, with confidence, exactly what that change will cost. Good customers generally stay out of the way and let the producer do the job. But sometimes the customer representative knows something that is needed. Then the rep has to ask and the producer has to answer in dollars and cents. Each one of those extra requests is decided on and the decision includes whether the cost should come out of the producer's pocket or whether the customer will pay for it with a supplemental fee called an *overage*.

Lesson #4: Projects rely on good decisions in planning and all the way through. Decisions come from people, which means that, to make a good decision, you need the right experts and you need to be able to make sure they speak up clearly and that you listen to them. When everyone can contribute his or her expertise—including what to do and why—we can make good decisions together.

LOCKING DOWN THE CONTRACT

In three days, Matt had his plan. He figured out how to do the shoot in one day. He had his people and his price for everyone and everything. And he went into the negotiation meeting. The customer laid out what they wanted and Matt let them know that they could get most of it in a day, but if they wanted it all, it would have to go do two days. The customer said to do what he could in one day. Then the price negotiation started. Matt wanted $12,000, and the customer wanted to pay $10,000. At that moment, Matt knew he would get the deal. But he had to show why his costs were higher. He presented his reasons and figures. These are some of the issues that were discussed:

- Using a better studio would cost more in the budget, but come out safer and cheaper in production because, with all equipment included, there was less chance of delay looking for a light they didn't have.
- Yes, Matt needed a production manager. If he tried to keep it all in his head, something would slip.

- OK, he agreed, we'll use one of your employees to pick up the bottle instead of hiring a hand model. Make sure she gets a manicure and bring a makeup kit. It won't look quite as good, but you'll save some money.

Each item was negotiated and planned out in detail, with consideration of and its cost and its effect on the timing of the day. Finally, they had a deal.

Lesson #5: Negotiate to close the contract, but also negotiate to get everything you need. You don't want to land a deal that will lose you money later or ruin your reputation with poor quality results.

PREPRODUCTION: PULLING THE TEAM TOGETHER AND GETTING READY TO SHOOT

Now, Matt had to make that plan into a reality in less than a week. First, he hired the production manager for three days of work and they split up all the work. He called everyone who had given an estimate and got most of them. He found substitutes for the others. The production manager found a few expenses—like lunch for the crew—that Matt had left off. They figured out how to make those affordable. Matt came from a background as a tabletop photographer and still likes to work with props, so, as they got down into the details, he focused on props and let his production manager take care of most of the other stuff. Together, they got what they needed and got ready for the day.

Lesson #6: Know your strengths and use them. Then pick the right people and rely on them to complement you with their strengths.

Lesson #7: Every project has a key moment—it may be filming, or writing computer code, or giving a big presentation, or running an event. Prepare for that moment in every way you can, so that you're ready for anything when that moment comes.

GET IT IN THE CAN: SHOOTING THE MOVIE

How do things work on shooting days? I've been learning the process by listening to and reading about how movies and TV are made, and Matt confirmed this picture of work on a film or TV set. Everyone is there to support the director in making his or her vision into a reality. The producer keeps a check on that to make sure it is affordable. Even controlling the budget supports the director—a director doesn't want to shoot half a perfect movie and then run out of money and have to stop. Project management is the result of the way the producer, the director, and the production manager work together, minute by minute. The director sets direction, the producer controls time and cost, and the production manager takes care of work flow, procurement, human resources, and all the other details. They receive information and work results from each team member and keep it going. They try not to let anything "let the air out of the day." A delay is like a flat tire, where all the air goes out and the trip has to stop. Instead, moment by moment, you move to an alternate plan to keep things moving.

Lesson #8: Every successful business does good project management. They may not call it project management, but they do it. They may split the project manager's job up across two or three people who communicate and keep it all together, but, however it is done, good project management must happen; it is essential to supporting good decisions, doing good work, and delivering good results.

As discussed in Chapter 3, good architecture comes from the ability to look at a single thing from several perspectives. When we apply that to making a movie, the key issue is how things will be ordered in time. The script lays out one order—the sequence of events we plan for the viewer to see. Filming is done in a completely different order. For example, wide shots need to be done before close-ups, because it takes five minutes to relight a set from a wide shot to a close-up, but an hour to relight a set from a close-up to a wide shot. Also, conversations are shot twice, once with the camera on one actor once with the camera on the other. Then, in postproduction, editing brings the various shot angles together into a series of seamless scenes. Postproduction might reassemble the scenes of the movie to match the script. But often there are changes. Perhaps the director saw a way to eliminate some long explanation by simply showing what viewers would need to know. Perhaps an actor improved a line. Perhaps one shot didn't work and something else had to be cut in, instead. Planning how to move a script through preproduction, the shoot, and postproduction is the architecture of making a movie, TV show, or commercial.

Lesson #9: Every profession has something equivalent to architecture, whatever it is called, that translates the customer's and technical perspectives and shows how they interact. In a film production, the sound crew, the lighting crew, the film crew, the actors, the postproduction people, the special effects people, and others all represent technical perspectives to consider. For every problem, the producer has to choose the least expensive technical solution good enough for the job from all of these areas of expertise.

Matt sees TV production and directing as management by contingency. Even with all the planning and with all the equipment and people ready, you still need to have three or four options for every problem you can imagine in your head and be able to decide what to do within 30 seconds.

For example, on the day of Matt's shoot, the labels for the medicine bottles had been sent over by courier. They came from a special printer who does extra-high-quality printing just for TV and advertising promotion. Unfortunately, they were sent over in a floppy envelope. They got bent on the way and couldn't be used.

The labels were needed for the first shoot of the day. Matt and his production manager agreed to reorder the morning, shooting scenes 2 and 3 first and then shooting scene 1 after the labels arrived, but before lunch. If they could do that, they could stay on schedule. Now, the new labels would arrive before scene 2 was done. Why not shoot scene 1 after scene 2? Because scenes 2 and 3 were a set, requiring very little change to the lighting between them. Keeping them together would save time. And—especially in making a movie—time is money.

The problem with the labels was the only major glitch. Matt and his team finished the 12-hour day on time with everything in the can—that is, with all the film they needed from the shoot.

Lesson #10: A day of work is a system. If one part fails, the whole thing might fail. We need a way to manage every contingency, to adjust to change, make new decisions, and keep everything going right.

The hard part was over, but the job wasn't done. After the film is shot, it needs to be developed and then edited in postproduction. The biggest post-production challenge in this case was color correction. The new film had to match the color, brightness, and tone of the original film exactly or the insert wouldn't work. It helped that Matt had worked on the original film. That let him match the lighting on the new set to the original. But color correction is still a demanding job, so Matt hired an expert who was able to make it work.

Lesson #11: Know which jobs are most crucial and when to pay for the expertise you need.

Lesson #12: After the production work, there is always some kind of wrap-up—follow-through and cleanup—essential to success.

CONCLUSION

Matt succeeded. He delivered the insert for the commercial with quality that satisfied himself and the customer, on time and within budget. He kept costs under control well enough that he could afford to do it again. And that was a good thing, because the customer asked Matt to do about one insert a month for the next six months. Matt had stepped up: his cinematography company was now a TV production company.

Lesson #13: Use project management to plan, prepare, do, and follow through to get it done right every time. Each success opens the door to a new opportunity.

Alignment to Our Customers

THIS CHAPTER DESCRIBES HOW ONE OF my clients, Phototake (www.phototakeusa.com), used the services of my company, Quality Technology & Instruction (www.qualitytechnology.com), to increase sales and by getting new customers and more repeat business. The client is a stock photography company providing images in medicine and technology. That is, it owns about 100,000 photographs and medical illustrations and sells the images or rights to the images to advertising firms and publishers to illustrate advertisements and textbooks. The company also does custom photo assignments and illustrations, but in this case study we're focusing on the stock side of the business.

A GOOD COMPANY NEEDS TO DO BETTER

At the beginning of this project, Phototake had been in business for over 15 years and had been on the Internet for three years. In 2002, the economy was slow, advertising slowed down, and Phototake's sales were slow, as well. The company had an excellent product and its customers really liked them. But we needed to figure out how to let other people know that. And we also needed to know what the customers wanted that they weren't already getting.

When a company is already doing a good job, it takes some research to figure out how to do better. So, we planned a project with five parts:

- Interview current customers to find out what they like about Phototake.
- Evaluate customer searches on the web site to see what customers were looking for but not finding.
- Analyze the information and decide what to do.
- Change the advertising campaign to reflect Phototake's strengths.

This case study is courtesy of Yoav Levy, owner of Phototake, at www.phototakeusa.com.

- Make any changes to customer support and the product line to bring what the company was providing into alignment with what the customers wanted.

We called the project Alignment to Our Customers because the term *alignment* gave the focus of our campaign. We were already serving our customers, but we wanted to focus on them more directly, to line up anything that was out of joint, so that the company was a smooth pipeline with no kinks, no twists, no delays in getting the customers what they wanted.

Lesson #1: A research project has three steps: research, where we gather information; analysis, where we decide what to do; and action, where we do what we think will work.

Lesson #2: If we want to improve a company that is already doing well, we will probably have to make changes that cut across multiple divisions of the company, aligning everything the company is doing to its customers and its goals.

SETTING SPECIFIC GOALS

We then set specific goals based on the general goals above. Here is the goal statement from the project plan.

Every two weeks, QTI will deliver useful research results to Phototake. Sid and Yoav will define:

- Specific action Phototake can take to make changes to improve alignment to customers.
- Specific experiments to try.
- Specific larger initiatives or projects that will start slowly or be put on hold, to be developed more rapidly when more resources are available.
- A revised, prioritized list of questions for QTI to take in the next research steps.

Ongoing research will include:

- Analysis of the behavior of current users of Phototake's web site. Input to gap analysis.
- Customer surveys, interviews, and focus groups. Input to gap analysis.
- Research into Phototake's competitors' activities. What are they doing? Is it working? Should Phototake ignore it, imitate it, or trump it?

I created this goal statement by interviewing Yoav with the goal of defining a research project that would answer the questions he needed answered and lead to specific action to improve business results.

Lesson #3: When doing a project for a customer, define what that customer needs and then turn it into a specific, clear goal.

FIND OUT WHAT YOUR CUSTOMERS LIKE ABOUT YOU, THEN TELL EVERYONE

Yoav arranged for me to talk with three long-time customers who said that they really like what Phototake had to offer. I prepared a survey before I did the calls. My key questions were: *Why* do you like what Phototake does? *What* do they offer that keeps you coming back? *How* does Phototake help you solve your business problems?

I created the questionnaire because I had two goals for the interviews that were somewhat in conflict. On one hand, I wanted to cast a wide net, to understand the customers' business and problems in general. On the other hand, I also wanted very specific details about what worked for them and what didn't. In a situation like that, planning the conversation with a questionnaire was essential.

Lesson #4: Use progressive elaboration to get more value from a project. When you sit down to do a small piece of work, plan that work in detail, create any tools you need, and then do and follow through.

Broad questions on the survey included:

- What are you working on?
- What business problems does Phototake's service help you solve?

To get more precise information, I also drilled down with questions like:

- When you're looking for pictures, what makes you choose one stock company's web site over another?
- What can a stock photography company do to lose you as a customer?
- What do you like most about Phototake's products? About its services?

It was important to get past generalities such as "It's easy to get the images I want." Every satisfied customer said that. What made the surveys valuable was learning how that worked and what made it true.

For example, one customer, a media buyer for a bunch of graphic designers, would get lots of requests, pile them up, call Phototake, and speak with a researcher who would select images for her. Another customer, a graphic designer, answered the same question, "How do you get your images? Why is it easy?" by saying, "I go to your web site. The search engine is great and I find what I want really quickly." From detailed answers like this, we learned how to keep running Phototake as a business and what to change. For example, from these two answers, we learned that good customer service included both a researcher on staff and the web site search engine—one could not replace the other.

For another example, many customers say they like fast delivery. But fast delivery can mean anything from "in stock and will arrive next week" to one-click sale with delivery over the web. Be sure to get your customer to *specify* what he or she wants.

We also asked customers why they chose different web sites and found that, to keep a customer, you have to do everything right. One customer said she used Phototake more because a competitor had great images but an unreliable web site. Another complained that a different web site had images that were too small to view. From all of this, we compiled a list of all the things Phototake did right. Since I was talking with people in advertising, I asked them about catch phrases that would get the idea across. As a result, by the time the interviews were done, our new advertising campaign was already being designed.

When the surveys were done, I analyzed the results and delivered a summary listing specific actions, questions, and recommendations for further research. You might note that this is plan, do, check, act (PDCA) in action. We gather information in research and then, in analysis, plan what to do. Then, every two weeks, we do it, check the results, and either keep doing it or go back to the drawing board.

Lesson #5: In an ongoing research project, build in frequent deliverables. You don't need to lock down everything you are doing. Instead, you can evaluate and change course using PDCA. But being flexible and experimental with PDCA requires being specific, not general or vague.

These were the most significant outputs from the interviews:

- A new flash (motion graphics) advertisement on the company's home page showing its images being turned into ads that showed the quality of Phototake products and the value of Phototake services.
- New text and images selected for a monthly e-mail advertising campaign. We took what current customers liked about Phototake and told everybody in our target market in clear images with snappy language.

Note that, in this case, we focused on what customers liked about Phototake. That wasn't an arbitrary decision nor did we want to avoid finding problems. Early research had shown us we had loyal customers. So the whole plan was to find out why they liked us, so we could get more loyal customers. If we had found that customers were leaving us, we would have researched why that was happening and worked to improve our alignment to customers.

Lesson #6: Take what you learn from research, decide what to do, and put it into action right away. The sooner you do it, the sooner you realize value.

Lesson #7: Whatever you do well, keep doing it, do it better, and let everyone know. Whatever you don't do well, fix it.

USE ALL THE INFORMATION YOU HAVE

The next piece of research used data that Phototake had in hand, but had never used. For three years, every time someone searched for a picture, typing in a word like "doctor" or "heart," the web site captured the search and the number of images found. We had data about over 100,000 searches. Have you ever watched a customer in a store—maybe your store—look around and walk out without buying anything? Wouldn't it be great if you could ask each one, "What were you looking for?" Well, that's what we had the chance to do.

Lesson #8: Look around your business. Where do you have information—customer requests, names and addresses, anything—that will tell you useful things if you only analyze it?

This job required some pretty powerful thinking, so I hired a statistical consultant. I worked with Anna to define what information would be useful. Then she took the data and ran it through a statistical program to generate Excel spreadsheets with summary data I could review. The lists she created for me included:

- *Customer searches that returned no images.* Here, Yoav and I looked at the list. If the request was for something that Phototake wanted to sell, we added it to our list of pictures we wanted.
- *Customer searches that returned fewer than ten images.* Here, we knew we would want more images like these.
- *The top 500 searches.* These searches were the most commonly requested items, indicating where we wanted to make sure we would keep getting fresh images from our vendors.
- *Searches resulting in the highest dollar sales.* Here, rather than focusing on quantity sold, we focused on the bottom line. We had to link several databases to do this, but it paid off in information that would grow the business.

In each case, the work required both a computer and a person. We needed the computer's power to organize the information and human intelligence to review the information to find the meaning. For example, separately, searches for "diabetes," "insulin," and "high blood sugar" might not be much. But, if all three showed up in the top 500, we would add them together. Then the single topic—diabetes, which has a symptom of high blood sugar and is treated with insulin—might be on our top 20.

Lesson #9: Combine brainstorming with the customer and a technical expert to define the questions you want to ask. You're looking for questions that will elicit answers that lead to business decisions and actions that grow the business.

Lesson #10: When analyzing data, combine computer power and human intelligence to get the answers to your questions.

We took the results of these surveys and did two things:

- Internally, the company focused on putting the most sought images on the web site first.
- We launched a newsletter for vendors, letting them know that customers were looking for

specific images. If the photographers could take these pictures, we would get them up on the web site and the images would be likely to sell. We also gave the photographers clearer instructions about how to organize the pictures for faster processing.

In this way, we streamlined internal activities to focus on what the customer would buy and we also widened the pipeline of new images from our vendors, getting more of what we needed sooner in a way that was easier and faster to process.

As a result, Phototake had more of what the customers wanted in stock and available on the web site to the customers sooner.

Lesson #11: See your business as a flow of products or services from vendor to customer. Fix the clogs in the pipes. Several small, inexpensive changes will end up increasing sales while reducing costs per sale. The result is pure profit.

CONCLUSION

Overall, our approach in the alignment campaign was what the Total Quality Management folks call *continuous improvement*. Continuous improve-ment means making many small changes that add up to big results. The neat thing about continuous improvement is that it can be done at low cost, without hiring new staff, using expensive consult-ants, or buying new equipment. You may want a consultant to guide you through your first proj-ects, but you can have your own staff do most of the work, so you can save money.

Lesson #12: Apply PDCA, work smarter, and realize pure profit with a small investment.

I noticed that, as I wrote this story, I kept using the word "we." I don't work for Phototake, but, when I take on a job for a client, I work with the people and it feels like a collaboration, like *we*. I was very glad when Phototake took what they learned from this research project, used, it, got through the economic slump, and started to pick up when the economy got moving again.

Lesson #13: When you do a project for a customer, care as much about their problems and their suc-cess as you would about your own.

Lesson #14: If a company faces its problems squarely in a difficult time, it can both survive and also position itself for growth.

CHAPTER 15

A Consulting Firm Launches Its First Product

THIS IS THE STORY OF THE DEVELOPMENT of a new industrial tool that could make a real difference in the manufacturing world wherever metals are coated or treated for durability. The folks at Surface Stress Technologies are really bright people—scientists and engineers who have come up with a solution to a longstanding problem that affects the automotive, aircraft, chemical, and other industries.

All metals wear out over time. Knowing how long a part will last—whether it's a piece of aircraft landing gear or a steam pipe in a power plant—is crucial to safety and productivity. But metal fatigue is the result of microscopic—nearly invisible—changes in the metal. Tiny differences in production in a single batch of products can result in big differences in durability. As a result, a whole bunch of pipes that look identical will age differently. One pipe might last only five years, while another lasts 30.

And there's no easy way to tell. Two pipes or wheels or whatever will look identical. Most of the tests that can detect metal fatigue require destroying the product being tested. As a result, a lot of manufacturing relies on taking a sample—perhaps ten percent of every unit made—and performing destructive tests on it. If the ten percent come up clean, then the batch is clean. (It's nowhere near that simple, but that gives you the idea.) Then items are overengineered, so that even the weakest units will last the needed field life.

If someone could come up with a technique for testing for the microscopic cracks that signal metal fatigue without destroying the part, it would solve a lot of expensive problems. And that's exactly what the team at Surface Stress Technologies did. In their laboratory, they have a device that puts an electrical charge into the metal object and then detects fatigue by how electricity moves

This case study is courtesy of Pete Dixon, President and Managing Partner of Surface Stress Technologies, www.surfacestress.com.

through the object. Their equipment can be adapted for many types of metals and coatings and can be set to detect fractures at different depths within the metal.

For several years, they made a living as consultants. They would get samples into their lab, use their equipment, and report the results to the client. In terms of what we discussed about programs in Chapter 4, Surface Stress Technologies was a projectized company making money from the engineering research they did for customers. They worked this way because their equipment worked well in a scientific laboratory with highly trained engineers operating it, but it could not work on a messy shop floor or be run by a technician without a lot of training.

Three years ago, they decided to change that. They decided to move from consulting to product development. Their goal was to produce an industrial-strength machine that companies could lease, put in a plant, and use to test hundreds of parts each day. In manufacturing, this would mean that 100 percent of parts could be tested, instead of only ten percent, and that all the parts that were good could be sold, rather than having to destroy ten percent of a batch to sell the other 90 percent. In maintenance, it could mean identifying failing parts sooner while allowing more durable parts to stay in place longer, reducing replacement costs.

The folks who run Surface Stress Technologies were right on the money with their ideas. And their science and technology were top-notch. I really admire them. I'm saying that now because the story includes a number of mistakes they made. In fact, they really gave themselves some headaches. So, before we look at the problems they created for themselves, I want to be clear: these guys are good at what they do and they have a real contribution to make. They also have two other very important qualities for entrepreneurial success—they are extremely persistent and they rec-

ognize and learn from their mistakes.

The mistakes they made are very common. In fact, I find them all over the place and most books on how to succeed as entrepreneurs warn people to avoid them. So this case study illustrates mistakes that you might be making right now! These mistakes can be prevented by good project management practice. There is a lot to learn in the details of this case study, but there are two main points.

- Good project management practices can really reduce start-up cost and time for a new venture—perhaps by a factor of five or more.
- If those practices are not used early, problems will come up. But project management still works—better late than never. Project management plus persistence can see a start-up company through difficult times.

Our story starts three years ago. The company had a patented technology and a consulting business that could solve industrial problems. The owners wanted to grow and to change their business by creating a device that they could sell to customers. The device would cost a bit under $50,000 and a single large company might want ten to a hundred of them. A full-blown plan for this situation would include the following:

- Technical planning to determine how to turn the laboratory device into a simple, robust prototype that would work on a shop floor.
- Project management planning to identify the best team for the job, create a schedule, budget, risk plan, and complete project plan for success.
- Business planning to write a business plan, acquire funding, and plan the development and operations of the new production line and service company.

Lesson #1: An entrepreneurial business plan should always be supported by an internal project plan that describes how the team will meet its goals.

The folks at Surface Stress did some of that. They hired an expert engineering consultant who estimated that it would cost $200,000 and take five months to create five industrial-strength prototype of their device. Unfortunately, the owner of the company—the chief scientist who invented the process—didn't believe the expert and thought he could do it himself for under $25,000 in six months.

Looking back, he sees he was wrong. This is a common mistake many experts and professionals make, which we discussed in Chapter 7, Ensuring Success by Completing the Plan. People tend to think that if they are experts in one area, they are experts in related areas. But the opposite is true.

Lesson #2: Identify all the types of expertise needed for your project in detail. Meet with experts and make good decisions about what you are and are not able to do yourself.

In a sense, the consultant they hired made a mistake, too. He was unable to make a convincing case for why it cost so much to turn a piece of laboratory equipment into an industrial device.

As a result, the Surface Stress people tried it on their own. They had set themselves up for trouble. They did not pick the right team for the job.

Let's take a look at the technical, project, and business challenges faced by Surface Stress over the last three years and how they handled them.

TECHNICAL CHALLENGES AND SOLUTIONS

The team has resolved these technical challenges:

- Analog-to-digital signal conversion
- Developing software to interpret test results
- Creating implements for special surfaces

The analog electrical signal from the sensitive coil had to be converted to a digital signal so that the computer could interpret it. (Don't worry if you don't know what that means.) The problem was that the signal had to be changed without losing very sensitive details of the signal. The Surface Stress people were used to handling that kind of problem in lab equipment. They didn't realize that doing it for an industrial-strength machine required a totally different type of engineering expertise. Once they didn't follow the consultant's advice, they hired two engineers who thought they could solve the problem, but couldn't, before they gave up on that approach. Then they went back to the plan they had discarded months before—hiring a firm that specializes in producing industrial equipment to come up with solutions to this and other industrial design problems.

Lesson #3: A job that is easy for the right team can be impossible for the wrong team, leading to human resource problems and a steep increase in project costs.

> ▼ **BOTTOM-LINE BASICS**
> ### Can You Beat the Expert?
>
> How many people think that, because they own a home, they can paint and do repairs? Some can. But almost no one can do it for less than it would cost to hire a professional. Many of us should stop and ask, "What makes me think I can do a better job at this faster and cheaper than a professional who does it for a living?" If we don't come up with a good answer, it's time to listen to the expert.
>
> We may want to get more than one expert opinion. We will want to listen to all the advice, understand it, and, particularly, understand *why* the process will cost what he or she says and take as long as he or she says. But the key is to make an informed decision on solid principles, rather than making a quick decision that can get you headed down the wrong road.
>
> The same is true for any project in a business. We need to realize that being expert in one thing often means *not* being an expert in a closely related area.

The second technical challenge involved developing computer software. As consulting engineers, the team could look at graphs generated by their equipment, interpret them, and explain the results to customers. For the machine they wanted to lease to customers on the shop floor, their intelligence had to be automated into a computer program. They needed to be able to define measurable results from the output of the coil and then have a computer program output a simple result—a green light for a good part, a red light for a bad one, and a yellow light if a retest was required—and a simple report of the results on each part. Fortunately, this part of the project went ahead without any big problems.

Their third technical problem had to do with making the machine work for parts with unusual shapes, that is, parts that weren't flat. Testing for fatigue requires a very good connection between the test coil and the surface of the metal to be tested. That's easy only if the metal is flat. If the metal has an odd shape—a curved surface, such as the inside or outside of a pipe, or the V of a groove in a gear—then a special implement needs to be developed for each job. That implement ensures a good, firm fit for the coil to the object.

The team encountered this type of problem several times in consulting work and when developing the prototype. In review, we found two types of problems:

- *Technical problems.* In these cases, there was no affordable solution—the particular part could not be tested. In one case, parts of uncertain quality went into valves before they were tested and the customer was looking for a way to test 100,000 valves at low cost, instead of discarding the whole batch because some might be bad. But there was no cost-effective way to attach the coil to the valve in a short enough time frame to make

the job affordable to the customer and profitable for the company.

- *Project communications problems.* In some cases, a solution for the custom implement was delayed because an assumption was made and the proper information was not communicated. In one case, a wheel that looked flat was actually an inverted cone with a very slight slope down to the center from all sides. The team wasted three months trying to get their flat coil to work before they requested the technical specification and saw the actual shape.

Each of these technical problems came up and was either solved or set aside. But the time it took to do that work—which had not been well planned for at the start—created real problems for the business.

I want to reinforce the point that this team did know how to solve these problems—but in a laboratory, not in a production environment. As we discussed in Chapter 4, Your Business and Your Projects, when we discussed the input-process-output model of work, a change in work environment can thoroughly change the tools and technical knowledge needed for success.

Lesson #4: Treating each technical or engineering job as a mini-project and fully documenting the process—input, process, output, tools, techniques, and work environment, as we discussed in Chapter 4—will reduce time and cost.

PROJECT MANAGEMENT CHALLENGES AND SOLUTIONS

The team has faced and resolved these challenges through project management:

- *Prototyping:* Finding the right client problem to solve
- *Communications:* Getting on the same page with the client

- *Improving support from a vendor*—a situation complicated because the vendor was slow in improving the prototype, which further delayed their timeline

Surface Stress Technologies made a good decision on how to launch their new equipment line. The idea was to find one client who had a problem, solve it for them with an industrial-strength prototype, and get them to commit a purchase order to buy a fairly large number of machines. Based on that commitment, Surface Stress could get funding to go into production for that customer and other customers to follow.

This method required finding a customer whose problem was a good match for the Surface Stress solution. That turned out to be a lot harder than anyone expected. Surface Stress took on eight clients. In three cases, their tool didn't solve the customers' problems. In four more, it did, but the customers only wanted consulting and didn't need to commit to a purchase. Only in the eighth case did Surface Stress find what it needed—a large company with an ongoing production problem that could be solved by buying a significant quantity of the new machine. As this book goes to press, they have just installed a prototype machine in that customer's factory after extensive testing. If it works for a month, Surface Stress will have the order that it needs.

Proper project management planning around finding the right client could have helped in these ways:

- *Casting a wider net to find customers.* Brainstorming techniques could have gotten many other ways of finding customers that were a good match.
- *Process definition and communications planning.* If Surface Stress had followed an input-process-output model for the work to be done on each job, they could have prevented miscommunications and delays. Some of the earlier client jobs might have worked with better planning. See the sidebar, Good Communications Saves the Client Relationship, for two examples.
- *Evaluation of customer requirements.* In several cases, the customer gained value from the consulting, but did not need to buy the production device. Good analysis of the customer's *business* problem—as opposed to the technical problem—could have foreseen this. For example, in one case, a customer needed to determine if a bend in a pipe would corrode. The Surface Stress team was able to determine that, indeed, some of the pipes were flawed. They hoped the customer would buy their device to test the pipes. Instead, the customer simply took the report from Surface Stress and told the company that had sold them the pipe to improve the quality of their products. It was cheaper to pass the cost of the problem back to the vendor than it was to buy expensive test equipment from Surface Stress. But that solution didn't occur to the folks at Surface Stress until they finished the consulting work— and found that they weren't going to sell their machine.
- *Work scheduling.* If the folks at Surface Stress had taken a project and business approach to planning these consulting/prototype jobs, they could have planned to have enough money to make it through several client relationships. Also, they could have planned to have each job be profitable as either a consulting engagement or an equipment sale, instead of expecting an equipment sale and sometimes ending up with nothing at all.

One interesting thing to note about Pete's experience is that some of the problems could be solved with either better engineering *or* better project

▼ SOMETHING SLIPPED!
Good Communications Saves the Client Relationship

The Surface Stress team would have been much better off if they had created a process model for their consulting engagements. They've done it now, because they've seen that not doing it cost them a couple of very expensive years. Now, they require the customer to provide technical specifications of the device to be tested as well as samples and they've developed an interview form for the customer. The proper way to use that form is to receive the technical information, do a simple project plan for the engagement, and then make an offer to the customer.

That planning would allow Surface Stress to go to each customer and tell them, upfront, if they were a candidate for consulting work, for a prototype machine, or neither. It would also allow them to set a price on the work to be done. Here are two specific examples where this kind of project planning for each engagement would have improved relationships with the client.

- With the customer who wanted part of a wheel tested, the surface stress engineer would have known the wheel was conical, not flat. That would have saved the project team three months. Since this is the customer who is waiting for a one-month manufacturing test before placing an order, this delayed the big breakthrough for Surface Stress by three months.

- With the customer who wanted to test assembled valves, Pete made the mistake of offering a price based on the cost of the test, rather than the cost of the test process, including setting up the coil on each valve. If Pete had evaluated the problem before committing to a price, he might have realized that, including time, his cost would be $2.50 per valve instead of $0.50 per valve. He then could have promised the customer to charge $5.00 or less per valve and the customer might have agreed to the job. But once Pete said it would be about 50 cents per valve, he couldn't credibly go back to the customer with a price five or ten times higher, even though the customer might have agreed to that price upfront.

management. Better engineering could reduce the cost of the job. Better project management and client communications could convince the client to pay more for the job. In some cases, either solution might work.

Lesson #5: Treating each client engagement as a project can reduce costs, improve communications, improve the chance of retaining the client, and make it easier to estimate the value of a client for your business.

Once the Surface Stress team realized that they needed a professional company to create an industrial-strength prototype of their equipment, they retained the services of a builder of custom electronic industrial equipment. However, they brought this vendor on board late, when they had little money left and did not have a clear business plan. For that vendor, building a one-off machine and then selling perhaps a hundred more made Surface Stress a very small client. And small clients have little leverage. The technical work has been good, but there have been long delays as the vendor's engineers are spending most of their time on jobs for more valuable clients. The Surface Stress team has not really brought this problem under management. Instead, they have simply borne with the delays, working, waiting, and hoping for completion that would move the company past prototyping and into production.

Lesson #6: Recognize your needs for expertise early.

Lesson #7: Have a convincing project plan and business model. Convey your needs to your vendors. Be ready to design contracts with incentives for timely performance.

ENTREPRENEURIAL BUSINESS CHALLENGES AND SOLUTIONS

- Negotiating with potential customers
- Staying in business

Because the Surface Stress team never really did in-depth planning for finding and negotiating with potential clients, they basically put up a web site, networked around, and dealt with each customer who knocked on the door. They were operating on the assumption that they could simply talk to a customer and find out if this customer was a good match for their prototyping efforts. Their thinking—we'll figure out if we can solve the customer's problem, then go from there—was too simplistic. They did not realize that they had to be able to talk effectively to production managers and business product managers, both of whom think very differently from laboratory engineers and both of whom have very different approaches to problem solving.

At first, they failed to convey their own technical requirements—for specifications and samples—to the customer. After that, when they had a technical solution, they often discovered that the customer—at a business level—had a business solution once they got information from Surface Stress and that the business solution—such as reporting a problem to a vendor or changing internal processes—was cheaper and less risky than becoming a prototype client for a start-up.

As a result, the Surface Stress team had to work with eight clients over three years, instead of working with one client over six months. That led to challenges in keeping the team together and

financing the company. One of the company owners had to pick up a day job to keep things going, creating further delays. Everyone had to put in more money. The greater investment and delay in starting up severely reduced the return on investment of the new company.

At Surface Stress, their major tool for overcoming the business challenges was simple persistence.

Lesson #8: Without good planning, delays can stretch a problem out tenfold, putting stress on a company's schedule, business plan, pocketbook, and team.

SUCCESS BRINGS MORE CHALLENGES

Because of good engineering—and in spite of some weaknesses in planning, project management, and communications—Surface Stress Technologies is on the edge of getting that first big order for production machines from a client. The moment that happens, everything changes. The company goes from being a venture that makes money by projects to one that makes money by production and sale of products. When I say everything changes, what do I mean?

- The business process flow changes completely.
- As a result, the methods of accounting and financing change.
- The crucial benchmarks of business success—the things we have to watch to make sure the company can stay in business—all change.
- The company needs to establish whole new departments to fulfill production management, sales, and customer service roles.

The company is going out of prototyping and into producing and introducing their product into its marketing life cycle, as we discussed in Chapter 2, Why Businesses Need Successful Projects. This will require the following new things:

- Business plan for financing the new divisions and departments
- Series of project plans for creating each of the new departments
- Set of technical plans for maintaining production and servicing equipment
- Set of business documents and contracts for leasing and service agreements

Lesson #9: As a company moves into a different marketing phase, it needs to launch a complete new program with several projects.

CONCLUSION

There is a lot to admire in the work of the Surface Stress team and a lot to learn from their errors. They have a good idea and it will probably become a good business through their engineering skill and persistence. At the same time, by applying good project management, they could have gotten there two years ago and spent $200,000 less. The value of applying project management concepts to changing small businesses is very clear when we see that. Project management is relatively easy to learn. The challenge is in knowing that it is worth learning. Clearly, in this case, it is. Highly capable scientists and engineers are getting a lot less value from their company because, as bright and capable as they are, they need expertise of a different sort. Using the expertise of project management:

- They could have realized that they needed expertise they didn't have, defined that expertise, and hired a company that could provide it in the beginning. Then they could have managed that vendor relationship to early success.

- They could have defined the requirements they, as a vendor, had for potential customers of their prototype. Surface Stress could have evaluated customers and chosen those that were likely to buy the prototype or charged more for consulting services if sale of the prototype was on the table.
- They could have defined the processes necessary to do consulting or prototype development work for a client, streamlining the process.
- They could have estimated the time and cost of the entire prototype program more accurately, so as to secure sufficient funding and plan their work time successfully.

As this book goes to print, Surface Stress Technologies is a couple of months from success on the prototyping project. I think they'll make it, because they are persistent and because they see and learn from their mistakes.

Have You Defined Your Projects?

After reading this case study, take a look at your own company. Are you in the middle of a big change? If so, have you defined what is involved? What will the company look like before and after? What projects will get you from here to there? If you're not using the tools in Part I, do that now. You'll save yourself lots of time and money.

Or, is there a change you've always wanted to make? Is there some way you want or need to run your business differently? Can project management help you define that opportunity and make your dreams come true?

CHAPTER 16

17 Years of Growth at Kirbo's

I ENJOYED TALKING WITH BRUCE, CO-OWNER of an office copier sales and service company in rural Texas, maybe because we're just such different people. He's a slow-talking Texan who doesn't think he's done anything special in running and growing a business for the last 33 years. He talks slower than I type, which made the interview easy. He's never defined a project; he's just thought his way through problems and made some good choices. He doesn't realize how much he knows or how much others could learn from him. But I learned a lot. I think you will, too.

He showed me that owners of a small business can grow it successfully, project after project, by doing good project management, even if they've never heard of the idea of project management, read any books, or taken any courses. Many small business owners are doing projects all the time and don't even know it. Once they know that

project management is what they're doing, they can overcome roadblocks more easily. As we do our work, we learn and grow, as the 12 lessons in this case study show.

Lesson #1: Experience becomes expertise, but that happens faster and more easily if we think about our experience. Looking at change, growth, and problem solving in terms of projects speeds and eases our growth.

Our story starts in 1988, when Kirbo's office supply had been selling and servicing office equipment for 16 years from one location in Brownwood, Texas. As a town less than 70 miles away, Stephenville, began to grow, it seemed to make sense to set up a new office. (Seventy miles is just around the corner in rural Texas.) But the owners didn't want to spend a lot of money. As co-owner Bruce Stewart put it, "It's a mistake to go in, spend a million dollars, and get it all at once. You may think it makes sense to get it all at

This case study is courtesy of Bruce Stewart, co-owner of Kirbo's Office Systems, www.kirbos.com.

once. But we grew slowly over five years, and, looking back, five years wasn't all that long." In fact, the Stephenville office was able to show profit most quarters from the very beginning.

Lesson #2: Slow, planned growth is often best for a small business.

Kirbo's started by renting storefront space, just a desk in someone else's print shop, and sending a part-time salesman. Then they added a service technician. Then the service technician needed to store some parts and it was time for Kirbo's to rent a building. When that seemed to be working, Bruce thought, "If we're going to be here forever, we don't want to pay rent." So they got some land and built a building of their own. They built it larger than they needed it to be at the time, but, over the years, they've outgrown it and now they're expanding the building. The Stephenville office has been profitable for Kirbo's for 17 years.

Adding the Stephenville office was a case of following the customer and growing into the territory. Potential customers in Stephenville needed photocopiers, faxes, and service, and there was no one nearby to help them out. Kirbo's came and met that customer demand. There are other reasons to start new locations. As you'll see, each of Kirbo's new locations came about for a different reason: following the customer, responding to competitive opportunity, and seizing an opportunity inside the team.

Lesson #3: One way to grow is to follow your customers and develop carefully, at the right speed. As they grow, you grow with them.

Lesson #4: There are many different problems that can become your opportunity for growth.

Kirbo's opened its third office in San Angelo in the year 2000. This time, the company learned that the local dealer for their products was, at the time, not doing the best job they could. Their competitor didn't know the newest equipment and wasn't selling it all that well. Kirbo's thought they could help out the parent company and make some money by opening an office in the same town as a competitor. This time, though, they faced challenges that hadn't come up in Stephenville. First of all, San Angelo is about 100 miles from Brownwood, too far to ask even a Texan to commute every day. Second, it turned out to be hard to find the right people for the job.

Things started well in San Angelo. Kirbo's sent an experienced salesman/manager from Stephenville to open the San Angelo office and business was good. But that employee wanted to stay in San Angelo for only six months and then he came back home to his family. The first service manager didn't work out due to a personal problem and Kirbo's had to let him go. The second salesman couldn't close a deal and he was told to leave as well. The same happened with a receptionist. Bruce says, "It's hard to let people go, but you can't keep people who aren't performing; it hurts you too much. We kept at it until we found the right people."

Lesson #5: Be compassionate, but also be direct about business problems with your team. Solve them quickly and cleanly; that way, actually, everyone is better off.

Now, though, the San Angelo team is doing well. With them in place, Bruce has been able to sleep well at night, not worrying about the San Angelo office. The current manager has joined the Chamber of Commerce and helped out on a number of local charities. Even though San Angelo has 100,000 people, it still operates like a small town and people want to give business to people who give back to the community. He is also very much oriented toward Kirbo's style of business: he makes a personal connection with each customer, understands his or her needs and concerns, and commits to being there. Their competitor simply faxes over a low-priced bid. That works for some customers, but the customers who want to be confident they will get reliable service choose Kirbo's.

The San Angelo office faced one other challenge. Once the Kirbo's office began to do well selling the newer models of copiers, their competitor saw that it was a good way to make money and did the same. So, instead of lagging behind, the competition caught up on the equipment pretty fast and, of course, had the home-court advantage in San Angelo. Kirbo's hadn't really expected that to happen.

Lesson #6: Remember: your competition is keeping an eye on you. As you change, expect them to change, too.

Kirbo's responded by accepting slower growth, keeping staff size to just three people for longer than they had originally planned. As Kirbo's developed its style of personal service and became known in the community, the right type of customers gravitated toward Kirbo's. The two copier service companies have different styles and customers have a choice.

Lesson #7: Your own personal style is an asset, especially when it comes to competition. Know how you like to do business, find customers that suit you, and, usually, you'll have all the work you need. You don't need to be number one; you just need to know yourself and do what you're good at doing in your own style.

Bruce and his partner never really planned to open a fourth location. The second had come from following their customers. The third was a competitive opportunity. The reason for opening the fourth store was more personal. A member of Bruce's partner's family had been in the office equipment business for about 30 years, but had always worked for one of the big dealers. He got fed up with corporate politics and he came to his

relative and asked for an opportunity to run his own store. Bruce and his partner looked at the situation from several angles before they decided to open their fourth office in Killeen in 2002.

On the plus side, they could start with a reliable, proven manager. The manager brought expertise and he knew the competition because he used to work for them. They asked several questions that, although not a formal marketing study, achieved the goal of a marketing study. Killeen is a fast-growing town with lots of new business. It is ten miles away from the town where the competitor is located and the competitor prefers business closer to their office. Kirbo's does well with smaller companies that don't interest the competitor and also has discovered that there are a number of companies that look small because they are not flashy local stores, but actually are large manufacturing businesses with customers across the globe. Personal service continues to be a big factor in Kirbo's growth. Just like the manager who joined Kirbo's, local companies don't like the impersonal corporate style of Kirbo's competitor. In the last three years, Kirbo's has found that they can grow a good business in Killeen, using their location, their style of personal service, and their willingness to get to know the neighborhood. One challenge that they faced early on was a customer concern. If Kirbo's had only one local technician, then how would a client get service if that technician was out sick or on a long call? Kirbo's promised four-hour response time if that happened, by sending someone from the home office in Brownwood about a hundred miles away. That was good enough for some customers. And, once they signed on, Kirbo's could afford to hire a second technician in Killeen, solving the problem permanently. As a result, the new Killeen office doing well—as are the other locations.

Lesson #8: Sometimes, we come up with a short-term solution to a problem and then grow into a permanent solution.

After hearing Bruce's stories, I asked him if he thought he was better off having grown the business and opened four stores, instead of just staying in Brownwood. He laughed and said, "We ask ourselves that all the time." Reflecting on that together, we saw several things he had gained:

- *Business equity—the value of the business— has grown.* Although Bruce and his partner have no thoughts of retirement, they know that, when they decide to retire, they have a larger, more valuable business to sell.
- *Kirbo's, being larger, is more robust.* For example, they recently lost a great salesman from the Stephenville office when he was called into active service from the army reserves. They reduced their losses by transferring a good salesman from another office into the key Stephenville territory and hiring someone for the other office. They couldn't have done that if they had only one office. Because they could transfer someone from one territory to another, they didn't have to hire a new salesperson for Stephenville, which could have slowed revenue for quite a while longer.
- *They've given more to more people in more local towns.* Business isn't all about money; it's about serving people and the community and providing employees with opportunities for growth, too. And they've done a lot more of that by growing.

Lesson #9: It always pays to look at value and opportunity cost, even after the fact.

The one thing that they didn't get was something that businesspeople always seem to expect from growth, but rarely actually get—more money for themselves. Somehow, most of the time in small business, costs seem to keep pace with revenues and net revenue isn't all that much greater for the owners of four stores than the owner of one. Bruce said that the other offices simply weren't as efficient as the home office, so he wasn't able to make as much money after the costs of hiring people and running the offices. When we looked at that, we saw that, while he and his partner had a good reason to be efficient—every dollar not spent was a dollar to keep in their pockets— their managers didn't have the same incentive.

So, at the end of the call, we defined a new problem and a new opportunity. How could the owners of Kirbo's share the benefits of cost savings with their managers, so that the incentive would make things more efficient and make more money for everyone? And how could managers at different stores share cost-saving techniques with one another, so the results would be even better? We looked at shifting the focus from growth of total revenue to growth of net revenue—pure profit.

Lesson #10: Today's situation is always worth a little attention. Your problems or your customers could be turned into an opportunity with a little thinking and a little work.

In reflecting on what I've learned from Bruce's story, I also see two larger patterns. The keys for successful growth for a small business are—not surprisingly—the same as the keys for project success. Whenever Kirbo's defined the problem clearly and put the right people on the job, they grew. Whenever they missed a step in defining the problem—such as when they didn't expect the competition to improve in San Angelo—or when they couldn't get the right people for the job, they ran into more problems and growth was slower.

Lesson #11: Business success and project success both come down to the same thing: the right people solving the right problem.

Last, I saw how much it helps to have the attitude that we can solve our problems and succeed. Most Texans may move at a slower pace than a transplanted Easterner like me, but we both see the world in basically the same way. Someone other than Bruce or myself might complain: "We can never get the right people," "In other towns, the competition is bigger and has a longer history," and so forth. Instead, Bruce, his partner, and the Kirbo's team took a practical attitude toward defining problems and working through them to success. And that attitude gave them the success they believed they could achieve.

Lesson #12: The project management approach—defining problems and solutions—is more than a way of thinking. It is an attitude that actually opens the door to solutions and success.

CHAPTER 17

Annual Strategic Planning at QTI

ONE OF THE FUN THINGS ABOUT learning, teaching, and consulting is that I get to take everything I've learned and apply it for the success of my own company. I like to take on big challenges—like writing two or three books in a year—so I need all the project management I can get to make each project efficient and keep track of everything. I start every year from the top down with strategic planning to set direction and program management to organize the year's projects.

A STRATEGIC PLAN ADDS FLEXIBILITY

The plan becomes my baseline for the year. Either I follow it or I do something better. As a result, I'm not locked into the plan. Actually, the plan makes it easier to decide when *not* to do the plan. For example, a few minutes ago, just before I started writing this case study, I got an e-mail announcing that a former client was looking for help at the beginning of a new, large project. It's the kind of work that I love to do. But I'm already pretty busy and this client, being in government, has to put the request out for competitive bid. So, I will need to decide if I want to take the time to go after the job.

That decision will be pretty easy. My administrative assistant will put together all the information. We will compare the value of the new project against the value of the work I will give up to do it—an opportunity-cost analysis. If the value of having this job is greater than the value of what I am already planning to do, then I'll put in the bid. In the analysis, I'll look at whether this job is aligned with how I want my company to grow and also at any risks related to the job—potential delays that would use up my time and so forth.

A company without an annual plan is under more stress and at more risk. Decisions take longer to make and, without practice making strategic decisions, it is too easy to jump after something that looks good, but actually won't pay off.

WHAT IS A STRATEGIC PLAN?

A company's strategic plan sets its direction and defines the context that then defines what projects will help the business succeed and grow. If your company doesn't already have a vision, mission, and values statement, I recommend that you read two books:

- *Built to Last: Successful Habits of Visionary Companies,* by James C. Collins and Jerry I. Porras (1997), which explains the value of a company defining an enduring vision, mission, and values and then developing a strategy, and gives specific instructions for creating a vision, mission, and values statement in Chapter 11.
- *The Seven Habits of Highly Effective People,* by Stephen R. Covey (1990), which can teach you how to create corporate and personal mission statements and can help you organize your work and time so that you can achieve your goals and lead others.

A company's vision, mission, and values statement should have one part that does not change and another part that changes in response to what our customers need. For example, Boeing will always build cutting-edge airplanes and spacecraft, but what defines "cutting edge" changes each decade. Also, in the first few years of strategic planning, we are still defining who we are and what the company stands for. So, we may revise and refine the existing plan.

QTI's vision, mission, and values plan has really helped me over the last few years. It has allowed me to do what I've wanted to do: write books, consult, and train, while balancing the workload so that I made enough money and delivered my books to the publisher, too. It has let me consider creative ideas and new possibilities and then focus on the ones that mattered most.

HOW TO PLAN STRATEGY EACH YEAR

Each year, I review and improve the permanent part of QTI's strategic plan, the core vision, mission, and values. I then update the mission or create a new mission for the year. This mission is about goals of corporate growth and opportunity and about solutions to major problems. I also review and revise my mission to customers. QTI succeeds by serving customers, but how will I serve them this year? Will I write books, reaching many people, or do consulting and training, providing more in-depth services to just a few clients? Last year, I got some new clients in state government. Is that a new direction or a temporary twist in the road? Strategic planning lets me make general plans into specific ones.

Strategic planning lets me put together two questions:

- What do I want to do this year?
- What is best for my business this year?

I get answers; those answers are the programs and projects for the year. Table 17-1 gives the process instructions for annual strategic planning.

Part of the work of creating a strategic plan should be on a retreat, but not all of it. Before the retreat, you should gather all the information you can and read and review everything. Also, don't assume you should go on retreat alone. Maybe the whole company should go! And after the retreat, we take the plan to our team and, with our team, add details and build it into the schedule. Have every director or manager make his or her part work: get input from each one and have each one develop his or her own schedule for delivering the results that will make your company succeed.

Work Environment	Business owners or senior executives taking time aside for an annual strategic planning session in an organization that uses the *Get It Done Right!* method.
Input	• Prior year's strategic plan • Any reviews of major projects or work from the prior year • Corporate financial statements • List of customers and revenue per customer • Any documents describing business issues or problems • Any other documents you find valuable in assessing your business
Tools	• Large pads, paper, sticky notes • Word processing program • Spreadsheet program
Resources	Time aside from work
Techniques	• Methods in *Built to Last* by Collins and Porras and *The Seven Habits of Highly Effective People* by Covey • Methods in these process instructions
Process	1. Read last year's strategic plan 2. Ask yourself where you want to be in three to five years. Review the part of the plan that discussed that and update it. 3. Create a spreadsheet listing goals and actual results achieved. Look for major variances only. Don't worry about details such as whether the work was done on time or completely within budget. 4. For each major variance, note whether there was a conscious decision to cancel the project or if it just drifted out of sight or if you kept at it, but didn't finish. 5. For each realized goal, ask, "Is this something I want to do again this year?" 6. For each problem solved, ask, "Was this problem permanently solved? Could the solution apply more widely?" 7. For each cancelled or unfinished goal, ask, "Do I want to do this in the coming year?" 8. Based on your answers in 5, 6, and 7, write up a partial draft list of goals for the next year. 9. Look at your list of clients. Are there any you want to do more business with? Any you want to drop? Any types of clients—market segments—you want to pursue further? Add these ideas to your draft plan. 10. Step way back and listen to your dreams. Is there anything new and different you want to do? Add those to your draft plan. 11. Look at your input documents and talk with your team members. Do they have any dreams? Do they have any major problems that need solving? Add those opportunities and problems to your plan. 12. Use the survey in Chapter 1 to create an updated list of problems and opportunities. 13. Use all the material in Chapters 1-4 to organize your business and its programs.

TABLE 17-1. Process instructions: Annual revision of a strategic plan (continued on next page)

Process	14. All of this is your draft plan. Now, you can use the techniques on brainstorming from Chapter 11 to organize the ideas.
	15. State items in the plan as goals.
	16. Organize those goals into groups, looking for the largest issues to be solved and looking for opportunities to align your business and align to your customers, as we discussed in Chapter 14.
	17. Define all of this into programs that serve customers for pay, develop new products, or improve operations.
	18. Figure out which programs add the greatest value.
	19. Decide how many programs you and your team can do this year.
	20. Include those programs in your plan.
	21. For each of those programs, define and prioritize the projects.
	22. In areas where you had an idea for a program, but you don't have the time and money to do it, see if there is a smaller project that will solve part of the problems.
	23. Throughout the whole document, make sure everything is clear, especially the goals.
	24. Share this with your team.
	25. Working with your team, schedule work and goals for each month of the year.
	26. Review and revise your strategic plan.
Output	A strategic plan that will guide your company for the year, realizing the greatest value and steering for success.

TABLE 17-1. Process instructions: Annual revision of a strategic plan (continued)

CONCLUSION

Project management, ultimately, is about making dreams into reality. Give yourself time to dream. Then create a strategic plan that will focus the work of the year to make your dreams and your team's dreams real.

A Customer Problem Opens a New Business

MY FRIEND MALCOLM RYDER HAS been an entrepreneur since childhood. He has an unusual mix of talents—in addition to being an excellent business marketing strategist, he is also an accomplished photographer. Photography was his first love. During college summers, Malcolm didn't want to work for anyone else; he wanted to make money on his own terms. One day, he had a need for some rush custom photography work and he learned it would cost $200, which was more than he was willing to pay. So he did it for himself. And he realized he'd be willing to do it again for less than $200. That "aha!" moment gave birth to a business idea.

Rush custom photography work is expensive for a reason: it is exhausting, it's not fun because of the late nights of work, and it is high risk. Sometimes, you just can't do a good job on time. In that case, the customer might not pay and, worse, he or she might let other folks know that you aren't good at your job.

Malcolm turned two problems into one big opportunity. His customers' problem was that they sometimes wanted rush custom work and they would like a lower price, just like he did. His problem was that, to launch a photography business, he had to distinguish himself in some way and build a portfolio.

Lesson #1: Your customer's problems are your opportunities.

He launched his business with a marketing campaign that offered 35 percent off rush custom work. He figured that, if he did that for two months, he could get four customers who would either want more work or be good referrals and he'd be building his portfolio at the same time. Looking back, he admits he was scared.

The first challenge he faced is that he was simply afraid. He was afraid that he'd make a

This case study is courtesy of Malcolm Ryder, President of Archestra—Consulting in Industry Analysis at www.archestra.com.

mistake and blow a job. He was afraid that customers wouldn't come back after the first time. How did he bring that fear under management? He turned it into a business risk and planned to mitigate that risk. He put out his discount offer, but he took only jobs he thought he could handle. He identified a need, took a risk, and then did whatever it took to succeed. Two months later, he didn't have just four good customers; he had about 12. And his business was up and running.

Lesson #2: Look at your anxiety and define it as risk. Then bring it under management.

Well, the business was up and running, but Malcolm was running himself ragged. He had never planned to stay in rush custom work, but now he needed to make the transition to doing high-quality custom work without the tight deadlines. This put him into a rough period where the business was in transition between being known for rush services and being known for quality. Malcolm did good work. But could he prove it in the market well enough to change his marketing strategy so he wouldn't have to keep up the exhausting custom work?

Lesson #3: Any transition in a business is stressful, so it's good to have a plan—a project plan.

With rush custom work, people went with Malcolm because he offered a better price and delivered on time. Then, after the fact, they saw he did good work. With photography, it's easy to show you've done a good job when you're done. The hard sell is to show that you're going to do a good job before the picture is taken. Malcolm had a running start. He had 12 customers who were coming back or giving him referrals. And he had the beginnings of a portfolio. But his next challenge was a timing question. When would he give up doing rush work and rely on getting work based on a reputation for quality?

The answer came in several steps:

- As he got more jobs that weren't on a tight deadline, he refused rush work because he didn't have time for it if he was already on a job.
- He never offered his discount twice to the same customer. The second time a customer asked for rush work, he charged the going rate in the market.
- The exhausting work finally caught up with him. He made two mistakes. The first time, he got off easy. He didn't get paid, but the customer didn't complain, because several other people had made mistakes as well. The second time, he delivered late and the customer refused to pay, saying, "Because you were late, we have an expensive mess. We need to take the money we would have paid you and pay someone else to clean up your mess." Worse, they let other potential customers know that they thought Malcolm wasn't reliable.

After the second mistake, Malcolm got the message that the time was right for the change. Although it felt risky to change his whole marketing approach, he gave up doing rush work. He relied on his reputation for quality and grew his business without the stress.

Lesson #4: If you have a strategy clear in your mind, then you'll be ready to make the right decision at the right time.

Malcolm's strategy for entering the market had worked. His low-price rush service offer got him in the door and he didn't need it any more. Now, he focused on quality photography. That created a new problem. Quality is expensive. He had good money coming in, but expenses were high enough that it was hard to make enough net revenue—profit—to achieve his goals. His solution was to specialize.

Lesson #5: Every situation has its problems. Define

them, come up with a goal, and solve your problems with projects, one at a time.

Malcolm specialized by photographing things that didn't move. He decided not to do sports events, social events like weddings, or anything else where he had only one shot to take the picture. Instead, he would do portraits of people and animals, pictures of buildings for architects, and pictures of artwork for collectors, museums, and libraries. There, he could achieve the quality he wanted to satisfy himself and to build his business, because, if he didn't like what he did the first time, he could go back and do it again.

He also specialized by focusing on the customers who were best for his business. He focused on customers who could afford to give him repeat business, which meant mostly working for businesses and wealthy art collectors.

With these two choices, he was able to do the same work and make more money on each job by reducing costs.

- He reduced marketing time and costs, because each customer would call him back for additional work.
- His experience led to expertise. He knew how to get a good image on less expensive photo paper and how to save money by renting lighting equipment, instead of buying it.
- He was able to explain choices like these to his customers, so that he could give them options and pass on higher costs if they wanted especially high-quality work.

Lesson #6: Focusing on a single issue clearly can improve your bottom line.

Lesson #7: If you get experience, then learn from your experience. Experience becomes expertise that will make you money.

As you can see, Malcolm is a pretty bright guy. Now, he spends his time thinking about ways businesses can get into a market and grow. Isn't that what he was doing all along? You can see more of his work on industry analysis and his general ideas on solving problems strategically, at www.archestra.com.

CHAPTER 19

Even a Kid Can Learn Project Managment

THIS CASE STUDY COMES FROM MATT Williams, the producer who taught us how to make a TV commercial. He's changed careers: he now teaches film and media at a high school. He has set up an amazing three-year program in television and film that teaches kids how to make professional-quality television and film projects. As part of that, they learn to work as a team, manage the project, and *get it done right.*

This case study illustrates several important things:

- Anyone can learn project management.
- Learning project management—learning to get it done right—is an important part of personal and professional growth that opens doors to new opportunities in life.
- Getting excited about a project and

learning project management can help a person change in ways that many psychologists will tell you is rare or impossible, helping people who are limited in life or who might even fail in life to have successful careers and grow in new ways.

At his high school, Matt has a reputation for helping kids who may be having difficulty in standard curricula. Kids who are faltering or failing in other subjects come into his media program and get excited about making a movie. When they see they really can do something—produce or direct or support a movie with their name on it— they see they can get things done. One thing they have to get done is homework, and they start doing their homework for other classes. Their grades improve. And, when it's all over, they haven't just made a movie. Matt also teaches them how to prepare, do, and

This case study is courtesy of Matt Williams, Head of the Television/Media Program at River Dell Regional High School in Oradell, NJ. To learn more, go to www.riverdell.k12.nj.us.

follow through on their SAT test—the standard test for getting into college—sometimes helping them boost their scores by 100 points out of a maximum of 1600. Other kids have discovered that they loved acting or have chosen a career in media after Matt's program.

Lesson #1: Learning a craft, and learning project management along with that craft, opens professional doors. The skill of delivering results is personally empowering and professionally marketable. More and more, businesses want to hire people—not just kids, but people of all ages—who can get a job done.

LEARNING ABOUT THE WORLD OF MOVIES

Matt's first challenge is to get these kids excited about making movies. He knows that success comes from a focused team. Here's his formula:

- *Share insider tips.* Tell them they will learn things that only moviemakers know. I can tell you this works—I got excited as Matt explained some details of cinematography to me.
- *Show them successful movies from other students.* Get the kids thinking, "We can do this, too!"
- *Show them the history of motion pictures from the ground up.* Let them develop a real understanding of the issues, culture, and history.
- *Immerse the kids in a world of things to learn.* Share the wide variety of movies, the different technical areas, and the history so that they see just how much there is to know.

To do this, Matt sees that the program needs enough time to teach the kids all of the knowledge and skills involved. Each class is one full school year with a 55-minute period each day. This may surprise you, but the kids don't make a film of their own until the third year. Even then, the whole

class—22 kids working in four teams of five or six students each—produces only four five-minute films or one film under 20 minutes. Matt sees that there is no point having kids run around with cameras, make mistakes, and be disappointed. He teaches them what they need to understand and what they need to know how to do before he goes out with them to make a movie.

Lesson #2: If your team needs to learn, give them the knowledge and let them practice the skills long enough to be able to do it right.

Matt does this by showing good and bad examples from the movies. He never shows errors from past student movies—that would be disheartening. Instead, he shows low-quality and high-quality movies and discusses the differences. He says that people learn what is good by getting a lot of exposure to as much film—or art, or anything else—as possible.

LEARNING HOW TO MAKE A MOVIE

Every profession has its inside knowledge and a language to express that. The kids learn the relationship between the technical aspects of film and the final aesthetic result. They learn how to position cameras effectively to communicate a clear message that isn't confusing. They learn that a close-up offers facial expressions and communicates an emotional message.

All of this builds to the end of the second year, where the kids take on a challenging project. They have to reproduce—second by second—five minutes of a major Hollywood film. The kids disassemble the scenes in the movie to production shots. Some kids work as actors, others as cinematographer, director, producer, and crew. The goal is to make a movie that matches action, dialog, camera angles, cuts, and lighting down to the second. Students learn a tremendous amount in this exercise. In project management terms, they are learning architecture and decomposition—the essential skills of planning and work breakdown structuring.

Lesson #3: The best way to learn from experts is to use their work as a model, learning from it by imitating it in detail, seeing what decisions the experts made, and why. Then, when we go on to do our own work, we'll know what decisions we have to make, the significance of each one, and how to get it done right.

Film making is a creative art. The best directors know the conventions—and know when to follow them to make a movie easy for the viewer and also when to go against them to produce something unique, creative, and inspired.

MAKING A MOVIE

Coming into the third year, Media 3, Matt helps the kids get ready by having them brainstorm ideas for the movie. He follows the brainstorming methods we taught in Chapter 11, with one very important addition. He explains to the kids that the goal is to get as many ideas—good and bad—out in the first session. When we first hear an idea, we may know if it's crazy or reasonable, but we can't know if it's good or bad. Most brainstorming sessions end up with three or four reasonable ideas, and people go on to choose the best. It is much better to have 20 ideas, even if 19 of them are lousy, because one just might be brilliant.

Lesson #4: We brainstorm in stages so that we can have lots of possibilities to choose from. If we evaluate too early, we'll miss out on the best ideas.

Matt guides the kids, ensuring that their plan is workable, but letting them make decisions within that plan. For example, they need to be able to shoot on school property, using kids in the class, Matt as an adult, and maybe an occasional "guest star" parent or other student. They have to make sure they can set up, shoot, and take down a scene, and then put everything away in 55 minutes so that they can get to their next class on time. Working in this time frame gets them ready for the real world of TV and movies, where three or four scenes are typically shot by one crew in one 12-hour day.

When teaching kids to make movies, Matt thinks in contingencies, just as he did when he was producing TV commercials. If a shoot can't go as scheduled—maybe a prop isn't ready or an actor is out sick—he has the kids observe another crew and learn from them. Matt expects an amount of finished work that leaves some room for lost production days.

Lesson #5: When people are learning, allow a lot of extra time for mistakes.

Their work in Media 2 imitating a Hollywood movie has given the kids the core skills that they need. In Media 3, they need a process, and Matt provides it:

- Create a draft script.
- Move into preproduction with the draft script, improving the script during preproduction and filming.
- Define the roles and jobs.
- Make a storyboard showing each shot, step by step.
- Using the storyboard, break down the production into scenes and shots. Make sure each shot can be done in one 55-minute period.
- Shoot, evaluate, and decide if you need to reshoot.
- Assemble the film in postproduction.

Lesson #6: To do good work, we need to know our technical skills and to have a clearly defined process for the work.

CONCLUSION

And so, the kids make their own movie. Some years, Media 3 produces four movies, each about five minutes long. Other years, they put the pieces together into a 20-minute show.

The kids think that the movie is the important thing. I think that what the kids have learned to do—how they have grown up and what they have learned about themselves—is what really matters. Some have really gotten it and learned to be excellent project managers. Others have found a passion and headed for a career. Some don't go quite that far; but each student learns something that helps with school with his or her life and for the future. And Matt helps them see that, by helping them apply what they've learned to other areas of their lives.

Here is Matt's project plan for doing well on the SAT standardized test—it will work for you if you need to take a GMAT for graduate school or if you want to pass the exam for your Project Management Professional (PMP) certification, too.

- Be prepared—do your work before you get there. The SAT exam is like the day of the shoot. Prepare beforehand, and know what you're going to do when you get there.
- Manage your time—be time managers. Look at the clock. Don't spend 20 minutes on a detail and two minutes on the big one shot that will make or break the movie—or the exam. For the SAT, you get 30 seconds per question. On a movie shoot, you get five minutes per setup.
- Practice problem-solving for when you hit a roadblock. Fast thinking and accurate expression are key. You need to articulate specifics clearly. Multiple-choice exams require quick accurate articulation of each answer.

- Always, always, always answer all the questions. Finish the project!!!

Some students look at what they did in a year and get scared. They say, "It took a year for one crew to make a five-minute movie. How am I ever going to make a short film, much less a full-length feature?"

Matt tells these students what I would tell them—a big movie is just a bunch of five-minute movies strung together. A project is a bunch of tasks. Break up the big job, do each task right, put it all back together, and the big job is done.

When you work on a project, you never know what you will learn. Sometimes, the technical skills matter the most. That happened for one student who had never thought about acting until Matt encouraged him to put himself in front of the camera. He's out of high school now and pursuing his love—a career in acting. For others, the key is in learning to *get it done right!* That is a transferable skill—from one project to the next, and from one job to the next in any career.

Grow Your Team

Think about each member of your team—and yourself as well. What could each of you learn by doing a project? What qualities does each staff person have that, right now, need improvement so that he or she can grow and the company can grow? What project would give that person the experience that allow him or her to gain the skills and confidence necessary to become better at what he or she does?

Answer that question. Plan a small learning project for each team member. Help them get excited. Help them grow and succeed.

Your success comes from theirs.

Glossary of Terms Used in This Book

THIS GLOSSARY INCLUDES ALL THE TERMS that you'll find used in this book. It's a good quick reference that I hope you will turn to regularly. Following this glossary is the glossary created by the Project Management Institute, which includes a broader array of terms and concepts.

Acceptable level of risk Amount of risk tolerable in a project.

Accuracy The degree to which an estimate is close to the actual result.

Action The smallest part of the work on a project: one job, done by one person or a small team, with a clearly defined deliverable. Also *step* or *task*.

Activity definition The process of identifying the specific schedule activities that need to be performed to produce the various project deliverables.

Activity duration estimating The process of estimating the number of work periods that will be needed to complete individual schedule activities.

Activity resource estimating The process of estimating the types and quantities of resources required to perform each schedule activity.

Activity sequencing The process of identifying and documenting dependencies among schedule activities.

Allocate To give a certain amount of money or a time or due date to a project. An allocation can be considered a project constraint imposed by the customer or sponsor.

Analogous estimation Estimation based on comparison with past projects or activities. To be accurate, it requires an experienced team and research to determine that the activities of the current project are, in fact, similar to the past activities used in the comparison or adjust for the differences.

Architecture The ability to design something while seeing it several ways at once—and explaining it to others who can only see it one way or another. Architecture particularly includes the ability to work within constraints of different types.

Baseline plan The project plan used when comparing the status of a project with the project plan.

Bias A type of error in estimation that causes a repeated similar difference between the estimate and the actual result, time after time.

Bottom-up estimation Estimations of the activities at the lowest level of the activity list or WBS, added up to produce a total estimate.

Budget A planned schedule for spending money.

Cancellation The ending of a project after it starts, but before it succeeds.

Cause Something that results in something else. When a problem is solved fully, any cause of the problem is eliminated.

Change request A request for a change to project scope, time, cost, constraints, or other defining aspects of the project plan or the product we are making. It may be verbal initially, but it must then be written down to be managed.

Checklist A form with checkboxes that helps ensure that no steps are missed.

Communications feedback A message from the receiver to the sender verifying receipt and comprehension of the sender's message.

Component One element in a system, a part. This could be a process, a physical object or tool, a person or team, or a subsystem.

Consequence A result of an action. All actions have consequences.

Consequence of a risk Whatever will happen if the risk event happens and is not managed—typically, project failure, increased time and/or cost, or loss of scope or quality.

Constraint A limit on how the project can be done. A constraint can be created by the business, from the project management perspective, or as a result of a technical requirement or limitation.

Continuous feedback Feedback information gathered and used at all times to keep a system in balance or on course.

Continuous improvement A Total Quality Management technique that seeks to constantly improve all procedures through PDCA.

Corrected course A new plan based on the status of a project and any changes in circumstances and/or expectations.

Corrective action Adjustment to plans and actions that will keep a project on course toward its goal.

Cost estimate The expected amount of money a project will take, based on analysis of the project plan.

Crisis A situation that, if not handled immediately, will result in things getting much worse. All crises are problems, but not all problems include a crisis.

Customer The primary recipient and user of the product, service, or work result created by a project, the central stakeholder.

Deliverable An end result to a step of work. It must be clearly defined and a person must be able to use it without calling on the person who made it.

Dependency A relationship between two schedule activities or an activity and a milestone, indicating a relationship between the start and end of one activity and the start and end of the other, usually because the output of one activity is the input of the other.

Destruct test A test that destroys the product to determine one of its features. A destruct test can be used on a sample of products from a batch to confirm that the rest of the batch meets standards.

Driver A direction for a project, such as soonest delivery, lowest cost, or highest quality.

Due The status of a project at the deadline or past.

Duration The length of a job from start to finish, no matter how many people are working on it and whether or not the job is continuous or stopped for something else.

Early estimate Estimate based on project information before the work breakdown structure is complete, validated, and approved.

Effective Having the desired effect, resulting in improvement, or producing a desired result.

Efficient Obtaining maximum results with minimum resources. Efficiency can be measured against time—if it's done quickly, it's efficient—and against cost—if it doesn't cost much, it's efficient—and in relation to other resources.

Effort The time, measured in person-hours, that it takes to complete a task or job.

Empowerment Giving people what they need to get the job done, including tools, skills, information, authority, and resources, and letting them do it themselves.

Estimate To attempt to figure out what future results will be, particularly how much a project will cost or how much time it will take.

Exclusion Something not to be included in project results, something that is not a goal of the project.

Execution Actually doing the job.

Feedback Information returned to a system that allows the system to adjust its functions to stay stable or reach a desired goal.

Forecast A prediction of what will happen. A first forecast is a prediction of what will happen if a project or any other activities continue without changing. The results of corrective actions and risk events can also be forecast.

Functional manager The manager of a department, responsible for production work.

Functional organization A company with a traditional hierarchical structure of departments and no provision for cross-departmental project management.

Gap analysis The approach of seeing any problem or opportunity as a space to be crossed between the current state and a desired future state.

Gate A review process at the end of the phase in which a project makes sure that the deliverables are all in good shape and a decision is made whether or not to continue the project.

Hard-dollar value Value that can be measured numerically.

Implementation Use of tools and/or plans to reach specified goals.

Important Of significant worth or consequence. If the value can be measured in dollars, then the bigger the difference to the bottom line, the more important. Some important things cannot be measured exactly, such as customer goodwill and employee retention.

Inclusion Something to be included in project results, a statement of a planned work result.

Initial baseline plan The project plan as approved at the end of the planning gate.

Input Ingredients that go into a process and end up as part of the product.

Iron triangle An image that expresses the relationship among scope, time, and cost, where, if one changes, at least one of the others must also change.

Late estimate An estimate based on the work breakdown structure as well as other project documents. With the work plan complete, the estimate is more accurate.

Leadership Setting direction for a group of people.

Lessons learned from the project What worked and what didn't work, as well as decisions about how to do better on the next project.

Life cycle cost Total cost of a product, service, or system, including development, maintenance during its productive years, and, if appropriate, decommissioning costs.

Likelihood An estimate of the chance that the risk event will happen.

Manage To define the job, plan the work to be done, and control the work according to plan. A project manager takes responsibility for planning and managing to deliver success on a project.

Management options for risks Choices for dealing with a risk before, or when, it happens.

Matrix An organization in which functional managers and project managers have equal authority in assigning people to routine work or projects.

Matrix management The art of balancing the needs of functional managers and a project.

Maximizing return Getting the most money or benefit within a particular period of time.

Milestone A defined set of deliverables due at the end of a phase or stage.

Mission A statement of what the organization is and how it serves.

Mock-up A prototype that is not fully functional.

On hold Status of a project task or job that can-

not start yet, usually because some information or input is missing, indicated by HOLD in our template.

Opportunity A chance to do something new, to make things better, to serve more, or to make more money.

Output The end result or deliverable of a process.

Overdue Status of a project that is still being worked on past its due date.

Parametric modeling An estimation method that uses a measurable factor (such as size, in feet, or a count of the number of units to be produced) times an expected cost or effort per unit to produce the estimate.

Periodic feedback Feedback information gathered at regular intervals, such as hourly or weekly, typical of status reporting.

Permanent preventative solution A change in a process that eliminates a root cause of a problem, so that it and similar problems cannot happen again.

Phase (or stage) A large, defined piece of a project that ends with a clearly defined set of deliverables.

Pilot project A small project that tests a proposed solution or other idea.

Planning Thinking through and writing down what a project team intends to do to succeed in the project.

Portfolio management Identifying, prioritizing, authorizing, and controlling projects and related activities to invest resources in the best projects in order to achieve strategic objectives and to get the return desired at an acceptable risk.

Present value The value of money expected in the future, adjusted for time, to allow for comparisons of money amounts at different times by the current value.

Problem A situation that, if not resolved, will create results that would be bad or interfere with operations and activities. Problems have *symptoms, consequences,* and *causes.*

Process A defined series of steps to change inputs to outputs.

Progress What a project has accomplished, from the starting point to its current status.

Progressive elaboration Defining something very broadly first and then in more and more detail, often in breaking down a work activity or a problem.

Project "A problem scheduled for solution," according to Joseph M. Juran, the Total Quality Management guru. Also, "an opportunity scheduled for realization."

Project change An approved change request and all supporting documentation, resulting in a revision of the baseline plan.

Project communications management Establishing and maintaining a system for obtaining information as needed and providing information as needed.

Project cost management Establishing, tracking, and controlling the costs of a project.

Project human resources management Securing, training, supporting, and retaining the people needed to work on a project.

Project integration management Keeping track of all the ways in which a change to one part of the plan changes other parts of the plan.

Project manager The person assigned to run a project and make sure it gets done.

Project plan A document that includes the starting point, the goal, the process by which the goal will be achieved, and anything else that will help make the project work.

Project procurement management Securing, tracking, and coordinating products, materials, and/or services need for a project.

Project quality management Ensuring that the deliverables of a project meet or exceed the specifications at each review gate.

Project risk management Planning for, monitoring, and controlling unexpected events that might have an impact on project outcomes. The focus is on expecting the unexpected and figuring out how to succeed anyway.

Project schedule The planned dates for performing project activities and the planned dates for meeting project milestones.

Project scope management Ensuring that project work is performed to deliver the expected results as specified.

Project time management Establishing, tracking, and controlling the time allocated for a project, including the start and end and the timing of project activities.

Projectized organization An organization in which every activity or almost every activity is run as a program or a project by program and project managers.

Proof-of-concept system A working model of an idea or concept that shows it can be done, but not that the idea is worth developing.

Proof of the business case Evidence that the project produced the expected results and provided the specified benefits.

Prototype An early model of something planned for production.

Quality That which adds value.

Ready to start Status of a job that could start at any time, indicated by READY in our template.

Rebaseline To change the plan being used as input to the status-reporting process.

Reconciliation The process of deciding how to close the gap between an allocation and an estimate or between an early estimate and a later one.

Requirements elicitation A dialog with customers and stakeholders that leads to a high-quality scope statement.

Requirements specification A detailed statement of the exact results that the organization or the customer wants to get from a project.

Requirements tracing The process of making sure that all customer and technical requirements are included in the work breakdown structure.

Resources Things that are needed for a process that are used up and do not become part of the output.

Return on investment (ROI) Ratio between the benefits and the costs of the project or time in which the project will pay off on the investment.

Revised baseline plan The project plan revised to include one or more approved project changes. From that point forward, the actual work of the project is compared with the revised baseline plan.

Risk Any event or situation that could prevent a project team from finishing the project, reduce the value of what it deliver, or force it to alter the plan, schedule, or budget.

Risk identification Creating a list of risks and naming each risk.

Risk management The attempt to bring uncertainty under control.

Risk name An identifier for the risk, usually the risk event itself.

Risk planning Creating a list of risks, describing each risk, and planning a response to each risk.

Robust Able to survive through change.

Root cause A deep underlying cause, a cause of other causes.

Schedule development The process of analyzing schedule activity sequences, schedule activity durations, resource requirements, and schedule constraints to create the project schedule.

Scope The results to be delivered by a project.

Scope creep The tendency to expand the results to be delivered by a project during development, generally to add features and/or functionality.

Scope specification A refined, precise scope statement detailed out through progressive elaboration.

Scope statement A statement of what the project is or is not doing, a statement of all work results, clarified by a listing of exclusions.

Shaping A psychological tool that reinforces many small changes to create a larger change.

Significance The measure of a consequence—cost in dollars, delay in time, or project failure.

Soft-dollar value Value that cannot be measured exactly, either because it is too early in the project to estimate accurately or because it is a type of value that can be recognized, but not measured.

Stage (or phase) A large, defined piece of a project that ends with a clearly defined set of deliverables.

Stakeholder Anyone affected by the project process or results.

Status Current situation, including a description of what work is done, what work is not yet done, and any risks or problems.

Status information Any information about how the project is proceeding and what is being done that is input to status reporting.

Status reporting The process of gathering feedback and status information, analyzing it, and deciding on any corrective action to take.

Step, task, or action The smallest part of the work

on a project: one job, done by one person or a small team, with a clearly defined deliverable. Also *task* or *action*.

Strategic planning Taking time aside from work to look at the big picture, to define the reasons for doing things, and set long-term goals.

Strategy Setting goals, based on the reasons for doing things.

Strong matrix An organization in which functional managers have less authority than project managers.

Subproject Subdivision of a project.

Subsystem Subdivision of a system.

Surrogate Substitute.

Symptom Sign and result of a condition, often a problem.

System Set of components that work together to perform a specific function inside an organism, an organization, or a larger system.

Tactic Use of tools and methods to achieve goals.

Task The smallest part of the work on a project: one job, done by one person or a small team, with a clearly defined deliverable. Also *step* or *action*.

Technique Method or instruction for doing something, such as a process.

Template A form with spaces for specifying key ideas.

Three-point estimation An analytical technique that uses three cost or duration estimates to represent the optimistic, most likely, and pessimistic scenarios. This technique is used to improve the accuracy of the estimates of cost or duration when the underlying activity or cost component is uncertain, sometimes in combination with other estimation methods.

Time value of money The idea that, due to interest rates, a given amount of money in the future is worth less than the same amount of money now.

Tool Something that is used in a process, but not used up. Tools can be reused.

Trigger Event that indicates that a risk is likely to happen or is happening already.

Uncertainty Starting point for risk management.

Urgent Status of a task that must be done by a certain time or it will have no value.

Value Quality, feature, or function that makes something desirable or more desirable. For a customer, it is what he or she receives for the price of a product or service. For an organization, it is what is increased by accomplishing its mission, serving its customers, making more money, spending less money, and improving its ability to continue operations and grow.

Values Key principles by which an organization lives and key terms that define what matters to the people in that organization.

Vision A picture of where the leaders of an organization want it to go.

Weak matrix An organization in which functional managers have more power and authority than project managers.

Work breakdown structure (WBS) A deliverable-oriented hierarchical decomposition of the work to be executed by the project team to achieve the project objectives and create the required deliverables, internal and external. It organizes and defines the total scope of the project. Each descending level represents an increasingly detailed definition of the project work. The WBS is decomposed into work packages.

Work breakdown structure (WBS) dictionary A document that describes each component in the work breakdown structure and includes a brief definition of the scope or statement of work, defined deliverables(s), a list of associated activities, and a list of milestones. Other information may include responsible organization, start and end dates, resources required, an estimate of cost, charge number, contract information, quality requirements, and technical references to facilitate performance of the work.

Work breakdown structuring The planning process that defines the components of a project product (work results) and outlines work process.

Work environment The situation in which a process is accomplished.

Work package The work result or deliverable component of a work structure, used to define project milestones.

Work process The activity we do in our work, the actions we take that result in a work product.

Work product The results of our work, the product we are making in any project, subproject, or task.

Work result Work product.

Working Status of a job in process, being worked on right now, but not yet due.

Working model A fully functional prototype.

Complete Project Management Glossary from the Project Management Institute

INCLUSIONS AND EXCLUSIONS

This glossary includes terms that are:

- Unique or nearly unique to project management (e.g., project scope statement, work package, work breakdown structure, critical path method)
- Not unique to project management, but used differently or with a narrower meaning in project management than in general everyday usage (e.g., early start date, schedule activity)

This glossary generally does not include:

- Application area-specific terms (e.g., project prospectus as a legal document—unique to real estate development)
- Terms whose uses in project management do not differ in any material way from everyday use (e.g., calendar day, delay)

- Compound terms whose meaning is clear from the combined meanings of the component parts
- Variants when the meaning of the variant is clear from the base term (e.g., exception report is included, exception reporting is not)

As a result of the above inclusions and exclusions, this glossary includes:

- A preponderance of terms related to Project Scope Management, Project Time Management, and Project Risk Management, since many of the terms used in these knowledge areas are unique or nearly unique to project management
- Many terms from Project Quality Management, since these terms are used more narrowly than in their everyday usage

- Relatively few terms related to Project Human Resource Management and Project Communications Management, since most of the terms used in these knowledge areas do not differ significantly from everyday usage
- Relatively few terms related to Project Cost Management, Project Integration Management, and Project Procurement Management, since many of the terms used in these knowledge areas have narrow meanings that are unique to a particular application area

COMMON ACRONYMS

AC	Actual Cost
ACWP	Actual Cost of Work Performed
AD	Activity Description
ADM	Arrow Diagramming Method
AE	Apportioned Effort
AF	Actual Finish Date
AOA	Activity-on-Arrow
AON	Activity-on-Node
AS	Actual Start Date
BAC	Budget at Completion
BCWP	Budgeted Cost of Work Performed
BCWS	Budgeted Cost of Work Scheduled
BOM	Bill of Materials
CA	Control Account
CAP	Control Account Plan
CCB	Change Control Board
COQ	Cost of Quality
CPF	Cost-Plus-Fee
CPFF	Cost-Plus-Fixed-Fee
CPI	Cost Performance Index
CPIF	Cost-Plus-Incentive-Fee
CPM	Critical Path Method
CPPC	Cost-Plus-Percentage of Cost
CV	Cost Variance
CWBS	Contract Work Breakdown Structure

DD	Data Date
DU	Duration
DUR	Duration
EAC	Estimate at Completion
EF	Early Finish Date
EMV	Expected Monetary Value
ES	Early Start Date
ETC	Estimate to Complete
EV	Earned Value
EVM	Earned Value Management
EVT	Earned Value Technique
FF	Finish-to-Finish
FF	Free Float
FFP	Firm-Fixed-Price
FMEA	Failure Mode and Effect Analysis
FPIF	Fixed-Price-Incentive-Fee
FS	Finish-to-Start
IFB	Invitation for Bid
LF	Late Finish Date
LOE	Level of Effort
LS	Late Start Date
OBS	Organizational Breakdown Structure
OD	Original Duration
PC	Percent Complete
PCT	Percent Complete
PDM	Precedence Diagramming Method
PF	Planned Finish Date
PM	Project Management
PM	Project Manager
PMBOK®	Project Management Body of Knowledge
PMIS	Project Management Information System
PMO	Program Management Office
PMO	Project Management Office
PMP®	Project Management Professional
PS	Planned Start Date
PSWBS	Project Summary Work Breakdown Structure
PV	Planned Value
QA	Quality Assurance

QC	Quality Control
RAM	Responsibility Assignment Matrix
RBS	Resource Breakdown Structure
RBS	Risk Breakdown Structure
RD	Remaining Duration
RFP	Request for Proposal
RFQ	Request for Quotation
SF	Scheduled Finish Date
SF	Start-to-Finish
SOW	Statement of Work
SPI	Schedule Performance Index
SS	Scheduled Start Date
SS	Start-to-Start
SV	Schedule Variance
SWOT	Strengths, Weaknesses, Opportunities, and Threats
TC	Target Completion Date
TF	Target Finish Date
TF	Total Float
T&M	Time and Material
TQM	Total Quality Management
TS	Target Start Date
VE	Value Engineering
WBS	Work Breakdown Structure

DEFINITIONS

Many of the words defined here have broader, and in some cases different, dictionary definitions. The definitions use the following conventions:

- Terms used as part of the definitions and that are defined in the glossary are shown in *italics*.
- When the same glossary term appears more than once in a given definition, only the first occurrence is italicized.
- In some cases, a single glossary term consists of multiple words (e.g., risk response planning).
- In many cases, there are multiple, consecutive glossary terms within a given definition. For example, *duration estimate* denotes two separate glossary entries, one for "duration" and another for "estimate." (There are even some definitions with a string of consecutive italicized words, not separated by commas, that represent multiple, consecutive glossary terms, at least one of which consists of multiple words. For example, *critical path method late finish date* denotes two separate glossary entries, one for "critical path method" and another for "late finish date.")

- In situations with multiple, consecutive glossary terms, an asterisk (*) will follow the last italicized word in the string to denote that multiple glossary terms are referenced.
- When synonyms are included, no definition is given and the reader is directed to the preferred term (i.e., see preferred term).
- Related terms that are not synonyms are cross-referenced at the end of the definition (i.e., see also related term).

Accept. The act of formally receiving or acknowledging something and regarding it as being true, sound, suitable, or complete.

Acceptance. See *accept*.

Acceptance Criteria. Those *criteria*, including performance *requirements* and essential conditions, which must be met before project *deliverables* are accepted.

Acquire Project Team [Process]. The process of obtaining the human resources needed to complete the *project*.

Activity. A *component* of *work* performed during the course of a *project*. See also *schedule activity*.

Activity Attributes [Output/Input]. Multiple attributes associated with each *schedule activity* that can be included within the *activity list*. Activity attributes include *activity codes, predecessor activities, successor activities, logical relationships, leads* and *lags, resource requirements, imposed dates, constraints,* and *assumptions*.

Activity Code. One or more numerical or text values that identify characteristics of the *work* or in some way categorize the *schedule activity* that allows filtering and ordering of activities within reports.

Activity Definition [Process]. The *process* of identifying the specific *schedule activities* that need to be performed to produce the various project *deliverables*.

Activity Description (AD). A short phrase or label for each *schedule activity* used in conjunction with an *activity identifier* to differentiate that project schedule activity from other schedule activities. The activity description normally describes the *scope* of work of the schedule activity.

Activity Duration. The time in *calendar* units between the start and finish of a *schedule activity*. See also *actual duration*, *original duration*, and *remaining duration*.

Activity Duration Estimating [Process]. The *process* of estimating the number of work periods that will be needed to complete individual *schedule activities*.

Activity Identifier. A short unique numeric or text identification assigned to each *schedule activity* to differentiate that *project activity** from other activities. Typically unique within any one *project schedule network diagram*.

Activity List [Output/Input]. A documented tabulation of *schedule activities* that shows the *activity description*, *activity identifier*, and a sufficiently detailed scope of work description so *project team members* understand what *work* is to be performed.

Activity-on-Arrow (AOA). See *arrow diagramming method*.

Activity-on-Node (AON). See *precedence diagramming method*.

Activity Resource Estimating [Process]. The *process* of estimating the types and quantities of *resources* required to perform each *schedule activity*.

Activity Sequencing [Process]. The *process* of identifying and documenting *dependencies* among *schedule activities*.

Actual Cost (AC). Total costs actually incurred and recorded in accomplishing work performed during a given time period for a *schedule activity* or *work breakdown structure component*. Actual cost can sometimes be direct labor hours alone, direct costs alone, or all costs including indirect costs. Also referred to as the actual cost of work performed (ACWP). See also *earned value management* and *earned value technique*.

Actual Cost of Work Performed (ACWP). See *actual cost (AC)*.

Actual Duration. The time in *calendar units* between the *actual start date* of the *schedule activity* and either the *data date* of the *project schedule* if the schedule activity is in progress or the *actual finish date* if the schedule activity is complete.

Actual Finish Date (AF). The point in time that *work* actually ended on a *schedule activity*. (Note: In some application areas, the schedule activity is considered "finished" when work is "substantially complete.")

Actual Start Date (AS). The point in time that *work* actually started on a *schedule activity*.

Analogous Estimating [Technique]. An estimating *technique* that uses the values of parameters, such as *scope*, *cost*, *budget*, and *duration* or measures of scale such as size, weight, and complexity from a previous, similar *activity* as the basis for estimating the same parameter or measure for a future activity. It is frequently used to estimate a parameter when there is a limited amount of detailed information about the project (e.g., in the early *phases*). Analogous estimating is a form of *expert judgment*. Analogous estimating is most reliable when the previous activities are similar in fact and not just in appearance, and the *project team* members preparing the *estimates* have the needed expertise.

Application Area. A category of projects that have common components significant in such projects, but are not needed or present in all projects. Application areas are usually defined in terms of either the product (i.e., by similar technologies or production methods) or the type of customer (i.e., internal versus external, government versus commercial) or industry sector (i.e., utilities, automotive, aerospace, information technologies). Application areas can overlap.

Apportioned Effort (AE). *Effort* applied to project *work* that is not readily divisible into discrete efforts for that work, but which is related in direct proportion to measurable discrete work efforts. Contrast with *discrete effort*.

Approval. See *approve*.

Approve. The act of formally confirming, sanctioning, ratifying, or agreeing to something.

Approved Change Request [Output/Input]. A *change request* that has been processed through the *integrated change control* process and *approved*. Contrast with *requested change*.

Arrow. The graphic presentation of a *schedule activity* in the *arrow diagramming method* or a *logical relationship* between schedule activities in the *precedence diagramming method*.

Arrow Diagramming Method (ADM) [Technique]. A schedule network diagramming *technique* in which *schedule activities* are represented by *arrows*. The tail of the arrow represents the start, and the head represents the finish of the schedule activity. (The length of the arrow does not represent the expected duration of the sched-

ule activity.) Schedule activities are connected at points called nodes (usually drawn as small circles) to illustrate the sequence in which the schedule activities are expected to be performed. See also *precedence diagramming method*.

As-of Date. See *data date*.

Assumptions [Output/Input]. Assumptions are factors that, for planning purposes, are considered to be true, real, or certain without proof or demonstration. Assumptions affect all aspects of *project* planning, and are part of the *progressive elaboration* of the project. *Project teams* frequently identify, document, and validate assumptions as part of their planning *process*. Assumptions generally involve a degree of *risk*.

Assumptions Analysis [Technique]. A *technique* that explores the accuracy of *assumptions* and identifies *risks* to the project from inaccuracy, inconsistency, or incompleteness of assumptions.

Authority. The right to apply *project resources**, expend *funds*, make decisions, or give *approvals*.

Backward Pass. The calculation of *late finish dates* and *late start dates* for the uncompleted portions of all *schedule activities*. Determined by working backwards through the schedule *network logic* from the project's end date. The end date may be calculated in a *forward pass* or set by the *customer* or *sponsor*. See also *schedule network analysis*.

Bar Chart [Tool]. A graphic display of schedule-related information. In the typical bar chart, *schedule activities* or *work breakdown structure components* are listed down the left side of the chart, *dates* are shown across the top, and *activity durations* are shown as date-placed horizontal bars. Also called a Gantt chart.

Baseline. The approved time phased plan (for a *project*, a *work breakdown structure component*, a *work package*, or a *schedule activity*), plus or minus approved *project scope*, *cost*, schedule, and technical changes. Generally refers to the current baseline, but may refer to the original or some other baseline. Usually used with a modifier (e.g., cost baseline, schedule baseline, performance measurement baseline, technical baseline). See also *performance measurement baseline*.

Baseline Finish Date. The finish date of a *schedule activity* in the approved *schedule baseline*. See also *scheduled finish date*.

Baseline Start Date. The start date of a *schedule activity* in the approved *schedule baseline*. See also *scheduled start date*.

Bill of Materials (BOM). A documented formal hierarchical tabulation of the physical assemblies, subassemblies, and *components* needed to fabricate a *product*.

Bottom-up Estimating [Technique]. A method of estimating a *component* of *work*. The work is *decomposed* into more detail. An *estimate* is prepared of what is needed to meet the *requirements* of each of the lower, more detailed pieces of work, and these estimates are then aggregated into a total quantity for the component of work. The accuracy of bottom-up estimating is driven by the size and complexity of the work identified at the lower levels. Generally smaller work scopes increase the accuracy of the estimates.

Brainstorming [Technique]. A general data gathering and creativity *technique* that can be used to identify *risks*, ideas, or solutions to *issues* by using a group of *team members* or subject-matter experts. Typically, a brainstorming session is structured so that each participant's ideas are recorded for later analysis.

Budget. The approved *estimate* for the *project* or any *work breakdown structure* component or any *schedule activity*. See also *estimate*.

Budget at Completion (BAC). The sum of all the *budgets* established for the *work* to be performed

on a *project* or a *work breakdown structure component* or a *schedule activity*. The total *planned value* for the project.

Budgeted Cost of Work Performed (BCWP). See *earned value (EV)*.

Budgeted Cost of Work Scheduled (BCWS). See *planned value (PV)*.

Buffer. See *reserve*.

Buyer. The acquirer of *products*, *services*, or *results* for an organization.

Calendar Unit. The smallest unit of time used in scheduling the *project*. Calendar units are generally in hours, days, or weeks, but can also be in quarter years, months, shifts, or even in minutes.

Change Control. Identifying, documenting, approving or rejecting, and controlling changes to the *project baselines**.

Change Control Board (CCB). A formally constituted group of *stakeholders* responsible for reviewing, evaluating, approving, delaying, or rejecting changes to the *project*, with all decisions and recommendations being recorded.

Change Control System [Tool]. A collection of formal documented *procedures* that define how project *deliverables* and documentation will be controlled, changed, and approved. In most *application areas* the change control system is a subset of the *configuration management system*.

Change Request. Requests to expand or reduce the *project scope*, modify policies, *processes*, plans, or *procedures*, modify *costs* or *budgets*, or revise *schedules*. Requests for a change can be direct or indirect, externally or internally initiated, and legally or contractually mandated or optional. Only formally documented requested changes are processed and only approved change requests are implemented.

Chart of Accounts [Tool]. Any numbering *system*

used to monitor *project costs** by category (e.g., labor, supplies, materials, and equipment). The project chart of accounts is usually based upon the corporate chart of accounts of the primary *performing organization*. Contrast with *code of accounts*.

Charter. See *project charter*.

Checklist [Output/Input]. Items listed together for convenience of comparison, or to ensure the actions associated with them are managed appropriately and not forgotten. An example is a list of items to be inspected that is created during *quality* planning and applied during quality *control*.

Claim. A request, demand, or assertion of rights by a *seller* against a *buyer*, or vice versa, for consideration, compensation, or payment under the terms of a legally binding *contract*, such as for a disputed change.

Close Project [Process]. The *process* of finalizing all *activities* across all of the project *process groups* to formally close the *project* or *phase*.

Closing Processes [Process Group]. Those *processes* performed to formally terminate all *activities* of a *project* or *phase*, and transfer the completed *product* to others or close a cancelled *project*.

Code of Accounts [Tool]. Any numbering *system* used to uniquely identify each *component* of the *work breakdown structure*. Contrast with *chart of accounts*.

Co-location [Technique]. An organizational placement strategy where the *project team members* are physically located close to one another in order to improve *communication*, working relationships, and productivity.

Common Cause. A source of variation that is inherent in the *system* and predictable. On a *control chart*, it appears as part of the random process variation (i.e., variation from a *process*

that would be considered normal or not unusual), and is indicated by a random pattern of points within the *control limits*. Also referred to as random cause. Contrast with *special cause*.

Communication. A *process* through which information is exchanged among persons using a common system of symbols, signs, or behaviors.

Communication Management Plan [Output/Input]. The *document* that describes: the *communications* needs and expectations for the *project*; how and in what format information will be communicated; when and where each communication will be made; and who is responsible for providing each type of communication. A communication management plan can be formal or informal, highly detailed or broadly framed, based on the requirements of the project *stakeholders*. The communication management plan is contained in, or is a subsidiary plan of, the *project management plan*.

Communications Planning [Process]. The *process* of determining the information and *communications* needs of the project *stakeholders*: who they are, what is their level of interest and influence on the *project*, who needs what information, when will they need it, and how it will be given to them.

Compensation. Something given or received, a payment or recompense, usually something monetary or in kind for *products*, *services*, or *results* provided or received.

Component. A constituent part, element, or piece of a complex whole.

Configuration Management System [Tool]. A subsystem of the overall *project management system*. It is a collection of formal documented *procedures* used to apply technical and administrative direction and surveillance to: identify and document the functional and physical characteristics of a *product, result, service,* or *component*; control any changes to such characteristics; record and report each change and its implementation status; and support the audit of the products, results, or components to verify conformance to *requirements*. It includes the documentation, tracking *systems*, and defined approval levels necessary for authorizing and controlling changes. In most *application areas*, the configuration management system includes the *change control system*.

Constraint [Input]. The state, quality, or sense of being restricted to a given course of action or inaction. An applicable restriction or limitation, either internal or external to the project, that will affect the performance of the *project* or a *process*. For example, a schedule constraint is any limitation or restraint placed on the *project schedule* that affects when a s*chedule activity* can be scheduled and is usually in the form of fixed *imposed dates*. A cost constraint is any limitation or restraint placed on the *project budget* such as *funds* available over time. A project *resource* constraint is any limitation or restraint placed on resource usage, such as what resource *skills* or *disciplines* are available and the amount of a given resource available during a specified time frame.

Contingency. See *reserve*.

Contingency Allowance. See *reserve*.

Contingency Reserve [Output/Input]. The amount of *funds, budget,* or time needed above the *estimate* to reduce the *risk* of overruns of project *objectives* to a level acceptable to the *organization*.

Contract [Output/Input]. A contract is a mutually binding agreement that obligates the *seller* to provide the specified *product* or *service* or *result* and obligates the *buyer* to pay for it.

Contract Administration [Process]. The process of managing the *contract* and the relationship between the *buyer* and *seller*, reviewing and documenting how a seller is performing or has performed to establish required *corrective actions* and provide a basis for future relationships with the seller, managing contract related changes and, when appropriate, managing the contractual relationship with the outside buyer of the *project*.

Contract Closure [Process]. The process of completing and settling the *contract*, including resolution of any open items and closing each contract.

Contract Management Plan [Output/Input]. The *document* that describes how a specific *contract* will be administered and can include items such as required documentation delivery and performance requirements. A contract management plan can be formal or informal, highly detailed or broadly framed, based on the requirements in the contract. Each contract management plan is a subsidiary plan of the *project management plan*.

Contract Statement of Work (SOW) [Output/Input]. A narrative description of *products, services, or results* to be supplied under contract.

Contract Work Breakdown Structure (CWBS) [Output/Input]. A portion of the *work breakdown structure* for the *project* developed and maintained by a *seller* contracting to provide a *subproject* or project *component*.

Control [Technique]. Comparing actual performance with planned performance, analyzing *variances*, assessing trends to effect *process* improvements, evaluating possible alternatives, and recommending appropriate *corrective action* as needed.

Control Account (CA) [Tool]. A management control point where *scope, budget* (resource plans), *actual cost,* and *schedule* are integrated and compared to *earned value* for performance measurement. Control accounts are placed at selected management points (specific *components* at selected levels) of the *work breakdown structure*. Each control account may include one or more *work packages*, but each work package may be associated with only one control account. Each control account is associated with a specific single organizational *component* in the *organizational breakdown structure* (OBS). Previously called a cost account. See also *work package*.

Control Account Plan (CAP) [Tool]. A plan for all the *work* and *effort* to be performed in a control account. Each CAP has a definitive *statement of work*, *schedule*, and time-phased *budget*. Previously called a Cost Account Plan.

Control Chart [Tool]. A graphic display of process data over time and against established *control limits*, and that has a centerline that assists in detecting a trend of plotted values toward either *control limit*.

Control Limits. The area composed of three standard deviations on either side of the centerline, or mean, of a normal distribution of data plotted on a *control chart* that reflects the expected variation in the data. See also *specification limits*.

Controlling. See *control*.

Corrective Action. Documented direction for *executing* the *project work* to bring expected future performance of the project *work* in line with the *project management plan*.

Cost. The monetary value or price of a *project activity** or *component* that includes the monetary worth of the *resources* required to perform and complete the activity or component, or to produce the component. A specific cost can be composed of a combination of cost components including direct labor hours, other direct costs, indirect labor hours, other indirect costs, and purchased price. (However, in the *earned value management* methodology, in some instances, the term cost can represent only labor hours without

conversion to monetary worth.) See also *actual cost* and *estimate*.

Cost Baseline. See *baseline*.

Cost Budgeting [Process]. The *process* of aggregating the estimated costs of individual activities or *work packages* to establish a cost *baseline*.

Cost Control [Process]. The *process* of influencing the factors that create variances, and controlling changes to the project budget.

Cost Estimating [Process]. The *process* of developing an approximation of the cost of the *resources* needed to complete *project activities**.

Cost Management Plan [Output/Input]. The document that sets out the format and establishes the *activities* and *criteria* for planning, structuring, and controlling the *project costs*. A cost management plan can be formal or informal, highly detailed or broadly framed, based on the requirements of the project stakeholders. The cost management plan is contained in, or is a subsidiary plan, of the *project management plan*.

Cost of Quality (COQ) [Technique]. Determining the costs incurred to ensure *quality*. Prevention and appraisal costs (cost of conformance) include costs for quality planning, quality control (QC), and quality assurance to ensure compliance to requirements (i.e., training, QC *systems*, etc.). Failure costs (cost of non-conformance) include costs to rework *products*, *components*, or *processes* that are non-compliant, costs of warranty work and waste, and loss of reputation.

Cost Performance Index (CPI). A measure of cost efficiency on a *project*. It is the ratio of *earned value* (EV) to *actual costs* (AC). CPI = EV divided by AC. A value equal to or greater than one indicates a favorable condition and a value less than one indicates an unfavorable condition.

Cost-Plus-Fee (CPF). A type of *cost reimbursable contract* where the *buyer* reimburses the *seller* for seller's allowable costs for performing the contract work and seller also receives a fee calculated as an agreed upon percentage of the costs. The fee varies with the actual cost.

Cost-Plus-Fixed-Fee (CPFF) Contract. A type of *cost-reimbursable contract* where the *buyer* reimburses the *seller* for the seller's allowable costs (allowable costs are defined by the contract) plus a fixed amount of profit (fee).

Cost-Plus-Incentive-Fee (CPIF) Contract. A type of *cost-reimbursable contract* where the *buyer* reimburses the *seller* for the seller's allowable costs (allowable costs are defined by the contract), and the seller earns its profit if it meets defined performance criteria.

Cost-Plus-Percentage of Cost (CPPC). See *cost-plus-fee.*

Cost-Reimbursable Contract. A type of *contract* involving payment (reimbursement) by the *buyer* to the *seller* for the seller's actual costs, plus a fee typically representing seller's profit. Costs are usually classified as direct costs or indirect costs. Direct costs are costs incurred for the exclusive benefit of the project, such as salaries of full-time project staff. Indirect costs, also called overhead and general and administrative cost, are costs allocated to the project by the performing organization as a cost of doing business, such as salaries of management indirectly involved in the project, and cost of electric utilities for the office. Indirect costs are usually calculated as a percentage of direct costs. Cost-reimbursable contracts often include incentive clauses where, if the seller meets or exceeds selected project objectives, such as schedule targets or total cost, then the seller receives from the buyer an incentive or bonus payment.

Cost Variance (CV). A measure of cost performance on a *project*. It is the algebraic difference between *earned value* (EV) and *actual cost* (AC).

CV = EV minus AC. A positive value indicates a favorable condition and a negative value indicates an unfavorable condition.

Crashing [Technique]. A specific type of project *schedule compression technique* performed by taking action to decrease the total *project schedule duration** after analyzing a number of alternatives to determine how to get the maximum schedule duration compression for the least additional cost. Typical approaches for crashing a schedule include reducing *schedule activity durations* and increasing the assignment of *resources* on schedule activities. See *schedule compression* and see also *fast tracking.*

Create WBS (Work Breakdown Structure) [Process]. The *process* of subdividing the major project *deliverables* and project *work* into smaller, more manageable *components.*

Criteria. *Standards*, rules, or tests on which a judgment or decision can be based, or by which a *product*, *service*, *result*, or *process* can be evaluated.

Critical Activity. Any *schedule activity* on a *critical path* in a *project schedule*. Most commonly determined by using the *critical path method*. Although some activities are "critical," in the dictionary sense, without being on the critical path, this meaning is seldom used in the project context.

Critical Chain Method [Technique]. A *schedule network analysis technique** that modifies the project schedule to account for limited resources. The critical chain method mixes deterministic and probabilistic approaches to *schedule network analysis.*

Critical Path [Output/Input]. Generally, but not always, the sequence of *schedule activities* that determines the duration of the *project*. Generally, it is the longest path through the project. However, a critical path can end, as an example, on a *schedule milestone* that is in the middle of the project schedule and that has a finish-no-later-than *imposed date* schedule *constraint*. See also *critical path method*.

Critical Path Method (CPM) [Technique]. A *schedule network analysis technique** used to determine the amount of scheduling flexibility (the amount of *float*) on various logical *network paths* in the *project schedule* network, and to determine the minimum total project *duration*. *Early start and finish dates** are calculated by means of a *forward pass*, using a specified *start date*. *Late start and finish dates** are calculated by means of a *backward pass*, starting from a specified completion date, which sometimes is the project *early finish date* determined during the forward pass calculation.

Current Finish Date. The current *estimate* of the point in time when a *schedule activity* will be completed, where the estimate reflects any reported work progress. See also *scheduled finish date* and *baseline finish date*.

Current Start Date. The current *estimate* of the point in time when a *schedule activity* will begin, where the estimate reflects any reported work progress. See also *scheduled start date* and *baseline start date*.

Customer. The person or *organization* that will use the project's *product* or *service* or *result*. See also *user*.

Data Date (DD). The *date* up to or through which the project's reporting *system* has provided actual status and accomplishments. In some reporting *systems*, the status information for the data date is included in the past and in some systems the status information is in the future. Also called *as-of date* and *time-now date*.

Date. A term representing the day, month, and year of a calendar, and, in some instances, the time of day.

Decision Tree Analysis [Technique]. The decision tree is a diagram that describes a decision under consideration and the implications of choosing one or another of the available alternatives. It is used when some future scenarios or outcomes of actions are uncertain. It incorporates probabilities and the costs or rewards of each logical path of *events* and future decisions, and uses *expected monetary value analysis* to help the *organization* identify the relative values of alternate actions. See also *expected monetary value analysis*.

Decompose. See *decomposition*.

Decomposition [Technique]. A planning technique that subdivides the *project scope* and project *deliverables* into smaller, more manageable *components*, until the project *work* associated with accomplishing the project scope and providing the deliverables is defined in sufficient detail to support *executing*, *monitoring*, and *controlling* the *work*.

Defect. An imperfection or deficiency in a project *component* where that component does not meet its *requirements* or *specifications* and needs to be either repaired or replaced.

Defect Repair. Formally documented identification of a *defect* in a project *component* with a recommendation to either repair the defect or completely replace the component.

Deliverable [Output/Input]. Any unique and verifiable *product*, *result*, or capability to perform a *service* that must be produced to complete a process, phase, or project. Often used more narrowly in reference to an external *deliverable*, which is a deliverable that is subject to approval by the project sponsor or customer. See also product, service, and result.

Delphi Technique [Technique]. An information gathering technique used as a way to reach a consensus of experts on a subject. Experts on the subject participate in this technique anonymously. A facilitator uses a questionnaire to solicit ideas about the important project points related to the subject. The responses are summarized and are then re-circulated to the experts for further comment. Consensus may be reached in a few rounds of this *process*. The Delphi technique helps reduce bias in the data and keeps any one person from having undue influence on the outcome.

Dependency. See *logical relationship*.

Design Review [Technique]. A management *technique* used for evaluating a proposed design to ensure that the design of the *system* or *product* meets the *customer requirements*, or to assure that the design will perform successfully, can be produced, and can be maintained.

Develop Project Charter [Process]. The *process* of developing the *project charter* that formally authorizes a *project*.

Develop Project Management Plan [Process]. The *process* of documenting the actions necessary to define, prepare, integrate, and coordinate all subsidiary plans into a *project management plan*.

Develop Preliminary Project Scope Statement [Process]. The *process* of developing the preliminary *project scope statement* that provides a high level *scope* narrative.

Develop Project Team [Process]. The *process* of improving the competencies and interaction of team members to enhance *project* performance.

Direct and Manage Project Execution [Process]. The *process* of executing the *work* defined in the *project management plan* to achieve the project's *requirements* defined in the *project scope statement*.

Discipline. A field of work requiring specific knowledge and that has a set of rules governing work conduct (e.g., mechanical engineering, computer programming, cost estimating, etc.).

Discrete Effort. *Work effort* that is separate, distinct, and related to the completion of specific *work breakdown structure* components and *deliverables*, and that can be directly planned and measured. Contrast with *apportioned effort*.

Document. A medium and the information recorded thereon, that generally has permanence and can be read by a person or a machine. Examples include *project management plans, specifications, procedures*, studies, and manuals.

Documented Procedure. A formalized written description of how to carry out an *activity, process, technique*, or *methodology*.

Dummy Activity. A *schedule activity* of zero *duration* used to show a *logical relationship* in the *arrow diagramming method*. Dummy activities are used when logical relationships cannot be completely or correctly described with schedule activity *arrows*. Dummy activities are generally shown graphically as a dashed line headed by an arrow.

Duration (DU or DUR). The total number of *work* periods (not including holidays or other nonworking periods) required to complete a *schedule activity* or *work breakdown structure component*. Usually expressed as workdays or workweeks. Sometimes incorrectly equated with elapsed time. Contrast with *effort*. See also *original duration, remaining duration*, and *actual duration*.

Early Finish Date (EF). In the *critical path method*, the earliest possible point in time on which the uncompleted portions of a *schedule activity* (or the *project*) can finish, based on the schedule *network logic*, the *data date*, and any schedule *constraints*. Early finish dates can change as the project progresses and as changes are made to the *project management plan*.

Early Start Date (ES). In the *critical path method*, the earliest possible point in time on which the uncompleted portions of a *schedule activity* (or the *project*) can start, based on the schedule *network logic*, the *data date*, and any schedule *constraints*. Early start dates can change as the project progresses and as changes are made to the *project management plan*.

Earned Value (EV). The value of *work* performed expressed in terms of the approved *budget* assigned to that work for a *schedule activity* or *work breakdown structure component*. Also referred to as the *budgeted cost of work performed* (BCWP).

Earned Value Management (EVM). A management methodology for integrating *scope, schedule,* and *resources,* and for objectively measuring project performance and progress. Performance is measured by determining the budgeted cost of work performed (i.e., *earned value*) and comparing it to the actual cost of work performed (i.e., *actual cost*). Progress is measured by comparing the *earned value* to the *planned value*.

Earned Value Technique (EVT) [Technique]. A specific technique for measuring the performance of work and used to establish the *performance measurement baseline* (PMB). Also referred to as the earning rules and crediting method.

Effort. The number of labor units required to complete a *schedule activity* or *work breakdown structure component*. Usually expressed as staff hours, staff days, or staff weeks. Contrast with *duration*.

Enterprise. A company, business, firm, partnership, corporation, or governmental agency.

Enterprise Environmental Factors [Output/ Input]. Any or all external environmental factors and internal organizational environmental factors that surround or influence the project's success. These factors are from any or all of the enterprises involved in the project, and include organizational culture and structure, infrastructure, existing resources, commercial databases, market

conditions, and *project management software*.

Estimate [Output/Input]. A quantitative assessment of the likely amount or outcome. Usually applied to project *costs, resources, effort,* and *durations* and is usually preceded by a modifier (i.e., preliminary, conceptual, feasibility, order-of-magnitude, definitive). It should always include some indication of accuracy (e.g., ±x percent).

Estimate at Completion (EAC) [Output/Input]. The expected total cost of a *schedule activity*, a *work breakdown structure component*, or the *project* when the defined *scope* of *work* will be completed. EAC is equal to the *actual cost* (AC) plus the *estimate to complete* (ETC) for all of the remaining work. EAC = AC plus ETC. The EAC may be calculated based on performance to date or estimated by the *project team* based on other factors, in which case it is often referred to as the latest revised estimate. See also *earned value technique* and *estimate to complete*.

Estimate to Complete (ETC) [Output/Input]. The expected cost needed to complete all the remaining work for a schedule *activity, work breakdown structure* component, or the *project*. See also *earned value technique* and *estimate at completion*.

Event. Something that happens, an occurrence, an outcome.

Exception Report. *Document* that includes only major variations from the plan (rather than all variations).

Execute. Directing, managing, performing, and accomplishing the *project work,* providing the *deliverables,* and providing *work performance information*.

Executing. See *execute*.

Executing Processes [Process Group]. Those *processes* performed to complete the *work* defined in the *project management plan* to accomplish the project's *objectives* defined in the *project scope statement.*

Execution. See *execute.*

Expected Monetary Value (EMV) Analysis. A statistical *technique* that calculates the average outcome when the future includes scenarios that may or may not happen. A common use of this technique is within *decision tree analysis.* Modeling and simulation are recommended for *cost* and schedule *risk* analysis because it is more powerful and less subject to misapplication than expected monetary value analysis.

Expert Judgment [Technique]. Judgment provided based upon expertise in an *application area, knowledge area, discipline,* industry, etc. as appropriate for the activity being performed. Such expertise may be provided by any group or person with specialized education, *knowledge, skill,* experience, or training, and is available from many sources, including: other units within the performing organization; consultants; *stakeholder*s, including *customers*; professional and technical associations; and industry groups.

Failure Mode and Effect Analysis (FMEA) [Technique]. An analytical *procedure* in which each potential failure mode in every *component* of a *product* is analyzed to determine its effect on the reliability of that component and, by itself or in combination with other possible failure modes, on the reliability of the product or system and on the required function of the component; or the examination of a *product* (at the *system* and/or lower levels) for all ways that a failure may occur. For each potential failure, an estimate is made of its effect on the total *system* and of its impact. In addition, a review is undertaken of the action planned to minimize the probability of failure and to minimize its effects.

Fast Tracking [Technique]. A specific project *schedule compression technique* that changes net-work logic to overlap *phases* that would normally be done in sequence, such as the design phase and construction phase, or to perform *schedule activities* in parallel. See *schedule compression* and see also *crashing.*

Finish Date. A point in time associated with a *schedule activity's* completion. Usually qualified by one of the following: actual, planned, estimated, scheduled, early, late, baseline, target, or current.

Finish-to-Finish (FF). The *logical relationship* where completion of *work* of the *successor activity* cannot finish until the completion of work of the *predecessor* activity. See also *logical relationship.*

Finish-to-Start (FS). The *logical relationship* where initiation of *work* of the *successor activity* depends upon the completion of work of the *predecessor activity.* See also *logical relationship.*

Firm-Fixed-Price (FFP) Contract. A type of *fixed price contract* where the *buyer* pays the *seller* a set amount (as defined by the *contract*), regardless of the seller's costs.

Fixed-Price-Incentive-Fee (FPIF) Contract. A type of *contract* where the *buyer* pays the *seller* a set amount (as defined by the contract), and the seller can earn an additional amount if the seller meets defined performance *criteria.*

Fixed-Price or Lump-Sum Contract. A type of *contract* involving a fixed total price for a well-defined *product.* Fixed-price contracts may also include incentives for meeting or exceeding selected *project objectives*, such as schedule targets. The simplest form of a fixed price contract is a purchase order.

Float. Also called slack. See *total float* and see also *free float.*

Flowcharting [Technique]. The depiction in a diagram format of the *inputs, process* actions, and *outputs* of one or more processes within a *system.*

Forecasts. *Estimates* or predictions of conditions and *events* in the *project's* future based on information and knowledge available at the time of the forecast. Forecasts are updated and reissued based on *work performance information* provided as the project is *executed*. The information is based on the project's past performance and expected future performance, and includes information that could impact the project in the future, such as *estimate at completion* and *estimate to complete*.

Forward Pass. The calculation of the *early start* and *early finish dates* for the uncompleted portions of all network activities. See also *schedule network analysis* and *backward pass*.

Free Float (FF). The amount of time that a *schedule activity* can be delayed without delaying the early start of any immediately following schedule activities. See also *total float*.

Functional Manager. Someone with management *authority* over an organizational unit within a *functional organization*. The manager of any group that actually makes a *product* or performs a *service*. Sometimes called a line manager.

Functional Organization. A hierarchical *organization* where each employee has one clear superior, staff are grouped by areas of specialization, and managed by a person with expertise in that area.

Funds. A supply of money or pecuniary resources immediately available.

Gantt Chart. See *bar chart*.

Goods. Commodities, wares, merchandise.

Grade. A category or rank used to distinguish items that have the same functional use (e.g., "hammer"), but do not share the same requirements for quality (e.g., different hammers may need to withstand different amounts of force).

Ground Rules [Tool]. A list of acceptable and unacceptable behaviors adopted by a *project team* to improve working relationships, effectiveness, and *communication*.

Hammock Activity. See *summary activity*.

Historical Information. Documents and data on prior projects including project files, records, correspondence, closed contracts, and closed projects.

Human Resource Planning [Process]. The *process* of identifying and documenting *project roles*, responsibilities and reporting relationships, as well as creating the *staffing management plan*.

Imposed Date. A fixed date imposed on a *schedule activity* or *schedule milestone*, usually in the form of a "start no earlier than" and "finish no later than" date.

Influence Diagram [Tool]. Graphical representation of situations showing causal influences, time ordering of *events*, and other relationships among variables and outcomes.

Influencer. Persons or groups that are not directly related to the acquisition or use of the project's *product*, but, due to their position in the *customer organization**, can influence, positively or negatively, the course of the *project*.

Information Distribution [Process]. The *process* of making needed information available to *project stakeholders* in a timely manner.

Initiating Processes [Process Group]. Those *processes* performed to authorize and define the *scope* of a new *phase* or *project* or that can result in the continuation of halted project *work*. A large number of the initiating processes are typically done outside the project's scope of control by the *organization*, *program*, or *portfolio* processes and those processes provide input to the project's initiating processes group.

Initiator. A person or *organization* that has both the ability and *authority* to start a *project*.

Input [Process Input]. Any item, whether internal or external to the project that is required by a *process* before that process proceeds. May be an *output* from a predecessor process.

Inspection [Technique]. Examining or measuring to verify whether an *activity*, *component*, *product*, *result* or *service* conforms to specified *requirements*.

Integral. Essential to completeness; requisite; constituent with; formed as a unit with another component.

Integrated. Interrelated, interconnected, interlocked, or meshed components blended and unified into a functioning or unified whole.

Integrated Change Control [Process]. The *process* of reviewing all *change requests*, approving changes and controlling changes to *deliverables* and *organizational process assets*.

Invitation for Bid (IFB). Generally, this term is equivalent to *request for proposal*. However, in some *application areas*, it may have a narrower or more specific meaning.

Issue. A point or matter in question or in dispute, or a point or matter that is not settled and is under discussion or over which there are opposing views or disagreements.

Knowledge. Knowing something with the familiarity gained through experience, education, observation, or investigation, it is understanding a *process*, *practice*, or *technique*, or how to use a *tool*.

Knowledge Area Process. An identifiable project management *process* within a *knowledge area*.

Knowledge Area, Project Management. See *Project Management Knowledge Area*.

Lag [Technique]. A modification of a *logical relationship* that directs a delay in the *successor activity*. For example, in a *finish-to-start* dependency with a ten-day lag, the successor activity cannot

start until ten days after the *predecessor* activity has finished. See also *lead*.

Late Finish Date (LF). In the *critical path method*, the latest possible point in time that a *schedule activity* may be completed based upon the schedule *network logic*, the project completion date, and any *constraints* assigned to the schedule activities without violating a schedule constraint or delaying the project completion date. The late finish dates are determined during the *backward pass* calculation of the project schedule network.

Late Start Date (LS). In the critical path method, the latest possible point in time that a *schedule activity* may begin based upon the schedule *network logic*, the project completion date, and any *constraints* assigned to the schedule activities without violating a schedule constraint or delaying the project completion date. The late start dates are determined during the *backward pass* calculation of the project schedule network.

Latest Revised Estimate. See *estimate at completion*.

Lead [Technique]. A modification of a *logical relationship* that allows an acceleration of the *successor activity*. For example, in a *finish-to-start* dependency with a ten-day lead, the *successor activity* can start ten days before the *predecessor activity* has finished. See also *lag*. A negative lead is equivalent to a positive lag.

Lessons Learned [Output/Input]. The learning gained from the process of performing the project. Lessons learned may be identified at any point. Also considered a project record, to be included in the *lessons learned knowledge base*.

Lessons Learned Knowledge Base. A store of historical information and *lessons learned* about both the outcomes of previous *project* selection decisions and previous project performance.

Level of Effort (LOE). Support-type *activity* (e.g.,

seller or *customer* liaison, project cost accounting, project management, etc.), which does not produce definitive end *products*. It is generally characterized by a uniform rate of *work* performance over a period of time determined by the activities supported.

Leveling. See *resource leveling.*

Life Cycle. See *project life cycle.*

Log. A document used to record and describe or denote selected items identified during execution of a process or activity. Usually used with a modifier, such as issue, quality control, action, or defect.

Logic. See *network logic.*

Logic Diagram. See *project schedule network diagram.*

Logical Relationship. A *dependency* between two *project schedule activities,* or between a project schedule activity and a *schedule milestone.* See also *precedence relationship.* The four possible types of logical relationships are: *Finish-to-Start; Finish-to-Finish; Start-to-Start;* and *Start-to-Finish.*

Manage Project Team [Process]. The *process* of tracking team member performance, providing feedback, resolving issues, and coordinating changes to enhance project performance.

Manage Stakeholders [Process]. The *process* of managing *communications* to satisfy the *requirements* of, and resolve *issues* with, project *stakeholders.*

Master Schedule [Tool]. A summary-level *project schedule* that identifies the major *deliverables* and *work breakdown structure components* and key *schedule milestones.* See also *milestone schedule.*

Materiel. The aggregate of things used by an *organization* in any undertaking, such as equipment, apparatus, tools, machinery, gear, material, and supplies.

Matrix Organization. Any organizational structure in which the *project manager* shares responsibility with the *functional managers* for assigning priorities and for directing the *work* of persons assigned to the *project.*

Methodology. A *system* of *practices, techniques, procedures,* and rules used by those who work in a *discipline.*

Milestone. A significant point or *event* in the *project.* See also *schedule milestone.*

Milestone Schedule [Tool]. A summary-level *schedule* that identifies the major *schedule milestones.* See also *master schedule.*

Monitor. Collect *project* performance data with respect to a plan, produce performance measures, and report and disseminate performance information.

Monitor and Control Project Work [Process]. The process of *monitoring* and *controlling* the processes required to initiate, plan, execute, and close a *project* to meet the performance *objectives* defined in the *project management plan* and *project scope statement.*

Monitoring. See *monitor.*

Monitoring and Controlling Processes [Process Group]. Those *processes* performed to measure and *monitor project execution** so that corrective action can be taken when necessary to *control* the execution of the *phase* or project.

Monte Carlo Analysis. A *technique* that computes, or iterates, the *project* cost or *project schedule* many times using input values selected at random from probability distributions of possible *costs* or *durations,* to calculate a distribution of possible total project cost or completion dates.

Near-Critical Activity. A *schedule activity* that has low *total float.* The concept of near-critical is equally applicable to a *schedule activity* or schedule *network path*. The limit below which *total float* is considered near critical is subject to *expert judgment* and varies from *project* to project.

Network. See *project schedule network diagram*.

Network Analysis. See *schedule network analysis*.

Network Logic. The collection of *schedule activity* dependencies that makes up a *project schedule network diagram*.

Network Loop. A schedule *network path* that passes the same *node* twice. Network loops cannot be analyzed using traditional *schedule network analysis* techniques such as *critical path method*.

Network Open End. A *schedule activity* without any *predecessor activities* or *successor activities* creating an unintended break in a schedule *network path*. Network open ends are usually caused by missing *logical relationships*.

Network Path. Any continuous series of *schedule activities* connected with *logical relationships* in a *project schedule network diagram*.

Networking [Technique]. Developing relationships with persons who may be able to assist in the achievement of *objectives* and responsibilities.

Node. One of the defining points of a schedule network; a junction point joined to some or all of the other *dependency* lines. See also *arrow diagramming method* and *precedence diagramming method*.

Objective. Something toward which *work* is to be directed, a strategic position to be attained, or a purpose to be achieved, a *result* to be obtained, a *product* to be produced, or a *service* to be performed.

Operations. An organizational function performing the ongoing execution of *activities* that produce the same *product* or provide a repetitive *service*. Examples are: production operations, manufacturing operations, and accounting operations.

Opportunity. A condition or situation favorable to the *project*, a positive set of circumstances, a positive set of *events*, a *risk* that will have a positive impact on project *objectives*, or a possibility for positive changes. Contrast with *threat*.

Organization. A group of persons organized for some purpose or to perform some type of *work* within an *enterprise*.

Organization Chart [Tool]. A method for depicting interrelationships among a group of persons working together toward a common *objective*.

Organizational Breakdown Structure (OBS) [Tool]. A hierarchically organized depiction of the *project organization* arranged so as to relate the *work packages* to the *performing organizational* units. (Sometimes OBS is written as Organization Breakdown Structure with the same definition.)

Organizational Process Assets [Output/Input]. Any or all *process* related assets, from any or all of the organizations involved in the *project* that are or can be used to influence the project's success. These process assets include formal and informal plans, policies, *procedures*, and guidelines. The process assets also include the organizations' knowledge bases such as *lessons learned* and *historical information*.

Original Duration (OD). The *activity duration* originally assigned to a schedule activity and not updated as progress is reported on the activity. Typically used for comparison with *actual duration* and *remaining duration* when reporting schedule progress.

Output [Process Output]. A *product*, *result*, or *service* generated by a *process*. May be an input to a successor process.

Parametric Estimating [Technique]. An estimating *technique* that uses a statistical relationship between historical data and other variables (e.g., square footage in construction, lines of code in software development) to calculate an *estimate* for activity parameters, such as *scope, cost, budget*, and *duration*. This technique can produce higher levels of accuracy depending upon the sophistication and the underlying data built into the model. An example for the cost parameter is multiplying the planned quantity of work to be performed by the historical cost per unit to obtain the estimated cost.

Pareto Chart [Tool]. A histogram, ordered by frequency of occurrence, that shows how many *results* were generated by each identified cause.

Path Convergence. The merging or joining of parallel schedule *network paths* into the same *node* in a *project schedule network diagram*. Path convergence is characterized by a *schedule activity* with more than one *predecessor activity*.

Path Divergence. Extending or generating parallel schedule *network paths* from the same *node* in a *project schedule network diagram*. Path divergence is characterized by a *schedule activity* with more than one *successor activity*.

Percent Complete (PC or PCT). An *estimate*, expressed as a percent, of the amount of *work* that has been completed on an *activity* or a *work breakdown structure component*.

Perform Quality Assurance (QA) [Process]. The *process* of applying the planned, systematic quality *activities* (such as audits or peer reviews) to ensure that the *project* employs all processes needed to meet requirements.

Perform Quality Control (QC) [Process]. The *process* of *monitoring* specific *project results** to determine whether they comply with relevant quality standards and identifying ways to eliminate causes of unsatisfactory performance.

Performance Measurement Baseline. An approved integrated *scope-schedule-cost** plan for the *project work* against which project execution is compared

to measure and manage performance. Technical and *quality* parameters may also be included.

Performance Reporting [Process]. The *process* of collecting and distributing performance information. This includes status reporting, progress measurement, and *forecasting*.

Performance Reports [Output/Input]. *Documents* and presentations that provide organized and summarized *work performance information, earned value management* parameters and calculations, and analyses of *project work* progress and status. Common formats for performance reports include *bar charts, S-curves, histograms*, tables, and *project schedule network diagram* showing current schedule status.

Performing Organization. The *enterprise* whose personnel are most directly involved in doing the *work* of the *project*.

Phase. See *project phase*.

Plan Contracting [Process]. The *process* of documenting the *products, services,* and *results* requirements and identifying potential *sellers*.

Plan Purchases and Acquisitions [Process]. The *process* of determining what to purchase or acquire, and determining when and how to do so.

Planned Finish Date (PF). See *scheduled finish date*.

Planned Start Date (PS). See *scheduled start date*.

Planned Value (PV). The authorized *budget* assigned to the scheduled work to be accomplished for a *schedule activity* or *work breakdown structure component*. Also referred to as the budgeted cost of work scheduled (BCWS).

Planning Package. A WBS *component* below the *control account* with known *work* content but without detailed *schedule activities*. See also *control account*.

Planning Processes [Process Group]. Those

processes performed to define and mature the *project scope*, develop the *project management plan*, and identify and schedule the *project activities** that occur within the *project*.

Portfolio. A collection of *projects* or *programs* and other work that are grouped together to facilitate effective management of that *work* to meet strategic business *objectives*. The projects or programs of the portfolio may not necessarily be interdependent or directly related.

Portfolio Management [Technique]. The centralized management of one or more *portfolios*, which includes identifying, prioritizing, authorizing, managing, and controlling *projects*, *programs*, and other related work, to achieve specific strategic business *objectives*.

Position Description [Tool]. An explanation of a *project team* member's *roles* and responsibilities.

Practice. A specific type of professional or management *activity* that contributes to the execution of a *process* and that may employ one or more *techniques* and *tools*.

Precedence Diagramming Method (PDM) [Technique]. A schedule network diagramming *technique* in which *schedule activities* are represented by boxes (or *nodes*). Schedule activities are graphically linked by one or more *logical relationships* to show the sequence in which the activities are to be performed.

Precedence Relationship. The term used in the *precedence diagramming method* for a *logical relationship*. In current usage, however, precedence relationship, *logical relationship*, and *dependency* are widely used interchangeably, regardless of the diagramming method used.

Predecessor Activity. The *schedule activity* that determines when the logical *successor activity* can begin or end.

Preventive Action. Documented direction to perform an *activity* that can reduce the probability of negative consequences associated with *project risks*.

Probability and Impact Matrix [Tool]. A common way to determine whether a *risk* is considered low, moderate, or high by combining the two dimensions of a risk: its probability of occurrence, and its impact on objectives if it occurs.

Procedure. A series of steps followed in a regular definitive order to accomplish something.

Process. A set of interrelated actions and *activities* performed to achieve a specified set of *products, results, or services*.

Process Group. See *Project Management Process Groups*.

Procurement Documents [Output/Input]. Those *documents* utilized in bid and proposal activities, which include *buyer's* Invitation for Bid, Invitation for Negotiations, Request for Information, Request for Quotation, Request for Proposal and *seller's* responses.

Procurement Management Plan [Output/Input]. The *document* that describes how procurement *processes* from developing procurement documentation through *contract closure* will be managed.

Product. An artifact that is produced, is quantifiable, and can be either an end item in itself or a component item. Additional words for products are *materiel* and *goods*. Contrast with *result* and *service*. See also *deliverable*.

Product Life Cycle. A collection of generally sequential, non-overlapping *product phases** whose name and number are determined by the manufacturing and control needs of the *organization*. The last product life cycle phase for a product is generally the product's deterioration and death. Generally, a *project life cycle* is contained within one or more product life cycles.

Product Scope. The features and functions that

characterize a *product*, *service* or *result*.

Product Scope Description. The documented narrative description of the *product scope*.

Program. A group of related *projects* managed in a coordinated way to obtain benefits and control not available from managing them individually. Programs may include elements of related *work* outside of the *scope* of the discrete projects in the program.

Program Management. The centralized coordinated management of a *program* to achieve the program's strategic *objectives* and benefits.

Program Management Office (PMO). The centralized management of a particular *program* or programs such that corporate benefit is realized by the sharing of *resources, methodologies, tools, and techniques*, and related high-level project management focus. See also *project management office*.

Progressive Elaboration [Technique]. Continuously improving and detailing a plan as more detailed and specific information and more accurate estimates become available as the project progresses, and thereby producing more accurate and complete plans that result from the successive iterations of the planning *process*.

Project. A temporary endeavor undertaken to create a unique *product*, *service*, or *result*.

Project Calendar. A calendar of working days or shifts that establishes those *dates* on which *schedule activities* are worked and nonworking days that determine those dates on which schedule activities are idle. Typically defines holidays, weekends and shift hours. See also *resource calendar*.

Project Charter [Output/Input]. A *document* issued by the project *initiator* or *sponsor* that formally authorizes the existence of a *project*, and provides the *project manager* with the authority to apply organizational *resources* to project *activities*.

Project Communications Management [Knowledge Area].

Project Cost Management [Knowledge Area].

Project Human Resource Management [Knowledge Area].

Project Initiation. Launching a *process* that can result in the authorization and *scope* definition of a new *project*.

Project Integration Management [Knowledge Area].

Project Life Cycle. A collection of generally sequential *project phases* whose name and number are determined by the *control* needs of the *organization* or organizations involved in the *project*. A life cycle can be documented with a *methodology*.

Project Management (PM). The application of *knowledge, skills, tools*, and *techniques* to *project activities** to meet the project *requirements*.

Project Management Body of Knowledge (PMBOK®). An inclusive term that describes the sum of *knowledge* within the profession of *project management*. As with other professions such as law, medicine, and accounting, the body of knowledge rests with the practitioners and academics that apply and advance it. The complete project management body of knowledge includes proven traditional *practices* that are widely applied and innovative practices that are emerging in the profession. The body of knowledge includes both published and unpublished material. The PMBOK is constantly evolving.

Project Management Information System (PMIS) [Tool]. An information *system* consisting of the *tools* and *techniques* used to gather, integrate, and disseminate the outputs of project management *processes*. It is used to support all aspects of the project from initiating through closing, and can include both manual and automated *systems*.

Project Management Knowledge Area. An identified area of *project management* defined by its *knowledge requirements* and described in terms of its *component processes*, *practices*, *inputs*, *outputs*, *tools*, and *techniques*.

Project Management Office (PMO). An organizational body or entity assigned various responsibilities related to the centralized and coordinated management of those *projects* under its domain. The responsibilities of a PMO can range from providing project management support functions to actually being responsible for the direct management of a project. See also *program management office*.

Project Management Plan [Output/Input]. A formal, approved *document* that defines how the projected is executed, monitored and controlled. It may be summary or detailed and may be composed of one or more subsidiary management plans and other planning documents.

Project Management Process. One of the 44 *processes*, unique to *project management* and described in the *PMBOK® Guide*.

Project Management Process Group. A logical grouping of the *project management processes* described in the *PMBOK® Guide*. The project management process groups include *initiating processes*, *planning processes*, *executing processes*, *monitoring and controlling processes*, and *closing processes*. Collectively, these five groups are required for any *project*, have clear internal *dependencies*, and must be performed in the same sequence on each project, independent of the *application area* or the specifics of the applied *project life cycle*. Project management process groups are not *project phases*.

Project Management Professional (PMP®). A person certified as a PMP® by the Project Management Institute (PMI®).

Project Management Software [Tool]. A class of computer software applications specifically designed to aid the *project management team* with planning, monitoring, and controlling the project, including: *cost estimating*, scheduling, *communications*, collaboration, configuration management, document control, records management, and *risk* analysis.

Project Management System [Tool]. The aggregation of the *processes*, *tools*, *techniques*, *methodologies*, *resources*, and *procedures* to manage a project. The *system* is documented in the *project management plan* and its content will vary depending upon the *application area*, organizational influence, complexity of the project, and the availability of existing *systems*. A project management system, which can be formal or informal, aids a *project manager* in effectively guiding a *project* to completion. A project management system is a set of *processes* and the related monitoring and control functions that are consolidated and combined into a functioning, unified whole.

Project Management Team. The members of the *project team* who are directly involved in *project management activities*. On some smaller *projects*, the project management team may include virtually all of the *project team members*.

Project Manager (PM). The person assigned by the *performing organization* to achieve the *project objectives**.

Project Organization Chart [Output/Input]. A *document* that graphically depicts the *project team* members and their interrelationships for a specific *project*.

Project Phase. A collection of logically related *project activities**, usually culminating in the completion of a major *deliverable*. Project phases (also called phases) are mainly completed sequentially, but can overlap in some project situations. Phases can be subdivided into *subphases* and then *components*; this hierarchy, if the project or portions of the project are divided into phases, is contained in the *work breakdown structure*. A project phase is a component of a *project life cycle*. A project phase is not a *project management process group**.

Project Process Groups. The five *process groups* required for any project that have clear dependencies and that are required to be performed in the same sequence on each project, independent of the *application area* or the specifics of the applied *project life cycle*. The process groups are initiating, planning, executing, monitoring and controlling, and closing.

Project Procurement Management [Knowledge Area].

Project Quality Management [Knowledge Area].

Project Risk Management [Knowledge Area].

Project Schedule [Output/Input]. The planned *dates* for performing *schedule activities* and the planned dates for meeting *schedule milestones*.

Project Schedule Network Diagram [Output/Input]. Any schematic display of the *logical relationships* among the project *schedule activities*. Always drawn from left to right to reflect project *work* chronology.

Project Scope. The *work* that must be performed to deliver a *product, service, or result* with the specified features and functions.

Project Scope Management [Knowledge Area].

Project Scope Management Plan [Output/Input]. The *document* that describes how the *project scope* will be defined, developed, and verified and how the *work breakdown structure* will be created and defined, and that provides guidance on how the *project scope* will be managed and controlled by the *project management team*. It is contained in or is a subsidiary plan of the *project management plan*. The project scope management plan can be informal and broadly framed, or formal and highly detailed, based on the needs of the *project*.

Project Scope Statement [Output/Input]. The narrative description of the *project scope*, including major *deliverables*, project *objectives*, project *assumptions*, project *constraints*, and a *statement of work*, that provides a documented basis for making future project decisions and for confirming or developing a common understanding of *project scope* among the *stakeholders*. The definition of the *project scope*—what needs to be accomplished.

Project Sponsor. See *sponsor*.

Project Stakeholder. See *stakeholder*.

Project Summary Work Breakdown Structure (PSWBS) [Tool]. A *work breakdown structure* for the project that is only developed down to the *subproject* level of detail within some legs of the WBS, and where the detail of those subprojects are provided by use of *contract work breakdown structures*.

Project Team. All the *project team members*, including the *project management team*, the *project manager* and, for some projects, the *project sponsor*.

Project Team Directory. A documented list of *project team* members, their project *roles* and *communication* information.

Project Team Members. The persons who report either directly or indirectly to the *project manager*, and who are responsible for performing *project work* as a regular part of their assigned duties.

Project Time Management [Knowledge Area].

Project Work. See *work*.

Projectized Organization. Any organizational structure in which the *project manager* has full authority to assign priorities, apply *resources*, and direct the *work* of persons assigned to the *project*.

Qualitative Risk Analysis [Process]. The *process* of prioritizing *risks* for subsequent further analysis or action by assessing and combining their probability of occurrence and impact.

Quality. The degree to which a set of inherent characteristics fulfills *requirements*.

Quality Management Plan [Output/Input]. The quality management plan describes how the *project management team* will implement the *performing organization's* quality policy. The quality management plan is a component or a subsidiary plan of the *project management plan*. The quality management plan may be formal or informal, highly detailed, or broadly framed, based on the *requirements* of the *project*.

Quality Planning [Process]. The *process* of identifying which quality standards are relevant to the *project* and determining how to satisfy them.

Quantitative Risk Analysis [Process]. The *process* of numerically analyzing the effect on overall project *objectives* of identified *risks*.

Regulation. Requirements imposed by a governmental body. These *requirements* can establish *product*, *process* or *service* characteristics—including applicable administrative provisions—that have government-mandated compliance.

Reliability. The probability of a *product* performing its intended function under specific conditions for a given period of time.

Remaining Duration (RD). The time in *calendar units*, between the *data date* of the *project schedule* and the *finish date* of a *schedule activity* that has an *actual start date*. This represents the time needed to complete a *schedule activity* where the *work* is in progress.

Request for Information. A type of *procurement document* whereby the *buyer* requests a potential *seller* to provide various pieces of information related to a *product* or *service* or *seller* capability.

Request for Proposal (RFP). A type of *procurement document* used to request proposals from prospective *sellers* of *products* or *services*. In some *application areas*, it may have a narrower or more specific meaning.

Request for Quotation (RFQ). A type of *procurement document* used to request price quotations from prospective *sellers* of common or standard *products* or *services*. Sometimes used in place of *request for proposal* and in some *application areas*, it may have a narrower or more specific meaning.

Request Seller Responses [Process]. The *process* of obtaining information, quotations, bids, offers, or proposals, as appropriate.

Requested Change [Output/Input]. A formally documented *change request* that is submitted for *approval* to the *integrated change control* process. Contrast with *approved change request*.

Requirement. A condition or capability that must be met or possessed by a *system, product, service, result*, or *component* to satisfy a *contract, standard, specification*, or other formally imposed *documents*. Requirements include the quantified and documented needs, wants, and expectations of the *sponsor, customer*, and other *stakeholders*.

Reserve. A provision in the *project management plan* to mitigate *cost* and/or schedule *risk*. Often used with a modifier (e.g., management reserve, contingency reserve) to provide further detail on what types of risk are meant to be mitigated. The specific meaning of the modified term varies by *application area*.

Reserve Analysis [Technique]. An analytical *technique* to determine the essential features and relationships of components in the *project management plan* to establish a *reserve* for the *schedule duration*, *budget*, estimated *cost*, or *funds* for a *project*.

Residual Risk. A *risk* that remains after risk responses have been implemented.

Resource. Skilled human resources (specific disciplines either individually or in crews or teams), equipment, *services*, supplies, *commodities*, *materiel*, *budgets*, or funds.

Resource Breakdown Structure (RBS). A hierarchical structure of *resources* by resource category and resource type used in *resource leveling* schedules and to develop resource-limited schedules, and which may be used to identify and analyze project human resource assignments.

Resource Calendar. A calendar of working days and nonworking days that determines those *dates* on which each specific *resource* is idle or can be active. Typically defines resource specific holidays and resource availability periods. See also *project calendar*.

Resource-Constrained Schedule. See *resource-limited schedule*.

Resource Histogram. A *bar chart* showing the amount of time that a *resource* is scheduled to work over a series of time periods. Resource availability may be depicted as a line for comparison purposes. Contrasting bars may show actual amounts of resource used as the project progresses.

Resource Leveling [Technique]. Any form of *schedule network analysis* in which scheduling decisions (start and finish dates) are driven by resource constraints (e.g., limited resource availability or difficult-to-manage changes in resource availability levels).

Resource-Limited Schedule. A *project schedule* whose *schedule activity*, *scheduled start dates* and *scheduled finish dates* reflect expected resource availability. A resource-limited schedule does not

have any early or late start or finish dates. The resource-limited schedule *total float* is determined by calculating the difference between the *critical path method late finish date* and the resource-limited scheduled finish date. Sometimes called resource-constrained schedule. See also *resource leveling*.

Resource Planning. See *activity resource estimating*.

Responsibility Assignment Matrix (RAM) [Tool]. A structure that relates the project *organizational breakdown structure* to the *work breakdown structure* to help ensure that each component of the project's *scope* of *work* is assigned to a responsible person/team.

Result. An output from performing project management *processes* and *activities*. Results include outcomes (e.g., integrated *systems*, revised *process*, restructured *organization*, tests, trained personnel, etc.) and *documents* (e.g., policies, plans, studies, procedures, *specifications*, reports, etc.). Contrast with *product* and *service*. See also *deliverable*.

Retainage. A portion of a *contract* payment that is withheld until contract completion to ensure full performance of the contract terms.

Rework. Action taken to bring a defective or nonconforming *component* into compliance with *requirements* or *specifications*.

Risk. An uncertain *event* or condition that, if it occurs, has a positive or negative effect on a *project's objectives*. See also *risk category* and *risk breakdown structure*.

Risk Acceptance [Technique]. A *risk response planning technique** that indicates that the *project team* has decided not to change the *project management plan* to deal with a *risk*, or is unable to identify any other suitable response strategy.

Risk Avoidance [Technique]. A *risk response planning technique* for a *threat* that creates changes to the *project management plan* that are meant to either eliminate the *risk* or to protect the *project objectives* from its impact. Generally, risk avoidance involves relaxing the time, cost, scope, or quality *objectives*.

Risk Breakdown Structure (RBS) [Tool]. A hierarchically organized depiction of the identified *project risks** arranged by *risk category* and subcategory that identifies the various areas and causes of potential risks. The risk breakdown structure is often tailored to specific project types.

Risk Category. A group of potential causes of *risk*. Risk causes may be grouped into categories such as technical, external, organizational, environmental, or *project management*. A category may include subcategories such as technical maturity, weather, or aggressive estimating. See also *risk breakdown structure*.

Risk Database. A repository that provides for collection, maintenance, and analysis of data gathered and used in the risk management *processes*.

Risk Identification [Process]. The *process* of determining which *risks* might affect the *project* and documenting their characteristics.

Risk Management Plan [Output/Input]. The *document* describing how *project risk management* will be structured and performed on the *project*. It is contained in or is a subsidiary plan of the *project management plan*. The risk management plan can be informal and broadly framed, or formal and highly detailed, based on the needs of the project. Information in the risk management plan varies by *application area* and project size. The risk management plan is different from the *risk register* that contains the list of project *risks*, the *results* of risk analysis, and the risk responses.

Risk Management Planning [Process]. The *process* of deciding how to approach, plan, and execute *risk* management *activities* for a *project*.

Risk Mitigation [Technique]. A *risk response planning technique** associated with *threats* that seeks to reduce the probability of occurrence or impact of a *risk* to below an acceptable threshold.

Risk Monitoring and Control [Process]. The *process* of tracking identified *risks*, monitoring *residual risks*, identifying new risks, executing risk response plans, and evaluating their effectiveness throughout the *project life cycle*.

Risk Register [Output/Input]. The *document* containing the *results* of the *qualitative risk analysis*, *quantitative risk analysis*, and *risk response planning*. The risk register details all identified *risks*, including description, category, cause, probability of occurring, impact(s) on objectives, proposed responses, owners, and current status. The risk register is a component of the *project management plan*.

Risk Response Planning [Process]. The *process* of developing options and actions to enhance opportunities and to reduce threats to *project objectives*.

Risk Transference [Technique]. A *risk response planning technique** that shifts the impact of a *threat* to a third party, together with ownership of the response.

Role. A defined function to be performed by a *project team member*, such as testing, filing, inspecting, coding.

Rolling Wave Planning [Technique]. A form of *progressive elaboration* planning where the *work* to be accomplished in the near term is planned in detail at a low level of the *work breakdown structure*, while the work far in the future is planned at a relatively high level of the work breakdown structure, but the detailed planning of the work to be performed within another one or two periods in the near future is done as work is being completed during the current period.

Root Cause Analysis [Technique]. An analytical technique used to determine the basic underlying reason that causes a *variance* or a *defect* or a *risk*. A root cause may underlie more than one variance or defect or risk.

Schedule. See *project schedule* and see also *schedule model*.

Schedule Activity. A discrete scheduled *component* of *work* performed during the course of a *project*. A schedule activity normally has an estimated *duration*, an estimated *cost*, and estimated resource requirements. Schedule activities are connected to other schedule activities or schedule milestones with *logical relationships*, and are decomposed from *work packages*.

Schedule Analysis. See *schedule network analysis*.

Schedule Compression [Technique]. Shortening the *project schedule duration* without reducing the *project scope*. See also *crashing* and *fast tracking*.

Schedule Control [Process]. The *process* of controlling changes to the *project schedule*.

Schedule Development [Process]. The *process* of analyzing *schedule activity* sequences, schedule activity *durations*, *resource requirements*, and schedule *constraints* to create the *project schedule*.

Schedule Management Plan [Output/Input]. The *document* that establishes *criteria* and the *activities* for developing and controlling the *project schedule*. It is contained in, or is a subsidiary plan of, the *project management plan*. The schedule management plan may be formal or informal, highly detailed or broadly framed, based on the needs of the *project*.

Schedule Milestone. A significant *event* in the *project schedule*, such as an event restraining future work or marking the completion of a major *deliverable*. A schedule milestone has zero *duration*. Sometimes called a milestone *activity*. See also *milestone*.

Schedule Model [Tool]. A model used in conjunction with manual methods or *project management software* to perform *schedule network analysis* to generate the *project schedule* for use in managing the execution of a *project*. See also *project schedule*.

Schedule Network Analysis [Technique]. The *technique* of identifying *early and late start dates**, as well as *early and late finish dates**, for the uncompleted portions of project *schedule activities*. See also *critical path method, critical chain method, what-if analysis,* and *resource leveling*.

Schedule Performance Index (SPI). A measure of schedule efficiency on a project. It is the ratio of *earned value* (EV) to *planned value* (PV). The SPI = EV divided by PV. An SPI equal to or greater than one indicates a favorable condition and a value of less than one indicates an unfavorable condition. See also *earned value management*.

Schedule Variance (SV). A measure of schedule performance on a project. It is the algebraic difference between the *earned value* (EV) and the *planned value* (PV). SV = EV minus PV. See also *earned value management*.

Scheduled Finish Date (SF). The point in time that *work* was scheduled to finish on a *schedule activity*. The scheduled finish date is normally within the range of *dates* delimited by the *early finish date* and the *late finish date*. It may reflect *resource leveling* of scarce *resources*. Sometimes called planned finish date.

Scheduled Start Date (SS). The point in time that *work* was scheduled to start on a *schedule activity*. The scheduled start date is normally within the range of *dates* delimited by the *early start date* and the *late start date*. It may reflect *resource leveling* of scarce *resources*. Sometimes called planned start date.

Scope. The sum of the *products, services,* and

results to be provided as a *project*. See also *project scope* and *product scope*.

Scope Baseline. See *baseline*.

Scope Change. Any change to the *project scope*. A *scope* change almost always requires an adjustment to the project *cost* or *schedule*.

Scope Control [Process]. The *process* of controlling changes to the *project scope*.

Scope Creep. Adding features and functionality (*project scope*) without addressing the effects on time, *costs*, and *resources,* or without *customer* approval.

Scope Definition [Process]. The *process* of developing a detailed *project scope statement* as the basis for future project decisions.

Scope Planning [Process]. The *process* of creating a *project scope management plan*.

Scope Verification [Process]. The *process* of formalizing *acceptance* of the completed *project deliverables*.

S-Curve. Graphic display of cumulative *costs*, labor hours, percentage of *work*, or other quantities, plotted against time. Used to depict *planned value, earned value,* and *actual cost* of project work. The name derives from the S-like shape of the curve (flatter at the beginning and end, steeper in the middle) produced on a *project* that starts slowly, accelerates, and then tails off. Also a term for the cumulative likelihood distribution that is a *result* of a *simulation*, a *tool* of *quantitative risk analysis*.

Secondary Risk. A *risk* that arises as a direct *result* of implementing a risk response.

Select Sellers [Process]. The *process* of reviewing offers, choosing from among potential sellers, and negotiating a written *contract* with a *seller*.

Seller. A provider or supplier of *products*, *services*, or *results* to an organization.

Sensitivity Analysis. A *quantitative risk analysis* and modeling *technique* used to help determine which *risks* have the most potential impact on the *project*. It examines the extent to which the uncertainty of each project element affects the *objective* being examined when all other uncertain elements are held at their *baseline* values. The typical display of *results* is in the form of a tornado diagram.

Service. Useful *work* performed that does not produce a tangible *product* or *result,* such as performing any of the business functions supporting production or distribution. Contrast with product and result. See also *deliverable*.

Should-Cost Estimate. An *estimate* of the *cost* of a *product* or *service* used to provide an assessment of the reasonableness of a prospective *seller's* proposed cost.

Simulation. A simulation uses a *project* model that translates the uncertainties specified at a detailed level into their potential impact on *objectives* that are expressed at the level of the total *project*. Project simulations use computer models and *estimates* of *risk*, usually expressed as a probability distribution of possible *costs* or *durations* at a detailed work level, and are typically performed using *Monte Carlo analysis*.

Skill. Ability to use *knowledge*, a developed aptitude, and/or a capability to effectively and readily execute or perform an *activity*.

Slack. See *total float* and *free float*.

Special Cause. A source of variation that is not inherent in the *system*, is not predictable, and is intermittent. It can be assigned to a defect in the *system*. On a *control chart*, points beyond the *control limits*, or non-random patterns within the control limits, indicate it. Also referred to as assignable cause. Contrast with *common cause*.

Specification. A *document* that specifies, in a complete, precise, verifiable manner, the *requirements*, design, behavior, or other characteristics of a *system*, *component*, *product*, *result*, or *service* and, often, the *procedures* for determining whether these provisions have been satisfied. Examples are: requirement *specification*, design specification, product specification, and test specification.

Specification Limits. The area, on either side of the centerline, or mean, of data plotted on a *control chart* that meets the *customer's* requirements for a *product* or *service*. This area may be greater than or less than the area defined by the control limits. See also *control limits*.

Sponsor. The person or group that provides the financial resources, in cash or in kind, for the *project*.

Staffing Management Plan [Process]. The *document* that describes when and how human *resource requirements* will be met. It is contained in, or is a subsidiary plan of, the *project management plan*. The staffing management plan can be informal and broadly framed, or formal and highly detailed, based on the needs of the *project*. Information in the staffing management plan varies by *application area* and project size.

Stakeholder. Person or *organization* (e.g., *customer*, *sponsor*, *performing organization*, or the public) that is actively involved in the *project*, or whose interests may be positively or negatively affected by execution or completion of the project. A stakeholder may also exert influence over the project and its *deliverables*.

Standard. A *document* established by consensus and approved by a recognized body that provides, for common and repeated use, rules, guidelines or characteristics for *activities* or their *results*, aimed at the achievement of the optimum degree of order in a given context.

Start Date. A point in time associated with a *schedule activity's* start, usually qualified by one of

the following: actual, planned, estimated, scheduled, early, late, target, *baseline*, or current.

Start-to-Finish (SF). The *logical relationship* where completion of the *successor schedule activity* is dependent upon the initiation of the *predecessor schedule activity*. See also *logical relationship*.

Start-to-Start (SS). The *logical relationship* where initiation of the work of the *successor schedule activity* depends upon the initiation of the work of the *predecessor schedule activity*. See also *logical relationship*.

Statement of Work (SOW). A narrative description of *products, services, or results* to be supplied.

Strengths, Weaknesses, Opportunities, and Threats (SWOT) Analysis. This information gathering technique examines the project from the perspective of each project's strengths, weaknesses, *opportunities*, and *threats* to increase the breadth of the *risks* considered by risk management.

Subnetwork. A subdivision (fragment) of a *project schedule network diagram*, usually representing a *subproject* or a *work package*. Often used to illustrate or study some potential or proposed schedule condition, such as changes in preferential schedule *logic* or *project scope*.

Subphase. A subdivision of a *phase*.

Subproject. A smaller portion of the overall *project* created when a project is subdivided into more manageable *components* or pieces. Subprojects are usually represented in the *work breakdown structure*. A subproject can be referred to as a project, managed as a project, and acquired from a seller. May be referred to as a *subnetwork* in a *project schedule network diagram*.

Successor. See *successor activity*.

Successor Activity. The schedule activity that follows a *predecessor activity*, as determined by their *logical relationship*.

Summary Activity. A group of related *schedule activities* aggregated at some summary level, and displayed/reported as a single activity at that summary level. See also *subproject* and *subnetwork*.

System. An *integrated* set of regularly interacting or interdependent *components* created to accomplish a defined *objective*, with defined and maintained relationships among its components, and the whole producing or operating better than the simple sum of its components. Systems may be either physically *process* based or management process based, or more commonly a combination of both. Systems for *project management* are composed of *project management processes, techniques, methodologies,* and *tools* operated by the *project management team.*

Target Completion Date (TC). An *imposed date* that constrains or otherwise modifies the *schedule network analysis.*

Target Finish Date (TF). The *date* that *work* is planned (targeted) to finish on a *schedule activity.*

Target Schedule. A *schedule* adopted for comparison purposes during *schedule network analysis,* which can be different from the baseline schedule. See also *baseline.*

Target Start Date (TS). The *date* that *work* is planned (targeted) to start on a *schedule activity.*

Task. A term for *work* whose meaning and placement within a structured plan for project work varies by the *application area,* industry, and brand of *project management software.*

Team Members. See *project team members.*

Technical Performance Measurement [Technique]. A performance measurement *technique* that compares technical accomplishments during *project* execution to the *project management plan's schedule* of planned technical achievements. It may use key technical parameters of the product produced by the project as a *quality* metric. The achieved metric values are part of the *work performance information.*

Technique. A defined systematic *procedure* employed by a human *resource* to perform an *activity* to produce a *product* or *result* or deliver a *service,* and that may employ one or more *tools.*

Template. A partially complete *document* in a predefined format that provides a defined structure for collecting, organizing and presenting information and data. Templates are often based upon documents created during prior *projects.* Templates can reduce the *effort* needed to perform *work* and increase the consistency of *results.*

Threat. A condition or situation unfavorable to the *project,* a negative set of circumstances, a negative set of events, a *risk* that will have a negative impact on a project objective if it occurs, or a possibility for negative changes. Contrast with *opportunity.*

Three-Point Estimate [Technique]. An analytical *technique* that uses three *cost* or *duration estimates* to represent the optimistic, most likely, and pessimistic scenarios. This technique is applied to improve the accuracy of the *estimates* of cost or duration when the underlying *activity* or cost *component* is uncertain.

Threshold. A *cost,* time, *quality,* technical, or *resource* value used as a parameter, and which may be included in *product specifications.* Crossing the threshold should trigger some action, such as generating an exception report.

Time and Material (T&M) Contract. A type of *contract* that is a hybrid contractual arrangement containing aspects of both *cost-reimbursable* and *fixed-price contracts.* Time and material contracts resemble cost-reimbursable type arrangements in that they have no definitive end, because the full value of the arrangement is not defined at the time of the award. Thus, time and material contracts can grow in contract value as if they were cost-reimbursable-type arrangements. Conversely, time and material arrangements can also resemble fixed-price arrangements. For example, the unit rates are preset by the *buyer* and *seller*, when both parties agree on the rates for the category of senior engineers.

Time-Now Date. See *data date*.

Time-Scaled Schedule Network Diagram [Tool]. Any *project schedule network diagram* drawn in such a way that the positioning and length of the *schedule activity* represents its duration. Essentially, it is a *bar chart* that includes schedule *network logic*.

Tool. Something tangible, such as a template or software program, used in performing an *activity* to produce a *product* or *result*.

Total Float (TF). The total amount of time that a *schedule activity* may be delayed from its *early start date* without delaying the project *finish date*, or violating a schedule *constraint*. Calculated using the *critical path method* technique and determining the difference between the *early finish dates* and *late finish dates*. See also *free float*.

Total Quality Management (TQM) [Technique]. A common approach to implementing a *quality* improvement program within an *organization*.

Trend Analysis [Technique]. An analytical technique that uses mathematical models to forecast future outcomes based on historical *results*. It is a method of determining the *variance* from a *baseline* of a *budget*, *cost*, *schedule*, or *scope* parameter by using prior progress reporting periods' data and projecting how much that parameter's variance from baseline might be at some future point in the project if no changes are made in *executing* the *project*.

Triggers. Indications that a risk has occurred or is about to occur. Triggers may be discovered in the *risk identification* process and watched in the *risk monitoring and control* process. Triggers are sometimes called *risk* symptoms or warning signs.

Triple Constraint. A framework for evaluating competing demands. The triple constraint is often depicted as a triangle where one of the sides or one of the corners represent one of the parameters being managed by the project team.

User. The person or *organization* that will use the project's *product* or *service*. See also *customer*.

Validation [Technique]. The *technique* of evaluating a *component* or *product* during or at the end of a *phase* or *project* to ensure it complies with the specified *requirements*. Contrast with *verification*.

Value Engineering (VE). A creative approach used to optimize *project life cycle* costs, save time, increase profits, improve *quality*, expand market share, solve problems, and/or use *resources* more effectively.

Variance. A quantifiable deviation, departure, or divergence away from a known *baseline* or expected value.

Variance Analysis [Technique]. A method for resolving the total *variance* in the set of *scope*, *cost*, and *schedule* variables into specific component variances that are associated with defined factors affecting the scope, cost, and schedule variables.

Verification [Technique]. The technique of evaluating a *component* or *product* at the end of a *phase* or *project* to assure or confirm it satisfies the conditions imposed. Contrast with *validation*.

Virtual Team. A group of persons with a shared *objective* who fulfill their *roles* with little or no time spent meeting face to face. Various forms of technology are often used to facilitate *communication* among team members. Virtual teams can be comprised of persons separated by great distances.

Voice of the Customer. A planning *technique* used to provide *products*, *services*, and *results* that truly reflect *customer requirements* by translating those customer requirements into the appropriate technical requirements for each *phase* of project product development.

War Room. A room used for *project* conferences and planning, often displaying charts of *cost*, *schedule* status, and other key project data.

Work. Sustained physical or mental effort, exertion, or exercise of *skill* to overcome obstacles and achieve an *objective*.

Work Authorization [Technique]. A permission and direction, typically written, to begin work on a specific *schedule activity* or *work package* or *control account*. It is a method for sanctioning *project work* to ensure that the work is done by the identified *organization*, at the right time, and in the proper sequence.

Work Authorization System [Tool]. A subsystem of the overall *project management system*. It is a collection of formal documented *procedures* that defines how *project work* will be authorized (committed) to ensure that the work is done by the identified *organization*, at the right time, and in the proper sequence. It includes the steps, *documents*, tracking *system*, and defined approval levels needed to issue work authorizations.

Work Breakdown Structure (WBS) [Output/Input]. A *deliverable*-oriented hierarchical *decomposition* of the *work* to be *executed* by the *project team* to accomplish the project *objectives* and create the required deliverables. It organizes and defines the total *scope* of the *project*. Each descending level represents an increasingly detailed definition of the *project work*. The WBS is decomposed into *work packages*. The deliverable orientation of the hierarchy includes both internal and external deliverables. See also *work pack-*

age, *control account*, *contract work breakdown structure*, and *project summary work breakdown structure*.

Work Breakdown Structure Component. An entry in the *work breakdown structure* that can be at any level.

Work Breakdown Structure Dictionary [Output/Input]. A *document* that describes each *component* in the *work breakdown structure* (WBS). For each WBS component, the WBS dictionary includes a brief definition of the *scope* or *statement of work*, defined *deliverable(s)*, a list of associated *activities*, and a list of *milestones*. Other information may include: responsible *organization*, start and end dates, *resources* required, an *estimate* of *cost*, charge number, *contract* information, *quality requirements*, and technical references to facilitate performance of the *work*.

Work Item. Term no longer in common usage. See *activity* and *schedule activity*.

Work Package. A *deliverable* or *project work component* at the lowest level of each branch of the *work breakdown structure*. The work package includes the *schedule activities* and *schedule milestones* required to complete the work package deliverable or project work component. See also *control account*.

Work Performance Information [Output/Input]. Information and data, on the status of the *project schedule activities* being performed to accomplish the *project work*, collected as part of the *direct and manage project execution processes**. Information includes: status of *deliverables*; implementation status for *change requests*, *corrective actions*, *preventive actions*, and *defect repairs*; forecasted *estimates to complete*; reported percent of *work* physically completed; achieved value of *technical performance measures*; start and finish dates of *schedule activities*.

Workaround [Technique]. A response to a negative *risk* that has occurred. Distinguished from *contingency* plan in that a workaround is not planned in advance of the occurrence of the risk event.

Index